An Evangelical Assessment

The Legacy of John Paul II

Edited by Tim Perry

IVP Academic
An imprint of InterVarsity Press
Downers Grove, Illinois

InterVarsity Press
P.O. Box 1400, Downers Grove, IL 60515-1426
World Wide Web: www.ivpress.com
E-mail: email@ivpress.com

InterVarsity Press® is the book-publishing division of InterVarsity Christian Fellowship/USA®, a student movement active on campus at hundreds of universities, colleges and schools of nursing in the United States of America, and a member movement of the International Fellowship of Evangelical Students. For information about local and regional activities, write Public Relations Dept., InterVarsity Christian Fellowship/USA, 6400 Schroeder Rd., P.O. Box 7895, Madison, WI 53707-7895, or visit the IVCF website at <www.intervarsity.org>.

Design: Cindy Kiple
Images: Pope John Paul II ©Okoniewski/The Image Works

ISBN 978-0-8308-2595-0

Printed in the United States of America ∞

Library of Congress Cataloging-in-Publication Data

The legacy of John Paul II: an evangelical assessment / edited by Tim Perry.
p. cm.
Includes bibliographical references and index.
ISBN-13: 978-0-8308-2595-0 (pbk.: alk. paper)
1. John Paul II, Pope, 1920-2005. I. Perry, Tim S., 1969-
BX1378.5.L44 2007
282.092—dc22

2007026757

P 20 19 18 17 16 15 14 13 12 11 10 9 8 7 6 5 4 3 2 1
Y 23 22 21 20 19 18 17 16 15 14 13 12 11 10 09 08 07

Contents

Foreword by J. I. Packer

Anyone who affirmed that the Roman Catholic Church had changed its position during the past half-century would be wrong. But anyone who denied that it has changed its posture would be wrong too. The old siege mentality has gone for good, and today's Roman Catholicism is outgoing, ecumenical, committed to evangelization and, despite everything, hopeful about its future in a way that is quite new. This is the *aggiornamento,* the sprucing-up, that John XXIII dreamed of when he called the Second Vatican Council; it has happened, at least in the upper reaches of the communion, which is where movements in Roman Catholicism usually begin. And it is the Council, plus the papacy of John Paul II, more than any other factors, that have brought about this change.

I have never been an enthusiast for the papacy, and I once put a Roman Catholic friend right off his dinner by describing the papal setup as a grotesque institution. (I am not proud of having done this, may I say.) The idea of one man being pastor-teacher of the entire Christian church, with supreme authority in all departments rising to doctrinal infallibility, and of communion with him and the bishops that he and his predecessors chose as being the test of whether or not one is fully in the church, has never seemed to me anything but strange, and the steady expansion of the Roman Catholic Church (for it does grow worldwide, whatever may be happening to it in the West) seems to me to increase rather than diminish its strangeness. For me, however, nothing has come closer to giving the institution credibility than the truly brilliant papacy of John Paul II.

John Paul, the first non-Italian pope since long before the Reformation and the first Polish pope ever, was a ten-talent man: philosopher, theologian, scholar, author, youth worker, ethicist, ecumenist, populist and more, he set a new style in "poping," if we may venture such a word. One cannot, for instance, imagine any of his predecessors putting his hand over an American evangelist's hand and saying to him, "We are brothers," as John Paul did to Billy Graham. When he became Pope he set himself to travel the world to put new heart into Catholics, and also to teach the world by means of the series of brilliant and weighty encyclicals with which this book interacts. Bible-based, humanity-focused, Christ-centered and mission-attuned, they were planned not just for domestic consumption but also to open conversations with non-Roman Christians and with the global village generally about the values and visions that should unite mankind at this time. In consequence, interaction with the encyclicals is extremely worthwhile, and we should be glad that this present fine collection of evangelical essays is leading the way at this point. And if the saints departed know what goes on in the world they left behind (and on that question, of course, the jury is still out), we can be sure that John Paul is glad too, for this is undoubtedly the level of response that he hoped for.

Foreword by Avery Cardinal Dulles

After working some fifteen years with the informal group Evangelicals and Catholics Together, I have come to appreciate the remarkable convergences that have been achieved in recent years. Members of that group have grown to recognize each other's firm commitment to the Scriptures, the early creeds, and to human dignity and freedom.

It did not surprise me, therefore, to learn that plans were being made for a commentary by evangelicals on the principal documents of John Paul II.

I expected the commentary to be a courteous and even-handed discussion reiterating the issues on which the two parties agreed and disagreed. To some extent the present book does this. The evangelicals express satisfaction with the Pope's extensive use of Scripture, his commitment to evangelization, and his strong defense of family values and innocent human life. While applauding these points, the evangelicals predictably distance themselves from the Pope's positions on good works, purgatory, indulgences, the Virgin Mary and the papal office.

The true significance of this book lies elsewhere. The authors have deeply pondered the thought of John Paul II on a broad spectrum of crucial issues. Far from looking at him as a misbeliever, they treat him with great respect as "our common teacher," to borrow the title used by Timothy George in his Epilogue. They gladly acknowledge that they and their colleagues have much to learn from the one whom some of them were perhaps taught in earlier days to regard as the antichrist.

I recommend this volume to all serious Christians. It will help Protestants to see how much they can profit from studying the official documents of the Catholic Church as helps for living out their faith in the face of contemporary secularism and relativism. Catholics, conversely, can find in these pages faithful presentations, thoughtful prolongations, and fresh applications of papal teaching. In this way all of us can come closer to one another and, most importantly, to Christ the Lord.

Introduction

For Such a Time as This: Living With(in) the Legacy of John Paul II

Tim Perry

As I have thought about how to introduce the essays that follow, I have been drawn again and again to a trio of photographs that hangs on my office wall. The first two are clearly related to each other. The third, at least at first glance, doesn't obviously fit. And yet, in my bones, I am convinced—and I suspect a growing number of traditional Protestant theologians in North America would also discern—that, in spite of the deep theological disagreements that they represent, "for just such a time as this" (Esther 4:14) these photographs belong together.

Obviously a pair, the first two photographs match in almost every conceivable way, down to the poses of their subjects. In one, Hendrik Kraemer hunches over his desk, writing furiously—presumably about the *sui generis* nature of the revelation of God in Christ. In another, an aging Karl Barth is even more hunched, even more furious and no doubt writing about the same subject. Kraemer was a phenomenologist of religion, missiologist, Bible translator and one of the first Dutch Reformed theologians to treat the thorny problem of theology of religions in an informed, systematic and extensive fashion; he remains one of that tradition's most creative thinkers on the subject.[1] Barth stands alongside John Calvin and Friedrich

[1] Kraemer's two major works are *The Christian Message in a Non-Christian World* (London: Edinburgh House, 1938) and *Religion and the Christian Faith* (London: Lutterworth, 1956). See my *Radical Difference: A Defense of Hendrik Kraemer's Theology of Religions* (Waterloo, Ont.: Wilfrid Laurier University Press, 2001) for a discussion of how Kraemer in fact anticipates themes later developed in certain kinds of postliberal theology.

Schleiermacher as one of the determinative voices of Reformed theology. Kraemer was the subject of my Ph.D. thesis; Barth is the theologian I turn to first and most frequently when preparing lectures, writing sermons and engaging in research.

And then there's the third photograph: John Paul II circa 1980. As much as the first two are alike, this one is just as different. The theological passion that so obviously animates Kraemer and Barth is replaced by John Paul's serene strength. The gray flannel suits of the Reformed theologians are set aside for the vestments of the Bishop of Rome. And of course, for any informed observer, five centuries of profound theological disagreement is quite close to the surface. For even though John Paul may well have been the most ecumenically minded and indeed evangelical-friendly pope since the Reformation, his deep and public Marian devotion, his insistence on the primacy of the Catholic Church and, perhaps especially, his endorsement of indulgences remind me (along with all contributors to this book) that he was still, well, a Catholic. And for me at least, a corollary follows immediately: I am not and, for the sake of conscience and the Word of God, cannot become one.[2] Why then does he take his stand alongside Barth and Kraemer on my wall and in my mind as a theologian worthy of serious consideration and emulation?

In the photo, John Paul is at the height of his powers. I don't remember this John Paul very well; I was nine when he became pope in 1978. The John Paul of my experience was the older, frail yet strangely charismatic pope. The one who received the accolade, "John Paul II, we love you!" on so many World Youth Days. No longer the one who made dictators tremble, the John Paul of my experience himself trembled with Parkinson's disease. He who had reminded both autocrats and democrats about humanity, liberty and the inevitable triumph of the Truth had been replaced by the no less compelling reminder of young people (Catholics, Protestants and all who had ears) about the adventure that ought to define the Christian life—one marked by chastity, fidelity and the capacity for holiness that can only develop in suffering.

I like this photograph and find myself contemplating it often, not because it points to a John Paul who is other than the one I remember, but because it gives

[2]I continue to demur from the opinion of William J. Abraham concerning my own future theological development, namely, that "it will be interesting to see whether or not Perry can avoid the move to some vision of papal infallibility, once he fully internalizes the robust vision of Mary adopted here" (William J. Abraham, "Foreword," in my *Mary for Evangelicals: Toward an Understanding of the Mother of Our Lord* [Downers Grove: IVP Academic, 2006], p. 12). With Paul Zahl, however, I confess that "every Anglican—even the most Protestant ones—can feel the tug toward Rome," and note that several theologians I admire, including R. R. Reno and Douglas Farrow, have already crossed the Tiber.

me a glimpse of the deep reserves of holy strength that helped end an evil empire, that were wrapped in weakness as his body failed him increasingly through the 1990s. As I reflect on the picture, I regularly pray that God will grant the same reserves to all of us on the narrow way to the Father's house, who have been charged with resisting the evil empires of our own age in the name of Jesus: a rampant, individualistic consumerism that knows no national boundaries and worships mammon on the one hand and a radical, nihilistic version of Islam that seeks violently to erase cultural and religious difference and worships death on the other. I pray that God will use the example of John Paul II to inspire Christians across confessional and continental divides as we engage in these twin struggles.[3]

Hence the words of Mordecai to Queen Esther in the title of this essay: "for such a time as this." The separation between the Catholic Church and the churches of the Reformation remains real and broad and deep, especially for those of us on both sides who persist in the conviction that there can be no reconciliation at the altar without first reconciliation in the truth. And yet, not only in the rapidly de-Christianizing West where the church is at once consumerized and marginalized, but also and perhaps especially in the West's confrontation with a demographically young and often militant Islam, those disagreements are recast in the light of the great truths that unite us. These truths were well expressed by the great fundamentalist of the first half of the twentieth century, J. Gresham Machen: "How great is the common heritage which unites the Roman Catholic Church, with its maintenance of the authority of Holy Scripture and with its acceptance of the great early creeds, to devout Protestants today!"[4] Of course, the unity Machen discerned was over against a theological liberalism that he described as "not Christianity at all."[5] Eight decades later, in the light of the challenges above and after the failure of liberal Protestantism to maintain an effective Christian witness, I can only echo, "How great, indeed!"

The witness of John Paul II, purified in the crucible that was Nazi-occupied Poland and honed by the thuggish repression of the Soviets, was providentially given to the whole church to remind all her members of the deep resources at her

---

[3]Under the tutelage not only of John Paul II, but also of Oliver O'Donovan, N. T. Wright and Stanley Hauerwas, I am coming to the conclusion that the two major protagonists in their respective attempts to dissolve difference—turning the world into one universal capitalistic democracy or bringing it by whatever means into the house of Islam—are in fact mirror images of each other. And while I am not a pacifist, I am increasingly convinced that—again, for such a time as this—both need to be opposed by a church radically committed to nonviolence.

[4]J. Gresham Machen, *Christianity and Liberalism* (1923; reprint, Grand Rapids: Eerdmans, 1999), p. 52.

[5]Ibid.

disposal for cultural resistance, renewal and re-evangelization. These deep resources will have to be drawn upon as the West seems determined to hurtle headlong toward a new technologically limitless, but spiritually and morally bankrupt Dark Age. For such a time as this, we evangelicals ought to join John Paul in his call to the world that it is time to open wide the doors to Christ, in his fearless proclamation that Jesus Christ is the answer to the question that is every human life, in his reminder that because of the sufferings of Christ, Christ's disciples need not fear any opposition.

It was with the deep conviction that evangelicals can and should follow John Paul into those common resources that I approached Dan Reid and Joel Scandrett, my editors at InterVarsity Press, with the idea that eventually became this volume. What better way, I proposed, for evangelicals to honor the leadership of John Paul II than to gather a team of scholars broadly representative of the movement's various wings and offshoots, to comment on his encyclicals (with one exception—more on that, below).[6] They agreed that this idea warranted further development, and I set about inviting people to contribute. I was amazed at the enthusiasm my invitations generated, even among folks who ended up having to decline. Of the twenty-six scholars I contacted, only two thought that the project was unwise (and these, ironically enough, for diametrically opposed reasons). The fourteen who accepted my invitation have produced a strong body of work that interacts with John Paul's thought, at times sympathetically, at others critically and always thoughtfully. Taken together, their essays provide a testimony to the abiding validity and value of John Paul's witness to the Truth that neither ignores nor downplays the realities of our ongoing division of our communities.

The book is divided into three parts. The first sets the scene. Mark Noll, whose involvement was undertaken during his move from Wheaton College to the University of Notre Dame, introduces readers to the legacy of John Paul II for North American evangelicalism. He detects a broad move from "intractable stand-off" to "cautious engagement" over the last fifty years or so. He notes that while the first moves were tentative, over the last thirty years subsequent ones have become more deliberate and more widespread. He credits the acceleration in good measure to John Paul II. Next, Derek S. Jeffreys engages with the pope's first encyclical,

[6]The encyclical is officially neither the only nor the most authoritative papal teaching document. In the case of John Paul II, however, it was a primary means for dissemination of his major doctrinal and social teachings within the Catholic Church and, indeed, to Christians around the world. While the encyclicals do not represent the entirety of John Paul's teaching, they provide a window into his thought for the purposes of this volume. The encyclicals may be found in English translation at the Vatican's website: http://www.vatican.va/holy_father/john_paul_ii/encyclicals/index.htm.

Redemptor hominis. The document, he says, teaches evangelicals about how best to engage in the challenging ethical conversations taking place in technology and biotechnology. While Jeffreys's thesis is clearly focused, his extended introduction to John Paul's philosophy and theology of the person justifies the inclusion of his essay in part one. For the personalism first enunciated in *Redemptor hominis* is the scarlet cord, tying all the documents together into one body of work.

Part two focuses on doctrine. The first two essays offer quite positive assessments of their respective documents. First, a fine essay by Michael Beaty and C. Stephen Evans applies John Paul's analysis of contemporary philosophy in *Fides et ratio* to specifically evangelical concerns. They conclude that evangelicals ought to agree with the pontiff that philosophy can and should help the university to remain faithful to its calling and that, conversely, a confidently Christian university ought to enable philosophy to be true to its own vocation. This is followed by Clark H. Pinnock's meditation on *Dominum et vivificantem.* Pinnock praises the document's presentation of the Triune God as self-giving love, the role of the Spirit as creation's life-giver and the often overlooked place of the Spirit in the doctrines of the incarnation and the church.

The next four, while continuing to cultivate no less a sympathetic stance, confront us with serious ongoing doctrinal disputes. My own essay responds to the invitation contained in *Redemptoris mater.* Although sensitive to the pope's desire to see Mary become a focus for unity and his biblical strategy to realize it, I conclude that, at best, evangelicals can follow only part way for now. If Mary is to be, as John Paul hopes, a sign of the church's unity, the realization of this hope remains in God's future. Mark Noll graciously does double duty by following with his own reflections on *Ecclesia de eucharistia.* Presenting the Eucharist as both a locus of doctrine and a way of life for John Paul, Noll argues that while evangelicals ought to honor, appropriate and, indeed, be edified by much of the document, in the end it breathes an ecclesiology foreign to evangelical Protestant convictions. William J. Abraham then turns our attention to the serious epistemic and canonical challenges posed by the doctrine of papal infallibility to serious ecumenical engagement as he examines *Ut unum sint.* There is, he concludes, no neat way to sidestep these challenges, and working through them will take some time yet. Finally, Andrew Goddard sets the stage for part three with a gracious and sustained interaction with *Veritatis splendor.* Like Noll, Goddard presents us with a vision of morality from which evangelicals can learn a great deal and against which they must continue to protest. Complicating matters, these are not easily disentangled, whether one is talking about the role of Scripture in moral reasoning, the function of law, the relationship of morality (works) to salvation (faith), the authority of the church, or the nature of freedom and truth.

Goddard's essay thus moves us into part three, essays addressing John Paul's moral and social visions. It opens with Nancy Pearcy's response to *Evangelium vitae.* She discerns therein a deep harmony between the pope's understanding of the human person and those of the evangelical philosopher Francis Schaeffer that led to quite similar understandings of beginning-of-life ethical issues, and hopes to discern just what gave both writers their prophetic insight.

From the pope's thoroughly pro-life stance, the next two essays move us to matters of social and economic justice, beginning with Mark Charlton's reading together of *Dives in misericordia* and *Sollicitudo rei socialis.* The relationship between the two documents is not immediately obvious, with the former being doctrinal[7] and the latter concerned with social justice. Nevertheless, Charlton discerns in both an integrated vision in which the transformation of justice by the mercy of God and a holistic vision of development can stimulate evangelicals to reflect on social justice as integral to evangelism. Next, Ronald Sider tackles the economic vision set forth in *Laborem exercens* and *Centesimus annus.* Though the documents deal directly with economic justice and the rights of labor, Sider argues that they enunciate a vision of the sanctity of human life, the family, environmental concern and peacemaking with which evangelicals are already in agreement and can therefore serve as a basis for the reinvigoration of American politics beyond its current polarization.

Rounding out part three is a series of essays falling broadly under the umbrella of Christian mission. Terrance Tiessen begins by noting the places in which evangelical responses to *Redemptoris missio* will be positive, where they will be mixed and where (again) they will evoke counterclaims. Much in each of these areas has been already presented in the summaries above. Especially striking in this essay is Tiessen's call for better implementation of the encyclical's insights, especially on religious freedom, at the parish level, where evangelicals and Catholics are often adversaries rather than allies in evangelization. Peter Kuzmič follows with a reading of *Slavorum apostoli,* John Paul's celebration of Saint Cyril and Saint Methodius. Praised as symbols of the spirituality of the Eastern (Byzantine) and Western (Latin) tradition of the undivided church, they are upheld as abiding models of both missionary activity and Christian unity. They are thus seen as bridge-building

[7]A meditation on the nature of God's mercy, *Dives in misericordia* naturally belongs with *Redemptor hominis* and *Dominum et vivificantem,* composing as they do an extended reflection on the doctrine of the Trinity.

figures between the East and the West, and as symbolically significant for modern-day reestablishment of European unity based on the common heritage of faith and culture. Third, evangelicals and Catholics have, in their own distinctive ways, focused on education as a key to the maintenance of identity and the extension of the church's mission. David L. Jeffrey, therefore, concludes part three by examining the apostolic constitution[8] *Ex corde ecclesiae* (this is the exception alluded to above) in the light of its sometimes stormy reception in the academy. Its enunciation of a clear account of the relationship between individual intellectual freedom, on the one hand, and the religious liberty of educational institutions to operate out of a commitment to a shared religious worldview, on the other, can provide evangelicals with deep insights as they pursue a similar agenda in their respective colleges and universities.

Finally, the last word goes to Timothy George, who reflects on the universal witness of John Paul II. Naming him "Our Common Teacher," George summarizes the compelling Christian witness that was and remains John Paul II. Serving as a wonderful epitaph and conclusion, George reminds all of us—evangelical, Catholic and others—why so many of us are reflexively adding "the Great" to the name of this shepherd of God's people.

---

[8]Ranking first in order of authority, an apostolic constitution is the most solemn teaching document issued in the Roman Catholic Church.

PART ONE

SETTING THE SCENE

1

Evangelicals and John Paul II

Mark A. Noll

Introduction

At the end of John Paul II's life, it was possible to hear strikingly contrasting statements from evangelical Protestants about this pope and the nature of his foundational convictions. To note the range of those opinions is to possess a snapshot of current evangelical attitudes toward John Paul and the Catholic faith he represented as pontiff. But since most of the commentary was mostly favorable, it is also to gain a sense of how much has changed in the recent past. The very existence of different evangelical assessments is in itself striking, since not many decades ago evangelical opinion on such matters was much more uniform: to simplify slightly, evangelicals only fifty years ago may have conceded that faithful Christians could be found in the Catholic church, but only *despite* the church's official teaching and only by *implicit rejection* of what the Catholic church claimed for and about its pope.[1]

The pontificate of John Paul II (1978-2005) began after that earlier evangelical consensus about the irremediable dangers of Roman Catholicism had begun to soften. Because of who this pope was and what he accomplished, that earlier consensus has undergone even more fragmentation. Evangelical-Catholic relations always concern more than just evangelical attitudes toward the pope. But in the case of John Paul, his great presence on the world stage—not to speak of the full theological record he left in scores of formal writings, hundreds of more personal communications and thousands of public addresses—has had a decisive effect on evangelical attitudes toward Catholics in general.

[1]I am grateful to Jeremy Wells, who provided indispensable research assistance for this introduction.

This book provides—with one exception—evangelical theological assessments of the pope's encyclicals, which are among the most formal and most official of his pontifical pronouncements. But for introducing these assessments, it is useful to attempt a sketch of more general evangelical attitudes toward the pope and his positions through the more than quarter century of his pontificate. We begin with a range of evangelical viewpoints that were expressed at his death. Then, in order to put the years of his papacy in context, it will be useful to cast a quick glance back to the late 1950s and early 1960s in order to understand how far evangelical-Catholic relations had traveled in the years immediately preceding the pope's investiture. From that point (1978), sampling from the pages of *Christianity Today* magazine will provide a sense of general evangelical attitudes toward the pope and his major actions. For this brief introduction, treatment is mostly limited to this American source, even though the question of international evangelical attitudes toward John Paul II is an important subject worthy of extensive attention in its own right. By undertaking this survey, it is possible to illustrate how different the modern era of cautious evangelical-Catholic engagement has become from the seemingly intractable stand-off that was once the norm. And it is possible to indicate how much the years of John Paul II contributed to deepening contemporary Catholic-evangelical discussion, dialogue, cooperation, debate and assessment.[2]

Evangelical Views of John Paul II at His Passing

One of the most interesting evangelical assessments of John Paul II appeared shortly after his death in a long essay entitled "The Pope We Never Knew," which appeared in *Christianity Today.* It was written by David Scott, who in the late 1980s had worked with Campus Crusade for Christ in Poland. His account told the story of Father Franciszek Blachnicki, who in the 1970s had organized a Polish youth movement named Oasis with help from Crusade staff and Crusade literature. Oasis had been thoroughly evangelical in its orientation and emphasis. The point of telling this story in the spring of 2006 was because this youth movement had been supported by Karol Cardinal Wojtyla, the Bishop of Krakow. The support continued in at least some measure after Cardinal Wojtyla became the pope. Scott then asked "was Pope John Paul II an evangelical?" and answered "in the technical historical meaning of the word, of course not." But he also went on

[2]A more general account of recent developments in Catholic-evangelical relations can be found in Mark A. Noll and Carolyn Nystrom, *Is the Reformation Over? An Evangelical Assessment of Contemporary Catholicism* (Grand Rapids: Baker, 2005).

to say that, even as Crusade leaders like Bill Bright had earlier commended the character of the late pope's faith, so now Scott was prepared to say something very positive: "Many American evangelicals saw in Wojtyla a man devoted to a biblical faith in Christ and committed to proclaiming the gospel to an increasingly lost secular world. He shared the core values of American evangelicalism: Christocentricism, Biblicism, evangelism, and anti-secularism."[3]

A different viewpoint could be found in a thoughtful volume published shortly before by a leader of the Evangelical Alliance in Italy. In this book, Leonardo De Chirico acknowledged that more Catholics and more evangelicals were finding it easier to work together on more projects, both doctrinal and practical. But he also reaffirmed in definite terms the traditional Protestant view that critical differences continued to divide Catholic and Protestant systems of doctrine. With much reference to John Paul II's encyclicals, De Chirico concluded that Catholicism's stress on the church as mediator of divine grace continued to define a complete worldview that was at odds with the classical Protestant assertion of free grace as a free gift from God mediated to humans by Christ alone.[4]

Equally thoughtful, though also somewhat whimsical, was the commentary of Stephen Long, an evangelical Wesleyan, who asked after the pope's passing whether Protestants needed a leader like John Paul II. Long was reflecting especially on the Protestant propensity to fall into "ever-repeating and deepening division and schism" and on the results of that division, which in his view entailed an ever-weakening ability to resist secular influences of several kinds. As opposed to that Protestant fragmentation and weakness in the face of secular society, he then pointed to the life of the late pope as a counterexample. Long acknowledged "the legitimate reasons why Protestants separated from the Catholic Church." But he then suggested that because John Paul II had functioned as the head of a united worldwide church, and because he had testified so faithfully to Christ, he had enjoyed an effectiveness denied to any Protestant:

> John Paul II taught us to risk truth and not be content with the modern assumption that peace can only be had when we confess power as the most basic reality of our lives. . . . This is the beautiful scandal of the papacy: it is an institution that proclaims that truth is more basic than power even when those of us weaned on a (Protestant)

[3]David Scott, "The Pope We Never Knew: The Unknown Story of How John Paul II Ushered Campus Crusade into Catholic Poland," *Christianity Today*, May 2005, p. 38. In a public email of May 12, 2006, Joe Losiak, who had pioneered the work in Poland with Father Blachnicki, offered qualifications and a few reservations about David Scott's account.

[4]Leonardo De Chirico, *Evangelical Theological Perspectives on Post-Vatican II Roman Catholicism* (Bern: Peter Lang, 2003).

hermeneutics of suspicion can only see the papacy as a contradiction.[5]

The testimony of prominent voices from American pentecostal and charismatic circles was similarly positive. In the issue of *Pneuma,* a scholarly journal of pentecostal studies, which was published shortly after the pope's passing, Cecil Robeck of Fuller Theological Seminary provided a lengthy memoir about his personal dealings with John Paul II through participation in formal pentecostal-Catholic dialogues. Robeck reported that he had been won over to a positive assessment of John Paul after hearing him profess his faith to a very mixed group of religious leaders in Los Angeles in 1987: "I had heard enough to know that this pope . . . was sufficiently 'Evangelical' for me to accept him and his witness to the Gospel without further hesitation."[6]

In the June 2005 issue of *Charisma,* several contributors said much the same thing. Although they raised a few issues of continued Catholic-evangelical disagreement, the overall tone was positive. According to author Stephen Mansfield, "John Paul II can truly be understood only in light of his absolute devotion to the supernatural, in light of his belief in a miracle-working God performing wonders in behalf of those who serve Him." David Aikman, writing out of his experience with newer Christian communities in China and elsewhere in the world, used his reflections on the life of the late pope to affirm that "the time has come to say publicly that vast numbers of Catholic bishops, priests and laypeople are indeed our Christian brothers. . . . The fruits of godliness so overflowed from the life of John Paul II that he showed us, more than anything else, who our brothers and sisters really are."[7]

When in succeeding issues, letters were published responding to these positive comments in *Charisma,* many respondents agreed, but some came back with negative opinions of the sort that had once been standard among evangelicals: "The Catholic Church is full of paganism and witchcraft, and the pope is worshiped to some extent. You should get away from all that mess. . . . The Catholic Church isn't another sect of Christianity; it's a cult. . . . Although some believers are Catholic, the Catholic church has always been at enmity with the true, believing church. . . . Catholic doctrines such as the theology of purgatory speak to the fact that Roman Catholicism does not reflect Christian-

---

[5]D. Stephen Long, "In Need of a Pope?" *Christian Century,* May 17, 2005, pp. 10-11.

[6]Cecil M. Robeck Jr., "John Paul II: A Personal Account of His Impact and Legacy," *Pneuma* 27 (Spring 2005): 6.

[7]Stephen Mansfield, "Keeper of the Flame," *Charisma,* June 2005, p. 41; David Aikman, "No More Walls," *Charisma,* June 2005, p. 74.

ity. In fact, it opposes it." But then, predictably, there were reactions to the reactions: "Casting stones at Catholics must stop. We are followers of Jesus Christ, too! . . . I was saddened to see so much Catholic bashing by your readers in the August issue. Thank you for your efforts to promote unity in the body of Christ."[8] What the letter pages of *Charisma* with their diverse commentary on John Paul II revealed clearly was a measure of continuity with the past—among evangelicals there remained pockets of serious reservations about Catholicism in general and this pope in particular. But they also revealed a range of positive attitudes that were unthinkable less than half a century before. To that earlier time, when evangelical attitudes were much more uniformly negative, we now turn as a way of introducing the more positive views that predominated about the late pope.

Catholics in Evangelical Perspective, 1956-1966

The great improvement in evangelical attitudes toward Catholicism can be demonstrated by comparing treatment in *Christianity Today* magazine during the mid-1950s (that is, before the papacy of John XXIII and the Second Vatican Council) and then in the late-1970s (that is, when Karol Wojtyla was elected pope). This periodical was begun in 1956 through the efforts of Billy Graham and with Carl F. H. Henry serving as founding editor. From the first, the magazine's leaders intended it to be a forthright, but also charitable, defender of evangelical theology, as well as a principled, but also discerning, advocate for evangelical public life. In its treatment of Catholicism, early issues of the magazine mostly offered carefully re-stated expressions of traditional Protestant opinion. In keeping with standard evangelical opinion of the time, it protested persistently against what editors and contributors saw as errors in Catholic doctrine. Yet even more, the magazine was concerned about what it viewed as Catholic tendencies toward political oppression. In *Christianity Today*'s early period, it is hard to discern a specific opinion on Pope Pius XII (1939-1958), except that he was implicated in Catholicism's conspiracies against freedom.

Thus, in the magazine's first year, 1956-1957, it went on record protesting Catholic opposition to the principle of the separation of church and state; it expressed fears about the "Thomistic philosophy of the Roman catholic Church" as leading to political theory that was "all too totalitarian"; it said of the pope that "he must look to his legions because he can no longer look to the gospel"; and in a rare mention by name, Pius XII was criticized for exalting the role of Mary in the pro-

[8]Letters quoted here are from the Feed Back column, *Charisma,* August 2005, pp. 10, 12; September 2005, p. 12; and November 2005, p. 12.

vision of salvation.[9] For the next several years, the main concern of the magazine with respect to such issues was the possibility that a Catholic might be elected president of the United States. Articles and editorials were quite stiff on this prospect, especially as the candidacy of John F. Kennedy emerged.[10] The most remarkable of the articles was a long "Open Letter to Sen. Kennedy," which included many questions like the following: "Can you, Senator Kennedy, reconcile your belief in the separation of church and state with [the] authoritative position of your church; or do you repudiate it for yourself."[11] What made this "open letter" so noteworthy was its authorship by Charles Clayton Morrison, the long-time editor of *The Christian Century*. The *Century* was the flagship periodical of American mainline Protestants whose influence Billy Graham and other founders of *Christianity Today* had deliberately sought to counter by establishing their own evangelical magazine. In other words, when it came to fears of Roman Catholicism in 1960, the evangelical *Christianity Today* stood closer to the mainline *Christian Century* than it did to anything Catholic.

If articles and editorials were firm in their anti-Catholicism during this era, most commentary published as letters from readers reflected even more extreme views. These opinions in letters were probably more typical of the evangelical populace as a whole than were the relatively measured voices of the magazine's own writers and editors. To be sure, when the magazine published material protesting Catholic restrictions on civil and religious freedom, a few readers would sometimes protest that Catholicism was being misrepresented. But the predominant reader response, especially as the election of 1960 drew near, was strident anti-Catholicism:

> If such facts as are pointed out in this article do not awake the Protestant population of America to evangelistic zeal and activity, the land for which our fathers died will go by default to that church from which we have sought to be a free nation under God. (Franklin, VA) . . . After more than a half century in a Catholic community I fear the Roman Catholic hierarchy far more than communism. I consider

---

[9]C. Stanley Lowell [of Protestants and Other Americans United, an organization defending the separation of church and state], "Rising Tempo of Rome's Demands," *Christianity Today*, January 7, 1957, pp. 11-13; Editorial, "Natural Law and Revelation," *Christianity Today*, June 24, 1957, p. 20; Editorial, "Billy Graham and the Pope's Legions," *Christianity Today*, July 22, 1957, p. 21; and John Gerstner, "Current Religious Thought," *Christianity Today*, January 21, 1957, p. 38.

[10]For only a sampling, see, "World News," *Christianity Today*, January 20, 1958, p. 28; quotations from Harold John Ockenga in Editorial, "Where Are We Drifting?" *Christianity Today*, December 22, 1958, p. 21; Editorial, "Should Americans Elect a Roman Catholic President?" *Christianity Today*, October 26, 1959, p. 22; Editorial, "Political Anxieties Rise as Party Conventions Approach," *Christianity Today*, July 4, 1960, p. 22.

[11]Charles Clayton Morrison, "Open Letter to Sen. Kennedy," *Christianity Today*, September 12, 1960, pp. 18, 32-33.

> it more anti-Christian. (Carroll, IA) . . . Let Protestants awaken to the dangers of the hour, and refuse to be tools of any totalitarian political power, whatever the garb. (Jackson, MN) . . . The rapidly growing power of Rome in our country is one of the greatest menaces to the fundamental principles of separation of church and state, and liberty of conscience and freedom of speech and of the press. (Hagerstown, MD)[12]

Yet consistently suspicious as *Christianity Today*'s writers and constituency were of all things Catholic, specific attention to the popes was relatively infrequent and, given the conventions of that earlier day, relatively gentle. When Pius XII died in the fall of 1958, the magazine commented that "the rule of Pius XII saw numerous pronouncements which went beyond scriptural license" and that he "expanded Roman dogma by defining the Virgin Mary's presumed assumption into heaven in body and soul." But otherwise the editors had little to say.[13] While there was some nervousness about the official United States delegation sent to the pope's funeral, the magazine also spoke with relative favor about the new pontiff, John XXIII, as looking to be probably "a religious more than a political pope."[14] During the first phases of the Second Vatican Council (1962-1965), there was some reporting of John XXIII's opening address and instructions, but noticeably less in-depth treatment than had earlier been devoted to the perceived threat of a Catholic U.S. president.[15]

Sometime during the pontificate of John XXIII, the tide of opinion among evangelicals turned, at least as represented in the pages of *Christianity Today.* The pope's encyclical *Pacem in terris* (1963) was greeted as "masterful and historic" and only gently criticized for being too optimistic about the potential of groups like the United Nations to make things better in a hurry. Then when John died, the magazine commented editorially on several aspects of Catholic teaching that opposed Protestant principles, but it also provided words of commendation that would once have been rare from any Protestant about any pope: "In the final hours of life, men marveled at the strength of Pope John's heart. Prior to that they had marveled at its warmth. . . . Perhaps history's most universally beloved pope, . . . John XXIII undoubtedly was largely responsible for a fresh spirit of charity which created happier

---

[12]Letters section, *Christianity Today,* December 8, 1958, p. 23; August 31, 1959, p. 16; September 28, 1959, p. 14; and March 14, 1960, p. 15

[13]"Catholicism Under Pious XII," *Christianity Today,* October 27, 1958, p. 32.

[14]"Church and State: The Tempter's Snares," *Christianity Today,* November 24, 1958, p. 29; "Pope John XXIII," *Christianity Today,* November 24, 1958, p. 32.

[15]For example, Stuart P. Garver, "Problems of Unity: Reflections on the Vatican Council," *Christianity Today,* December 7, 1962, pp. 27-28.

church relationships."[16] In later years, John's successor, Paul VI, would be praised for some of his actions (for example, in affirming human freedom) and criticized for others (for example, not relaxing the church's stance on birth control).[17] But a more irenic tone had replaced the antagonism of only a few years before.

From the magazine's pages themselves, it is difficult to pinpoint exactly why evangelical attitudes moderated toward Catholicism and its papal head. Beyond question, the fact that the election of John Kennedy as the first Catholic president did not lead to the predicted political disasters played a role. Doubtless the positive impression made by John XXIII was also a factor. But shifting currents within American society also certainly came into play.

Some of these straws in the wind were indicated by letters to *Christianity Today* from this earlier period. There was first a personality factor, as when a reader from San Diego commented in early 1960 about the positive Christian character of individual pontiffs: "I submit that present and immediately past incumbents of the papal throne were and are men of such saintly lives and such palpable piety that it ill becomes us Protestants of lesser devotional caliber to drag out an ancient document [referring to a Reformation-era statement that called the pope the Antichrist]."[18] The influence of what would later be called "culture wars" was also beginning to emerge. In late 1960, a reader from Canterbury, Connecticut, praised Catholic attitudes toward public culture that almost all Protestants had once feared: "Why should it be considered an 'alien phenomenon' that Catholics want their children to hear about God and Christ in a non-public, non-secular parochial school." To this reader, American public schools had become a real problem: "Such atheism-aiding, socialism-aiding education is further backed by the presence in public schools of the God-opposing theories, the anti-Christ ideologies (evolution, etc.). Why should not Protestants have Christian schools instead of public? Why condition the children against God? Are Catholics more smart, Christian, and loyal to the children's deepest needs than we are?"[19]

These positive assessments of Catholic piety and Catholic cultural wisdom were not typical in the late 1950s and early 1960s. Yet they did herald the sort of opinion that in the not too distant future would characterize much evangelical commentary on John Paul II.

---

[16]Editorial, "A Pontiff's Love and a Council's Anathemas," *Christianity Today,* June 21, 1963, p. 27.

[17]Editorial, "The Pope and World Peace," *Christianity Today,* August 28, 1964, p. 32; Editorial, "The Pope Who Fails to Speak," *Christianity Today,* November 25, 1966, p. 27.

[18]Letter, *Christianity Today,* January 18, 1960, p. 16.

[19]Letter, *Christianity Today,* October 24, 1960, p. 14.

EVANGELICALS ON JOHN PAUL II, 1978-2005

Once again, the pages of *Christianity Today* offer a reliable guide for charting evangelical attitudes toward John Paul II. Besides articles and full news reports, a lively letters column offered many different angles to perceiving and assessing the Roman pontiff.

Coverage of Karol Wojtyla as pope got off to an unusually propitious start with an article published in October 1978 that featured news of a trip by Billy Graham to Poland. In words written before the death of John Paul I, but brought out as his successor was being selected, the magazine reported that Graham's Polish journey had been resisted by many in the church's hierarchy, but not "the archbishop of Krakow, Cardinal Karol Wojtyla," who "is friendly to it."[20] Positive relationships that had been nurtured with the Oasis program for youth seemed to be expanding, and those relationships included positive connections with the archbishop who now had become John Paul II.

Early treatment of the new pope was unusually favorable, and for a reason rooted in earlier political perspectives. The first news story on John Paul II was almost entirely positive, especially as it stressed Wojtyla's resistance to political tyranny: "But most unique about John Paul II is the way he has guided Polish Catholics, people who live in a Communist state where atheism is the national policy." Similarly, the first editorial mention, while cautious in its assessments, likewise stressed the new pope's political position: "John Paul's experience under Nazi, then Communist, rule should make him more sensitive to the plight of religious minorities."[21] For Americans who had associated Catholicism with political despotism, it seemed to be a sharp reversal for the church now to be led by one who had spent his life defending Christianity against the twentieth century's most notorious despots.

Once initial impressions gave way to more deliberate assessments, evangelical opinions remained cautious, but were also expressed with unusual marks of respect. Two of the most mature of such assessments were published in 1985, after seven years of John Paul's tenure, and then at the end of his life in May 2005. Together they offer an example of evangelical balance in evaluating the work of John Paul II, but also (at twenty years' separation) of the ever-increasing approval that developed over time among at least some evangelicals.

The full assessment in 1985 was written by *Christianity Today* editor Kenneth

---

[20]Robert D. Linder and Richard V. Pierard, "Poland Opens the Door to Billy Graham," *Christianity Today,* October 6, 1978, p. 45.

[21]Anonymous, "The Papacy: Time for Catholicity," *Christianity Today,* November 3, 1978, p. 60; Editorial, "John Paul II," *Christianity Today,* November 17, 1978, p. 12.

Kantzer, who began by suggesting that John Paul had become "the most popular pope of this century" and by acknowledging that this pope "is determined not to let things drift." To Kantzer, it was an almost palpable relief to recognize that "he will not restore the Roman church to its narrow isolation and rigid conservatism of the nineteenth and early twentieth centuries." Again, the pope's political provenance—"with a faith forged in the hot battle against communism that fought the Polish church at every turn"—loomed large; such a valiant champion against such an enemy deserved a great deal of respect. For evangelicals, Kantzer thought this pope's deep sense of mission—"John Paul II is nothing if not a man of deep convictions and a sharp sense of duty"—made him an estimable figure. To be sure, the editorial acknowledged that this same burden of conviction had made things difficult for some ecumenical ventures; it singled out especially dialogue between Catholics and Anglicans as suffering because of the pope's rigor in upholding Catholic distinctives in dogma and practice. But for evangelicals who had their own reasons for worrying about ecumenism, the pope's record on this score was not necessarily a bad thing. It seemed rather that evangelicals should applaud the pope's willingness to slow down an ecumenical movement that, in Kantzer's eyes, often featured "extreme liberal theology and ethics."

With evangelical convictions specifically in view, Kantzer offered a nuanced assessment for why the pope had won many admirers. For its balance, it is worth quoting at length:

> John Paul II's personal appeal to evangelicals cannot be denied. Despite his Mariology, his adamant opposition to contraception, to all divorce on any grounds, his emphasis on priestly celibacy, his teaching on the role of women (which sometimes comes across as though the only legitimate place of women is in the home), and his strong clericalism, their enthusiasm has not been dimmed. Their appreciation is based on his strong support of certain fundamental doctrines of biblical faith; his willingness to discipline the most blatant opponents of evangelical faith; his biblical emphasis in which his messages are invariably sprinkled with scriptural teaching; his strong commitment to the family, to a biblical sexual ethics, and to prolife positions; his insistence upon justice and true freedom of religion everywhere; and his bold stand for the priority of the Christian message over political involvement. All these endear him to the hearts of evangelicals.[22]

As Kantzer made very clear, however, he wanted evangelical readers not to be swept away by these positive aspects of the pope's work. In particular, he reminded

[22]Kenneth Kantzer, "A Man Under Orders: Where Is Pope John Paul II Taking the Roman Catholic Church?" *Christianity Today*, September 6, 1985, pp. 14-15.

them of the specific doctrinal issues that "have, since the days of Luther and before, divided a biblically rooted evangelicalism from a Roman Catholicism based partly on biblical revelation and partly on human tradition." In Kantzer's view, significant Catholic dogmas still violated the Reformers' insistence on faith alone, grace alone, Christ alone and the Scriptures alone. They included the pope's insistence on sacramental penance, his frequent reference to his "hope" in Mary, his defense of Rome as the final interpreter of Scripture, his advocacy for papal infallibility and his inclusion of loving works alongside faith as grounds for salvation. With such matters in view, Kantzer concluded by acknowledging that "Pope John Paul II has moved many things in [the Catholic church] toward the good. But on many other vital matters that affect the souls of men and their relationship to God, Rome is still Rome."[23]

Both the appreciation and the caution that marked Kantzer's assessment from 1985 also characterized the magazine's summary assessment of John Paul's entire papal career twenty years later. But in the intervening decades the tone had improved even more. Now appreciation triumphed over caution, and the unsigned editorial expressed admiration with startling frankness. This editorial began by recounting the first meeting between the pope and Billy Graham, which had taken in place in 1981. According to Graham's account, which he had not made public until several years later, at the end of a friendly half-hour of conversation, "John Paul II reached over, clutched Graham's thumb, and told him, 'We are brothers.'" The *Christianity Today* editors then explained why telling this story now would not cause the consternation that may have greeted it a quarter of a century before:

> John Paul II offered a winsome face of Christianity to the world and leaves behind a Roman Catholic church firmly opposed to moral relativism. He reinforced the Second Vatican Council's commitment to seek renewal in the sources of classic Christianity—Scripture and the church fathers. And while significant differences remain—examples include ecclesiastical authority, the means of grace, and the relationship of justification to sanctification—evangelicals can confidently engage a Catholic Church committed to fundamental Christian truths.[24]

Alliances forged in the era's culture wars loomed large for this editorial, especially the Catholic and evangelical opposition to abortion-on-demand. But even larger loomed positive conversations about Christian doctrine and practice, as tes-

---

[23]Ibid., pp. 14-15.

[24]Editorial, "'We Are Brothers': John Paul II's Legacy of Orthodoxy Bodes Well for Evangelical Engagement," *Christianity Today*, June 2005, pp. 28-29.

tified particularly by the collaborative statements that began in 1994 under the rubric of "Evangelicals and Catholics Together." The editorial did not shy away from mentioning many of the same doctrinal issues that had troubled Kenneth Kantzer twenty years before, including the pope's "disturbing embrace of Marian devotion" and "the central issue of ecclesiology, especially in areas of papal authority and infallibility." Speaking practically, the editors also pointed out that many of America's megachurches were filled with ex-Catholics who had not found in their original church the positive evangelization they were seeking.

But the editorial's last words were once again positive. If Catholics still needed to learn about free grace and personal lay commitment from evangelicals, so too did evangelicals need to learn "about the role of community" and the benefits of "Catholic social teaching" that the pope had promoted. In a word, "so long as the Catholic Church adheres to John Paul II's firm orthodoxy, evangelicals will gain from this ecumenical effort."[25]

The measured and balanced assessments that the major *Christianity Today* statements provided for the pontificate of John Paul II did not, of course, speak for all evangelicals. When, for example, Kantzer's editorial appeared in 1985, a reader from Fulton, Michigan, responded by saying that the very title *pope* contradicted the positive judgments the magazine had offered; to truly follow the apostles John and Paul, the pope would have to give up calling himself a pope. But another reader, from Port Saint Lucie, Florida, quoted several passages of Scripture to suggest that it was the Catholic teaching on Mary, not evangelical nervousness about her, that should provide the norm for all believers.[26] Similarly, after the generally positive assessment of 2005, a reader from British Columbia urged others "not to be fooled"; the Catholic church was still an unreformed menace—"A chameleon may conveniently change its color, but it is still a chameleon." But another reader from New York was so enthusiastic about the editorial and an accompanying story about the new pope, Benedict XVI, that he had mailed them off to the new pontiff for his edification![27]

Alongside the set-piece editorials, which almost always conveyed a strong but cautious sense of approval for the pope, and the strikingly diverse letters, which could range from extreme praise to extreme censure for everything having to do with John Paul II, the pages of *Christianity Today* contained many other specific bits of information and many other informed assessments on the pope's tenure.

---

[25]Ibid., pp. 28-29.
[26]Letters, *Christianity Today,* October 18, 1985, p. 8.
[27]Letters, *Christianity Today,* August 2005, p. 17.

A full-scale compilation of such commentary would turn into a book-length work itself, but highlights are notable for underscoring many areas in which evangelicals praised the pope and a few in which traditional reservations received fresh expression.

The strongest opposition to the pope surfaced when his Marian devotion was juxtaposed to his pastoral leadership in areas of the world where Protestants had historically suffered at the hands of Catholics. Thus, in a report on John Paul II's first trip to Latin America, William Conrad offered a cautiously guarded assessment that stressed the worries of Latin American evangelicals who feared what the pope's visit might entail for them: "Some evangelicals are concerned by the Pope's adoration of Mary, saying that when devotion to the Virgin increases, so does persecution of evangelicals."[28] Similarly, a reporter from Poland relayed concerns from Polish Protestants that the pope's trips to his native country had made things worse rather than better for them.[29] Sometimes the pope's devotion to Mary was in the spotlight, as when John Stott expressed the fear that the pope in a visit to Brazil, "because of his outspoken veneration of Mary, will not speak out (as he should) against those attitudes and practices that undermine the sufficiency of Jesus Christ."[30] But often it was the combination of this Marian emphasis with his trips to regions where ancient Catholic-Protestant antagonisms remained that prompted criticism.[31] Predictably, whenever such assessments appeared, letters in the next issues accented criticisms in more extreme terms or rebutted criticisms with counterarguments. Beyond doubt, however, the evangelical constituency continued to harbor reservations about John Paul II's Mariology, especially when it was manifest among populist Roman Catholicism in Latin America, Poland and a few other historically Catholic parts of the world.

On other matters, especially in the early days of the pope's tenure, more traditional Protestant suspicion could also be heard, though usually expressed with considerable balance. Thus, in 1981, a Lutheran conceded that John Paul II was "a downright amiable person," but he also carefully defended the sense in which any pope might be considered by Protestants as an antichrist because of support

[28]William Conrad, "Puebla: All Things to All Bishops," *Christianity Today*, March 23, 1979, p. 58.

[29]Kenny Waters, "Polish Pastors Meet and Pledge Evangelism Thrust," *Christianity Today*, August 7, 1981, p. 40.

[30]John Stott, "Brazil: The Spiritual Climate," *Christianity Today*, April 4, 1980, p. 32. See also David Neff, "Let Mary Be: Why the Pope Shouldn't Give Mary That Which Belongs to Her Son," *Christianity Today*, December 8, 1997, pp. 14-15.

[31]See, for example, Stephen R. Sywulka, "John Paul Woos Straying Flock: Protestants Object to Being Labeled as 'Sects,'" *Christianity Today*, April 8, 1996, p. 94.

for traditional Catholic teaching. A year later a Presbyterian took note of favorable reactions to a papal visit to North America but reminded readers that the Catholic "church is still officially committed by its creed to doctrines evangelicals cannot accept—and some of them lie at the heart of biblical faith."[32]

Despite continued evangelical nervousness about such important themes in the pope's public activities, the much more prevalent attitude expressed in the magazine was approval that at times even verged toward the reverential. The full range of news stories, articles and letters conveying these opinions provides the raw material for understanding why John Paul II became such a widely admired figure for so many evangelicals. But for our purposes a sampling must suffice.

John Paul II's first trip to Poland became an opportunity to praise him for his Christ-centered speeches and to recall his courageous opposition to Communist tyranny.[33] His crack-down on theological liberalism—whether of Hans Küng in Europe or liberation theology in Latin America—won favorable comment.[34] He was praised for speaking up for the pro-life cause in private conversation with President Clinton.[35] And an editorial commended him for wisely parsing the tangled issues surrounding creation and evolution.[36]

It was also a small, but significant step toward broader evangelical recognition when brief comments by John Paul II began to appear in *Christianity Today*'s "Reflections" column, a page in each issue of the magazine given over to short quotations on a common theme. Beginning with the issue of December 11, 1987, when he was quoted about the need to enter the kingdom of God as a child (from Mark 10:15), words from John Paul II regularly joined words from well-known evangelicals (like Corrie Ten Boom, A. J. Gordon, Vance Havner, Martyn Lloyd-Jones, John Stott, Oswald Chambers) and a wide range of other spiritual mentors (Martin Luther, C. S. Lewis, Dorothy L. Sayers, G. K. Chesterton, Henri Nouwen) in providing food for spiritual thought.[37]

On more directly theological and ethical issues, it was intriguing not only that the pope was being cited favorably, but also by whom he was being cited. Thus, John

[32]David Scaer, "The Pope as Antichrist: An Anachronism?" *Christianity Today,* October 23, 1981, p. 66; W. Stanford Reid, "The Divisions in Christendom," *Christianity Today,* October 22, 1982, p. 13.
[33]Editorial, "The Pope in Poland," *Christianity Today,* June 29, 1979, p. 11; Anonymous, "The Pope's Triumph Pushes Polish Regime Off Balance," *Christianity Today,* June 29, 1979, p. 50.
[34]Anonymous, "The Pope Draws the Theological Line," *Christianity Today,* January 25, 1980, pp. 38-39; "Why Is Latin America Turning Protestant?" *Christianity Today,* April 6, 1992, pp. 28-29.
[35]Steve Rabey, "In Search of Catholic Youth," *Christianity Today,* September 13, 1993, p. 68.
[36]David Neff, "The Pope, the Press, and Evolution," *Christianity Today,* January 6, 1997, pp. 18-19.
[37]"Reflections," *Christianity Today,* December 11, 1987, p. 32; December 12, 1994, p. 49; November 13, 1995, p. 69; September 6, 1999, p. 104; January 8, 2001, p. 82; March 2003, p. 70.

Stott praised John Paul for stressing Christ in his early public pronouncements.[38] Richard John Neuhaus (while still a Lutheran before his conversion to Catholicism) commended the pope as "a profound teacher of the dignity of the human person and of the societal structures appropriate to that dignity."[39] Philip Yancey reported on the striking contrast between responses by the public in Chile to the pope and to their own political leaders: "Through sheer moral force, the Pope commanded more of Chile's loyalty than did President Pinochet with all his vaunted power."[40] The noted historian Elizabeth Fox-Genovese explored and approved his stance on women in church and society.[41] Charles Colson recounted with delight the pope's fortitude in standing fast for Christian truth in a well-publicized visit with Indian religious leaders.[42] And the secular, but strongly pro-life and anti-discrimination Michael Horowitz spoke of the pope in the same breath with William Wilberforce and Ronald Reagan as leading defenders of freedom.[43] It would be fair to say that no evangelical leader was receiving the same breadth of commendation as John Paul II regularly received in the pages of this evangelical periodical.

For the subject closest to the purpose of this book, it is also significant that authors in *Christianity Today* made regular reference to the pope's formal writings, including his encyclicals, and that this commentary was overwhelmingly positive. *Veritas splendor* (The Splendor of Truth) was singled out for the guidance it might offer evangelicals in becoming more intellectually responsible, as well as guidance for all people in finding a sure moral compass for modern life and thought.[44] *Ut unum sint* (That They Might Be One) was treated with respect in a balanced report on its main points.[45] And *Dominus Iesus* (The Lordship of Christ) was praised for its clear guidelines concerning ecumenical cooperation, despite the fact that some observers read this encyclical as reprising an older Catholic triumphalism.[46] In general, although coverage of the encyclicals was not extensive, it opened the kind of fruitful dialogue that the chapters of this book intend to carry further.

---

[38]John Stott, "Poland's Power of the Proletariat," *Christianity Today,* October 10, 1980, pp. 50-51.

[39]Richard John Neuhaus, "Who, Now, Will Shape the Meaning of America?" *Christianity Today,* March 19, 1982, p. 20.

[40]Philip Yancey, "The Pope's New Weapon," *Christianity Today,* August 7, 1987, p. 56.

[41]Elizabeth Fox-Genovese, "A Pro-Woman Pope," *Christianity Today,* April 27, 1998, pp. 73-75.

[42]Charles Colson, "The Ugly Side of Tolerance," *Christianity Today,* March 6, 2000, p. 136.

[43]Michael Horowitz, "Cry Freedom," *Christianity Today,* March 2003, p. 50.

[44]Nathan O. Hatch, "Our Shackled Scholars," *Christianity Today,* November 22, 1993, pp. 12-13; Richard John Neuhaus, "A Voice in the Relativistic Wilderness," *Christianity Today,* February 7, 1994, pp. 33-35.

[45]Anonymous, news story, *Christianity Today,* July 17, 1995, pp. 56-57.

[46]Editorial, "Honest Ecumenism," *Christianity Today,* October 23, 2000, pp. 28-29.

CONCLUSION

The extensive treatment of John Paul II that appeared in *Christianity Today* from the start of his pontificate in 1978 to its conclusion in 2005, as well as the more episodic but also significant treatment in *Charisma,* provides useful background for the more detailed theological studies that follow. Clearly, for many American evangelicals, the implacable suspicion of the pope that once prevailed widely is no more. To be sure, significant sections of the evangelical community maintain the older criticisms of Catholicism, and sometimes with the old vigor. But most evangelicals who have taken the time to study what John Paul II actually spoke and wrote know that these older attitudes are no longer helpful. His words, combined with the courage of his pre-papal life and the ceaseless humanitarian energy of his papal career, made this pope an object of interest, respect and (surprising) authority for many evangelicals. That development, which almost no one could have anticipated only short years ago, lay behind a conversation reported by Richard John Neuhaus, after he had himself become a Roman Catholic. After listening to a friend, who is a Baptist, praise one of the pope's encyclicals, Neuhaus pointed out that it and other papal writings were not just for Catholics, but for all who were committed to the moral meaning of life. At which point, "My Baptist friend who says that that this pope sure knows how to pope adds, 'He's your pope, but I hope you don't mind if we borrow him from time to time.'"[47] Gauging how much and in what ways to borrow, rather than whether to borrow, have become the pressing questions.

John Paul II was obviously a theologian of fundamental trinitarian orthodoxy who employed the Scriptures and classical church teachings to exalt Jesus Christ as the sole Savior of the world. That he was also obviously a Catholic theologian who insisted on a prominent role for Mary in the history of salvation, a preeminent role for papal authority in defining Christian teaching, and an exalted place for the institutional church in all matters of Christian life and practice adds (for evangelicals) the complexity that it is the purpose of this book to explore.

[47]Richard John Neuhaus, "A Voice in the Relativistic Wilderness," *Christianity Today,* February 7, 1994, p. 35.

2

"A Deep Amazement at Man's Worth and Dignity"

Technology and the Person in Redemptor hominis

Derek S. Jeffreys

Efforts to expand the scope of bioethical reflection, meanwhile, will likely be stifled first and foremost by the overwhelming predominance of "the life question" in our public considerations of bioethical topics. This has certainly been one of the most frustrating aspects of public bioethics as I have experienced it these past three years. All too often in public debate, bioethical controversy is fought out on the plane of what one may call the "the life principle," the principle that calls for protecting, preserving, and saving human life.

Leon R. Kass

As many others in the West, we have had such a faith in science and its doctrine of progress that we are unprepared for the choices biotechnology brings us.

For the Health of the Nation: An Evangelical Call to Civic Responsibility

INTRODUCTION

American discussions of bioethics focus heavily on issues like cloning and embryonic stem cell research. Often, evangelicals approach them by considering only the value of human life. The embryo is a person, they maintain, and any attempt to manipulate it is immoral. Since embryonic stem cell research requires manipulating the embryo, we cannot permit it. U.S. President George Bush employed such moral reasoning when announcing his 2001 decision to restrict federal funding for embryonic stem cell research, remarking that "I also believe human life is a sacred gift from our Creator. I worry about a culture that devalues life, and believe as your President I have an important obligation to foster and encourage respect for life in America and throughout the world."[1] Others have used similar arguments about in vitro fertilization, abortion and euthanasia.

Unfortunately, by focusing exclusively on the moral value of the embryo or fetus, many evangelicals neglect important challenges confronting twenty-first-century humanity.[2] Specifically, they fail to develop a philosophy of technology that considers how technology affects our lives. For example, biotechnology's significance far exceeds questions about killing persons. At its heart, it "appears as a most recent and vibrant expression of the technological spirit, a desire and disposition rationally to understand, order, predict, and (ultimately) control the events and workings of nature, all pursued for the sake of human benefit."[3] Biotechnology forces us to think about human nature, freedom, the purposes of science and moral agency. Recently, these questions entered public discourse when President Bush appointed a President's Council on Bioethics. In a fascinating report, this body considered aspects of biotechnology requiring urgent attention. For example, it noted that millions of American children and adults now use pharmacology to treat mental illness. Unquestionably necessary for many people, pharmacological intervention nevertheless affects how we think about moral agency. Does it mitigate moral responsibility or undermine the connection between effort and character development? Similarly, the council discussed memory-altering therapies for those overwhelmed by combat or sexual abuse. Should we use them only for the severely ill or permit others to employ them to

---

[1]George W. Bush, "President Discusses Stem Cell Research," White House Office of the Press Secretary (August 9, 2001) <http://www.whitehouse.gov/news/releases/2001/08/20010809-2.html>.

[2]To forestall misunderstanding, I want to say I strongly oppose abortion, euthanasia and embryonic stem cell research.

[3]*Beyond Therapy: Biotechnology and the Pursuit of Happiness*, President's Council on Bioethics, Washington, D.C. (October 2003), p. 2, <http://www.bioethics.gov/reports/beyondtherapy/index.html>. This is a superb report, and I draw heavily on it throughout this essay.

enhance their memories? How do these therapies affect our identity, which is tightly linked to memory? The council also considered genetic enhancement and engineering. The Human Genome Project (the recently completed attempt to map the human genetic structure) is increasing our power to eliminate disease and enhance personality characteristics. Should we use this power to alter the personalities of future children or restrict it to combating disease? These questions are vitally important, but many Americans ignore them. They believe that if biotechnology is safe and affects none of the life issues, consumers should be allowed to use it.

In contrast, the late Pope John Paul II repeatedly called for a philosophically sophisticated approach to technology. Throughout his long papacy, he engaged in extensive dialogue with scientists and issued documents addressing technological change. To discussions of technology he brought a complex philosophical vision informed by European thought. In this essay, I explore this vision by focusing on his first encyclical, *Redemptor hominis.* First, I introduce John Paul II's concept of the person, exploring human action, self-determination and self-possession. Second, I discuss his "personalistic norm," which proscribes using persons merely as a means to an end. Third, turning to *Redemptor hominis,* I consider the person in the modern world, emphasizing how Christ's kingship reveals the primacy of spiritual over material values. Fourth, I examine what the encyclical teaches about technology, exploring how human beings can become alienated from their products. I show how John Paul II analyzes intransitive action and alienation, and discuss how he uses the work of French philosopher Gabriel Marcel (1889-1973) and Polish poet Cyprian Norwid (1821-1883). Finally, after describing how evangelicals use technology, I maintain that John Paul II's personalism can help them respond critically to biotechnology.

Persons and Action

When he ascended to the papacy in 1979, John Paul II brought with him a well-developed philosophical vision. Trained as a Thomist (someone who takes Thomas Aquinas as his philosophical inspiration), he developed Thomistic thought at Poland's Lublin University, embracing thinkers like Jacques Maritain and Etienne Gilson. However, he also wrote extensively about phenomenology, the philosophical approach that emphasizes experience and consciousness. In particular, he critically retrieved the work of Max Scheler, a remarkable German phenomenologist. Scheler taught him to focus carefully on our experience of values. John Paul II used all these philosophical resources as a participant in the

Second Vatican Council, writing about the momentous changes the council brought. Finally, he developed his philosophical vision while living under the Nazi and Soviet regimes in Poland, which systematically destroyed the person. Like others in the twentieth century, he responded to these horrors by embracing personalism, an outlook that makes the person the center of ethical and political analysis. He resolved to defend the person's dignity against the many modern attempts to eliminate it.[4]

In his personalism, John Paul II maintains that we experience a fundamental distinction between persons and things. For him, there exists a "great gulf which separates the world of persons from the world of things."[5] Unlike persons, things lack an inner life, cannot exercise freedom and have no sense of moral responsibility. They cannot relate to truth and goodness, cannot ask questions of themselves and others, and cannot ponder why they exist. We understand these differences between persons and things, John Paul II maintains, because persons act on us. For example, I recognize the difference between my computer and my students because students act on me in ways that reveal their inner lives. Action enables us to understand that persons exist and have a nature.[6]

According to John Paul II, we also experience a difference between what happens to us and what we do. When we do something, we have "a sense of efficacy," an experience of our own causality.[7] We also feel responsible for what we cause, recognizing the link between our will and the consequences of our acts. Drawing on a classical distinction in Aquinas, John Paul II distinguishes transitive from in-

---

[4]For the best introductions to John Paul II's philosophy, see Rocco Buttiglione, *Karol Wojtyla: The Thought of the Man Who Became John Paul II* (Grand Rapids: Eerdmans, 1997); Kenneth L. Schmitz, *At the Center of the Human Drama: The Philosophical Anthropology of Karol Wojtyla/John Paul II* (Washington, D.C.: The Catholic University of America Press, 1993); and Jaroslaw Kupczak, *Destined for Liberty: The Human Person in the Philosophy of Karol Wojtyla/John Paul II* (Washington, D.C.: The Catholic University of America Press, 2000). Given the complexity of John Paul II's ideas, I will be selective in my discussion of his account of the person.

[5]Karol Wojtyla, *Love and Responsibility,* trans. H. T. Willetts (New York: Farrar, Strauss & Giroux, 1960), p. 24.

[6]For other Thomists who emphasize action, see Joseph de Finance, *Être et agir dans la philosophie de Saint Thomas* (Rome: Università Gregoriana, 1960) and W. Norris Clarke, "Action as the Self-Revelation of Being," in *Explorations in Metaphysics: Being, God, Person* (Notre Dame, Ind.: University of Notre Dame Press, 1994).

[7]Karol Wojtyla, "The Personal Structure of Self-Determination," in *Person and Community: Selected Essays,* trans. Theresa Sandok, Catholic Thought from Lublin 4 (New York: Lang, 1993), p. 189. In my essay, I draw primarily from the essays in this volume. In 1969, John Paul II published his major work in phenomenology, *The Acting Person,* but its English translation (trans. Andrzej Potocki [Boston: Reidel, 1979]) has been beset by controversy over its accuracy. For a discussion of this controversy, see Schmitz, *At the Center,* pp. 58-60, and Kupzcak, *Destined for Liberty,* pp. 67-68. I will, however, occasionally refer to the 1979 English translation.

transitive action. With transitive action, the subject's action goes beyond her, seeking "an expression and effect in the external world" that is "objectified in some product."[8] Intransitive action, in contrast, remains in the person, determining her "immanent quality or value."[9] Human action may be simultaneously intransitive and transitive, shaping both the outside world and the person.

Importantly, intransitive action reveals self-determination, a key characteristic of persons. Willing to act, I go out "toward a value," transcending my own ego.[10] For example, when I visit Florence, Italy, I am drawn to its beautiful churches and monuments. I experience a "horizontal" transcendence, moving toward aesthetic values.[11] I also "simultaneously determine myself."[12] Human acts are reflexive, rebounding back on the person and shaping character. Repeatedly viewing Brunelleschi's *Duomo* in Florence, I may become more attuned to architectural beauty. By being willing to relate to moral values like truthfulness, I shape a basic orientation toward good and evil. Gradually, I alter my personhood, either fulfilling myself by embracing moral values or degenerating into an evil person who rejects them. Self-determination thus involves exercising efficacy to develop character and constitutes our most immediate experience of the person.

Self-determination also "in some sense points to self-possession and self-governance as the structure of the person."[13] Through it, I appear as a being possessing and governing itself. As philosopher W. Norris Clarke puts it, the person is *dominus sui* (the master of itself), aware of itself "as present and as a source" of its actions.[14] Self-possession may suggest excessive self-concern, but in fact, "both self-possession and self-governance imply a special disposition to make a 'gift of oneself,' and this is a 'disinterested' gift."[15] Only a being possessing itself has something to give to another. Throughout his writings, John Paul II continually links self-possession and self-giving. The two concepts are par-

[8]Karol Wojtyla, "The Constitution of Culture Through Human Praxis," in *Person and Community: Selected Essays,* trans. Theresa Sandok, Catholic Thought from Lublin 4 (New York: Lang, 1993), p. 266.

[9]Ibid. For a wonderful treatment of the intransitive values of the person, see Josef Pieper, *Leisure: The Basis of Culture,* intro. Roger Scruton, new trans. Gerald Malsbary (South Bend, Ind.: St. Augustine's Press, 1998).

[10]Wojtyla, "Personal Structure of Self-Determination," p. 191.

[11]Ibid. For a detailed discussion of transcendence, see Wojtyla, *Acting Person,* pp. 255-58, 135-48. See also Karol Wojtyla, "The Person: Subject and Community," in *Person and Community: Selected Essays,* trans. Theresa Sandok, Catholic Thought from Lublin 4 (New York: Lang, 1993), pp. 232-33.

[12]Wojtyla, "Personal Structure of Self-Determination," p. 191.

[13]Ibid., p. 192.

[14]W. Norris Clarke, S.J., *Person and Being* (Milwaukee: Marquette University Press, 1993), p. 43.

[15]Wojtyla, "Personal Structure of Self-Determination," p. 194.

ticularly important for thinking about love and the family because self-giving characterizes love between spouses and love between parents and children. Through it, the family can develop a remarkable community of giving and sharing.[16]

Because a person has self-possession and self-determination, we should never use him merely as a thing. To articulate this insight, John Paul II presents the "personalistic norm," which states that "the person is the kind of good which does not admit of use and cannot be treated as an object of use and as such the means to an end."[17] Naturally, we often use others in our families and workplaces, but we should always recognize them as independent centers of activity and self-determination. The personalistic norm has roots in the work of the German philosopher Immanuel Kant, but John Paul II gives it a unique interpretation by emphasizing how we experience the person's value. It rules out any utilitarian approach to ethics that employs persons as mere means for social or political ends. Throughout his papacy, John Paul II employed the personalistic norm to criticize totalitarian and democratic regimes that used persons as mere means.

THE PERSON AND REDEMPTION

In *Redemptor hominis,* John Paul II links our experience of persons to redemption in the modern world. The church, he maintains, "continually seeks ways of bringing" the mystery of Christ "to humanity –to the peoples, the nations, the succeeding generations, and every individual human being" (*Redemptor hominis,* §7).[18] Redemption speaks to a world marked by positive technological change but also containing unprecedented possibilities for destruction. Amidst these changes, the person's value often seems to disappear. Many modern philosophical and scientific movements reduce persons to biological or psychological processes. Or, they deny that we have a human nature altogether. Totalitarian regimes have destroyed millions of people, utterly disregarding their value in the name of utopian schemes. Jesus Christ penetrates all these developments by vividly revealing the person's value. Assuming human nature, he shows that "by the very fact that it was as-

---

[16]For one discussion of the self-giving love and the family, see John Paul II, *"Familiaris consortio"* . . . *on the Role of the Christian Family in the Modern World,* Libreria Editrice Vaticana (November 22, 1981) <http://www.vatican.va/holy_father/john_paul_ii/apost_exhortations/documents/hf_jp-ii_exh_19811122_familiaris-consortio_en.html>.

[17]Wojtyla, *Love and Responsibility,* p. 41.

[18]In this essay, I use the Vatican translation of John Paul II, *Redemptor hominis*, Libreria Editrice Vaticana (March 4, 1979) <http://www.vatican.va/edocs/ENG0218/_INDEX.HTM>. Unless otherwise noted, all of the following in-text citations to this encyclical will be identified by section number only.

sumed, not absorbed, in him, [humanity] has been raised in us also to a dignity beyond compare" (§8). In every age, the church directs our gaze toward this dignity, opposing all philosophical and political tendencies denying it.

Jesus reveals human dignity because he expresses divine love, which forms the basis for a true humanism. In a moving paragraph, John Paul II insists that "man cannot live without love. He remains a being that is incomprehensible for himself, his life is senseless, if love is not revealed to him, if he does not encounter love, if he does not experience it and make it his own, if he does not participate intimately in it" (§10). Many philosophical and theological views contain important truths but remain incomplete because they ignore divine love. Human beings fully understand their own value only when experiencing this love. Modern people may be unaware of Christ's love, but it exerts its force by vivifying "every aspect of authentic humanism," and our amazement at it is another name for the gospel (§10).[19] In his years as pope, John Paul II redefined humanism to allow for its transcendent dimension, considering suffering, war, biotechnology and other issues.

Authentic humanism considers both human nature and our unique individuality. Christ, John Paul II maintains, directs his love toward concrete persons. Redemption addresses "each man in all the unrepeatable reality of what he is and what he does, of intellect and will, of his conscience and heart" (§14). Its object is "man in his unique unrepeatable human reality, which keeps intact the image and likeness of God himself" (§13). Christ unites with each person, becoming "present with the power of the truth and the love that are expressed in him with unique unrepeatable fullness" (§13). In these words, John Paul II expresses one of personalism's fundamental insights, the idea that each person has irreplaceable and incommunicable value. Discussing our shared human nature, philosopher John F. Crosby notes that "each human being, besides sharing in this common nature, also has something of his own—something his own and not another's—incommunicably his own."[20] We also cannot identify a person's unique dignity with a common human nature. His self-possession is uniquely his own, which "nobody else can exercise or execute."[21] We cannot reduce it to a social or psychological phenomenon, and cannot subsume human dignity into an abstract metaphysical theory. Instead,

---

[19]John Paul II was influenced by the French philosopher Jacques Maritain, who developed a Christian humanism in the 1930s and 1940s. For Maritain's most famous work on this subject, see Jacques Maritain, *Integral Humanism, Freedom in the Modern World, and a Letter on Independence* (Notre Dame, Ind.: University of Notre Dame Press, 1996).

[20]John F. Crosby, "A Neglected Source of the Dignity of Persons," in *Personalist Papers* (Washington, D.C.: The Catholic University of America Press, 2004), p. 7.

[21]Wojtyla, *Acting Person*, p. 107.

before the person, we must pause and wonder at the "irreducible."[22] True humanism must avoid adopting vague generalities about humanity, and instead embrace each person's unique value.

True humanism, John Paul II also insists, must never separate freedom from truth. Acknowledging modernity's strong aspirations toward freedom, the church values "what man has himself worked out in the depths of his spirit concerning the most profound and important problems" (§12). Consequently, the Second Vatican Council strongly affirmed religious liberty even though the church has historically often failed to embrace it. Rather than rejecting diverse approaches to truth, the church should accept their positive teachings. However, it must never abandon the truth about the human person because it is a "condition for authentic freedom" (§12).[23] John Paul II rejects all forms of relativism, which see truth as relative to the individual, culture or history. He also repudiates the idea that freedom is maximal choice, arguing that this leads to confusion and social disorder. Maximal choice without guidance or maturity is a counterfeit form of freedom. Christians thus confront the delicate task of affirming one truth while acknowledging truths in non-Christian thought.

WHAT DO WE FEAR? TECHNOLOGY AND THE PERSON

Part of this truth concerns technology and the person, and in the decade before he issued *Redemptor hominis,* John Paul II considered technology carefully. Beginning with *Person and Act* in 1969 (his major work in phenomenology) and continuing with essays in the 1970s, he developed a phenomenological approach to it. He wrote in an intellectual climate in which technology was a matter of serious philosophical reflection. Among others, philosophers Martin Heidegger, Jürgen Habermas and Jacques Ellul wrote extensively about how technology affects humanity.[24] Often, they expressed deep worries about how we are losing control of our products. For example, Ellul famously analyzed how techniques degrade social relations. Heidegger argued against an instru-

[22]For a good discussion of the irreducibility of the person, see Karol Wojtyla, "Subjectivity and the Irreducible in the Human Being," in *Person and Community: Selected Essays,* trans. Theresa Sandok, Catholic Thought from Lublin 4 (New York: Lang, 1993), pp. 209-19.

[23]John Paul II defends this close link between freedom and truth in his controversial 1993 encyclical, *Veritatis splendor,* Libreria Editrice Vaticana (August 6, 1993) <http://www.vatican.va/edocs/ENG0222/_INDEX.HTM>.

[24]Martin Heidegger, "The Question Concerning Technology," in *The Question Concerning Technology and Other Essays,* ed. William Lovett (New York: Harper Torchbooks, 1977), pp. 3-35; Jürgen Habermas, *The Theory of Communicative Action,* vol. 1, *Reason and the Rationalization of Society* (Boston: Beacon, 1985); Jacques Ellul, *The Technological Society* (New York: Vintage, 1967).

mental understanding of technology, seeking instead to define its essence. Habermas discussed how technology affects democracy and human nature. Unfortunately, few North Americans today are aware of this rich debate about technology, despite the last decade's tremendous advances in information and other technologies.

Like many in this debate, John Paul II describes how we become estranged from technology. Modern man "seems ever to be under threat from what he produces, that is to say from the result of the work of his hands and, even more so, of the work of his intellect and the tendencies of his will" (§15). Modern human beings fear technology will bring "an unimaginable self-destruction, compared with which all the cataclysms and catastrophes of history known to us seem to fade away" (§15). Too often, man's activity "is not only subjected to 'alienation,' in the sense that it is simply taken away from the person who produces it, but rather it turns against man himself, at least in part, through the indirect consequences of its effects returning on himself. It is or can be directed against him. This seems to make up the main chapter of the drama of present-day human existence in its broadest and universal dimension. Man therefore lives increasingly in fear" (§15). Because action is both transitive and intransitive, technology invariably shapes our moral characters. In the modern world, it may affect us in extremely negative ways. With advances in military hardware and biotechnology, we are left wondering why creative forces can quickly become so destructive.

In this threatening environment, Christ's kingship reveals the priority of spiritual over material values. We must always ask if "in the context of this progress man, as man, is becoming truly better, that is to say more mature spiritually, more aware of the dignity of his humanity, more responsible, more open to others" (§15). Because Jesus Christ makes Christians "so universally sensitive about the problem of man," they cannot avoid developing ethical norms for technological progress. Warning against technological euphoria, John Paul II insists that new technologies must "accord with man's moral and spiritual progress" (§15). The church, in particular, must consider the "fundamental need for solicitude by man for man, for his humanity, and for the future of people on earth" (§15). However, it must also avoid endorsing easy political solutions to complex technological problems. Christ's kingship is not a political one, but "consists in the priority of ethics over technology, in the primacy of the person over things, and in the superiority of spirit over matter" (§16). It requires us to constantly strive to retain a proper order of values that elevates the spiritual over the material. This is particularly difficult in the face of technological progress, which too often leads people to embrace a shallow consumerism.

Christ's kingship also obliges us to remember that humanity exercises a responsible dominion over material things.[25] Unless man vigilantly monitors technology, he becomes its slave, relinquishing "the place in the visible world that belongs to him" (§16). Sadly, modern materialism dethrones humanity from its central place in creation, viewing the person merely as an animal with an advanced brain.[26] Even those who reject materialism find themselves trapped by technology used in ways "contrary to the intentions and the very premises of its pioneers" (§16). We sometimes invent a product for one purpose, only to find others using it for another.[27] Too often, we rush to develop new technologies, disregard their social and spiritual consequences, and surrender our dominion over the material world.

To respond to technological change, John Paul II emphasizes intransitive action. In a fascinating address he gave two years before *Redemptor hominis* ("The Constitution of Culture Through Human Praxis"), he insisted that intransitive values are more valuable than transitive ones. Technological achievements presuppose a subject actualizing herself. Using the controversial term *praxis,* John Paul II maintains that it "consists in realizing ourselves and, at the same time, in making the nonhuman reality outside of ourselves more human."[28] While "not denying the fundamentality" of production, we must not "allow the human being to become an epiphenomenon and, in a sense, a product."[29] *Praxis* reveals our capacities for self-determination and transcendence. Through it, the person remains superior to her products, never becoming merely one of them.

Through self-determination, persons can also humanize technology by allowing it to reflect goodness and beauty. We not only determine ourselves through action, but our products also "involve a certain radiation of humanity, by virtue of which the effects of culture are properly inscribed in the effects of nature."[30] Too often, we ignore beauty in artifacts, failing to experience "wonder

---

[25]For another discussion of Christ's kingship, see *Veritatis splendor,* §§38-39.

[26]Steven Pinker is a contemporary materialist who dethrones humanity; see Steven Pinker, *The Blank Slate: The Modern Denial of Human Nature* (New York: Penguin, 2002).

[27]This is an important theme in the President's Council on Bioethics report, *Beyond Therapy,* which frequently discusses how biotechnological advances arise in one context, only to be used in completely different ones.

[28]Wojtyla, "Constitution of Culture," p. 267. Rocco Buttiglione discusses this essay at length, and I have learned much from his discussion; see Buttiglione, *Karol Wojtyla,* pp. 292-305.

[29]Wojtyla, "Constitution of Culture," p. 267.

[30]Ibid., p. 269.

and awe at reality."[31] Technology has a contemplative aspect, a communion with aesthetic values that is "something completely internal; it is an immanent activity of the human soul, and it leaves its mark and brings forth fruit in this same dimension. It is from this communion that we mature and grow inwardly."[32] Through contemplation, we appreciate not only what technology does *for* us, but also what it does *to* us.

In this analysis, Gabriel Marcel and Cyprian Norwid play an important role. Sometimes John Paul II cites Marcel's famous distinction between "being" and "having."[33] Having relates a person to something external to her, a thing she assimilates and possesses.[34] It implies a contrast between the internal and external. For example, when I own a car, I use an external object to get around, possessing it to serve my purposes. In contrast, being lacks possession and use, and remains within the person rather than relating her to something external. It involves a presence we have difficulty conceptualizing because "it is almost impossible for us to avoid a picture of activity which would be in some sense physical. We can hardly help seeing it as the starting-up of a machine, a machine of which our bodies are the spring and perhaps also the mold."[35] Being also lacks the acquisitive character we find in having because the person seeks to rest with an object's presence.[36] For example, standing before Michelangelo's famous statue *David,* I admire its form, without seeking to possess it for mundane purposes. Finally, being includes a joyful and active reception of another, a willingness to welcome its presence.

Marcel uses the having/being distinction to draw attention to the characteristics of modern techniques. Techniques are indispensable to human life, and we cannot regard "either technical progress in general, or the progress of some particular technique, as having of its very nature a necessarily negative value for the hu-

---

[31]Ibid., p. 270.

[32]Ibid., p. 271.

[33]For an extended discussion of this distinction, see Gabriel Marcel, *Being and Having: An Existentialist Diary,* trans. Katherine Farrer (New York: Harper Torchbooks, 1965). We know that John Paul II read Marcel's work because he cites it in "Constitution of Culture." He also refers to Marcel in his first encyclical on economics; see *Sollicitudo rei socialis,* Libreria Editrice Vaticana (December 30, 1987), §28 <http://www.vatican.va/edocs/ENG0223/_INDEX.HTM>. In this encyclical, John Paul II applies the having/being distinction to economic development, arguing that consumerism reflects the unhealthy dominance of having. Schmitz is one of the few thinkers to recognize connections between John Paul II and Marcel; see Schmitz, *At the Center,* p. 35, n. 137.

[34]Marcel, *Being and Having,* p. 155.

[35]Ibid., pp. 187-88.

[36]Marcel develops the remarkable concept of disposability *(disponibilité),* the active reception of another person. For a discussion of *disponibilité,* see Gabriel Marcel, "Belonging and Disposibility," in *Creative Fidelity,* trans. and intro. Robert Rosthal (New York: Farrar, Straus, 1964), pp. 38-58. W. Norris Clarke also explores the metaphysics of receptivity; see Clarke, *Person and Being.*

man spirit."[37] However, techniques have important characteristics that distinguish them from intransitive values. For example, we can divorce techniques from particular subjects, appealing to anyone who employs them. Given proper instructions, anyone can turn on my computer in the morning. Moreover, with techniques, I try to control things outside of me, and succeed the more control I exercise. Intransitive values, in contrast, are intimately linked to concrete persons. It is senseless to take my love for my wife, create a love algorithm and urge others to employ it. I cannot manipulate and control love like I do my computer. Moreover, unlike techniques, intransitive values are not subject to quantitative gain or loss. If I "have four things and give two away, it is obvious that I only have two left, and that I am correspondently *impoverished.*"[38] Such arithmetic is inapplicable to intransitive values, which differ from a "statistical unit which can be noted in the calculations of a sociologist employing the methods of an engineer."[39] Philosopher Kenneth Schmitz helpfully calls this dimension of intransitive values "communication without loss."[40] Unlike things, persons can give of themselves without loss. A teacher, Schmitz notes, shares her knowledge with students without losing it. Rather than being a zero-sum game, a genuine community of learning enriches both students and teachers.

Like Marcel, Norwid emphasizes intransitive values, depicting how modern techniques often undermine our experience of beauty. Near the end of his papacy, John Paul II noted that he had been "bound by a deep spiritual kinship" with Norwid since his "secondary school years."[41] An exile from Poland, Norwid fre-

---

[37]Gabriel Marcel, *Man Against Mass Society,* foreword by Donald Mackinnon (Chicago: Henry Regnery, 1962), p. 56. For a good discussion of Marcel and technology, see Bernard A. Gendreau, "The Cautionary Ontological Approach to Technology of Gabriel Marcel," paper presented at the Twentieth World Congress of Philosophy, Boston, Mass., August 10-15, 1998, Paideia: Philosophy of Technology, <http://www.bu.edu/wcp/Papers/Tech/TechGend.htm>. See also Gabriel Marcel, "Some Remarks on Irreligion Today," in *Being and Having: An Existentialist Diary,* trans. Katherine Farrer (New York: Harper & Row, 1965), pp. 176-99. Jacques Ellul discusses the elements of technique extensively; see Ellul, *Technological Society,* chap. 2.

[38]Marcel, *Being and Having,* p. 69 (italics original).

[39]Gabriel Marcel, "The Ego and Its Relation to Others," in *Homo Viator: Introduction to a Metaphysics of Hope,* trans. Emma Craufurd (New York: Harper and Row Torchbooks, 1962), p. 25.

[40]Kenneth L. Schmitz, "Created Receptivity and the Philosophy of the Concrete," in *The Texture of Being: Essays in First Philosophy,* ed. Paul O'Herron (Washington, D.C.: Catholic University of America Press, 2007), chap. 7.

[41]*Address of John Paul II to the Representatives of the Institute of Polish National Patrimony* (July 1, 2001), §2 <http://www.vatican.va/holy_father/john_paul_ii/speeches/2001/documents/hf_jpii_spe_20010701_norwid_en.html>. For another discussion of beauty, see *Letter of His Holiness John Paul II to Artists,* Libreria Editrice Vaticana (April 4, 1999) <http://www.vatican.va/holy_father/john_paul_ii/letters/documents/hf_jp-ii_let_23041999_artists_en.html>. For a good discussion of Cyprian Norwid, see Buttiglione, *Karol Wojtyla,* pp. 25-26. John Paul II discusses Norwid in many places; see John Paul II, *Crossing the Threshold of Hope* (New York: Knopf, 1995), p. 224; John Paul

quently wrote about beauty in the modern world. Confronting the Industrial Revolution's dehumanization, he describes how work can reflect human spirituality.[42] Norwid believed that "the main problem is that work is alienated from creativity, the artifact is merely useful, instead of satisfying man's innate sense of beauty."[43] Drawing explicitly on Norwid, John Paul II suggests that the material world shows a "kind of readiness to put itself at our disposal: to serve human needs, to welcome within it the superior scale of human ends, to enter in some way into the human dimension and participate in human existence in the world."[44] As spiritual creatures, human beings are not aliens in a cold, hostile material world. Instead, they find receptivity in the universe, and integrate the spiritual and material. To avoid dehumanization, technology should reflect this relationship between the spiritual and material. Moreover, it should allow human beings to cultivate a contemplative life that allows them to relate to properly to products. For example, architecture and urban planning ought to reflect our inner life and promote quiet contemplation. They should never simply serve utilitarian purposes.

To underscore this proper scale of values, John Paul II transforms the concept of alienation, a common theme in twentieth-century political philosophy.[45] For Marxists, alienation means that human beings are estranged from their "economic and political systems, their property, and their work."[46] They suggest that to end it, "all we have to do is transform the world of products, change the economic and political systems, and rally against religion."[47] For John Paul II, Marxists simply

---

II, *Memory and Identity: Conversations at the Dawn of the Millennium* (New York: Rizzoli, 2005), pp. 60-61. For Norwid's influence on John Paul II, see George Weigel, *Witness to Hope: The Biography of Pope John Paul II* (New York: Cliff Street Books, 1999), pp. 34-36.

[42]John Paul II links work, contemplation and the person in his encyclical on work, which he issued two years after *Redemptor hominis.* Many of the themes I discuss in this essay appear in that encyclical; see *"Laborem exercens"... to All Men and Women of Good Will on Human Work on the Ninetieth Annniersay of Rerum novarum,* Libreria Editrice Vaticana (September 14, 1981) <http://www.vatican.va/edocs/ENG0217/_INDEX.HTM>.

[43]George Gomori, *Cyprian Norwid* (New York: Twayne, 1974), p. 33. For a good collection of Norwid's poems in English, see Cyprian Kamil Norwid, *Selected Poems,* trans. Adam Czerniawski, intro. Bogdan Czaykowski (London: Anvil Press Poetry, 2004).

[44]Wojtyla, "Constitution of Culture," p. 270.

[45]For a detailed discussion of alienation, see Karol Wojtyla, "Participation or Alienation?" in *Person and Community: Selected Essays,* trans. Theresa Sandok, Catholic Thought from Lublin 4 (New York: Lang, 1993), pp. 197-209. John Paul II links alienation to the phenomenological concept of participation, which describes the person's relationship to a community.

[46]Ibid., p. 205.

[47]Ibid. For a careful treatment of how Wojtyla responds to Marxism, see Buttiglione, *Karol Wojtyla,* pp. 292-305. Buttiglione notes that Wojtyla makes few direct references to Marxism because he operated in a dangerous climate in Poland, where censors monitored and deleted any critical remarks about it.

transfer the problem of alienation outside of persons, ascribing it to "structures of our social existence, while ignoring what is essential."[48] Nevertheless, despite its imprecise and materialistic origins, alienation "seems needed in the philosophy of the human person" because it expresses the contingency of communal life.[49] However, it pertains to "the human being not as an individual of the human species" but to "the human being as a personal subject."[50] Here again, we see John Paul II highlighting the irreducible person, rather than simply discussing the alienation of the human species (as many nineteenth-century thinkers did). Alienation occurs when communities and institutions create "an occasion for depriving people in some respect of the possibility of fulfilling themselves in community."[51] Work arrangements stifling self-possession and self-determination alienate us from our personhood. John Paul II thus alters the modern concept of alienation by making it a matter of the person's interior life and intransitive values.

EVANGELICALS AND BIOTECHNOLOGY

John Paul II's sophisticated response to technology contrasts sharply with many North American approaches to it. The Pew Research Center, a polling organization, has tracked American attitudes toward technology, finding that "Americans are near unanimous in their confidence that life will get better for themselves, their families and the country as a whole."[52] They often uncritically and enthusiastically embrace in vitro fertilization, pharmaceutical intervention and other technologies. They think little about what these technologies mean for American society. The consequences of this naïve approach to technology can be disturbing. For example, in the last decade, pharmaceutical companies have gained enormous economic power and now advertise extensively on television. Confronting cultural and other pressures, many Americans find it increasingly difficult to resist new pharmaceutical products.

When using technology, evangelicals apparently differ little from other Americans. The Barna Group, another polling organization, recently did extensive surveys of how evangelicals use technology. It concluded that research "points out that born again Christians account for a significant slice—40%, to be exact—of

---

[48]Wojtyla, "Participation or Alienation?" p. 205.
[49]Ibid.
[50]Wojtyla, "Person: Subject and Community," p. 255.
[51]Ibid., p. 256.
[52]"Optimism Reigns, Technology Plays Key Role," Pew Research Center for the People and the Press (October 24, 1999) <http://people-press.org/reports/display.php3?ReportID=51>. Since 1999, the Pew Center has continued to follow these attitudes, and has found the same optimism in this century.

the consumer technology market. In fact, evangelical Christians—who are a subset of the born again segment—are more likely than the norm to have cell phones, desktop computers, and Internet access."[53] However, evangelicals engage in little serious theological reflection about the moral meaning of technology. If a technology is safe and has no impact on the life issues, they seem willing to allow free market forces to dictate its use.

Evangelicals have noticed John Paul II's strong stances on abortion and other life issues. Obviously, his personalistic norm provides direct guidance for thinking about embryonic stem cell research and human experimentation. For example, if embryos have the same moral value as persons, we should refrain from using them as mere research tools. Similarly, we should refuse to clone one child to serve as an organ donor for another, a clear case of using a person merely as a means. Finally, the personalistic norm bars us from doing human subject research without informed consent. On these and other matters, John Paul II forcefully applied the personalistic norm. Evangelicals applauded him, joining with the Vatican in its public condemnations of cloning, abortion and embryonic stem cell research.

Despite this convergence, however, evangelicals have ignored how John Paul II challenges naïve and superficial approaches to biotechnology. *Redemptor hominis* teaches us to be skeptical about any emerging technology. Each change brings benefits and burdens, and we often ignore potential burdens or construe them too narrowly. Safety concerns also dominate public discussions of biotechnology. For example, debates about human cloning focus on its safety, given the complications scientists have encountered with animal cloning. However, some people believe

---

[53]The Barna Group, "Americans' On-the-Go Lifestyles and Entertainment Appetites Fuel Increasing Reliance upon Technology," The Barna Update (February 7, 2006) <http://www.barna.org/FlexPage.aspx?Page=BarnaUpdate&BarnaUpdateID=217>. In this survey, the Barna group says the following about evangelicals: "Born again Christians" are defined as people who said they have made a personal commitment to Jesus Christ that is still important in their life today and who also indicated they believe that when they die they will go to heaven because they had confessed their sins and had accepted Jesus Christ as their savior. Respondents were *not* asked to describe themselves as "born again." "Evangelicals" meet the born-again criteria (described above) plus seven other conditions. These include saying their faith is very important in their life today; believing they have a personal responsibility to share their religious beliefs about Christ with non-Christians; believing that Satan exists; believing that eternal salvation is possible only through grace, not works; believing that Jesus Christ lived a sinless life on earth; asserting that the Bible is accurate in all that it teaches; and describing God as the all-knowing, all-powerful, perfect deity who created the universe and still rules it today. Being classified as an evangelical is not dependent upon church attendance or the denominational affiliation of the church they attend. Respondents were *not* asked to describe themselves as "evangelical." For a critical look at Barna's data, see John G. Stackhouse Jr., "What Scandal? What Conscience? Some Reflections on Ronald Sider's *Scandal of the Evangelical Conscience*," *Books and Culture* (July/August 2007) available at <http://www.christianitytoday.com/bc/2007/004/12.20.html>.

that once the federal government determines a product's safety, the ethical argument ends.[54] Yet, as the President's Council on Bioethics recently noted, the "bigger ethical issues in this area [therapy and enhancement] have little to do with safety; the most basic questions concern not the hazards associated with the techniques but the benefits and harms of using the perfected powers, assuming that they may be safely used."[55] Once we establish a technology's safety, we have only begun serious ethical reflection, and should proceed to consider how it may affect the person.

Similarly, appeals to individual autonomy or consumer freedom plague public discussions of biotechnology. Celebrating freedom, geneticist Lee Silver notes that "in a society that values individual freedom above all else, it is hard to find any legitimate basis for restricting the use of reprogenetics [technology combining reproduction and genetics]."[56] For Silver, after we have satisfied our safety concerns, we should allow individuals to freely decide to use new technology. This remarkably shallow approach to bioethics ignores the person's inner life. It recognizes no distinction between technique and intransitive values, leaving individuals morally adrift in a sea of technical choices. Moreover, it disregards the communal consequences of individual choices, which create problems that individual choosers may misunderstand. Finally, it pays no attention to alienation, falsely assuming that we can easily control biotechnology. Once we understand the person's nature, vague appeals to individual autonomy appear ethically impoverished, incapable of guiding us through rapid biotechnical changes.

Rather than endorsing free choice as an ethical standard, John Paul II urges us to cultivate self-possession, and think critically about our desires. We need to develop our personhood, because we constantly confront internal and external stimuli. We forget that self-possession is particularly vulnerable to degradation. Excited by gadgets, we lose sense of how to become a self-giving person. Believing ourselves to be autonomous, we forget how many of our desires arise from external sources. In fact, with many new biotechnologies, "desires can be manufactured almost as effectively as pills, especially if the pills work more or less as promised to satisfy the newly stimulated desires. By providing quick solutions for short-term problems or prompt fulfillment of easily satisfied desires, the character of human longing itself could be al-

---

[54] I am simplifying a complex debate about cloning and safety. For an excellent discussion of this and other issues related to cloning, see the President's Council on Bioethics, *Human Cloning and Human Dignity: An Ethical Inquiry*, Washington, D.C. (July 2002) <http://www.bioethics.gov/reports/cloningreport/index.html>.

[55] *Beyond Therapy*, p. 303.

[56] Lee Silver, *Remaking Eden: How Genetic Engineering and Cloning Will Transform the American Family* (New York: Avon, 1998), p. 11.

tered, with large aspirations for long-term flourishing giving way before the immediate gratification of smaller desires."[57] For John Paul II, we should never uncritically accept these desires because they often reflect societies marred by the culture of death, government manipulation and consumerism. More importantly, desire-satisfaction cannot ground the moral life. Instead, the person's self-possession and love provide the normative standard for evaluating desires.

To illustrate how self-possession can serve this normative function, let me return to the example of pharmaceutical technologies. The President's Council on Bioethics recently drew attention to the many American children using Ritalin and related drugs (to treat attention-deficit/hyperactivity disorder or ADHD). The council questioned whether so many children should be using these drugs (an estimated three to four million), but focused primarily on how they affect character and promote social conformity.[58] It argued that in some cases, Ritalin might undermine the link between effort and accomplishment. The council also warned that educational institutions might be using medications to enforce social conformity. By emphasizing these issues, the council enriched public debate about children and pharmacology. I would add to its account a concern about pharmacology and self-possession. Pharmaceutical interventions often help a person by altering brain chemistry. They have been remarkably successful for many children, but how do they affect self-possession? Are children taking Ritalin encouraged to develop inner values and to open themselves up to the spiritual gifts of others? Does pharmaceutical intervention cultivate the "communication without loss" characterizing intransitive values? Or, does it provide an easy substitute for the hard work of developing as a person? We cannot answer such questions in the abstract and should avoid generalizing without considering individual cases. Throughout such reflection, however, self-possession and love can serve as a normative standard guiding pharmaceutical intervention.

This normative standard also undermines deterministic and pessimistic approaches to biotechnology. For some twentieth-century thinkers, the "technological system has become overwhelming, runaway, and autonomous."[59] In their analyses, systems remove responsibility for action, creating a dangerous climate in which people disregard the consequences of their action. In contrast, John Paul II refuses to concede technology the power to completely overwhelm us. We shape our characters, cultivate or disregard intransitive values, and remain responsible

---

[57]*Beyond Therapy*, p. 304.

[58]For this discussion, see *Beyond Therapy*, chap. 2.

[59]John Paul Russo, *The Future Without a Past: The Humanities in a Technological Society* (Columbia: University of Missouri Press, 2005), p. 9. Russo offers an excellent analysis of recent changes in information technology.

for our acts and characters. Writing about sin, John Paul II notes that "it is a truth of faith, also confirmed by our experience and reason, that the human person is free. This truth cannot be disregarded in order to place the blame for individuals' sins on external factors such as structures, systems or other people. Above all, this would be to deny the person's dignity and freedom, which are manifested—even though in a negative and disastrous way—also in this responsibility for sin committed."[60] Confronting technology, the person has an irreplaceable moral responsibility that only he can exercise. Technological systems may appear autonomous and severely constrain our freedom. However, the person can always respond to them self-consciously, actively shaping his character and community.

We see John Paul II's opposition to technological determinism when he discusses euthanasia in *Evangelium vitae.* Strongly condemning it, he nevertheless argues that we are morally permitted to refuse life-sustaining treatment. In such circumstances, a strong prohibition against euthanasia offers little guidance. When should I refuse end-of-life treatment? How do I know when to accept my own death? Addressing this question, John Paul II maintains that we should consider our characters. Powerful medications at life's end severely threaten personhood, and the elderly often seem helpless to respond to them. One person might choose to "voluntarily accept suffering by forgoing treatment with pain-killers in order to remain fully lucid and, if a believer, to share consciously in the Lord's Passion."[61] Another might take strong medications knowing he might die. Highly individual circumstances will dictate a person's choices, but self-possession and love provide guidance. In no case does medical technology necessitate choice. John Paul II repeatedly rejected technological determination, powerfully witnessing to self-possession when his own health declined.[62]

This approach to end-of-life care illustrates a final lesson of *Redemptor hominis,* which teaches that redemption extends beyond individual salvation to communal

---

[60]John Paul II, *Reconciliation and Penance . . . on Reconciliation and Penance in the Mission of the Church Today,* Libreria Editrice Vaticana (December 2, 1984), §16 <http://www.vatican.va/holy_father/john_paul_ii/apost_exhortations/documents/hf_jp-ii_exh_02121984_reconciliatio-et-paenitentia_en.html>.

[61]John Paul II, *Evangelium vitae . . . on the Value and Inviolability of Human Life,* Libreria Editrice Vaticana (March 25, 1995), §65 <http://www.vatican.va/edocs/ENG0141/_INDEX.HTM>.

[62]A few years before he died, John Paul II issued a beautiful letter about the elderly that considered old age and intransitive values; see John Paul II, *Letter of His Holiness John Paul II to the Elderly,* Libreria Editrice Vaticana (October 1, 1999) <http://www.vatican.va/holy_father/john_paul_ii/letters/documents/hf_jp-ii_let_01101999_elderly_en.html>. In this letter, he continued reflections on Jesus and suffering that he had begun in his 1984 apostolic letter on suffering; see *"Salvifici Doloris" . . . on the Christian Meaning of Human Suffering* (February 11, 1984) <http://www.vatican.va/roman_curia/pontifical_councils/hlthwork/documents/hf_jp-ii_apl_11021984_salvifici-doloris_en.html>.

life. Politics and policy alone cannot define our response to technology. Instead, we need a spiritual response that acknowledges divine grace and transformation in Christ. Moreover, confronting technology's dangers, we cannot leave individuals to their own devices, subject to market and other forces assaulting them. To withstand technological threats, we must see Jesus Christ as "the stable principle and fixed centre of the mission that God himself has entrusted to man" (§11). Christians should reflect systematically about technology within a context of grace and the body of Christ. Ecclesial institutions ought to carefully consider how parishioners use technology. Commenting about churches and technology, George Barna (the director of the Barna Group), states that "we expect increased broadband access, podcasting, and ubiquitous adoption of handheld mobile computing devices by consumers to further alter the way churches conduct ministry."[63] Before uncritically endorsing such technologies, churches might evaluate their moral significance. How do they affect the inner lives of those using them? Do they help people become self-giving persons, open to receiving the gifts of others? Because redemption provokes such questions, churches cannot avoid them by retreating into an individualistic approach to technology.

Conclusion

The generation born in the mid-1980s, John Paul Russo writes, "was reared not only under conditions of mass culture, which had been true for at least the previous fifty years, but also in the midst of a communications revolution and its decisive impact on all fields of technology and globalization."[64] Biotechnology is only one trend confronting technologically advanced societies. Unfortunately, few evangelicals have contemplated its meaning, focusing only on life issues like abortion, euthanasia and stem cell research. In contrast, John Paul II was fully aware of technology's dangers, and frequently warned about its dehumanizing effects. When he issued *Redemptor hominis,* he had been thinking about technology for more than a decade. He had developed a conception of the self-determining and self-possessing person, and articulated the personalistic norm. Drawing on Marcel and Norwid, John Paul II argued that we should protect and cultivate intransitive values threatened by modern technology. The spiritual character of these values might give evangelicals pause before they uncritically endorse biotechnical developments. With each new technology, we should con-

---

[63]The Barna Group, "Technology Use Is Growing Rapidly in Churches," The Barna Update (September 13, 2005) <http://www.Barna.org/FlexPage.aspx?Page=BarnaUpdate&BarnaUpdateID=199>.
[64]Russo, *Future Without a Past*, p. 1.

sider if it hinders or enhances self-determination and self-possession. We have no easy recipes for dealing with technological change, with new problems emerging on a case-by-case basis. In all cases, however, the person remains the "primary and fundamental way for the Church, the way traced out by Christ himself" (§14).

When he ascended to the papacy, John Paul II extorted people to "be not afraid; open wide the doors for Christ. To his saving power open the boundaries of states, economic and political systems, the vast fields of culture, civilization, and development."[65] Confronting dictatorships, a culture of death, wars and personal suffering, he never lost his fundamental conviction that humanity need not fear what it creates. As they confront this century's dizzying changes in biotechnology, Americans would do well to heed John Paul II's remarkable message.

---

[65]Quoted in Weigel, *Witness to Hope*, p. 262.

PART TWO

Witnessing to Truthful Doctrine

3

FIDES ET RATIO

The Role of Philosophy and the Christian University

Michael Beaty and C. Stephen Evans

INTRODUCTION

"Faith and reason are like two wings on which the human spirit rises to the contemplation of truth; and God has placed in the human heart a desire to know the truth—in a word, to know himself—so that, by knowing and loving God, men and women may also come to the fullness of truth about themselves."[1] In this beautiful metaphor of the Christian and intellectual life, Pope John Paul II concisely captures a biblically inspired wisdom that evangelical Christians, along with all believers, ought to embrace wholeheartedly. By offering in this encyclical a clear, cogent and culturally aware *cri de coeur* for the sake of well-formed Christian persons, the late pope gives not only Catholics but also evangelical Christians an excellent tool for sustaining vital faith in a post-Christian age. Our aim in this essay is mainly appreciative; however, we shall offer some critical perspective that we think will help evangelicals to appropriate the insights of the encyclical in a way that honors their own tradition and its concerns.

While the encyclical is most directly addressed to the bishops of the Catholic Church, John Paul II ends it by speaking to theologians (especially seminary

---

[1]John Paul II, *Fides et ratio: On the Relationship Between Faith and Reason* (Boston: St. Paul Books and Media, 1998), p. 7; *Fides et ratio . . . on the Relationship Between Faith and Reason,* Libreria Editrice Vaticana (September 14, 1998), blessing <http://www.vatican.va/edocs/ENG0216/_INDEX.HTM>.

professors), philosophers, scientists and "everyone." So, not only is it clearly addressed to those who practice philosophy as a professional discipline (such as the authors of this essay), but it is aimed more broadly at Christians everywhere, both lay and religious. For these reasons, we intend to discuss what we evangelicals[2] can learn from a careful reading of *Fides et ratio.* We think that an evangelical reading of this document is not only beneficial for those of us who are evangelical, but that our perspective on the document may offer insights that will be helpful to the wider church.

We begin the chapter by peering through a narrow lens at the practice of philosophy, one of John Paul II's vocations. Much of *Fides et ratio* directly addresses the state of philosophy in the West, its present condition and John Paul II's critique of it, and his aspirations and exhortation that philosophy recover its true calling. By focusing on his discussion of philosophy in relation to faith and reason for evangelicals, we intend to apply his critique and insights more generally for evangelicals.

In section one, we suggest that the role the department of philosophy typically plays in the contemporary university is an instrumental one and explain why that is so. In section two, we ask if this instrumentalist conception would change were we speaking of a Christian university. We argue that in many Christian universities this conception is not fundamentally changed. In sections three and four, we explore how and why it would change if the conception of philosophy and reason sketched by John Paul II in *Fides et ratio* were recovered. On the whole, then, we endorse the view of philosophy outlined in the encyclical. However, we add a caution about this embrace of reason and philosophy that is rooted in our evangelical Protestant tradition. It is vital to remember the way that our human sinfulness mars every aspect of human life, and reason and philosophy are not an exception to this principle. This caution is not a criticism of the encyclical; it is rather present at several points in the document itself, but it deserves more emphasis.

In section five, we discuss two problems or social ills which John Paul II addresses in *Fides et ratio* because they are, we suggest, especially germane to evangelicals. In combating skepticism, we evangelical philosophers make common cause with John Paul II against much of the modern academy. In combating various forms of fideism, we make common cause with John Paul II against many of our own evangelical brothers and sisters. Again, our agreement with John Paul II

[2]By evangelical we mean those Christians whose primary concerns are (1) conversion, (2) faithfulness to the Bible, (3) activism and (4) a focus on the cross. See David Bebbington, *Evangelicalism in Modern Britain: A History from the 1730s to the 1980s* (London: Unwin Hyman, 1989), pp. 2-19; Mark Noll, *The Scandal of the Evangelical Mind* (Grand Rapids: Eerdmans, 1994), p. 8.

on this point is tempered by a caution that is related to our earlier worry. We should carefully define the term *fideism* so that it does not improperly designate views that call attention to the limits of human reason and the ways in which faith can help overcome those limits.[3] Finally, in section six, we sketch what a department of philosophy at a contemporary Christian university would look like were it to take seriously what we think evangelicals can learn from *Fides et ratio*. We contend that, among other things, evangelicals can learn the following two things from this important encyclical. First, one important role of philosophy is to help the university be true to its highest purposes or ideals, its true calling. Second, a Christian university can assist philosophy in being true to its authentic calling.[4]

The Truncated Role of Philosophy in the Contemporary University

Our initial topic is how *Fides et ratio* helps evangelical philosophers understand and defend the role of philosophy in the contemporary university. Let's make our first approach to this topic by asking two related questions: (1) What is the role of philosophy in the contemporary university? (2) What is the proper role or function of the university?

In the contemporary university, we find at least four competing answers to the question: What is the proper role or function of the university?

1. To provide the kind of education that enables the student to perfect his or her human capacities: intellectual, moral, physical, religious and social.
2. To provide the sort of education that enables its graduates to perform well in the role of citizen of the polis or state.
3. To provide the sort of education that enables its graduates to be successful in a career or profession.
4. To provide the resources and sustain the practices necessary to discover and disseminate new knowledge by research, publication and application.

In most contemporary American universities, these four ends rest in an uneasy

[3]One of the present authors has actually defended what he terms "responsible fideism," in C. Stephen Evans, *Faith Beyond Reason* (Grand Rapids: Eerdmans, 1998). In this book, responsible fideism is defined as a recognition by reason itself of the limits of reason and the ways in which faith can help heal reason. It should be evident that John Paul II's criticism of fideism is directed at views that reject or denigrate reason and not at this kind of view.

[4]Several sections of this chapter are taken from or are based on a paper that was delivered at the University of Notre Dame at a conference, "Joy in Truth: The Catholic University in the New Millennium," September 30, 2005, by one of the authors, Michael Beaty.

and disordered relationship to one another, both in rhetoric and in practice.[5] In many private secular or religiously identified universities, (1) and (2) dominate their rhetoric, while (3) typically dominates their practices. In America's great research universities, both private and state-supported, (4) is the engine that pushes and pulls the train, often to the detriment of both (1) and (2), at least some critics contend.[6]

Notice that (3) clearly regards education in instrumental or utilitarian terms and that it encourages a narrow, specialized education. While (4) may be understood in non-instrumental terms, it clearly encourages narrow and specialized studies rather than broad, deep, comprehensive, non-instrumentalist understandings of education.

What would be the role of philosophy if the aim of the university were either (3) or (4)? Philosophy, like any other department or academic unit in the university, will understand that it must justify its existence by reference to one or the other or both of these goals. One common strategy, then, will be to convince students that a major in philosophy will secure success for its graduates in a wide variety of careers, in the esteemed professions, and in the culture, especially in mainstream economic and political life.

So the philosophy faculty will attempt to convince its colleagues and the consumers (parents and students) of the desirability of its product—a major in philosophy. One way to do this is to argue that there are some highly marketable skills—let's call them transferable skills: critical thinking and writing, oral and written persuasiveness, analytic and synthetic reading comprehension, creative powers of imagination and creativity—that are especially well taught by philosophers, can be acquired at a high rate by the industrious and disciplined student, and permit that student to compete very effectively for entrance into the leading professions (law, medicine, management, government, the academy and business).

On this view, the role of philosophy is essentially instrumental—that of providing transferable skills to students interested in being successful in various highly valued professions and in our democratic and capitalist culture.[7] Of course, a few of them will go on to graduate school and enter the highly special-

---

[5]This claim has been made frequently over the past three decades at least, though its lineage is at least as old as John Henry Cardinal Newman, *The Idea of a University* (London: Longmans, Green, 1931). For a more recent discussion of this kind of worry, see Jaroslav Pelikan, "The Storm Breaking upon the University: The University in Crisis," in *The Idea of the University: A Reexamination* (New Haven, Conn.: Yale University Press, 1992), pp. 11-21.

[6]To cite just two examples, see Mark Schwehn, *Exiles from Eden* (Oxford: Oxford University Press, 1993), pp. 4-12; Douglas Sloan, *Faith and Knowledge: Mainline Protestantism and American Higher Education* (Louisville: Westminster John Knox, 1994), pp. 17-19.

[7]Pope John Paul II decries reduction of reason to mere "instrumental reason" (*Fides et ratio,* §47).

ized profession of philosophy. Naturally the competencies, information, knowledge and skills necessary for success in graduate school will have significant utilitarian value.

On this instrumentalist view of the role of philosophy in the contemporary university, one might expect to find a few philosophy courses offered as ways of meeting various distribution requirements in a general education curriculum and occasionally as ways of meeting requirements for other non-philosophy majors as well. Some of these courses might have content valuable for those other majors. For example, business or management majors might be required by their faculty to take a business ethics or professional ethics course. Likewise, environmental studies majors might be required by their faculty to take an environmental ethics course. If the department and its chair are especially enterprising and well-connected politically in a university that embraces the notion that its education should produce good citizens of our pluralist democracy[8] or good citizens of the world,[9] then there might be a philosophy course that is a university-wide requirement because of its alleged contribution to enabling students to become good citizens. Maybe the requirement will be Introduction to Logic or Introduction to Critical Thinking or Introduction to Philosophy because of the general view that citizens of a democratic culture must be equipped to reason well to meet their obligations to participate in a democratic culture, since such a culture prizes reasoned debate and deliberation before political decisions are made. With these possible exceptions, the philosophy department competes for students and resources just like any other discipline, and its appeals will be largely instrumental and utilitarian. Thus, most philosophy departments will be small, for their role is small, and their existence tenuous.

If the university is a research university and believes that it could advance its status by directing a substantial portion of its resources into a Ph.D. program in philosophy, it would have an instrumental reason to do so. It then has the additional task of creating a demand for its classes. If it manages to position itself politically to have some philosophy courses required for all or most students, what will be its justification or rationale?

The Truncated Role of Philosophy in Evangelical/Denominational Colleges

Would adding the adjective *Christian* make any difference to this instrumentalist

[8]Amy Gutmann, *Democratic Education* (Princeton, N.J.: Princeton University Press, 1987).
[9]Martha C. Nussbaum, *Cultivating Humanity: A Classical Defense of Reform in Liberal Education* (Cambridge, Mass.: Harvard University Press, 1997).

conception of the role of philosophy in the contemporary university we have just sketched? It depends on what one means by *Christian*. If *Christian* is narrowed and flattened to mean something like "a personal relation to Jesus that is expressed primarily in attending church, private prayer, and devotional Bible reading," then the answer to this question will probably be, "No, Christianity will not make much of a difference." Sadly, a narrowing and flattening of Christian faith of this kind has been all too characteristic of evangelicals in America, at least in the last sixty to seventy-five years. The problem with this understanding of Christianity is that it tends to denude historic Christian faith of its intellectual and historical content, or at least of any content that might make a difference in education or the public sphere more generally. On such an understanding, Christian faith is disconnected from the attempt to use reason to understand God, the natural world and the place of humans in that world. This understanding also severs Christian faith from an understanding of the Good and the possibility of serious reflection on moral responsibility. Historically, this is of course an aberration; Christians have traditionally been committed to an intellectual effort to think through their faith commitments and faith's implications for understanding all of reality. Abandoning this intellectual commitment results in a false dichotomy between head and heart and, consequently, abandonment by Christians of our calling to unify faith and intellect, or as St. Paul puts it, to "take every thought captive to obey Christ" (2 Cor 10:5).

Even recognizing Paul's admonition here may not be enough, however, since the admonition can be given an instrumentalist or utilitarian reading in which it sanctions primarily apologetic endeavors directed toward those indifferent or hostile to the Christian faith. Christian universities (and we shall use this phrase to include colleges as well) whose vision is essentially instrumentalist in this way will usually require some religion classes, typically a study of the Bible, and perhaps a course in apologetics or a philosophy course that is largely apologetic in nature. In addition, Christian universities of this sort will make available lots of extracurricular religious activities (Bible studies, prayer groups and mission trips), will require attendance at chapel, and will, perhaps, encourage annual campuswide revivals. These requirements may be highly valuable as means to genuine goods; nevertheless, if that is all that the Christian school offers, then it implicitly presents a truncated view of the university and of human persons, as well as a truncated view of philosophy's value to human beings and of its role in the university.

Many evangelical universities have made great efforts to overcome this kind of model by emphasizing the importance of the formation of a Christian world and life view. However, progress has not been uniform, and the instrumental view of philosophy remains dominant at many schools. For example, this is particularly true of Baptist universities, at least in the South, that part of the United States whose practices we know best. In many of these institutions, it is easy to see that philosophy has not been regarded as essential to a liberal arts education but is regarded as merely instrumentally valuable. Indeed, a review of the universities aligned with the Association of Southern Baptist Colleges and Schools (ASBCS) shows that philosophy and theology are often regarded as the stepchildren in a department of religion or a school of Christian studies.

Consider, for example, a fairly typical Baptist university affiliated with the ASBCS. This university's School of Christian Studies has five departments and eleven faculty members. Biblical Studies has four faculty, Christian Ministries and Christian Missions, combined, have five, and Christian Theology and the Philosophy departments each have one faculty member. How should we read the distribution of faculty to discipline? At the very least, it reminds us that Baptists have traditionally viewed the study of philosophy or theology as relatively insignificant, in comparison to biblical studies and education for professional ministry and missions. We contend that the implicit assumption of the School of Christian Studies at this Baptist university is that the study of philosophy is largely instrumental and pragmatic, and not demonstrably different from our initial depiction of it. The school we selected, sadly, is by no means unrepresentative, and in fact philosophy is probably better represented there than in many other schools. We suspect that at many Christian universities, Baptist and otherwise, philosophy is not taught at all, and if it is, it is not taught by someone professionally trained in philosophy.

Many Baptist and evangelical philosophers toil faithfully and dutifully in institutions which embrace a similar assumption about philosophy and theology. Such schools could gain an alternative view of the university, of the role of philosophy in it, and of philosophy's value to human beings through a careful reading and thoughtful appropriation of *Fides et ratio.*

Fides et Ratio, the University and Philosophy

Let us hear once more the greeting with which John Paul II begins the encyclical, and with which we began this essay:

> Faith and reason are like two wings on which the human spirit rises to the contemplation of truth; and God has placed in the human heart a desire to know the truth—in a word, to know himself—so that, by knowing and loving God, men and women

may also come to the fullness of truth about themselves (cf. Ex 33:18; Ps 27:8-9; 63:2-3; Jn 14:8; 1 Jn 3:2).[10]

In this passage, John Paul II reminds his readers that our lives may be understood as a journey toward truth, a journey for which both faith and reason are necessary co-laborers. The journey would ideally include appropriation of truths of various kinds: truths about particular aspects or parts of reality, truths about how these partial truths fit into larger and more comprehensive understandings of nature and the cosmos, and truths that answer questions about the ultimate meaning of human existence, ultimately leading us toward an absolute, "something ultimate, which might serve as the ground of all things."[11]

The late pontiff claims that the more we human beings understand reality and the world, the more we understand ourselves as human beings and as individuals.[12] As John Paul II sees the matter, the search for truth includes the recognition that there are different modes of truth or ways of knowing and thus different methods of inquiry. Some are the methods employed in everyday life and in scientific experimentation and confirmation. Some are speculative inquiries into cosmology and metaphysics; these are necessarily philosophical, with the results often intrinsically linked to religious truths. Moreover, philosophy, when properly pursued, is no enemy of these religious truths, because faith and reason both aim at a truth that comes from a common source.[13] So, even when reason, like John the Baptist, prepares the way for the apprehension of the truths of faith, reason, whether in the form of philosophy or scientific inquiry, is not merely instrumentally valuable.[14]

In *Three Rival Versions of Moral Enquiry,* Alasdair MacIntyre suggests that we answer the question, "What are universities for?" by asking "What peculiar goods do universities serve?" This latter question requires us to specify the peculiar and essential function(s) which no institution other than the university is equipped to do.[15] John Paul II's sweeping vision suggests that the university is that institution whose principal function is to order a variety of intellectual modes of inquiry so that we human beings might better understand ourselves and all of reality. The ul-

[10]John Paul II, *Fides et ratio,* p. 7, blessing.
[11]Ibid., p. 40, §27.
[12]Ibid., p. 9, §1.
[13]Ibid., pp. 49-65, §§36-48. In these pages, John Paul II discusses the essential complementary relationship between faith and reason and the negative consequences of abandoning this conception. In the next section, we add some qualifying remarks about this affirmation of reason that note the impact of sin on human thought.
[14]Ibid., pp. 42-48, §§64-79.
[15]Alasdair MacIntyre, *Three Rival Versions of Moral Enquiry: Encyclopedia, Genealogy, and Tradition* (Notre Dame, Ind.: University of Notre Dame Press, 1990), p. 222.

timate aim is a wide and deep notion called understanding or wisdom. Since the attainment of understanding depends on a variety of methods of inquiry oriented to differing modes of truth in the natural sciences, the social sciences, the humanities and the like, a genuine university will be a place that honors and orders these various methods of inquiry and the modes of truth to which such inquiries provide us access.[16]

John Paul II is especially eloquent in speaking about the nature and role of philosophy:

> Men and women have at their disposal an array of resources for generating greater knowledge of truth so that their lives may be ever more human. Among these is *philosophy,* which is directly concerned with asking the question of life's meaning and sketching an answer to it. Philosophy emerges, then, as one of the noblest of human tasks.[17]

John Paul II then lists a variety of practices and modes of inquiry whose aim is understanding, reminding us of philosophy's original meaning as the love of wisdom. On John Paul II's view, then, philosophy is both an essential and constitutive feature of a genuine university, a university that is true to its original and most important purposes.

On this alternative view of philosophy and its role in the university we are sketching, philosophy has three essential tasks: (1) inquiry-related tasks, (2) integrative tasks and (3) regulative tasks.[18] Like Aristotle, John Paul II insists that philosophy begins with wonder—wonder about the existence of something rather than nothing; about the intricate regularities, visible and invisible to the naked eye on whose existence the cosmos and even our own lives depend; about the patterns of good and evil that bless and mar our social order; about the internal struggles

---

[16]What we infer from John Paul II about the distinctive aim of the university includes but goes beyond the answer MacIntyre gives in *Three Rival Versions of Moral Enquiry.* In it, MacIntyre asserts that the specifying feature of the university is to be the place where conceptions and standards of rational justification are developed, applied in varied forms of rational inquiry, and then further evaluated so that the wider society can learn how to conduct its own debates, theoretical or practical, in rationally defensible ways (p. 222). In our view, MacIntyre is correct, but these forms of rational inquiry serve the further goods or ends of understanding and wisdom.

[17]*Fides et ratio,* p. 11, §3.

[18]Clearly, until the twentieth century, philosophy understood itself as including inquiry, integrative tasks, and regulative tasks. This is seen by examining *The Republic, Nicomachean Ethics, Summa Contra Gentiles* or the role of the moral and mental philosophy courses taught in nineteenth-century American colleges, ideals derived in part from Scottish universities of the seventeenth and eighteenth centuries. See, for example, Francis Wayland, *The Elements of Moral Science,* ed. and intro. Joseph L. Blau (Cambridge, Mass.: Harvard University Press, 1963). John Henry Newman draws from this same vision in his *The Idea of the University.*

whose result is a good or bad character; and many more. Wonder begins by virtue of an innate[19] and natural desire to know[20] and is often occupied with questions and pursued by divergent modes of inquiry whose aim is to achieve as complete an understanding of nature (the natural world, the social world, the individual) as possible. It is this natural desire for truth and for a comprehensive and ultimate or foundational understanding of the cosmos, nature and human existence that distinguishes human beings from other animals.

John Henry Cardinal Newman identifies this expansive notion of understanding with education, whose aim is "the true enlargement of the mind."[21] One, though only one, important constituent of this kind of education is philosophy. Indeed, what Aristotle, John Henry Newman and John Paul II share in common is the notion than the human quest for understanding or wisdom includes not only the search for truth in discrete and autonomous aspects of the natural and social world, by a variety of methods of inquiry, but also the search for truth by attention to larger, more comprehensive, integrated and unified bodies of knowledge and meaning. On this view, a university education enables the properly educated individual to obtain an understanding larger than the understanding obtained by education in one discipline. Essential to the achievement of this kind of education is the integration of the contributions of a variety of disciplines and subdisciplines into larger and larger units of meaning. Philosophy's special task, according to John Paul II, is the search for wisdom, the ultimate and overarching meaning of life. This "sapiential" task of philosophy includes as one element critical reflection on the nature of inquiry, both in its own discipline and as found in other disciplines, using its emphasis on unity and comprehensiveness to prompt the effort to integrate these partial perspectives into larger units with the aim of moving our common human understanding to a larger and deeper unity and better representation of all that is.[22] In short, a university which includes philosophy as understood here is committed to being true to its widest and deepest purposes.

BEING CHRISTIAN AND THE CALLINGS OF PHILOSOPHY AND THE UNIVERSITY

What does *Christian* add to this conception of the university? To answer this question, recall once more the image of faith and reason as two "wings." This image

---

[19] *Fides et ratio,* p. 11, §3.

[20] Ibid., p. 38, §25. In this passage, John Paul II quotes Aristotle in *Metaphysics* 1.1: "All human beings desire to know."

[21] Newman, *The Idea of a University,* discourse 6.6.

[22] Pope John Paul II, *Fides et ratio,* pp. 30, 36-48, §§16-20.

evocatively suggests a bird flying upward toward its natural object. Quite clearly, if one of its wings were damaged and failed to work properly, the bird would progress upward to its destination only with great difficulty at best; more likely, it would be unable to achieve its aim at all. At worst, it might plummet to the earth. Similarly, John Paul II implies that if either faith or reason fails to do its proper work, then human beings are seriously hampered in realizing our natural desire to know and live in the truth. Moreover, just as it is necessary for the two wings of a bird to function together harmoniously, so it is for faith and reason to work together. He puts it this way, "Therefore, reason and faith cannot be separated without diminishing the capacity of men and women to know themselves, the world and God in an appropriate way."[23] "[E]ach without the other is impoverished and enfeebled."[24]

John Paul II also insists that faith and reason must function in a complementary manner: "There is no reason for competition of any kind between reason and faith . . . : each has its own scope for action."[25] The truths obtained by reason and those obtained by faith are "neither identical nor mutually exclusive."[26] On the one hand, like the great philosophers of the classical period, he affirms that reason's tasks of intellectual inquiry and exploration, with truth as its aim, is both a noble and ennobling human activity.[27] Thus, on his view we surmise that in a Christian university, being Christian helps the university, as well as philosophy, be true to its own callings and purposes.

At the same time, John Paul II reminds us that on the Christian view of things, even if human reason functioned perfectly, our understanding of nature would be incomplete. There are truths unavailable to natural reason, "mysteries hidden in God" which are known only by revelation, that is, by God's testimony and the supernatural assistance of grace. Thus, the deepest truths about God, human fulfillment and human salvation become available to us via revelation, the supreme revelation of God in Christ.[28]

However, one might wonder whether John Paul II's embrace of reason is too uncritical. After all, human reason is not just finite but also fallen. Protestants have often been critical of Catholics for failing to recognize the degree to which human reason has been damaged by the fall. Does this encyclical ignore this problem? It

---

[23]Ibid., p. 30, §16.
[24]Ibid., p. 64, §48.
[25]Ibid., p. 30, §17.
[26]Ibid., p. 18, §9.
[27]Ibid., §§11-12.
[28]Ibid., p. 19, §12.

certainly does not. John Paul II insists that our natural understanding is not only extended but sometimes corrected by means of revelation. This implies that even though ideally reason and faith should always function harmoniously, in reality conflicts will occur. From the beginning, John Paul II insists, "Christian thinkers were critical in adopting philosophical thought."[29] The late pontiff goes on to give a "rapid survey of the history of philosophy" in the West, the moral of which seems to be that philosophy has progressively impoverished itself by distancing itself from faith and the insights provided by the Christian revelation.[30] There is some irony here, in that John Paul II's account of the history of Western philosophy as involving a decline that is grounded in the separation of reason from faith in many ways reminds us of the view, quite influential in evangelical circles, made popular by Francis Schaeffer.[31] The irony is that Schaeffer was a Reformed thinker who blamed the divorce of reason from faith on the Catholic philosophers of the Middle Ages. We think that John Paul II's sketch of the dire consequences of separating reason from faith shows that he is aware of the problem that Schaeffer highlights (and also that Schaeffer's diagnosis of the cause of the problem is probably mistaken).

However, we do want to add a caution at this point. If this warning about the damaging effects of sin is not emphasized, there is a danger that John Paul II's affirmation of reason could make invisible what Protestant theologians often call "the antithesis" between faith and unbelief. In every area of human life, sin and the forces of evil are at war with God and God's redemptive work, and the same is true in our intellectual lives. We think that the encyclical could have more strongly emphasized this point by distinguishing reason as God intended it to function and reason as it actually functions in a fallen world. Such a distinction is clearly implied by the document but deserves greater prominence.

This awareness of fallenness should not, however, lead Christians to turn from the intellectual life; rather it should help Christians do their work in a discerning way. The work of the Christian university must include not only the exploration of what is known by means of all the various means of rational inquiry available to finite and fallen creatures, but also the integration of such investigations with the truths given by revelation into a larger, more complete whole. This integrative work must include a critical aspect. This ideal is not possible,

---

[29]Ibid., p. 53, §39.
[30]Ibid., pp. 61-62, §§45-48.
[31]See Francis Schaeffer, *The God Who Is There* (Downers Grove, Ill.: InterVarsity Press, 1968) and also *Escape from Reason* (Downers Grove, Ill.: InterVarsity Press, 1968).

claims John Paul II, unless "faith and philosophy recover the profound unity which allows them to stand in harmony with their nature without compromising their mutual autonomy."[32] When faith and reason are linked in the fashion described by John Paul II, they enable the university to be true to its own calling. However, this conception requires that "[t]he *parrhesia* of faith must be matched by the boldness of reason."[33]

Christian Philosophers and the Defense of Reason

In this section we want to focus on two problems or societal ills to which John Paul II devotes much attention, and connect these problems with the initial sketch of a philosophy department whose aims are largely instrumental, pragmatic and utilitarian, a conception we contend is either implicitly or explicitly embraced by most American universities, whether religious or secular. The first of these is a set of ailments associated with defective understandings of reason in modern culture and modern philosophy that we, for want of a better term, will refer to as *skepticism,* a problem especially endemic to secular institutions.[34] The second is the problem of *fideism,*[35] a problem especially germane, in our judgment, to Baptist as well as other universities. Both share a common malady: the separation of faith and reason. We will address each in turn, though we will spend substantially more time on the latter than the former.

At the beginning of the encyclical, John Paul II connects the innate human desire for truth with philosophy as the love of wisdom. One dimension of the love of wisdom is the effort to order a variety of partial truths into larger and more systematic bodies of knowledge so that possible answers to the meaning of human existence are identified and explored critically. He then notes that the church (1) sets great value on philosophy understood in this way, (2) regards philosophy as "an indispensable help for deeper understanding of faith," and (3) sees it as a way for communicating the truth of the gospel to those who have not yet come to faith.[36] He makes it clear that all human beings, and not only Christians, ought to value philosophy highly as a special exercise of the human capacity to reason, not

---

[32]Ibid., p. 65, §48. Actually, given that John Paul II himself says that faith and philosophy should not be separated, we wonder if *autonomy* is the right term; perhaps it would be better to say that philosophy has its own distinct task and integrity as a form of human inquiry, since *autonomy* suggests a kind of separation.

[33]Ibid.

[34]Ibid., p. 14, §5.

[35]Ibid., p. 74, §55.

[36]Ibid., p. 13, §5.

merely instrumentally but as an end in itself. Yet, in this encyclical, he warns of the growing distrust of reason's "great capacity for knowledge."[37] He chides philosophers and other scholars for resting "content with partial and provisional truths, no longer seeking to ask radical questions about the meaning and ultimate foundation of human, personal and social existence."[38] He worries that when men and women forget that they are always on a journey toward a truth which transcends them that individual dignity will be at the mercy of caprice; our human state or status will be judged merely by pragmatic criteria; and pleasure, power and technology will dominate over higher human goods.[39] We concur with John Paul II that as long as a community or culture is skeptical about reason in the ways described above, its task will largely be instrumentally defined. Skepticism about reason's ability to be more than an instrument for securing arbitrarily chosen ends helps explain the status of most departments of philosophy in American universities, both religious and secular.

In opposition to instrumentalist understandings of philosophy, John Paul II writes in large measure to challenge these more radical versions of *skepticism* about philosophy. More pointedly, he writes to encourage philosophers to resist these perversions of reason in modernity, the tendency to reduce rationality to instrumental reason whose ultimate ends are individual self-interest or some version of utilitarianism. Such a view of philosophy is implicitly skeptical because it gives up on any aspiration to give us knowledge of the real. More particularly, he exhorts philosophers to regain their faith in reason's capacity to know, not only partial and provisional truths but also vital, transcendent truths in deep and profound ways, which he calls wisdom. Finally, John Paul II calls philosophers to be bold in the defense of reason. He calls Christian philosophers to be bold in defense of the mutually enhancing relation of faith and reason, especially in light of the indissoluble unity of faith and reason and the mystery of personal existence.[40]

We contend that evangelicals have good reasons to embrace John Paul II's account of reason, its integral relation to a vibrant and vital understanding and practice of faith, and his rejection of skepticism about reason's capacity to be more than merely instrumental or pragmatic. Evangelicals emphatically embrace John's identification of God with the eternal logos, the logos with Christ and with Truth:

[37]Ibid., p. 15, §5.
[38]Ibid.
[39]Ibid., p. 14, §5.
[40]Ibid., pp. 21, 29, §§12, 16.

"The true light which enlightens everyone, was coming into the world" (Jn 1:9).[41] While the mysteries of these identities are many and perplexing, the central affirmation is that God and Truth are one or unified. Not surprisingly, evangelicals should be and have been uncompromising in their steadfast search for substantial and unmoving truth, rather than merely relative and instrumental truths. Indeed, Christian universities which embrace the view of faith and reason articulated in *Fides et ratio* will understand the role of philosophy quite differently from those seduced by the sirens of modern skepticism. The position of such a department of philosophy in the university and its practices will be noticeably different. We shall return to this point later in the essay.

What, by contrast, does John Paul II mean by *fideism,* and why, in his and our judgment, is it a problem for departments of philosophy, especially those in evangelical Christian universities? By *fideism,* John Paul II means a view "which fails to recognize the importance of rational knowledge and philosophical discourse for the understanding of faith, indeed for the very possibility of belief in God."[42] It is important to define this term *fideism* carefully. We should not use it carelessly to denigrate Christian thinkers such as Kierkegaard who call attention to the ways in which *fallen* human reason can and does fall into conflict with faith. John Paul II does not have in mind what one of us has called "responsible fideism," defined as the need for reason to recognize its own limits and seek help where it needs help.[43] Rather, by *fideism* John Paul II has in mind the rejection of reason or the improper denigration of this God-given faculty.

This kind of objectionable fideism can be found in the evangelical world. All too often we evangelicals are committed to a piety, which for all its attractive features, is impoverished by its ambivalence about reason or, perhaps worse, by its embrace of reason in an impoverished form. Such maladies are often expressed in the form of a naïve biblicism and an aversion or even a "disdain for philosophy or theology."[44] In *The Scandal of the Evangelical Mind,* Mark Noll, acclaimed evangelical historian, provides a sustained critique of evangelical culture.[45] Noll

---

[41] Also, see Pope John Paul II's discussion of the "Splendor of Truth" which "shines forth in all the works of the Creator and, in a special way, in man, created in the image and likeness of God" (John Paul I, *Veritatis splendor* [Boston: Pauline Books and Media, 1993], p. 1; *Veritatis splendor,* Libreria Editrice Vaticana [August 6, 1993], blessing <http://www.vatican.va/edocs/ENG0222/_INDEX.HTM>).

[42] *Fides et ratio,* p. 74, §55.

[43] See C. Stephen Evans, *Faith Beyond Reason* (Grand Rapids: Eerdmans, 1998). For an argument that Kierkegaard is not a fideist in an objectionable sense, see C. Stephen Evans, *Kierkegaard on Faith and the Self* (Waco, Tex.: Baylor University Press, 2006).

[44] Nicholas Wolterstorff, "Faith and Reason," *Books and Culture* (July/August 1999), p. 28.

[45] Noll, *Scandal of the Evangelical Mind.*

is trenchant and pointed in his indictment:

> *The scandal of the evangelical mind is that there is not much of an evangelical mind.* An extraordinary range of virtues is found among the sprawling throngs of evangelical Protestants in North America, including great sacrifice in spreading the message of salvation in Jesus Christ, open-hearted generosity to the needy, heroic personal exertion on behalf of troubled individuals, and the unheralded sustenance of countless church and parachurch communities. Notwithstanding all their other virtues, however, American evangelicals are not exemplary for their thinking, and they have not been so for several generations.[46]

Noll goes on to observe that while evangelicals "have nourished millions of believers in the simple verities of the gospel" they "have largely abandoned the universities, the arts, and other realms of 'high' culture," noting that despite sponsoring dozens of seminaries, scores of colleges, hundreds of radio stations and thousands of diverse parachurch groups, evangelicals have "not a single research university."[47]

According to Noll, the single greatest vice with which evangelicals or the evangelical culture is beset is an all-too-pervasive anti-intellectualism displayed in both characteristic attitudes and habits. The anti-intellectualism of evangelicals is of two sorts. The first is a function of an evangelical ethos that "is activist, populist, pragmatic, and utilitarian."[48] Entrepreneurial and free-wheeling, evangelicals have typically focused on immediate opportunities, understood as means to the propagation of the gospel, and on the technical know-how necessary to create new opportunities to spread the good news both far and wide, or, at best, on the problem-solving necessary to overcome obstacles that constrain these practical goals. Typically very little energy is expended on relating this simplistic, other-worldly understanding of "spreading the gospel" to larger and deeper Christian intellectual traditions. For example, too often in the twentieth century, little thought was given to the implications of the doctrine of creation and our human role as stewards of creation and for our human responsibility for the organization and governing of human communities. Clearly, on our view, the knowledge the natural and social sciences aim to achieve is crucial to good stewardship of both the natural environment and of human communities. We need more disciplined biblical, philosophical and theological inquiries that attempt to integrate Christian convictions with these sciences and share the results of such

---

[46]Ibid., p. 3 (italics added).
[47]Ibid.
[48]Ibid., p. 12.

cross-disciplinary inquiry.[49] Noll quotes a Canadian scholar, N. K. Clifford, who describes well the first kind of anti-intellectualism.

> The Evangelical Protestant mind has never relished complexity. Indeed its crusading genius, whether in religion or politics, has always tended toward an oversimplification of issues and the substitution of inspiration and zeal for critical analysis and serious reflection. The limitations of such a mind-set were less apparent in the relative simplicity of a rural frontier society.[50]

In our own view, the kind of anti-intellectualism identified by Clifford is not only connected to activist, populist, pragmatic and utilitarian habits of an evangelical ethos that has been successful precisely because of its pragmatic and entrepreneurial approach to spreading an other-worldly gospel, but also to the pietism characteristic of evangelicalism, an approach to the Christian faith that, according to James Burtchaell, emphasizes "spirit over letter, commitment over institution, affect over intellect, laity over clergy, . . . and . . . [which] looked to the earliest Christian communities for their model."[51]

Burtchaell commends the original pietist reformist and positive impulses. He observes that, when confronted with "a snarled tangle of custom, construal, and protected interests,"[52] capable, intelligent, insightful first-generation pietists often were able to discern a simple truth obscured in the morass of both divine and human constructions. These insights prompted needed reformation and renewal. Unfortunately, the ability to apprehend profound but simple truths displayed by first-generation pietists often degenerates, notes Burtchaell, into repetition of mindless simplicities in the face of genuine complexities by subsequent generations of pietists. These later generations often have lost touch with the intellectual and religious traditions which schooled pietism's exemplary reformers and provided the necessary intellectual background that made the simple truths intelligible. Over time simple formulas—such as heart over head, feeling over ideas, action

---

[49]We hasten to add that the last decade or so has seen increased evangelical attention to these issues in intellectually and socially responsible, though often controversial, ways. See, for example, the Evangelical Environment Network and *Creation Care* magazine at <www.creationcare.org>. In October 2005, the National Association of Evanglicals, a thirty-million-member group, adopted an "Evangelical Call to Civic Responsibility," which insisted that all Christians have a duty to care for the environment and that the government has a duty to protect the environment on behalf of the public. *Washington Post*, February 6, 2004, A01.

[50]Noll, *Scandal of the Evangelical Mind,* p. 13. N. K. Clifford, "His Dominion: A Vision in Crisis," *Sciences Religieuses/Studies in Religion* 2 (1973): 323.

[51]James T. Burtchaell, *The Dying of the Light: The Disengagement of Colleges and Universities from Their Christian Churches* (Grand Rapids: Eerdmans, 1998), p. 839.

[52]Ibid.

over scholarship, commitment over institution—or slogans and clichés such as "Jesus is the answer" and "If you have Jesus, you don't need Socrates" become associated with pietism's emphases on the priority of an individual profession or confession of faith. Thus, rather than faith and reason acting as two wings to propel a person toward truth, reason has been separated from faith to the detriment not only of the individual but of the communities within which individuals are cultivated, well or poorly, for now their conceptions of faith and learning are defective and impoverished.

Burtchaell perceptively draws out the consequences of a shallow and unstable pietism for Christian universities. Arising from a legitimate pietist reform, what began as the deep theological conviction that too much energy among Christians often has been devoted to controversies about theologically inessential doctrines devolves into the conviction that theology does not matter.[53] All that matters is inward conviction (faith as feeling or subjective commitment) and moral or mission-related activism. Combine this shallow pietism with the modern university's commitments to positivism (knowledge is only what is empirically testable; everything else is private) and political liberalism's commitment to solve political conflict by tolerating a wide range of diverse belief systems by relegating them to the private rather than the public square (e.g., public institutions such as the modern university), then it becomes inevitable, suggests Burtchaell, "that religious endeavors on campus should be focused upon the individual life of faith, as distinct from the shared labor of learning."[54] This bifurcation of the public and the private has the unintended consequence of isolating or severing religious piety (faith, worship and moral behavior) from "secular" learning.[55] Not surprisingly, Christian universities over which shallow pietism exert considerable influence will regard the life of the mind in largely instrumental and pragmatic ways. If, for example, philosophy as a discipline has a place in the college, it will largely serve the ends of providing transferable skills (logic and argumentation and persuasive speaking and writing)

---

[53]Here we agree with Noll that the "intellectual disaster of fundamentalism" includes the assumption that the distinctive teachings of various fundamentalist groups (such as dispensationalism and the Holiness and Pentecostal movements) are among those that are essential to the Christian faith. In short, we agree with Noll that the distinctive teachings of these various movements are not among those essential to the Christian faith. One evidence for this is the obvious fact that the doctrines seen by one fundamentalist group as essential (such as dispensationalism) are rejected by other groups that have their own distinctive doctrines. Thus, we affirm a pietist insight that some theological wranglings are about matters inessential (though not necessarily unimportant). See Noll, *Scandal of the Evangelical Mind,* p. 142.

[54]Burtchaell, *Dying of the Light,* p. 842.

[55]Ibid.

for those interested in the professions (business, law, medicine and ministry) and of defending the faith (apologetics). Both philosophy and theology will be regarded as perhaps useful but secondary when compared to biblical studies in preparation for ministry and missions.

We contend that an antidote for the relegation of philosophy (and theology) to merely instrumental roles in evangelical Christian universities is that evangelicals embrace John Paul II's treatment of the relationship of faith and reason in *Fides et ratio.* Fundamentally, John Paul II affirms the capacity of the intellect (reason), despite both its natural limitations and its fallenness, to explore reality in all its diversity and fullness, with its aim as truth about God, the cosmos, and the natural and social worlds.[56] He affirms the integrity of the distinct, though related, tasks of both faith and reason, but denies the exaggerated separation that has been promoted by, on the one hand, various schools of philosophy, especially since the Enlightenment, and, on the other, by various forms of pietism. Furthermore, he insists on what we believe to be a vital point—that faith and reason ideally form an essential unity, which both excessive forms of rationalism and shallow forms of pietism undermine to the detriment of both faith and reason.[57] We evangelical philosophers need to embrace John Paul's image of faith and reason as "two wings on which we arise to the contemplation of truth" with each having its proper function or role, thus, integrity as distinct spheres of human activity, but integrally related, which produces both mutual enhancement and ultimate unity. Otherwise we face the continued marginalization of philosophy as a primarily instrumental and secondary human endeavor with its attendant consequences for the role and place of philosophy in Christian universities.[58] Here we evangelical philosophers need to be bold in our defense of reason.[59]

Perceptively, Mark Noll identifies a second kind of anti-intellectualism that besets the evangelical culture. This form expresses itself not so much as inattention and dismissal of scholarly debates but "as the wrong kind of intellectual attention"[60] or "the sometimes prosecution of the wrong sort of intellectual life."[61] This latter form of anti-intellectualism sometimes is birthed from a willful and all-too-happy ignorance of both the intellectual riches of the Christian tradition and an all-too-deep familiarity with non-Christian or even anti-Christian patterns of

---

[56]John Paul II, *Fides et ratio,* pp. 9-16, §§1-6.
[57]Ibid., p. 64, §§45-48.
[58]Ibid., pp. 61-65, §§45-48.
[59]Ibid., p. 65, §48.
[60]Noll, *Scandal of the Evangelical Mind,* p. 24.
[61]Ibid., p. 12.

thought and habit. However, anti-intellectualism does not always stem from such deplorable sources; often the problems come from a commendable, sometimes even sophisticated, attempt to pursue knowledge within a biblical or Christian point of view that is wedded to wooden interpretations of the Scriptures and outmoded intellectual paradigms. Thus, however intellectually sophisticated, pietistic intellectualism is ultimately at odds with Christianity's deepest impulses and commitments.[62]

Noll indicates some of the ways in which, for example, creation science is problematic and in tension with traditional Christian views.[63] First, it rejects the view, expressed by Augustine and reaffirmed over and over again throughout Christian history (though with obvious counterexamples), that the best theology and biblical interpretation must incorporate the best of our scientific knowledge.[64] (We want to claim that this principle is consistent with the claim that scientific claims are fallible and should not be accepted uncritically when they appear to conflict with revealed truth; there are complex hermeneutical issues here that we cannot deal with in this chapter.) Second, by adopting a kind of Manichaeism or "super supernaturalism"[65] in its effort to defend the Bible or harmonize the Bible and science, it demonizes "the ordinary study of nature."[66] Third, it fails to appreciate the value of adding to the study of the Bible knowledge of its appropriate cultural and historical contexts. Rather, it encourages an ahistorical study of the Bible by means of the already limited methods of Baconian science.[67]

The damage done by creation science to the evangelical mind is extensive, argues Noll, for it violates deep Christian convictions and dispositions. First, it encourages Christians to be inherently or intrinsically distrustful of either our empirical grasp of the world or the empirical sciences as they currently exist.[68] Second, creationist commitments and practices "foster a stunted ability to perceive the world of nature."[69] Third, evangelicals who think they are defending the Bible when they defend creation science are merely defending a human idol because

[62]Ibid.

[63]Note here that we (and Noll) by "creation science" do not mean to refer to the contemporary "intelligent design movement," which deserves more careful comment than we can here give. By creation science we mean the view that holds to a static "young earth" creation and rejects any process of natural evolution, either in the organic or inorganic sphere.

[64]Noll, *Scandal of the Evangelical Mind,* pp. 186, 202-3.

[65]Ibid., p. 188.

[66]Ibid.

[67]Ibid., pp. 191, 197.

[68]Ibid., p. 196.

[69]Ibid., p. 197.

they have given ultimate authority to a nineteenth-century interpretation of the Bible based upon limited methodology in science (Baconism).[70] Fourth, "evangelicals lost the ability to look at nature as it was and so lost out on the opportunity to understand more about nature as it is."[71]

No doubt, universities that embrace and legitimize views of philosophy and the Bible that are truncated and distorted in ways similar to those that led to creation science will understand the role of philosophy in largely instrumental and apologetic ways. However intellectually sophisticated such defenses of the faith may be, we contend that they depend on, or operate with, narrow and stultifying understandings of both faith and reason and thus are defective. Necessarily, then, as intellectual or scholarly artifacts or constructions, they are grossly defective accounts, and inevitably harmful with respect to God's full intentions for human flourishing and God's redemptive activity in the world. In short, they are anti-intellectual, especially when seen from the vantage point of the much more robust understanding of faith and reason articulated in *Fides et ratio.*

The Role of the Department of Philosophy in a Contemporary Christian University

We wish to end our chapter with a sketch of a department of philosophy at a contemporary Christian university that takes seriously the conception of faith and learning sketched in *Fides et ratio.* In doing so, we are suggesting concrete applications of what evangelicals might learn from this great encyclical.

First, if we may dare say so, in this contemporary Christian university one or more philosophy courses should be required of all undergraduate students. We imagine these required courses being of two types. One type would be courses for students at the earliest stages of their collegiate experience in which they are introduced to philosophy as a set of fundamental questions, and a mode or modes of inquiry, whose ultimate aim is wisdom, best understood as a lifelong quest, something which is wide and deep, and deeply important, yet always unfinished business for finite and sinful creatures. One constituent of the course is helping students to see the encounter with the texts they are reading, the modes of inquiry they are exploring, the intellectual virtues and the cognitive skills they are acquiring as intrinsically and not merely instrumentally good. Such courses would not primarily be "introductions to the discipline" designed for potential philosophy majors, though they could serve that function as well, but should be designed to

[70]Ibid., p. 199.
[71]Ibid.

help students develop a deeply Christian mind with which to understand themselves and their world.

In this contemporary Christian university, a second order of courses that should be required would be capstone or bridge courses. These are courses that presuppose the students have been exposed to a subset of modes of inquiry or disciplines. The aim of these courses is to see how the variety of intellectual inquiries characteristic of these disciplines might be integrated and unified into larger and larger wholes. A course entitled Worldviews in Literature might help literature students think about the ways in which the worldviews of writers have shaped their novels, plays and poems and the ways such worldviews affect people's lives today. A course called History and Meaning might look at whether any kind of purpose or telos can be discerned in human history, whether human history has some kind of overall meaning and what the study of history might mean to the individual today. A course called Human Nature and Economics might look at the assumptions about human persons made in economic theory and how well such assumptions fit or do not fit biblical and philosophical understandings of the self. Obviously, many such courses should not be taught by philosophers alone, but should either be team taught or taught by those in other departments who have philosophical expertise.

Second, how will a department of philosophy in a contemporary Christian university of this sort think about a major in philosophy? We think the answer is clear enough: the aim of the department is not so much to produce professional philosophers as to enable the university to expose its students to, and to inculcate all of its students with, philosophical thinking and the unity of faith and learning. To be sure, the department will welcome majors. Some will major in philosophy because they recognize or will come to recognize that scholarship and teaching in a university setting is their calling. However, many will major in philosophy just to get the kind of education a good university aims to provide. They recognize that their natural gifts and interests will flourish best in the educational environment provided by the philosophy department and its courses. Other students have other gifts and interests, and other majors that will best serve their gifts and interests. Clearly, the philosophy department will be heavily involved in the task of liberal arts education since its aim is the education of the whole person. Indeed, one aim the philosophy department will share with other departments involved in liberal arts education is the formation and transformation of its students. One way of expressing this ideal is helping students to desire what they ought to desire rather than merely be clever at getting whatever it is they want. On this, Socrates, the biblical prophets and John Paul II agree.

Third, the department of philosophy at a contemporary Christian university of the sort we are describing will be firmly grounded in the history of philosophy understood as the history of human reflection in the quest for wisdom. Because the university is a child of the Christian church in the West, the department will pay special attention to the riches of the Christian intellectual traditions, the long history of Christians reflecting on perennial philosophical questions, and their engagement with other Western and non-Western philosophies and religions.

Fourth, such a department will affirm the scholarly gifts of the philosophers working in that department. Those philosophers will see themselves as teacher-scholars with a calling to share their gifts not just with their students but with a broader public. Some will do scholarship of a broad and general nature that has as its primary audience educated Christian laity or the general public. Some will have particular gifts that allow and require them to work in specialized areas of expertise. Such specialized research and publication are still regulated by a recognition of how these interests fit in and contribute to a larger whole that inspires and guides the work of the Christian intellectual community as a whole and the department in particular. Often the questions raised and the modes of inquiry posed as a means to address the questions and answers offered for reflection will not be explicitly Christian in character. Nonetheless, they are expressions of reason at work for the sake of its appropriate end—truth with respect to some domain of philosophical inquiry. As Christians, however, they will always ask about the meaning and value of that truth, and ask what truth means for me—and for you.

Fifth, the department will have, as a department, a special interest in philosophical problems that arise especially out of the Christian story about God, God's activity and God's relation to the world and humankind. It will not follow that every person in the department is an expert in these philosophical issues, but some surely will be. And it will follow that some courses address these sorts of issues and that some in the department have research programs which advance our collective understanding as Christians in these fundamental areas.

Sixth, the department will have a responsibility in the matters of imitation and edification. Here is what we mean. In the end, the aim for all of us is to become persons of a certain sort, to become, as far as possible, reconciled to God in Christ and transformed. Or, as we Baptists often say, the aim is to become the sort of person God wants us to be, the sort of person Paul speaks of in Colossians, for example:

> As God's chosen ones, holy and beloved, clothe yourselves with compassion, kindness, humility, meekness, and patience. Bear with one another and, if anyone has a complaint against another, forgive each other; just as the Lord has forgiven you, so

> you also must forgive. Above all, clothe yourselves with love, which binds everything together in perfect harmony. (Col 3:12-14)

To embrace this goal is to embrace edification, or the edifying role of philosophy. One of the more important things Christian philosophers must do to accomplish this aim is to model for our students the intellectual, moral and religious virtues that reflect the new life we have found in Christ through participation in the body of Christ, the church, both local and universal, visible and invisible. Our special charism, as philosophers, is to affirm that faith and reason are not enemies but co-collaborators in God's divine economy. Since some students come to us afraid of new ideas and of reason, we model for them a confidence in reason and a fearlessness in reading and discussing—in taking ideas seriously, even those distant or hostile to our faith. Others come to us in rebellion against the simplistic and stultifying versions of the faith in which they have been nurtured. With such students, we model a sympathetic understanding for their pilgrimage and a patient effort to show that faith is not afraid of truth, and that truth is far wider and deeper than most of us suppose. We exhibit humility and rigor in discussing a formidable argument, charity and tenacity in disagreement with some point of view, and patience and honesty in the face of genuine perplexity. In short, each person in the department, to the best of his or her ability, has a responsibility to model for our students a faithfully formed intellect and an intellectually formed faith.

CONCLUSION

More needs to be said, to be sure, to fill out the conception of a department of philosophy in a contemporary Christian university.[72] But were there such a department in a contemporary Christian university of the sort we describe, that philosophy department would aid the university in being true to its calling. Finally, in a Christian university, being Christian helps philosophy and philosophers be true to their own callings, for we Christian philosophers affirm reason's dogged pursuit of truth and faith's gracious efficacy toward that same end.[73]

---

[72]For example, both mentoring and service are issues that should be addressed, had we both time and space.

[73]We wish to thank the many colleagues whose close reading of earlier drafts afforded us the opportunity to improve this essay dramatically. To begin, we thank the following Baylor philosophy graduate students: Mike Cantrell, Emily Glass, Sean Riley, Mark Tietjen and Mark Boone, who did the index. Their suggestions saved us from many errors. Next, we thank Daniel McInerny (University of Notre Dame), Scott Moore, Robert Kruschwitz and especially Doug Henry (Baylor University).

4

DOMINUM ET VIVIFICANTEM

The Breath of Divine Life

Clark H. Pinnock

CONTEXT

At the same time that Pope John Paul II was working on Jewish-Christian relations, he was pondering his fifth encyclical, which would be a meditation on the Holy Spirit *(Dominum et vivificantem)* and be signed at Pentecost 1986. I was happy when I heard about the theme and moved by his boldness to speak of a great Jubilee which would mark the passage from the second to the third Christian millennium. John Paul wanted the church to remember the gift of Jesus Christ through the Spirit on that special occasion. He wrote: "The Church's mind and heart turn to the Holy Spirit as this twentieth century draws to a close and the third Millennium since the coming of Jesus Christ into the world approaches, and as we look toward the great Jubilee with which the Church will celebrate the event" (*Dominum et vivificantem,* §49).[1] It reminds me of the prayer of Pope John XXIII, when he called the council and prayed: "Renew thy wonders in our day as by a new Pentecost."[2] In his message to the world at the opening session of the Second Vatican Council, he said: "In this assembly, under the guidance of the

---

[1]John Paul II, *Dominum et vivificantem: On the Holy Spirit in the Life of the Church and the World,* Libreria Editrice Vaticana (May 18, 1986) <http://www.vatican.va/edocs/ENG0142/_INDEX.HTM>. Unless otherwise noted, all in-text citations are to this encyclical.

[2]John XXIII, *Humanae salutis,* in *The Documents of Vatican II,* ed. Walter M. Abbott (New York: Guild Press, 1966), p. 709.

Holy Spirit, we wish to inquire how we ought to renew ourselves, so that we may be found increasingly faithful to the gospel of Christ."[3]

As an evangelical and charismatic, I respond enthusiastically to such a call. What a warm heart and comprehensive vision John Paul had! Here is a pastor, the very Bishop of Rome, saying that the church needs to be moving in the power of God and be open to being drawn into the mystery of God's love. He knew too that our knowledge of the Spirit will not come by way of the intellect alone. It will require the conversion of the human heart waiting in poverty of spirit.

May the windows of all churches be open to God's breath and let it sweep away the cobwebs and unleash refreshing renewal.

CONTENT

The content of the papal letter is divided into three parts. It is unassuming in appearance but profound in scriptural reflection. It is chock full of biblical verses which ought to impress and delight evangelicals. The aim of the encyclical is to profess the faith of the Roman Catholic Church in the Holy Spirit, named "the Lord and giver of life" by the Nicene-Constantinopolitan creed. It is also responding to deep spiritual desires felt by many people in the postmodern situation, wanting to draw us closer to the Spirit and discover again (as if for the first time), the transforming gift of the divine Breath.

Part one begins with the promise of the Spirit that was given by the Father through the Son to the church. Jesus spoke of the promise of the Father and of the coming of the Paraclete who will lead us ever deeper into the fullness of gospel truth and into an ever deeper relationship with God. Initially the letter delves into the self-giving of God in sending the Spirit to us. From the Gospel of John, he points to the mystery of the relations of love which lie at the heart of creation and redemption. They are surely among the matters of which Christ said, you cannot receive them now—not until Christ's self-emptying occurs through his passion and death on the cross. First there will be a departure of Christ by the cross and then a coming of the Counsellor who will be sent by the risen Christ to transform believers into his own exalted image. Having accomplished the work that God had entrusted to the Son on earth, God sent the Spirit at Pentecost to save and sanctify the church, so that we may have access to the Father through Christ in the Spirit.

Part two of the letter is given over to the work of the Spirit convincing the

[3]"Message to Humanity," in *The Documents of Vatican II*, ed. Walter M. Abbott (New York: Guild Press, 1966), pp. 3-4.

world concerning sin, righteousness and judgment. The "original sin" of humanity was and is the unbelief and incredulity that Jesus encountered among the people and that ultimately became the rejection that led to the cross. The righteousness that Christ had in mind was the justice which God would restore to him in the resurrection, having been condemned to death. And judgment refers to the guilt of the world in condemning him to death. This world has tragically forgotten its own purpose and story. It does not know where it comes from, what sustains it or where its destiny really lies, although it proudly assumes that it knows all these things. The sending of the Spirit will reveal to the world the truth about itself. It will assist sinners to recognize their need for redemption. It will teach them that the refusal of communion with God is the deepest sin. We have turned away and refused our true good and calling. We think that we can decide for ourselves what constitutes good and evil. The letter goes on to conduct a profound analysis of the workings of sin in our human lives. It brings out the fact that every sin, wherever and whenever it is committed, has reference to the cross of Christ. What is the sin against the Holy Spirit then? It is the radical refusal to accept the forgiveness which God offers and the turning away from truth, as if God were an enemy of his own creatures, a source of danger and a threat.

Part three considers the Spirit as the life-giver and explains reasons for the coming Jubilee in the year 2000. It will be a celebration of the incarnation of the Word twenty centuries ago by the power of the Spirit. The definitive self-communication of God in human history was accomplished by the power of the Spirit. Therefore the church celebrates the grace that has been manifested in order to bring salvation to all. Since Christ died for all, the Spirit, in a manner known only to God, offers to everyone the possibility of salvation and of being associated with the paschal mystery. The letter testifies to a universal access to salvation which has characterized Catholic teaching since Vatican II. The coming of the Spirit still encounters resistance and opposition. There is a struggle and a tension in the human heart. Sometimes we see openness to God and other times opposition to God's gift, something that is evident in so many aspects of contemporary life. We see death in the midst of life. Nevertheless, there is liberation through the preaching of the gospel in the power of the Spirit which can strengthen the inner man and provide a way of escape that we may be able to bear it. The Spirit is continually present with his people, making them a community which is a sign of the coming salvation of God.

In conclusion, the encyclical letter ends with a reassurance that the Spirit in his mysterious bond with Jesus Christ will accomplish what he has been sent to do.

ASSESSMENT

Now the time has come to interact with some important topics which are raised in the letter. First, notice how the letter begins with a discussion of the nature of God, theology's most important topic. This occurs in the fullest way in part one of the letter. In line with the creedal foundations of the faith, the claim is made that the Spirit of God participates in the everlasting and loving communion of the Holy Trinity. As the apostle writes: God is love and the love flows between the Father and the Son to overflow into us (1 Jn 4:7). God is a loving and relational being, and mutual love circulates among the persons of the Trinity. The Spirit participates in the communion of persons and engages in what John of Damascus calls the "dance" *(perichōrēsis),* a happy metaphor for the mutual love which the Father, Son and Holy Spirit share,[4] a fellowship into which (remarkably) we creatures are summoned to participate, thanks to the grace of God *(theōsis).*

The Spirit is somewhat less defined as a person in comparison with the Father and the Son. We are familiar with fathers and sons in earthly experience, but spirit, that is more nebulous. The "face" is not so clear in fire, water and wind. The Spirit seems content to remain more mysterious and less focused. One sees it also in the fact that the third "person" is simply called "spirit," a functional and general term that is used for the Godhead itself (Jn 4:24). Nevertheless, the Spirit seems to be associated with the love of Father and Son, as witness to it and participant in it, and is identified by theologians such as Augustine and Richard of Saint Victor as the link between the Father and Son in their love for each other (the *condilectus*). Richard used an analogy drawn from the context of marriage. Somewhat as a husband and a wife fashion community and open it up to a third person, a child, so do the Father and the Son perfect the love between them by sharing it with a third Person. In this way their own love for one another is enriched by sharing it with the Spirit who occupies (as it were) the space in the relationship of Father and Son.[5] The Spirit proceeds from their mutual love in a mysterious way, making it a love which is open and not exclusive. God is communion, and the Spirit brings communion about. Not only the communion on the level of the Godhead but as God's creative presence in every creature, he fosters communion.

The Spirit does not call attention to itself but plays a more modest and self-

---

[4]See, e.g., John of Damascus, *An Exact Exposition of the Orthodox Faith* 1.8 Christian Classics Ethereal Library, Calvin College <http://www.ccel.org/ccel/schaff/npnf209.iii.iv.html>.

[5]Richard of Saint Victor, *De Trinitate* 3.11, as quoted in William J. Hill, *The Three-Personed God: The Trinity as a Mystery of Salvation* (Washington, D.C.: Catholic University of America Press, 1982), p. 78.

effacing role. It seems to want to be known, not in ways that highlight its own distinctiveness ontologically but as the power of love which facilitates the purposes of God. As Paul writes, "God's love has been poured out into our hearts through the Holy Spirit" (Rom 5:5). Though there must be much more to know about the identity of God's Breath, the Spirit is revealed as the power of the Father's love, which touches, quickens and warms us. Tertullian imagined the Father as the orb of the sun, Jesus as the beam of light emanating from it, and the Spirit as its warmth and energy.[6] The Spirit is the irradiation of God's love, which ravishes our hearts and enables them to love in return. The Spirit is the mystery of God's engagement with the world and his empowering presence from the beginning of time. It is midwife to the new, conveying us through much groaning to new creation.

The encyclical directs one to a model of God in which the deity shines forth in self-giving love, sweeping away our fears and summoning us to enjoy union with God. The relevance of this vision to modern materialism is apparent. Instead of an ultimate reality which is devoid of purpose and value, we have the captivating vision of God as loving communion and dynamic communication. More basic than the question, "Does God exist?" is the question, "What do you mean by God?" Atheism will exist if this captivating vision of God as open, loving and dynamic communion is eclipsed. If it is not eclipsed, we can look for a new age of faith.

Second, moving beyond the place of the Spirit in the triune life, the encyclical points in a fruitful way to its role in creation as the life-giver which causes all creation to flow to its ultimate end in the infinite ocean of God. This theme is scattered through the letter. We read how the Spirit breathes life into the world and renews life through the mystery of the incarnation. It is present everywhere, drawing creatures to their destiny in God (§§47, 74, 95). God the Holy Trinity, because its nature is overflowing love, creates a world with creatures in it capable of loving God and fellow creatures. Because God is love, he seeks to make mutual love abound and sends forth the Spirit to implement this goal and bring it to fruition. The psalmist writes, relating the Spirit and nature, "When you send forth your spirit, they are created; and you renew the face of the ground" (Ps 104:30). The Spirit breathes life into creation and is the source of the new in the emergent universe. Therefore, the world does not stagnate and prove fruitless but is enabled and empowered to develop. The Spirit's job is to draw creation into the future of God's promise.

[6]Tertullian, *Against Praxeas* chap. 8, Christian Classics Ethereal Library, Calvin College <http://www.ccel.org/ccel/schaff/anf03.v.ix.viii.html>.

This is a time in history when people are very interested in natural history and the evolution of the planet, and a good occasion to link the Spirit and nature for people. Science now recognizes that nature is not machinelike but a dynamic and interrelated process. This development encourages us to see the Spirit as the ground of life in the world and as the power who calls on it to perform its marvels. Spirit is the power present in the universe from the earliest stirrings of history, sustaining the world and moving its creatures to self-transcendence. The encyclical invites us to view Spirit as God's immanent creative activity, alive in all that happens in nature and forming the ecology in which creatures can flourish. Doing so will help us understand the doctrine of creation better in an age of scientific cosmology. It is wonderful to be given the liberty to think of nature in relation to the Spirit as hovering over the universe like a mother bird, hatching order from chaos, and not to have to think of the creation event as a one-time action that produces a world and then ceases to operate. Instead, image a continual energizing of the world by the Spirit throughout its long history *(creatio continua)*. It is helpful to be able to think of the Spirit as pervading the universe, knitting things together and holding the world open for divine love.

Unlike some evangelicals, the Roman Catholic Church accepts "deep time" and the evolutionary outlook.[7] Hence believers in the Catholic Church do not face the unhappy dualism that we often face between materialistic evolution and young-earth creationism. They are free to think of the Spirit as drawing the process forward and teasing out the huge variety of potentials latent in it. By referring to the Spirit in nature, it is possible to combine creation and evolution by thinking of the Spirit guiding the process that leads to life and calling into existence the many conditions which make it possible. From the exuberance of trinitarian love comes the desire for creatures capable of loving, and from the Spirit come the power and wisdom to make this possible and actual. Spirit stands behind the creative processes which produce much more than is expected and move toward ever more complex forms of life. As one of Job's friends put it: "The spirit of God has made me, and the breath of the Almighty gives me life" (Job 33:4). In the service of the Creator, the Spirit supplies the inner-worldly direction and drive toward the goal of humanization, a trajectory which finds fulfillment in Jesus Christ.

A third contribution, which links Spirit and the incarnation (§§69-77), calls for comment. Often the incarnation is thought of apart from the Spirit despite the strong biblical witness concerning Christ's conception and ministry in the power

---

[7]John Paul II, "To the Pontifical Academy of Sciences: Truth Cannot Contradict Truth," *L'Osservatore Romano* (English edition), October 30, 1996, pp. 3, 7.

of the Spirit. I applaud the way in which the encyclical invites us to place a Spirit Christology alongside a logos Christology, a Christology from below and from above—Jesus as the Spirit-anointed wisdom of God, as the one who is radically open and completely receptive to the Holy Spirit. God's breath inspires Jesus in new and transforming ways in the successive stages of his life, ministry, death and glorification, enabling Jesus to be prophet of the reign of God. Faithful to the Spirit, Jesus witnesses to the coming kingdom in preaching, in healing, in an open table, in priority for sinners. He lived a life of radical openness to the Spirit, which led him to the cross. The Spirit does not abandon him but remains with him through the suffering and the death. And what was a savage act of murder became an event of liberation by the Spirit.

Bringing the Spirit into proximity with Christology lets us think of the work of Christ differently. It lets us view it in terms of a vicarious mission through the Spirit and to conceptualize his work as a Spirit-empowered representative on behalf of human life which fulfills the purpose of creation and heals humanity through a recapitulation of our human journey. It draws us to want to recover the soteriology of Irenaeus and the early Greek fathers who taught in these terms.[8] In a Spirit Christology, we see Jesus rendering his yes to God on our behalf and completing a representative journey which brings us back into relationship with God. The true prodigal travels our broken path and replaces our no with his yes, dying in obedience and rising to new life. Redemption comes through solidarity with Christ and his representative journey. Jesus is the gift of God's self-communication and the fulfillment of creation. In him, God gives himself a human heart and communicates the grace of sonship to us humans by the Spirit. Jesus is God's act of healing humanity, providing a new beginning through his recapitulation of our life. Salvation is through Christ's participatory journey accomplished in the power of the Spirit, who enabled him to take the journey and enables us to enter it.

In projecting a world of significantly free creatures, God reveals a longing for creatures who would say yes to his love for them. But in so doing, he took the risk that such creatures might say no instead. According to the biblical story, prodigal humanity decided to leave the Father's house for a far country. God's love allowed this choice but did not leave it there. The beloved Son who was baptized with the Spirit followed them into the far country to heal the broken relationship and bring them back to union with the triune love. The Spirit empowered the Son to be the fulfillment of what God longs for in the creature and to become the healer of our

[8]Irenaeus *Against Heresies* 5.21.3, Christian Classics Ethereal Library, Calvin College <http://www.ccel.org/ccel/schaff/anf01.ix.vii.xxii.html>.

brokenness. In his vicarious human life, Jesus says yes to the Father, experiences the spirit of sonship and pursues the path which leads him through death to resurrection on our behalf. In Christ, humanity itself is subjected to God and reunited to him as a new humanity (§40).

Jesus works atonement, not by appeasing an angry God but by taking a representative journey of obedience, on the basis of which the Spirit can form Christ in us and initiate our transformation, breaking the power of sin and death over us and leading us to share glory with the risen Lord. We are not saved by an external transaction so much as by a vicarious human journey which leads to union with God and redemption of creation. This insight may help us with the proclamation of the gospel. Too often people have been given the distorted idea that God is angry and will not forgive until a third party (Jesus) takes the punishment for them. A Spirit Christology can help correct this impression. It was love, not wrath, which brought Jesus, and the cross is an expression of God's desire to save us, not his reluctance. Part of a larger substitution, the cross was the moment of triumph when Christ accepted the will of the Father, absorbed the evil of humanity and confronted death itself in order to heal and forgive us. Bringing the Spirit into the narrative of salvation can help us clarify the rationale of atonement and re-evangelize people who have not heard the good news in these more biblical and appealing accents.

A fourth point that commends the document is its ecclesiology. It seems that, as bishop and pastor of the major Christian church, this pope is concerned about the power of the Holy Spirit, not only in the incarnation, but also in the life and mission of the people of God. Therefore, he wishes to celebrate the outpouring of the Spirit on the community which says yes to God through Jesus. As Christ's body, the church is filled with the Holy Spirit and experiences the presence of Christ in both its sacramental and its charismatic life. Often we are required in our churches to choose between two modes of the real presence of Christ, but not here where both dimensions are valid and integrated.

As a papal document, the encyclical enunciates the ancient traditions concerning the sacramental dimension of church life. In the various sacraments, people are acted on by God through faith; the sacraments are far more than mere human actions. Though an evangelical of a Baptist stripe, I take this point seriously. We have often impoverished ourselves by skepticism about the power of the Spirit in the sacramental life and have often discarded ancient liturgies and practices which have characterized church life from the beginning. As if to mimic secular rejection of mystery, we have sung the same tunes and turned away from the means of grace through which the Spirit renders material things and actions efficacious. This is a mistake. The Spirit enables believers to benefit from the bread and the wine, from the preaching, from the fellowship, and from many other such signs. We need to take more seriously the Catholic tradition on this point. God's presence makes itself felt among us in all sorts of material ways, and God acts among us and meets us through the words and actions of fellow human beings. The encyclical points us to a recovery of the power of the Holy Spirit in the symbols and languages of the heart.

The pope also refers to the charismatic dimension of the presence of Christ, speaking of gifts, both hierarchical and charismatic (§34). This is another area in which expectations of the power of the Spirit need to be rekindled among us. As the early church experienced and as modern pentecostalism has rediscovered, there is power in the midst of weakness for the life and mission of the church—power to proclaim the gospel and heal the sick. Power is expressed in Easter life and the possibility of exalted praise, fearless witness, inspired speech and other signs. Let us be done with limited expectations in regard to the Spirit and allow him to fall upon us both in our gathering and in our being sent out. In spite of some dangers and risks inherent in charismatic spontaneity, we should be open without restriction to manifestations of the Spirit in and through us.

The letter would have us less skeptical about the real presence of God and have us seek that presence through the Spirit in both sacramental and charismatic dimensions. To do so would not only enrich our lives but would facilitate the healing of church divisions, if only the two dimensions could be brought back into unity as they were together in the first centuries of church life. Certainly the original Baptists viewed the Lord's table as a place where people experience the real presence of Christ and not a mere memorial.

Another theme in the encyclical which I appreciated is its depiction of salvation from the point of view of the Holy Spirit (§47). It speaks of the Spirit calling men and women to a growing friendship with God and having them participate in the trinitarian life. It speaks of God coming to dwell within us and abide in us and of our sharing in the life of God. It says that God gives himself to us by the Spirit and intends to transform us from within. It envisages the goal of creation and salvation as a marriage feast, which symbolizes union and communion in the love of God. Orthodox theology would call this "divinization" *(theōsis),* by which is meant our being restored into the image of God and united to him. The letter, which was written from the standpoint of the Western church, makes an effort to use the language of the Eastern church, which is an ecumenical gain. The salvation of persons is viewed as an awakening to the love of God through the Spirit, the experience of sonship and conformity into the image of the Son. We are enabled to love because we belong to God who first loved us.

The image of healing is used in describing salvation. The loving Spirit wants to heal individuals, communities and ultimately the whole world in the process of redemption. The Spirit is poured out to make us new in body and soul. The letter omits any mention of a "third event" alongside conversion and sanctification, which some Christians call "baptism in the Spirit." I think these believers would lean toward interpreting such an event as a fuller realization in experience of sonship. It would be viewed as an actualization in experience of the life which was conferred upon the believer in baptism and at confirmation. It would be seen as a release of the Spirit into conscious experience of the power of the promised Spirit who has come. In creation, the Trinity throws itself open for the world by sending the Spirit who will lead the world back to the Father through the Son. The letter views salvation not solely as a change of legal status from guilty to innocent but in more relational and affective terms. "This is eternal life, that they may know you, the only true God, and Jesus Christ whom you have sent" (Jn 17:3).

Another theme of interest today and discussed in the letter is universal access to salvation. John Paul both here and in many speeches in his pontificate chose to handle the question of religious pluralism by referencing the Spirit. When he wants to render God's universal salvific will more intelligibly, he looks to the Spirit and cites this text from the Second Vatican Council: "The Holy Spirit in a manner known only to God offers to every man the possibility of being associated with this Paschal Mystery" (§53). He seems to be saying that the Spirit creates opportunities of salvation even among the unevangelized and that, regardless of the time and place in which a person lives, it is possible to receive God's offer of salvation because of the Spirit who is active everywhere and at all times in the universe, enfolding every human being in grace.

Elsewhere he writes:

> The universality of salvation means that it is granted not only to those who explicitly believe in Christ and have entered the Church. Since salvation is offered to all, it must be made available to all. But it is clear that today, as in the past, many people do not have an opportunity to come to know or accept the gospel revelation or to enter the Church. The social and cultural conditions in which they live do not permit this, and frequently they have been brought up in other religious traditions. For such people salvation in Christ is accessible by virtue of a grace which, while having a mysterious relationship to the Church, does not make them formally part of the Church but enlightens them in a way which is accommodated to their spiritual and material situation. This grace comes from Christ; it is the result of his Sacrifice and

> is communicated by the Holy Spirit. It enables each person to attain salvation through his or her free cooperation.[9]

Such openness is not original to John Paul (it is right there in the documents of Vatican II),[10] and even his reference to the Spirit as the one who implements it in the world is not completely new, but John Paul does emphasize it very strongly. In interfaith settings, he likes to bring the universal presence of the Spirit to bear on the issues. Rather than saying that non-Christian religions mediate God's grace structurally (as even Rahner does),[11] John Paul prefers to focus on the Spirit of Jesus touching every human heart. The Spirit goes ahead of the mission (prevenience) and the preaching of the gospel, and through the Spirit God's love finds a way such that no one will miss a genuine opportunity to be saved. This is an urgent issue for many today, and the pope appeals to the Spirit in seeking an intelligent solution.

Appealing to the Spirit in relation to the salvation of the unevangelized was an option in the documents of Vatican II but rare. In John Paul's work, on the other hand, it is his principle theme when speaking about and to non-Christians. He speaks of the working of the Holy Spirit in non-Christian religious and secular contexts, without recognizing the non-Christian religions themselves as a means of salvation. This is a conservative pope, and he is cautious at this point, but it seems to be a wise caution which avoids the difficulties that the progressive theologians have created by their bolder moves. They have to explain how the very different truth claims made by the various world faiths can possibly serve the salvation of Christ. But John Paul does not have to do this because he simply posits the work of the Spirit on the level of the human heart.

The letter makes a contribution to world peace and world evangelism because of its transparent openness to all the world's people. This willingness to recognize God's light and truth among them all supplies a basis for good relations and mutual respect. We have come a long way from the days of mutual recrimination and anathemas of only a few decades ago. Acknowledgment of this letter would move us in a truly positive direction.

---

[9]John Paul II, *Redemptoris missio: On the Permanent Validity of the Church's Missionary Mandate,* Libreria Editrice Vaticana (December 7, 1990), §10 <http://www.vatican.va/edocs/ENG0219/_INDEX.HTM>.

[10]Paul VI, *Dogmatic Constitution on the Church: "Lumen gentium,"* Second Vatican Council (November 21, 1964) §16 <http://www.vatican.va/archive/hist_councils/ii_vatican_council/documents/vat-ii_const_19641121_lumen-gentium_en.html>.

[11]Karl Rahner, "Christianity and the Non-Christian Religions," in *Theological Investigations,* trans. Karl-H. Kruger (London: Darton, Longman and Todd, 1966), 5:115-34.

CONCLUSION

There is great value in the pope's call to celebrate the Holy Spirit during the coming great Jubilee. There is a depth and breadth to his vision, and we are enriched by listening to his words. At the deepest level, he is calling us to be assured that, if God's Spirit gives life to the creation and renews it through the incarnation and Pentecost, we may be confident of receiving grace sufficient for each and every new challenge with which the new millennium will certainly confront us.

The document *Dominum et vivificantem: On the Holy Spirit in the Life of the Church and the World* is the longest and most complex meditation on the Holy Spirit in the history of the papal teaching office. It responds to the complaint of the Eastern churches, that theology in the West does not take the doctrine of the Spirit seriously enough. Six weeks after the encyclical was released, John Paul welcomed a delegation from the ecumenical patriarchate of Constantinople to the annual celebration of the Feast of Saint Peter and Saint Paul and told his Orthodox guests that the theological dialogue must proceed all the way to con-celebration of the Eucharist and to unity at the Lord's table.

Thanks to you, Johannes Paulus, *resquiat in pace.*

5

REDEMPTORIS MATER

A Bridge Too Far?

Tim Perry

INTRODUCTION

John Paul II oversaw the most paradoxical of pontificates.[1] On the one hand, it was perhaps the most ecumenically minded in history. Having lived through the two defining and demonic ideologies of the twentieth century—Nazism and communism—in his native Poland and having resisted into the twenty-first century Western culture's twin love affair with wealth and death, Karol Wojtyla was convinced that only a unified Christian witness to the life-transforming power of the gospel could meet the crises of the contemporary world. As a result, the "Supreme Pontiff"[2] sought to build and/or strengthen bridges to churches in the Christian East, to various Protestant denominations in the West, and, indeed, to people and organizations associated with the diverse movement known as evangelicalism.[3] Although his achievements with such organizations as the World Council of Churches, the Anglican Communion and the Orthodox family of Churches must

---

[1]A number of people contributed to this essay by commenting on earlier drafts. I wish especially to thank two Catholic scholars, Dana Dillon and Ralph Del Colle, for their incisive comments.

[2]A Latin title, *Pontifex maximus,* was once an epithet for pre-Christian emperors. From Constantine to Gratian, Christian emperors retained the title. Indeed, it was as Supreme Pontiff that Constantine convened the Council of Nicea in 325. Gratian transferred the title to Pope Damasus I in the fourth century, and it has been associated with the Bishop of Rome ever since. Translated, it means "principal bridge-maker."

[3]Such overtures, of course, preceded his elevation to the See of Peter. As Cardinal Wojtyla, he permitted Billy Graham to preach in Saint Anne's Church in Krakow. George Weigel, *Witness to Hope: The Biography of John Paul II* (New York: Harper Collins, 1999), p. 248.

be seen as modest, those conversations of which "Evangelicals and Catholics Together"[4] is the best example "would have been difficult to imagine without the ecumenical witness of John Paul II."[5]

On the other hand, to outsiders at least,[6] this papacy also seemed to accentuate those distinctives that prevented the (re-)building of bridges in many ways. Perhaps the prime example is *Dominus Iesus,* published by the Congregation for the Doctrine of the Faith on August 6, 2000, with John Paul II's explicit apostolic authority.[7] This document clarifies that, whatever good relations are to be fostered among Christian traditions, the Catholic Church is not one among equals.[8] Even Orthodox bodies—which are "true particular churches" because of their preservation of apostolic succession and a valid Eucharist—lack full communion with the one true church. Other ecclesial bodies "are not Churches in the proper sense."[9] It can be argued that this clear statement of Catholic identity vis-à-vis other Christian bodies and non-Christian religions is actually a help to clear-headed ecumenical discussions; nevetheless, many have concluded that it is too harsh. Of course, other examples can be mentioned: Reformation debates five centuries old took on renewed vitality in the light of John Paul II's endorsement of indulgences[10] and his deep, personal and public devotion to the Blessed Virgin Mary.[11]

---

[4]"Evangelical & Catholics Together: The Christian Mission in the Third Millennium," *First Things* 43 (May 1994): 15-22.

[5]Weigel, *Witness to Hope,* p. 859.

[6]This is an important qualification, for John Paul II has had many critics within the Roman Catholic Church who accused him of being insufficiently Catholic. And that charge tended to be expanded along ideological lines. For critics on the left, "insufficiently Catholic" tended to mean being too authoritarian in matters of personnel, too dogmatic in matters of theology and ethics, and too willing to abandon reforms of the Second Vatican Council. For critics on the right (who did not get as much press), "insufficiently Catholic" meant just the opposite: being too willing to tolerate dissent, too open to dogmatic and ethical exploration, and too tied to the reforms of the Second Vatican Council.

[7]Joseph Cardinal Ratzinger, *Declaration "Dominus Iesus" on the Unicity and Salvific Universality of Jesus Christ and the Church,* Congregation for the Doctrine of the Faith (August 6, 2007) §23 <http://www.vatican.va/roman_curia/congregations/cfaith/documents/rc_con_cfaith_doc_20000806_dominus-iesus_en.html>.

[8]Ibid., §§16-17.

[9]Ibid., §17. Assertions such as these stirred controversy in some Protestant (and, indeed, some Catholic) circles. It must therefore be noted that the documents of Vatican II say substantially the same thing. See, for example, Paul VI, *Dogmatic Constitution on the Church: "Lumen gentium,"* Second Vatican Council (November 21, 1964) §8 <http://www.vatican.va/archive/hist_councils/ii_vatican_council/documents/vat-ii_const_19641121_lumen-gentium_en.html>.

[10]See, for example, John Paul II, *"Incarnationis mysterium": Bull of Indiction of the Great Jubilee of the Year 2000,* esp. §9; see also the appended "Conditions for Gaining the Jubilee Indulgence" <http://www.vatican.va/jubilee_2000/docs/documents/hf_jp-ii_doc_30111998_bolla-jubilee_en.html>.

[11]Even a casual reader of John Paul's writings will be struck by the constant presence and integration of three threads on virtually every page: a commitment to thorough biblical exegesis, a dedication to

The desires to build bridges to other Christian communities and to maintain a strong Catholic identity come together in *Redemptoris mater.* Nowhere save in the encyclical *Ut unum sint* is the pope's concern for the visible unity of the church more evident. Nowhere is his Marian theology and devotion so explicit and developed. Its style—heavily reliant on biblical exegesis and with frequent recourse to pious language—is one readily recognizable to evangelical Protestants. Its tone—contemplative and warm-hearted—draws from and is aimed at the Marian piety of Orthodoxy. And throughout, its content is thoroughly Catholic. The assessment of one Canadian newspaper is apt: "Paradoxical. She who has been seen in the past as a divisive factor between Protestants and Catholics, she who has undergone an eclipse even in the Catholic Church since Vatican II, often in the name of ecumenism, is now proposed as a path of unity."[12]

This essay falls into three sections. The first places the encyclical in the context of Mariology in and after the Second Vatican Council. The second offers a sympathetic reading of the encyclical. The third engages with its contents. This hermeneutical exercise will, finally, allow me to consider whether the Mary of *Redemptoris mater* represents a point of contact for ecumenical overtures, or if she in fact remains a "bridge too far," exposing just how deep and wide the Reformation impasse remains.

Mary in and After Vatican II

The Second Vatican Council's document, "The Blessed Virgin Mary, Mother of God in the Mystery of Christ and the Church,"[13] has its own context.[14] It follows

---

the documents of Vatican II and a warm-hearted Marian piety. The strength of the latter—we may cite as evidence the *M* on his papal shield, his conviction that Mary had directly intervened to save his life after he had been shot, and his personal motto of utter Marian devotion, *totus tuus,* "all to you"—links John Paul II with Popes Pius IX and Pius XII, the popes responsible for the dogmatic definitions of the immaculate conception and bodily assumption, respectively. The form it takes, however, is (unsurprisingly) distinctly Polish. Devotion to Mary in Poland is deep and finds expression in devotion to Our Lady of Czestochowa. According to pious tradition, the icon, painted by Luke and approved of by the Virgin herself, fell into the hands of a Polish duke, Wladyslav, who in turn built a monastery to house it near the village of Czestochowa. As Poland became Europe's battlefield in the late medieval and early modern eras, the monastery at Czestochowa remained untouched, a miracle attributed to the special care of the Virgin Mary. In 1656, after a long but failed siege by Swedish armies, Mary was proclaimed the Queen of Poland. For a full retelling of the legend, see the anonymous article, "Our Lady of Czestochowa (Between East and West)," *Eastern Churches Quarterly* 10 (1954): 385-90.

[12]"Une prophécie pour le 3e millénaire," *L'informateur,* May 3-16, 1985, p. 7. Quoted in Thomas Ryan, "Ecumenical Responses to the Papal Encyclical *Redemptoris mater,*" *Ecumenism* 87 (1987): 26.

[13]*Lumen gentium,* chap. 8.

[14]Much of the material in this section appears in Tim Perry, *Mary for Evangelicals: Toward an Understanding of the Mother of Our Lord* (Downers Grove, Ill.: InterVarsity Press, 2006), chap. 11.

on the heels of "the Marian century" that spans the dogmatic definitions of the immaculate conception[15] in 1854 and the bodily assumption[16] in1950. According to the former, Mary was, by the miraculous intervention of God and in the light of the salvation won by Christ on the cross, conceived without original sin. The latter teaches that at the end of earthly life, Mary was taken, body and soul, into heaven. Many have pointed out that unlike these documents, *Lumen gentium,* chapter eight, is more biblically engaged, more patristically grounded and more modest in tone. This observation, while accurate in and of itself, can imply a departure from the previous pronouncements that is not entirely true. It is better seen as the culmination of a trend begun in 1854 rather than as a break with tradition.

In order to justify this understanding, I turn first to the history of the dogmas themselves. The immaculate conception, in some form or other, had been defended since the Middle Ages and has roots extending to Justin Martyr.[17] Similarly, the assumption in some form or other has been defended since the fifth century.[18] Neither doctrine was new. Furthermore, *Lumen gentium,* chapter eight, whatever its relative modesty, affirms the two declarations.[19] Second, the previous documents subtly curb Marian excesses. *Ineffabilis deus*[20] explicitly affirms that Mary is protected from original sin by an act of God. Mary needs to be saved by grace and is saved in a unique way: she is kept from sin in view of the merits of her Son and her Savior. The bull officially excludes those forms of belief and piety that placed her beyond the need of salvation.[21] Similarly, *Munificentissimus Deus*[22] takes no position on Mary's death; its language can accommodate both those who held that Mary died and then was raised and those who held that Mary never died. It thus avoids discussing the nature of Mary's coredemption even though, in the eyes of some, this was a natural implication to

---

[15]See Pius IX, *The Bull "Ineffabilis" in Four Languages,* trans. and ed. Ulick J. Bourke (Dublin: John Mullany, 1868).

[16]See Pius XII, *Apostolic Constitution of Pope Pius XII: "Munificentissimus Deus": Defining the Dogma of the Assumption* (November 1, 1950) http://www.vatican.va/holy_father/pius_xii/apost_constitutions/documents/hf_p-xii_apc_19501101_munificentissimus-deus_en.html.

[17]Justin is the first Christian theologian that we know of to speak of Mary as "the New Eve," language that, according to defenders of the dogma, finds its complete expression in the immaculate conception of Mary. See Justin, *Dialogue* 100, in *Ante-Nicene Fathers* 1:248-49.

[18]See R. L. P. Milburn, "The Historical Background of the Doctrine of the Assumption," in *Women in Early Christianity,* vol. 14 of *Studies in Early Christianity,* ed. David M. Scholer (New York: Garland, 1993), pp. 55-66.

[19]*Lumen gentium,* §59.

[20]See note 15.

[21]For an example, see Mary of Agreda, *Mystical City of God,* trans. George J. Blatter, 4 vols. (Wheeling: Corcoran Publishing, 1949).

[22]See note 16.

address.[23] *Lumen gentium* thus does not break from a tradition of Marian exaltation so much as it extends a century-long trend in moderation.[24]

What does set the document apart from its Marian predecessors is the means by which it pursues this moderation and the goal to which it puts it. Both the means and the goal are discerned in the council's use of ancient texts. From its opening citation of Galatians 4:4 to its final allusion to 2 Peter 3:10, it almost overwhelms the reader with its many scriptural and patristic citations,[25] easily surpassing medieval and modern references. This is clear evidence that the council deliberately wished to ground Marian teaching in the earliest (common) Christian faith in order to ease some of the ecumenical tensions. Does *Lumen gentium* succeed in its goal? To that question we now turn.

According to the text, all Mary's privileges follow from her motherhood, to which she has been predestined from all eternity and to which she freely assented in time (*Lumen gentium,* §53). Because of her maternity, she is an exalted creature: occupying a "place in the Church which is the highest after Christ and yet very close to us" (*Lumen gentium,* §54). Although it is far from a complete Mariology (*Lumen gentium,* §54), and in spite of its ecumenical aim (*Lumen gentium,* §§68-69), the document embraces those privileges that had proved ecumenically problematic, understanding the immaculate conception to be the completion of the patristic parallel of Eve and Mary (*Lumen gentium,* §56) and reiterating the bodily assumption (*Lumen gentium,* §59). Her privileges, however, do not so much divinize her as they display in her what God intends his church, and indeed each believer, to become. So it is that Mary is "one with all those who are to be saved" (*Lumen gentium,* §53) and a "pre-eminent and singular member of the Church, and as its type and excellent exemplar in faith and charity" (*Lumen gentium,* §53).

Mary's privileges, in other words, highlight her representative and exemplary

---

[23]For an example, see Gabriel M. Roschini, "The Assumption and the Immaculate Conception," *The Thomist* 14 (1951): 60-68. This continues to be an open debate. In 1996, the Theological Commission of the Pontifical International Marian Academy recommended against a papal definition of co-redemption. See the full text of "Request for the Definition of the Dogma of Mary as Mediatrix, Coredemptrix and Advocate," posted by The Marian Library/International Marian Research Institute from *L'Osservatore Romano* (June 4, 1997) at <http://campus.udayton.edu/mary// resources/internationalmarianacademy.htm>. I thank Ralph Del Colle for pointing me to this document.

[24]One could argue that this trend actually has its roots in the sober Mariology of John Henry Cardinal Newman. See John Henry Newman, *Certain Difficulties Felt by Anglicans in Catholic Teaching Considered,* vol. 2 (London: Longmans, Green, and Co., 1900).

[25]Numbering only eighteen paragraphs, *Lumen gentium,* chap. 8, manages to quote or allude to Scripture twenty-two times and to patristic writings twenty-seven times.

roles in the church's pilgrimage of faith. Consider first the former: as a daughter of Adam, she represents humanity's passive need for God; as the new Eve, the potential active acceptance of God's gift (*Lumen gentium,* §64). As for the latter, Mary is now where all believers aim to be and "so they turn their eyes to Mary who shines forth to the whole community of the elect as the model of virtues" (*Lumen gentium,* §65). It is in this ecclesiological context that the council situates the notion of Mary's mediation. She does not stand outside the church, nor is she Christ's equal (*Lumen gentium,* §62). Mary is unique only in the fullness of her response to and participation in the singular mediation of God's grace through Christ (*Lumen gentium,* §60). She is a representative of grace-enabled human potential and an example to believers.

In summary, *Lumen gentium,* chapter eight, seeks, without diluting church teaching, to present a moderate portrait of Mary in order that she might be a point of contact for ecumenical discussion.[26] This effort has, over the last twenty-five years or so, begun to bear good fruit as Protestants and Catholics have come to read the Bible, weigh the claims of tradition and engage in constructive debate together. Not only has this meant a joint engagement with the biblical material using hermeneutics that Protestants, over the last 250 years, have come to take for granted. It has also meant employing other methodologies from diverse academic disciplines to interpret Scripture and weigh tradition. It is this critical openness that motivates *Redemptoris mater,* allowing John Paul to see Mary both as a definer of Catholic doctrine and devotion and as an aid toward church unity. With that in mind, let us proceed to the text itself.

THE MOTHER OF THE REDEEMER

The first of two noteworthy points in the introduction to *Redemptoris mater* is the quotation of Galatians 4:4, with which *Lumen gentiumm,* chapter eight, also opens.[27] John Paul intends to offer a biblical reflection following the guidelines of Vatican II.[28] For him, the Pauline phrase "the fullness of time" denotes two facets of a singular event: both the incarnation of God the Son in Mary's womb and the beginning of the church in Mary who, as the recipient of the Word in both heart

[26]This is made explicit in Pope Paul VI's *Apostolic Exhortation, "Marialis cultus," for the Right Ordering and Development of Devotion to the Blessed Virgin Mary* (February 2, 1974), which sought to direct the Marian renewal begun by *Lumen gentium,* chap. 8. See <http://www.vatican.va/holy_father/paul_vi/apost_exhortations/documents/hf_p-vi_exh_19740202_marialis-cultus_en.html>.

[27]See *Lumen gentium,* §52.

[28]John Paul II, *Redemptoris mater: On the Blessed Virgin Mary in the Life of the Pilgrim Church,* Libreria Editrice Vaticana (March 25, 1987) §1 <http://www.vatican.va/edocs/ENG0224/_INDEX.HTM>.

and body, is the first and model disciple (*Redemptoris mater,* §1).[29] These form the bases of parts one and two of *Redemptoris mater.* The second is the announcement of a Marian Year, which itself foreshadows the Jubilee Year 2000 (§3).[30] In the light of its advent, John Paul explores how Mary precedes the church in its pilgrimage of faith. This forms the basis of part three.

Mary in the mystery of Christ. The encyclical is painstakingly organized with each part further subdivided into three. Thus, part one of *Redemptoris mater* reflects on the grace operative in Mary's life, the nature of her faith and her place in the drama of redemption. Turning first to grace, John Paul meditates on the angelic description of Mary as she who is "full of grace" (his rendering of, *kecharitōmenē* in Lk 1:28). Drawing on 1 John 4:8, 2 Peter 1:4 and especially Ephesians 1:3-14, John Paul presents "grace" as that sharing of the divine life through which God has planned to save all who believe in and through Christ (§8). It is a wondrous gift both planned from all eternity (i.e., election, §§7-9) and given in time (i.e., the incarnation, §11). This, in turn, leads to a balanced view of Mary as both one of the human family and "the favorite daughter of the Father" (§9).[31] With all who believe, she is included in the plan of election from all eternity (§7); the grace that she receives is available to all (§8); she stands among the poor and humble (§8). At the same time, Mary's place in God's plan is "special" (§8); in a unique way, she was *full* of grace (§8); she stands out as one who "remains perfectly open" to the gift of grace (§8).

Mary is full of grace "because it is precisely in her that the Incarnation of the Word, the hypostatic union of the Son of God with human nature, is accomplished and fulfilled" (§9). It is therefore to the glory of God's grace that the mother of God has been "redeemed in a more sublime manner" than the rest of the race (§10);[32] i.e., she was immaculately conceived. Her unique place in the drama of redemption is foreshadowed in Genesis 3:15 (the seed of the *woman*) and confirmed in Revelation 12:1 (the *woman* clothed with the sun). She is thus

---

[29]It is at this point that John Paul first mentions the immaculate conception, tying it specifically to its ecclesiological dimension, writing "in the liturgy the Church salutes Mary of Nazareth as the Church's own beginning, for in the event of the Immaculate Conception the Church sees projected, and anticipated in her most noble member, the saving grace of Easter. And above all, in the Incarnation she encounters Christ and Mary indissolubly joined: he who is the Church's Lord and Head and she who, uttering the first fiat of the New Covenant, prefigures the Church's condition as spouse and mother" (*Redemptoris mater,* §1). All following in-text citations to *Redemptoris mater* will be referred to only by section number, unless otherwise noted.

[30]That year ran from June 7, 1987, to August 15, 1988.

[31]Quoting *Lumen gentium,* §53: "beloved daughter of the Father."

[32]Quoting *Lumen gentium,* §53.

at the heart of "that struggle which accompanies the history of humanity on earth and the history of salvation itself" (§11). Before God and before humanity, Mary is the "unchangeable and inviolable sign of God's election" and, as such, remains "a sign of sure hope" (§11).

From the divine gift, John Paul moves to consider Mary's response and focuses on the words of Elizabeth's blessing: "'blessed is she who believed that there would be a fulfillment of what was spoken to her from the Lord' (Lk. 1:45). . . . The fullness of grace announced by the angel means the gift of God himself. Mary's faith . . . indicates how the Virgin of Nazareth responded" (§12). John Paul stresses here the active "obedience of faith" that finds its first expression in her acceptance as recorded in Luke 1:38. This "'let it be to me'—was decisive, on the human level, for the accomplishment of the divine mystery" (§13). It signals, in other words, Mary's active cooperation with grace which made possible, "as far as it depended on her" the realization of the plan of salvation (§13).

These words, however, do not simply frame that singular moment when the Son of God was conceived. They also mark the beginning of Mary's own pilgrimage of faith that she pursued throughout her life. It opens in a moment of complete trust in which Mary abandoned herself to God and God's plan for her (§15). It continues alongside the "historical situation in which the Son is to accomplish his mission, namely, in misunderstanding and sorrow" (§16). She will, as foretold by Simeon (Lk 2:25-35), "live her obedience of faith in suffering, at the side of the suffering Savior. . . [her] motherhood will be mysterious and sorrowful" (§16). This is obvious, of course, in the flight to Egypt documented by Matthew (Mt 2:12-22), but it also defines Mary's hidden life—that is, the life she lived with Jesus before his ministry began (§17). So it is that the blessing offered by Elizabeth and apprehended by Mary in faith comes to fruition only through a lifetime of mystery and suffering. John Paul's striking image of Mary growing in her understanding of her role, as of that of her Son, as she lives the obedience of faith throughout her life is not only true to Luke's text but also to Luther's 1521 Commentary on the Magnificat![33]

This blessing reaches its climax at the cross. Even here, at her darkest hour, Mary "faithfully preserved her union with her Son" (§18).[34] Here, at what John Paul evocatively calls "the complete negation" of the annunciation (§18), Mary remained united to her Son through a faith that can only be called "heroic" (§18).

---

[33]Martin Luther, *The Sermon on the Mount and Magnificat,* vol. 21 of *Luther's Works,* American Edition, ed. H. T. Lehmann (St. Louis: Concordia, 1955-), pp. 297-358.

[34]Quoting *Lumen gentium,* §58.

At this point, John Paul moves from a meditation on Mary's disposition (that of faith) to set the stage for a consideration of her ongoing role. So deep was her faith at the foot of the cross that through it Mary comes to share in the sacrifice of Christ (§19) and becomes "in a certain sense the counterpoise to the disobedience and disbelief embodied in the sin of our first parents" (§19). Mary's faithful obedience even to the cross thus undoes the unbelief of Eve such that it is appropriate to call her the "mother of the living" and to lay claim to the ancient phrase, "death through Eve, life through Mary" (§19).[35]

This role is then explored further as John Paul takes up the words "behold your mother" (Jn 19:27) to conclude this first section. He opens with a strong statement opposing any linkage of Mary's ongoing role to her genetic relatedness to Jesus (§20). Taking his cue from Luke 11:27-28, John Paul presents Jesus' teaching, "Blessed rather are those who hear the word of God and keep it," not as a rejection of Mary. Rather, Jesus' words "divert attention from motherhood only as a fleshly bond, in order to direct it towards those mysterious bonds of the spirit which develop from hearing and keeping God's word" (§20). Mary's ongoing maternal role in the drama of redemption is due to her election in grace to divine motherhood and her response of faith to that gift; it is a role that Mary herself slowly discovered and continuously accepted throughout her life.

At this point, John Paul shifts his reflections to the two Marian appearances in the Gospel of John—the wedding at Cana (Jn 2:1-12) and under the cross (Jn 19:25-27). Beginning with the former, John Paul documents the apparently strange conversation between Jesus and his mother that resulted in, first, his apparent refusal of her request, followed by her directive to the servants and, finally, the performance of a miracle. The exegetical challenges associated with this passage are well documented.[36] Nevertheless, John Paul insists that it "is certain that that event already quite clearly outlines the new dimension, the new meaning of Mary's motherhood" specifically, her "solicitude for human beings" (§21). This solicitude, further, is mediatory. She presents the needs of humanity before her Son, wishes the saving power of her Son to be made real in the lives of human beings, and speaks on his behalf, pointing out those things humans can do in order that his saving power might be revealed (§21). For John Paul, "the episode at Cana in Galilee offers us a sort of first announcement of Mary's mediation, wholly oriented towards Christ and tending to the revelation of his salvific power" (§22).

Turning to the latter, John Paul admits that the account reflects Jesus' concern

---

[35]Quoting ibid., §56.

[36]For more on this, see below.

for his mother, and insists on a more fundamental meaning. By entrusting the beloved disciple to his mother, Jesus gives her "as mother to every single individual and all mankind" (§23). Here, the "motherhood" generated by Mary's faith and glimpsed at the wedding comes to its fullest expression for, through Jesus' words, it finds a new "continuation in the Church and through the Church, symbolized . . . by John" (§24). Mary's motherhood of the church, in other words, is to be understood as "the reflection and extension of her motherhood of the Son of God" (§24). So intimate is the Marian link between the incarnation of the Son and the birth of the church that Mary's maternal presence continues to be felt (§24).

The mother of God at the center of the pilgrim church. This maternal link then forms the basis of part two of *Redemptoris mater,* in which John Paul applies the just enunciated Marian perspective to the universality of the church, the unity of the church and what he calls "the 'Magnificat' of the pilgrim Church." Before these can be unpacked, however, a word on the motif of pilgrimage is necessary, for it ties the three subsections together. Like Israel in the desert, so the church journeys through both space and time, and through the history of souls. And in that sojourn, Mary is present as the first disciple. Thirty years before the birthday of the church, she had begun her pilgrimage of faith at the annunciation. "The moment of Pentecost in Jerusalem had been prepared for by the moment of the Annunciation in Nazareth, as well as by the Cross." She therefore meets the first disciples as one who "goes before them" and who "leads the way" (§26). Just how she led and continues to lead the pilgrim church will be the focus of John Paul's remarks.

She leads, first of all, by being a teacher of the apostles. Although Mary did not receive the great commission to take the gospel to the ends of the earth, she was present in the Upper Room with them, as the mother of Jesus. "Thus, from the very first moment, the Church 'looked at' Mary through Jesus, just as she [i.e., the Church] 'looked at' Jesus though Mary. For the Church of that time and of every time Mary is a singular witness to the years of Jesus' infancy and hidden life at Nazareth" (§26). She does so, second, by being not only the first to believe among the disciples of the Lord but also the only disciple whose faith did not fail at the cross (§26). For these reasons, John Paul insists that Pentecost is better understood not as the beginning of the church but as the first public manifestation thereof. "It is precisely Mary's faith which marks the beginning of the new and eternal Covenant of God with man in Jesus Christ; this heroic faith of hers 'precedes' the apostolic witness of the Church, and ever remains in the Church's heart hidden like a special heritage of God's revelation" (§27).

So it is that Mary's faith has accompanied the apostolic witness to the gospel throughout the world to the degree that it and she remain present and living realities in the church (§28). As a result, a commitment to the mission of the church and to the gospel will invariably accompany various examples of Marian devotion, in the household, church communities, religious institutions, and even whole nations, societies and continents. And this Marian devotion, in turn, serves to strengthen devotion to Jesus by infusing the faithful with that same faith that stood firm at the cross. Thus, Mary precedes the pilgrim people of God throughout the world as the church "strives energetically and constantly to bring all humanity . . . back to Christ its Head in the unity of his Spirit" (§28).[37]

Not only does Mary serve the universal church and its mission. She also is a largely untapped resource in the Catholic Church's ecumenical discussions both in the West and in the East (§29). Consider first the former set of conversations. It is of course clear to all Western Christians that beliefs about the role of Mary in the plan of salvation have in fact been a source of disunity. John Paul, however, is optimistic that this is a transitional phase (albeit a rather long one). Encouraged by the fruit borne of the dialogues between the Catholic Church and the churches and ecclesial communities of the West, he is hopeful that dialogues will soon tackle the complicated issues of the nature of the Church and Mary's role in the work of salvation: "By a more profound study of both Mary and the Church, clarifying each by the light of the other, Christians who are eager to do what Jesus tells them—as their Mother recommends (cf. Jn. 2:5)—will be able to go forward together on this 'pilgrimage of faith'" (§30).

With the churches of the East, on the other hand, the barriers are less difficult. The deep Marian devotion of the East finds its fullest expression and its deepest roots in the Council of Ephesus, and also in the poetry of Saint Ephrem the Syrian and the panegyric of Saint Gregory of Narek (§31). The praise of the mother of God suffuses Byzantine liturgy, where it is always linked to the praise of her Son (§32). Her icons and images rightly preserve, foster and strengthen the devotion of Eastern Christians to the holy *Theotokos* (§33). In and through these various manifestations, and especially in "the Icon of the Virgin of the Cenacle, praying with the Apostles as they awaited the Holy Spirit" (§33), Mary is a sign of hope for all those involved in these dialogues. Indeed, the vast amount of piety could provide the resources to "hasten the day when the Church can begin once more to breath fully with her 'two lungs,' the East and the West" (§34).

Thus far, John Paul has taught that as the church universal presses on in its

[37]Quoting *Lumen gentium*, §1.

rediscovery of its unity in Christ, Mary remains present in and with it. He concludes part two reflecting on the Magnificat (Lk 1:46-55) and just how she does so. Through her utterance of this simply expressed yet literarily profound song, Mary demonstrates first to Elizabeth and then to all disciples that she "is the first to share in this new revelation of God and, within the same, in this new 'self-giving' of God" (§36). Thus, in her parallel pilgrimage of faith, the church constantly repeats her words (§37) and seeks to recapitulate the mission they express. "Drawing from Mary's heart, from the depth of her faith expressed in the words of the Magnificat, the Church renews ever more effectively in herself the awareness that the truth about God who saves, the truth about God who is the source of every gift, cannot be separated from the manifestation of his love of preference for the poor and humble" (§37).

Maternal mediation. The last matter to be taken up is the nature of Mary's mediation of grace from Jesus to the church in the church and its significance for the upcoming Marian Year. First, John Paul insists that Mary's mediation be understood in relation to the mediation of Jesus. On the one hand, there is only one mediator (1 Tim 2:5-6). Whatever mediatory role Mary continues to fulfill in the life of the church, it is not one equal to or over against the mediation of her Son. At the same time, however, it is a real mediation flowing from her election and faithful response to the gift of divine motherhood. "Since by virtue of divine election Mary is the earthly Mother of the Father's consubstantial Son and his 'generous companion' in the work of redemption 'she is a mother to us in the order of grace.' This role constitutes a real dimension of her presence in the saving mystery of Christ and the Church" (§38).[38] It is rooted, in other words, in Mary's recognition of her status as the handmaid of the Lord (Lk 1:38).

In this first moment of submission, Mary consents to be the mediator of the Mediator. It is a moment of complete consecration to God and God's plan that can only be described as "spousal" that then came to define the entirety of Mary's life. And this "entirety" extends both forward and backward in time—forward to her "entire maternal sharing in the life of Jesus Christ, her Son" (§39) and backward "in a way that matched her [prior] vocation to virginity" (§39).[39] Through

---

[38]Quoting *Lumen gentium,* §61.

[39]I have inserted the word *prior* here to indicate John Paul's allusion to the ancient belief, found in the following excerpt from the same paragraph, that Mary's *ante partum* virginity was the result of a lifelong vow of devotion to God that precluded marriage: "It can be said that a consent to motherhood is above all a *result* of her total selfgiving to God in virginity. Mary accepted her election as Mother of the Son of God, guided by spousal love, the love which totally 'consecrates' a human being to God" (*Redemptoris mater,* §39, emphasis added).

her words, she indicates her complete openness to the person and mission of her Son, an openness perfected as she advanced in her pilgrimage of faith to the crucifixion, an openness in which she cooperated with the mission of her Son through her own actions and suffering (§39). Thus, while it is true to say that God chooses to mediate the grace of Christ through many of his creatures, "Mary entered, in a way all her own, into the one mediation 'between God and men' which is the mediation of the man Christ Jesus. . . . [S]he was especially predisposed to cooperation with Christ, the one Mediator of human salvation. And such cooperation is precisely this mediation subordinated to the mediation of Christ" (§39).

Having been entrusted the welfare of the church by her Son (cf. Jn 19:26), "Mary, who from the beginning had given herself without reserve to the person and work of her Son, could not but pour out upon the Church, from the very beginning, her maternal self-giving" (§40). Now assumed into heaven, this (subordinate) maternal mediation and intercession continues, through which Mary "contributes in a special way to the union of the pilgrim Church on earth with the eschatological and heavenly reality of the Communion of Saints" (§41). In this role, she foreshadows the future of the church in its resurrected glory, and powerfully demonstrates that to serve the Lord through her mediation is to reign alongside him. In her "Assumption into heaven, Mary is as it were clothed by the whole reality of the Communion of Saints, and her very union with the Son in glory is wholly oriented towards the definitive fullness of the Kingdom, when 'God will be all in all'" (§41). Although thus exalted, Mary's maternal mediation remains subordinate to the singular mediation of Jesus.

Having established the reality and subordinate nature of Mary's mediation, John Paul reflects on that mediation, worked out in the corporate life of the church and in the individual lives of believers. With respect to the church, Mary is, first of all, "present . . . from generation to generation through faith and as the model of hope which does not disappoint (cf. Rom. 5:5)" (§42). Like Mary, the church becomes a mother when it accepts and proclaims God's word and, through baptism, brings forth children of God. Just "as Mary is at the service of the mystery of the Incarnation, so the Church is always at the service of the mystery of adoption to sonship through grace" (§43). Like Mary, the church is a faithful spouse. Mary, espoused to God, maintained her virginity throughout her life. The church, similarly, maintains its fidelity to Christ.[40] Like Mary, the church receives, keeps

[40]At this point, John Paul adds that Mary's virginity has value as a model for "total self-giving to God in celibacy. . . . Precisely such virginity, after the example of the Virgin of Nazareth, is the source of a special spiritual fruitfulness: it is the source of motherhood in the Holy Spirit" (*Redemptoris mater,* §43).

and ponders the Word of God, in order to proclaim it faithfully. The mystery of the life and mission of the church, in other words, is disclosed in the mystery of the life and mission of Mary.

Second, Mary is present in the church also as she who cooperates in the accomplishment of the church's mission, in bringing the sons and daughters of God to (re-)birth. She exercises her maternal care of the church continually by imploring the Holy Spirit to pour himself out on his church, that he might raise up new children of God, that he might redeem through the sacrifice of Christ. This maternal presence is especially experienced, John Paul continues, in the celebration of the Eucharist, where the "true body born of the Virgin Mary, becomes present" (§44). There is therefore, says John Paul, a profound link between authentic Marian devotion in its various manifestations and the central liturgical celebration of the church: the Eucharist.

Turning from the church to individual believers, John Paul states that there is an analogy between the union of mother and child according to the order of nature and the union of Mary to the believer according to the order of grace (§45). Just as the bond between mother and child is unique regardless of how many children any one woman has, so the bond between Mary and each believer is unique and unrepeatable. Just as maternal love is necessary for a child to mature, so Mary's maternal love is necessary for a believer to attain spiritual maturity. Revealed when Christ entrusted John to the care of Mary (Jn 19:27), Mary's maternal care is a gift of Jesus intended not just for John, but also for every believer. And like the Beloved Disciple, believers are to take Mary into our homes. That is, believers are to cultivate with her an intimate relationship, which in turn will only deepen our relationship with her Son.

The individual believer's relationship to Mary, that is to say, can in no way detract from his or her relationship to Jesus. Not only is it a gift of Jesus to be gratefully received and carefully nurtured, but also it is definitively directed toward him. Mary, our mother in faith, remains the woman at Cana who said, "Do whatever he tells you" (Jn 2:5). Jesus alone remains "the way, and the truth, and the life" (Jn 14:6) while Mary remains throughout the humble handmaid of the Lord. As believers devote themselves to Mary, therefore, she "with her faith as Spouse and Mother" will lead "them to the 'unsearchable riches of Christ' (Eph. 3:8)" even as he, in turn, will disclose more clearly the true dignity calling of humanity to them (§46).[41] So it is that Mary, "the exalted Daughter of Sion [*sic*],

[41]This is especially the case for disciples who are women: "the figure of Mary of Nazareth sheds light on womanhood as such by the very fact that God, in the sublime event of the Incarnation of his Son,

helps all her children, wherever they may be and whatever their condition, to find in Christ the path to the Father's house" (§47).

It is the special bond between humanity and Mary that is the reason for the proclamation of a Marian Year. Just as the previous Marian Year of 1954 accentuated the holiness of Mary as expressed in her immaculate conception and her bodily assumption, so the Marian Year of 1987-1988 is intended to accentuate the special presence of Mary in the mystery of Christ and his church. John Paul continues here in the furrow begun by Vatican II, emphasizing the biblical and incarnational roots and the ecclesiological focus of Marian doctrine and devotion. He explicitly directs people to study *Lumen gentium,* chapter eight, and the contents of this encyclical to bolster their Marian doctrine, and to study the writings of Saint Louis Marie Grignion de Montfort "who proposes consecration to Christ through the hands of Mary, as an effective means for Christians to live faithfully their baptismal commitments" (§48). In these ways, John Paul calls the church to remember its deep Marian doctrine and devotion in order that it might prepare for the challenges of the new millennium, chief of which is the undoing of the Great Schism between East and West.

As the encyclical moves into its conclusion, John Paul's deep Marian piety is given explicit expression through a short commentary on a Marian invocation from the Liturgy of the Hours:

> Loving Mother of the Redeemer, gate of heaven, star of the sea,
> assist your people who have fallen yet to strive to rise again.
> To the wonderment of nature you bore your Creator! (§51)

For John Paul, this prayer emphasizes the central place that Mary occupies in Christian faith. As the mother of the Redeemer, she was the first to experience the redemption of her Son. As the mother-in-grace of the church, of each believer and indeed of humanity, she accompanies us in our transformative striving from falling to rising, from death to life, responding to our prayers for assistance. The church thus

> sees Mary deeply rooted in humanity's history, in man's eternal vocation according

---

entrusted himself to the ministry, the free and active ministry of a woman. It can thus be said that women, by looking to Mary, find in her the secret of living their femininity with dignity and of achieving their own true advancement. In the light of Mary, the Church sees in the face of women the reflection of a beauty which mirrors the loftiest sentiments of which the human heart is capable: the self-offering totality of love; the strength that is capable of bearing the greatest of sorrows; limitless fidelity and tireless devotion to work; the ability to combine penetrating intuition with words of support and encouragement" (*Redemptoris mater,* §46).

> to the providential plan which God has made for him from eternity[.] She sees Mary maternally present and sharing in the many complicated problems which today beset the lives of individuals, families and nations; [the Church] sees [Mary] helping the Christian people in the constant struggle between good and evil, to ensure that it "does not fall," or, if it has fallen, that it "rises again." (§52)

It has been, concludes John Paul, the task of this encyclical to renew this vision in the hearts of believers.

SPANNING THE CHASM?

A bridge... In contrast to the concise *Lumen gentium,* chapter eight, John Paul has left 52 paragraphs containing 147 endnotes that display a theological commitment to a deep ecumenism and an awareness of the challenges such a commitment must overcome. Without compromising what he believes to be the truth of Roman Catholic Marian doctrine, John Paul appeals to East and West, showing that Mary can be a sign of unity rather than a point of division. And what must be observed at the outset is the ecumenical goodwill that infuses this text. The invitations to reflect together on Mary's place in the incarnation, the life of the church and the life of the believer are genuine. Max Thurian is therefore absolutely right to say, "this encyclical will provide an opportunity for many still-divided Christians to reflect on the place of Mary in the mystery of Christ and of the Church."[42]

Of course, opportunity for shared reflection does not necessarily entail the agreement for which John Paul so obviously hoped and prayed. In order to determine whether and what kinds of agreement have been achieved, I turn first to those separated churches for whom there is a deep affection for Mary: the churches of the East.[43] The issues here are not so much Marian as they are ecclesiological. That is, they have less to do with the content of Roman Catholic Mariology as they do with the manner in which the modern dogmas have been defined. Thus, while the immaculate conception might be challenged in the East for assuming an (allegedly faulty) Augustinian doctrine of original sin, Mary's holiness from the instant of her conception is celebrated every December 9, the Feast of the Conception.[44] Similarly, while there is no Eastern counterpart to the dogma

---

[42]Quoted in Ryan, "Ecumenical Responses," p. 27.

[43]I do so as an interested, yet hesitant, observer. I cannot but feel a little like a child overhearing his parents argue: I understand the broad strokes of the conversation and may even have my own point of view on the problem, but a full understanding of the contents, motivations and history of the argument continues to elude me. As a result, I offer the following comments with caution.

[44]Indeed, Western theologians formulated the doctrine of the immaculate conception to justify the inclusion of the Feast of the Conception of Mary in the Western liturgical calendar.

of the assumption, the event itself is commemorated every August 15, the Feast of the Dormition (or Falling Asleep). It is not surprising therefore that John Paul stresses Mary's place in the worship and devotion of the East (§§31-34, 50) as a point of contact around which paths to reunion might be struck. He does not, however, address the central problem between East and West for over a millennium: the nature and scope of the authority of the Bishop of Rome. Until that is addressed, it is doubtful that the recognition of a common Marian devotion will prove ecumenically fruitful.[45]

John Paul employs a different strategy in his overtures to the Protestant churches of the West for whom the major objection to Marian doctrine and devotion is its apparent lack of connection with the Bible. To this audience, John Paul offers extended meditations on the Gospels of Luke and John and the book of Acts, bolstered with some 204 further biblical citations and allusions. This strategy is to be commended. In the light of five centuries of sharp division, in which disagreements about Mary have played so prominent a role, turning to a commonly held authority for theological data is wise. And, on the one hand, we may even say that this strategy is successful. That is to say, as Protestants turn to the pages of Luke/Acts and John under the guidance of John Paul, they will quickly come to agree with John Paul that the Bible teaches that Mary is present in the church and in the lives of the believers as a prototype. On the other hand, we need also to say that the strategy points out just how much work remains, for it is clear that what John Paul finds in Luke/Acts and John is for many exegetes (especially, but not only, Protestant ones) simply not there. Both claims need to be unpacked further.

First, consider areas of agreement: in Luke/Acts, Mary fills three roles.[46] She is called to a prophetic office (Lk 1:26-38), which she executes in the Magnificat (Lk 1:46-55). She declares that the God who has been mindful of her has always cared for the lowly and, in such care, remembers and fulfills his promise to Abraham and the patriarchs. She is a pondering mother who does not fully understand all that is going on, even though she receives divine revelation concerning Jesus' identity and destiny. Rather, she assembles bits and pieces—from the angel, Elizabeth, the shepherds and even Jesus himself—weighing them over a long period of time. Finally, it is only when Luke numbers Mary among the first disciples awaiting Pen-

---

[45]John Paul has addressed this issue especially in the encyclical *Ut unum sint*. And in the light of that remarkable document, I am convinced that the ball is in the Eastern court. For text, see <http://www.vatican.va/holy_father/john_paul_ii/encyclicals/documents/hf_jp-ii_enc_25051995_ut-unum-sint_en.html>.

[46]The following claims are more fully developed in my *Mary for Evangelicals*, chaps. 4-5.

tecost (Acts 1:14) that it becomes clear that in addition to prophet and mother, Mary was also a disciple. She models persistent discipleship that agrees to what is not yet understood because her confidence lies not in the revelation but in the character of him who revealed.

Prophet, mother and disciple: taken together, they testify to one overarching purpose for Mary within the Lucan narrative: she is Luke's prototype and model for God's people. Mary is the specially elected crucible in which the general election of Israel receives its fullest expression. Her election uniquely discloses the purpose of God's general election of Israel: through her prophetic speech, Luke's readers discover that it is through Mary's child that God's promises to Abraham and his descendents will be fulfilled (Lk 1:54-55). Accordingly it ought not to surprise readers that the sword of judgment prophesied by Simeon (Lk 2:34-35) is both a sword of judgment passing through the land (Ezek 14:7), causing the falling and rising of many in Israel, and a sword of judgment passing through the soul of Mary, disclosing her thoughts also. The winnowing visited upon Israel is the same as that visited upon the mother of Jesus. Just as the nation has been elected to bless the world, so has Mary. Just as the nation has been the recipient of divine disclosure, so has Mary. Just as the nation will be judged by that same revelation, so will Mary. She is the daughter of Zion: a symbolic portrayal of the nation as a whole.

At the same time, she is a prototype and model of faith to believers. Like all believers, Mary is the recipient of the good news of God's electing grace. Her confident assent to this sovereign choice is held up as an example, not of female acquiescence to the divine (male) Father, but as an example of the secure obedience that is to mark the lives of all disciples, whether male or female (cf. Gal 3:28). Her daring adoption of the title "servant of the Lord" (Lk 1:38) signals that she has freely accepted her role in the plan of salvation, a role that links her to the great liberators of God's people. She bids all disciples live in slavery to Christ wherein is found true liberation and vocation. Her confident obedience and free acceptance, moreover, are given not because of the clarity of the revelation, but because of her trust in him who revealed. With respect to the content of God's disclosure, it appears her understanding is limited even as her will is determined to continue weighing matters until coherent conclusion emerges. In the same way, all believers are to strive to trust in God even as they continue to ponder the meaning of the divine revelation entrusted to them.

Moving from the Lucan corpus, it is clear that John has adopted and significantly developed the symbolic imagery. Early readers of the Cana miracle (Jn

2:1-12) may well have seen in Jesus' refusal to act on his mother's request a reminder that the people through whom the Messiah was given for the world's sake cannot manipulate him. Like his mother, they have no role in Jesus' earthly ministry. It stems from the will of the Father, is designed to reveal the glory of the Son and is intended to produce belief in Jesus' followers. She performs a similar function at the cross, where John re-presents a theme close to the heart of the synoptic tradition: Jesus' family is created not by bloodlines but by discipleship to the crucified and risen Lord (cf. Mk 3:31-35; Mt 12:46-50; Lk 8:19-21). The advent of Jesus' hour reveals that Jesus' true family can no longer be thought of as constituted by blood because of their unbelief (cf. Lk 7:1-9). Rather, Jesus' true family is created near the cross, composed of the Beloved Disciple, who, in his position as an especially loved nonrelative, symbolizes the individual follower of Jesus and Jesus' mother, who retains her symbolic status as the people of God. They are established in a relationship of mutual care that begins "from that hour" (Jn 19:27).

This extended exegetical exercise, I hope, proves the following points: (1) When John Paul leads us to the pages of holy Scripture, we Protestants find a wealth of Marian material that we have often overlooked. (2) His broad claims, namely, that Mary has an ongoing, active role in the life of the church and the believer, are biblically sound, defensible and therefore to be commended. He has, in his turn to holy Scripture, therefore, begun work on yet another bridge, this time to the churches of the Reformation, and to believers in those churches most likely to take the biblical witness with utmost seriousness, namely, evangelicals.

. . . too far. And it is also those readers who take the biblical witness with utmost seriousness who will be the first to point out the significant exegetical problems that lie just beneath these areas of agreement. Simply put, while we can agree that Luke and John present Mary as a prototype of God's people and an example to believers, our exegesis prevents us from wholly subscribing to John Paul's Marian vision.

Turning first to Luke, John Paul reads Luke as emphasizing Mary's holiness and active cooperation with the divine decision to enter into human history. I find both emphases to be textually implausible. With respect to Mary's holiness, as I understand her, Luke's Mary is presented as a foil to the terribly old, terribly righteous and terribly barren Elizabeth and Zechariah. When Gabriel comes to Mary in Luke 1, she is young, her piety is not mentioned, and she is engaged to be married and is presumably fertile. She is troubled and surprised by the angelic announcement. Where John Paul reads *kecharitōmenē* as God's prevenient gracious preparation of Mary to receive her role as mother of the Incarnate Lord, one that invariably includes an immaculate conception, I understand it as indicating something quite different. In contrast to Elizabeth and Zechariah, whose miracle child can be explained as a reward for piety and a response to prayer, Mary's miracle child is the unexpected result of God's unmerited favor. Mary is she on whom God's favor rests for no reason other than God's determination to be gracious.

For John Paul, grace is an infused righteousness that prepares Mary to receive even more grace, culminating in the incarnation of God the Son. For me, grace is God's unmerited favor. (We are back to a central Reformation debate, yet to be resolved in spite of the very positive movements on both sides in recent years.) This fundamental disagreement, in turn, leads to very different interpretations of Mary's words of assent to the angel. Her "let it be with me" (Lk 1:38) is understood by John Paul to indicate active agreement without which, on the human level, the incarnation could not have occurred. I, on the other hand, understand Mary's words to denote a free acceptance of what God has decreed. In the former reading, she is an active participant with grace; in the latter, the passive recipient of grace. Given the latter reading of Mary's words, the tenor of the chapter is summed up not so much by Mary's acceptance as by Gabriel's insistence that "nothing will be impossible with God" (Lk 1:37). This text testifies not to Mary's active cooperation in God's plan to save the world but to the power of God to do the impossible. Luke's answer to the question "Why Mary?" as I understand the text, is simply, "God."

Similar interpretive problems arise as we move from Luke to John and Mary's place at the wedding and the cross. John Paul reads Mary's words and actions at the Cana wedding as straightforward indicators of Mary's ongoing willingness to act as an intercessor and mediator between human needs and the power of her Son to meet those needs. The same "motherhood of faith" is to be seen at the foot of the cross, where the mother of the Son becomes, at his invitation, the mother of the church and all believers. We ought to be thankful that, in his exegesis of these passages, John Paul has clearly distanced himself—and sound Catholic teaching—from the pious Catholic view that the Mother of Mercy can sway her Son, the Righteous Judge that so exercised the Reformers. Nevertheless, as my own exegesis above makes clear, I simply do not see any evidence in the text for John Paul's reading. Rather, I see modest claims about the nature of the church's ongoing mission—always and only to point people to Jesus—and about the nature of the church—created by bonds of obedience rather than bloodlines. While I have written elsewhere that there are good reasons to think of Mary as the preeminent member of the church triumphant who continues to intercede for us, the church militant, and that such intercessions can be called mediatory and even co-redemptive,[47] I cannot find support for these arguments in these texts.

John Paul directs his Protestant readers to the biblical text, but when we read the same text, we come to very different conclusions about what the text means. And this, in turn, culminates in very different theological conclusions about Mary's presence and role in the life of the church and of believers. Interpretative disagreement, however, is not the core of the problems for Protestant readers of *Redemptoris mater.* Rather, the major issues raised by our conflicting exegeses are these. First, John Paul seems to take his exegesis for granted, as though all Christians read these texts similarly.[48] This is far from being the case; many biblical scholars, including many Catholics, would balk at the Marian maximalism that John Paul finds in Luke 1 and John 2 and 12.[49] This leads directly to the second issue: the Mariogical doctrines that John Paul draws from his exegesis and, indeed, takes for granted in *Redemptoris mater* (immaculate conception, bodily assumption) remain persistent points of controversy for Protestant readers. Had *Redemptoris mater* been an exhortation to only the Catholic faithful to deepen their Marian devotion according to the guidelines set out by *Lumen gentium,* chapter eight, these points would not be problematic. It is because he wants Mary to become an ecumenical opportunity that these points of ongoing hermeneutical and theological disagreement need to be acknowledged before they can be overcome.

CONCLUSION? I HOPE NOT

I may now turn to the question first posed in the introduction. Is the Mary of *Redemptoris mater* a point of contact for ecumenical overtures, or is she in fact a "bridge too far," exposing just how deep and wide the Reformation impasse remains? The answer, based on the exposition and analysis offered above, is as follows. Yes, Mary is a point of contact for ecumenical overtures, and, yes, she remains "a bridge too far" on the reading of *Redemptoris mater* I have offered. However much Protestant readers may come to accept Mary's ongoing and even

---

[47]See Perry, *Mary for Evangelicals*, chap. 13.

[48]Again, this observation brings us back to a central Reformation debate. Even as I question central conclusions of John Paul's exegesis, I acknowledge that these conclusions are hardly unique to him. As he reads, he stands within "the living tradition of the whole Church" (*Catechism of the Catholic Church* [Canadian Conference of Catholic Bishops, 1994], §113). As I read, I presume the power of the Word of God to call into question even long-accepted matters of interpretation. This is the *sola scriptura* debate in a nutshell.

[49]A helpful guide into the exegetical challenges on these issues remains Raymond Brown et al., *Mary in the New Testament* (Philadephia: Fortress, 1978).

active presence in the church and to believers as a prototype and model, there remains too much disagreement over the biblical exegesis that underlies very different definitions of these terms to conclude that concord has been reached or, indeed, is even possible at least at this time. But I do not want to conclude on a note of exegetical disagreement, ecumenical frustration and existential disappointment—not least because such a conclusion would not do justice to the optimistic Christian witness of John Paul II, as embodied in his oft repeated words, "Be not afraid."

Gathering with John Paul around the biblical witness is a step whose importance cannot be underestimated. I have shown, however, that in itself, it is insufficient. If we Protestants who have come broadly to agree that Mary is of central importance to unity in the truth, and can become a sign of hope in that quest for unity, are to take further steps in Marian investigation with John Paul and the fathers of the Second Vatican Council, then, I respectfully propose that the anathemas attached to the two modern Marian dogmas be lifted.

In 1974, Avery Cardinal Dulles, made just this proposal,[50] and the remarkable invitation issued by John Paul in 1987 has only sharpened my sense of the necessity of this action. It was Dulles's conviction, and it is mine, that the major difficulty Protestants have with Marian dogma is not Mary. Indeed, as I have shown above, we can agree broadly if not on particulars about Mary's place in the church and in the lives of believers. Rather, it is the insistence that those who demur from the immaculate conception "have suffered the shipwreck to their faith and have fallen away from the unity of the church," while those who deny the bodily assumption have "certainly abandoned divine and Catholic faith."[51] These anathemas, which are not, unlike the declarations themselves, understood to be infallible, make the kind of reconciliation around Mary for which John Paul and I pray impossible, for they exclude from the church (and perhaps even salvation) those of us who, "convinced by conscience and the Word of God," are compelled to disagree.[52] Dulles opines that the Catholic Church should lift the anathemas while continuing to present the dogmas as true beliefs. The intricacies of Dulles's argument concerning how this can be done without violence to the dogmas themselves and ought to be done for

[50]Avery Cardinal Dulles, "A Proposal to Lift Anathemas," *Origins* 4 (1974): 417-21.

[51]Ibid., p. 419. The citations are from the bulls *Ineffabilis deus* and *Munificentissimus deus,* respectively.

[52]In reviewing this essay, a Catholic colleague pointed out this sentence as particularly jarring. She directed me to the relevant passages in *Lumen gentium*, which presented Protestants as in real but imperfect communion with the Catholic Church. I confess that I do not understand how the more positive assessments in *Lumen gentium* may be said to square with the dire pronouncements of the two earlier bulls. All the more reason, it seems to me, to lift them.

the sake of ecumenical witness are beyond the scope of this essay.

What is relevant is the ecumenical purpose of just this action. It would neither automatically provide Marian reconciliation in the present nor guarantee it in the future. But it would further demonstrate that the invitation given in *Lumen gentium,* chapter eight, and *Redemptoris mater* to reflect together on Mary for the sake of unity in the truth is genuine. Moreover, it would, in my opinion, not only do great honor to the mother of God but also, and infinitely more importantly, do great honor to her Son who prayed that, "they might be one" (Jn 17:21).

6

Ecclesia de Eucharistia

Locus of doctrine, Way of Life

Mark A. Noll

Context

John Paul II issued the encyclical *Ecclesia de eucharistia: On the Eucharist in Its Relation to the Church,* on the Thursday of Easter Week 2003. The encyclical appeared during the twenty-fifth year of his pontificate, a year which he hoped to observe by involving "the whole Church more fully in this Eucharistic reflection, and also as a way of thanking the Lord for the gift of the Eucharist and the priesthood" (*Ecclesia de eucharistia* §7, p. 12).[1] Earlier he had also named 2003 "the Year of the Rosary" from his desire "to put this, my twenty-fifth anniversary, *under the aegis of the contemplation of Christ at the school of Mary*" (§7, p. 12, emphasis original).

Ecclesia de eucharistia amounts to a full statement of Catholic teaching and Catholic practice, but it is by no means a document standing on its own. Early in his tenure, John Paul published a letter to the church's bishops, *Dominicae cenae: The Mystery and Worship of the Eucharist,* in which he drew particular attention "to certain aspects of the Eucharistic Mystery and its impact on the lives of those who are the ministers of It."[2] The strong connection in the pope's mind between the

---

[1]All references to the encyclical are from John Paul II, *Ecclesia de Eucharistia: To the Bishops, Priests and Deacons, Men and Women in the Consecrated Life, and All the Lay Faithful on the Eucharist in Its Relation to the Church* (Boston: Pauline, 2003); references are by section and page number in this edition. See text online at <http://www.vatican.va/holy_father/john_paul_ii/encyclicals/documents/hf_jp-ii_enc_17042003_ecclesia-de-eucharistia_en.html>.

[2]John Paul II, *Dominicae cenae: The Mystery and Worship of the Eucharist* (Boston: Pauline, 2000), §2, p. 4. See text online at <http://www.vatican.va/holy_father/john_paul_ii/letters/documents/hf_jp-ii_let_24021980_dominicae-cenae_en.html>.

priesthood and the Eucharist was underscored by the fact that *Ecclesia de eucharistia* was promulgated on Holy Thursday and *Dominicae cenae* was distributed so that it might be read by the bishops on the same day in the liturgical calendar. Traditionally, the Eucharistic celebration on Holy Thursday is a time for priests to renew "the promises and commitments undertaken at the moment of ordination" (§1, p. 2). In the pope's view, "The Eucharist is the principal and central *raison d'être* of the sacrament of the priesthood" (§2, p. 4).

The pope's own formal writings on the subject rested, in turn, on many earlier formal statements, especially an encyclical of Paul VI issued toward the close of the Second Vatican Council, *Mysterium fidei* (September 3, 1965); the voluminous proclamations of the council itself; yet further encyclicals of modern popes; and, in the background, the pronouncements of the Council of Trent from the mid-sixteenth century—all supported by copious references to Scripture, patristic authorities and later Catholic teachers. In addition, the *Catechism of the Catholic Church,* which after many years of preparation was published in 1994 under the imprimatur of Joseph Cardinal Ratzinger, contains a substantial section directed entirely to "The Sacrament of the Eucharist," as well as many other Eucharistic references scattered throughout this long document.[3] Thus, although John Paul's encyclical from 2003 is a formidable tract, it is only part of a much larger mosaic of authoritative Catholic teaching on the subject. This fact should restrain evangelical readers from leaping too rapidly to conclusions drawn from this document alone; both apparent evangelical-Catholic convergences and evangelical-Catholic stand-offs need to be subjected to broader study of the fuller corpus of Catholic teaching.

In evaluating John Paul's encyclical, it is important to note that it expressed a strong experiential testimony. *Ecclesia de eucharistia* begins with the pope's reflection on the multitudinous places he has said Mass: "so many basilicas and churches in Rome and throughout the world . . . in chapels built along mountain paths, on lakeshores and seacoasts . . . on altars built in stadiums and in city squares" (§8, p. 13). It ends with an explanation of why, in discussing the Eucharist, "my heart is filled with gratitude":

> For over a half century, *every day,* beginning on 2 November 1946, when I celebrated my first Mass in the Crypt of Saint Leonard in Wawel Cathedral in Krakow, my eyes have gazed in recollection upon the host and the chalice, where time and space in

[3]*Catechism of the Catholic Church* (Liguori, Mo.: Liguori, 1994), pars. 1322-1415, pp. 334-56 of this edition.

> some way "merge" and the drama of Golgotha is represented in a living way, thus revealing its mysterious "contemporaneity." *Each day* my faith has been able to recognize in the consecrated bread and wine the divine Wayfarer who joined the two disciples on the road to Emmaus and opened their eyes to the light and their hearts to new hope (cf. Lk 24:13-35). (§59, p. 73)[4]

For the assessment I attempt at the end, the fact that the Catholic Eucharist was for the pope a way of life as well as locus of doctrine will be an important feature of my analysis.

SUMMARY

Ecclesia de eucharistia consists of an introduction, six chapters and a conclusion. The encyclical is tightly packed with both scriptural references and allusions to many Catholic sources—especially the Second Vatican Council and early church fathers, but also the pope's own earlier writings, the Catechism and (twice) the Council of Trent. It combines extensive discussion of technical points with zealous exhortations in everyday language. For evangelicals concerned about questions of biblical authority, controversies of the Reformation era, the once-standard Protestant depictions of Catholic doctrine (and vice versa) and recent breakthroughs of evangelical-Catholic dialogue, nearly every paragraph merits close analysis.

The introduction begins with a précis of the whole:

> The Church draws her life from the Eucharist. This truth does not simply express a daily experience of faith, but recapitulates *the heart of the mystery of the Church.* In a variety of ways she joyfully experiences the constant fulfilment of the promise: "Lo, I am with you always, to the close of the age" (Mt 28:20), but in the Holy Eucharist, through the changing of bread and wine into the body and blood of the Lord, she rejoices in this presence with unique intensity. (§1, p. 7)

The Eucharist is of fundamental importance because it "contains the Church's entire spiritual wealth: Christ himself, our passover and living bread" (§1, p. 7). The church "was born of the paschal mystery"; now in the Eucharist this "sacrament of the paschal mystery . . . *stands at the centre of the Church's life*" (§3, p. 8). Every celebration of the Eucharist returns the church "spiritually" (§3, p. 9) to the events of Holy Work. It is the redemption won by Christ on the cross that the Eucharist represents and to which priests lead the church "in spirit" (§4, p. 10) whenever they celebrate Mass.

This *mysterium fidei* (mystery of faith) reveals also the mystery of the church: "By

---

[4]In this quotation I have added the italics; in all other quotations, italics are from the encyclical.

the gift of the Holy Spirit at Pentecost the Church was born and set out upon the pathways of the world, yet a decisive moment in her taking shape was certainly the institution of the Eucharist in the Upper Room" (§5, pp. 10-11). The church's main function is now "the perennial making present of the paschal mystery" (§5, p. 11). When a priest says the words of institution—"or rather . . . *puts his voice at the disposal of the One who spoke these words in the Upper Room*"—he invokes "a truly enormous 'capacity' which embraces all of history as the recipient of the grace of the redemption" and by so doing provokes "profound amazement and gratitude" (§5, p. 11).

The pope trusts that this encyclical will aid in the effort to contemplate Mary as well as Christ, although in the introduction and throughout the document his stress is on the contemplation of Christ, since "above all in the living sacrament of his body and his blood . . . *the Church draws her life from Christ in the Eucharist;* by him she is fed and by him she is enlightened" (§6, p. 12). The results of that contemplation are so strikingly far-reaching they are difficult to put into words: the Eucharist possesses

> universal and, so to speak, cosmic character. Yes, cosmic! Because even when it is celebrated on the humble altar of a country church, the Eucharist is always in some way celebrated *on the altar of the world.* It unites heaven and earth. It embraces and permeates all creation. The Son of God became man in order to restore all creation, in one supreme act of praise, to the One who made it from nothing. He, the Eternal High Priest who by the blood of his Cross entered the eternal sanctuary, thus gives back to the Creator and Father of all creation redeemed. He does so through the priestly ministry of the Church, to the glory of the Most Holy Trinity. (§8, p. 13)

The introduction closes with reference to earlier papal pronouncements on the subject, with an expression of John Paul's intention to proclaim "the Eucharistic mystery" (§10, p. 15) as a way of continuing liturgical reform, with recommendations for the laity to adore the Blessed Sacrament and to take part in Eucharistic processions, with warnings against "*shadows*" or "abuses" (§10, p. 15) that have crept in over recent years, and with combined cautions and encouragements concerning "ecumenical initiatives" that involve the Eucharist (§10, p. 16).

The first chapter, "The Mystery of Faith," offers the heart of the pope's positive teaching and so, predictably, takes up many of the key issues that have long been in dispute between Catholics and Protestants. The Pauline recital of "the night when he was betrayed" (1 Cor 11:23) introduces a brief summary of the essential teaching: the Eucharist "is not only a reminder [of the Lord's passion and death] but the sacramental re-presentation. It is the sacrifice of the Cross perpetuated down the ages" (§11, p. 17).

The Protestant Reformers rejected the Catholic Mass because they held that it was conducted as *another* sacrifice (thus, displacing the once-for-all sacrifice of Christ on the cross), that it was treated as a sacrificial *work* (thus, denying God's free grace in Christ), and that it was *mandated* in terms of transubstantiation (thus, again choking God's free gift, this time with a required, but man-made formula).[5]

John Paul's exposition of Catholic teaching continues to use some of the same phrases that the Reformers rejected, but his treatment stays much closer to scriptural terms and to themes of grace. The church, in his view, "has received the Eucharist from Christ her Lord not as one gift—however precious—among so many others, but as *the gift par excellence,* for it is the gift of himself, of his person in his sacred humanity, as well as the gift of his saving work" (§11, p. 17). The sacrifice that is re-presented in the Mass is fully efficacious—it is "this central event of salvation" (§11, p. 18)—but it remains in the end a mystery of divine charity, "a love which knows no measure" (§11, p. 18).

Because the pope's description of the Mass as a sacrifice is so central, it must be given in his own words:

> The Church constantly draws her life from the redeeming sacrifice; she approaches it not only through faith-filled remembrance, but also through a real contact, since *this sacrifice is made present ever anew,* sacramentally perpetuated, in every community which offers it at the hands of the consecrated minister. The Eucharist thus applies to men and women today the reconciliation won once for all by Christ for mankind in every age. "The sacrifice of Christ and the sacrifice of the Eucharist are *one single sacrifice*" [quoting the *Catechism*]. Saint Chrysostom put it well: "We always offer the same Lamb, not one today and another tomorrow, but always the same one. For this reason the sacrifice is only ones. . . . Even now we offer that victim who was once offered and who will never be consumed." (§12, p. 19)

The Mass "does not add to that sacrifice [of the cross] nor does it multiply it." Rather, it is "repeated" as a "*memorial* celebration" that renders "Christ's one, definitive redemptive sacrifice always present in time" (§12, pp. 19-20).

When the church in the Mass celebrates the death of Christ, it also, however, celebrates his resurrection. Because of the resurrection, "it is as the living and risen One that Christ can become in the Eucharist the 'bread of life' (Jn 6:35, 48), the 'living bread' (Jn 6:51)" (§14, p. 21).

When he discusses transubstantiation, the pope moves gingerly. The Mass involves "a most special presence . . . 'real' . . . a presence in the fullest sense: a sub-

[5]These criticisms are taken up again below.

stantial presence whereby Christ, the God-Man, is wholly and entirely present" (§15, p. 21). In describing this "presence," the pope then offers one of the document's two quotations from the Council of Trent, which uses terms from Aristotle to describe how the "substance" of bread and wine are changed through "transubstantiation" into the body and blood of Christ in the Eucharist (§15, pp. 21-22). But then, as if not to dwell on the Aristotelian formula, the pope hastens on, in his own words, to say that "the Eucharist is a *mysterium fidei,* a mystery which surpasses our understanding and can only be received in faith. . . . Before this mystery of love, human reason fully experiences its limitations" (§15, p. 22). For all efforts to fathom the character of the Eucharistic presence, the key is to recognize the boundary laid down by one of his predecessors, Paul VI: "Every theological explanation which seeks some understanding of this mystery, in order to be in accord with Catholic faith, must firmly maintain that in objective reality, independently of our mind, the bread and wine have ceased to exist after the consecration, so that the adorable body and blood of the Lord Jesus from that moment on are really before us under the sacramental species of bread and wine" (§15, p. 23).[6]

John Paul then uses the language of John 6 ("unless you eat the flesh of the Son of Man . . . my blood is true drink") to affirm that the Eucharist unifies "the faithful" (§16, p. 23) to Christ, and that in this celebration Christ bestows upon communicants the Holy Spirit. Finally, because the Eucharist is also strongly eschatological—it "*expresses and reinforces our communion with the Church in heaven*" (§19, p. 25)—its celebration spurs on communicants in this life to act with hope by carrying out their duties and in "the building of a more human world, a world fully in harmony with God's plan" (§20, p. 26).

From a consideration of the Eucharist in itself, John Paul turns in the next three chapters to focus on the announced theme of the encyclical, *Ecclesia de eucharistia* (or, roughly translated, "the church is of the Eucharist"). Just as much as in his positive exposition of sacrifice, real presence and transubstantiation, these chapters address main Protestant concerns, for it was objections to the church's claims and actions with respect to the Eucharist that brought sharply into focus the great Reform movement of the sixteenth century.[7]

[6]Quoting from Paul VI, *Solemn Profession of Faith*, 30 June 1968, §25: *Acta apostolicae sedis* 60 (1968): 442-43.

[7]A signal contribution of at least some recent sixteenth-century studies is to show how absolutely critical was debate over the church in connection with the Eucharist, as, for example, in the willingness to die for, or to kill for, a proper understanding of Eucharistic practice, which is the central theme of Brad S. Gregory, *Salvation at Stake: Christian Martyrdom in Early Modern Europe* (Cambridge, Mass.: Harvard University Press, 1999).

The positive teaching in these three chapters explains why an accounting of the Eucharist is at the same time an accounting of the church, considered both as an apostolic institution and as a servant of God in the world. The practical implications concern the pathway of godliness for Catholics and the ecumenical consequences for others.

In chapter two, "The Eucharist Builds the Church," the pope explains why "the celebration of the Eucharist is at the centre of the process of the Church's growth," which began with the participation of the apostles (who are "both the seeds of the new Israel and the beginning of the sacred hierarchy") in the Last Supper, and continues to this day (§21, p. 29). In chapter three, "The Apostolicity of the Eucharist and of the Church," the pope affirms the "profound relationship" between church and Eucharist (§26, p. 37). In chapter four, "The Eucharist and Ecclesial Communion," the pope expounds upon "the Eucharist . . . as the culmination of all the sacraments in perfecting our communion with God the Father by identification with his only-begotten Son through the working of the Holy Spirit" (§34, p. 45).

Critical to all three chapters is the closest possible connection between the nature and benefits of the Eucharist, on one side, and the apostolic character of the Catholic priesthood, on the other. The logic unfolds like this:

- The Eucharist, inaugurated by Christ at the Last Supper, created the apostles as leaders of the church.
- Apostolic faith always "remains unchanged" (§27, p. 38).
- The church is "taught, sanctified and guided by the Apostles until Christ's return, through their successors in pastoral office: the college of Bishops, assisted by priests, in union with the Successor of Peter, the Church's supreme pastor" (§28, p. 38).
- For this apostolic ministry to be carried out, it "necessarily entails the sacrament of Holy Orders," by which "succession is essential for the Church to exist in a proper and full sense" (§28, p. 38).
- Thus, only a priest who has been ordained in this apostolic succession "brings about the Eucharistic Sacrifice" and can "recite the Eucharistic Prayer, while the people participate in faith and in silence" (§28, p. 39).
- Thus, the community established by the Eucharist "is a communion with its own *Bishop* and with the *Roman Pontiff*. The Bishop, in effect, is the *visible* principle and the foundation of unity within his particular Church" (§39, p. 50).

- And, thus, communion with the local bishop and with the Bishop of Rome "is intrinsically required for the celebration of the Eucharistic Sacrifice" (§39, p. 51).

Manifold theological realities and practical results flow directly from this conception of the Eucharist in relation to the church. Theologically, because the Holy Spirit is so intimately tied to the Eucharist, celebrating Mass exalts "the joint and inseparable activity of the Son and of the Holy Spirit" (§23, p. 32). It also accentuates "*the unifying power* of the body of Christ," and so roots out "the seeds of disunity" (§24, p. 33). In addition, the Eucharist "presupposes the life of grace, by which we become 'partakers of the divine nature'" (2 Pet 1:4), but is also expressed through "the virtues of faith, hope and love" (§36, p. 47). Faith by itself is not "sufficient," since believers "must persevere in sanctifying grace and love, remaining within the Church 'bodily' as well as 'in our heart'; what is required, in the words of Saint Paul, is 'faith working through love' (Gal 5:6)" (§36, p. 47).

Practically, because "the Eucharist *creates communion* and *fosters communion*" (§40, p. 51), attendance at Sunday Mass is "fundamental for the life of the Church and of individual believers" (§41, p. 52). As communicants share in the Mass, "*the Lord's Day* also becomes *the Day of the Church,* when she can effectively exercise her role as the sacrament of unity" (§41, p. 52).

Likewise, since the transformed bread and wine truly present Christ, "the *worship of the Eucharist outside of the Mass* is of inestimable value for the life of the Church" (§25, p. 33). A life of prayer oriented toward the Eucharist—"Eucharistic adoration . . . prayer of adoration before Christ present under the Eucharistic species"—is what the pope himself has often experienced as a source of "strength, consolation and support" (§25, p. 34). "By not only celebrating it but also by praying before it outside of Mass we are enabled to make contact with the very wellspring of grace" (§25, pp. 34-35).

To prepare for celebrating the Eucharist, those who are aware of "a grave sin," must receive the Sacrament of Reconciliation before communicating (§36, p. 48), since "the two sacraments of the Eucharist and Penance are very closely connected" (§37, p. 48). The theological reasoning behind this connection features a Catholic understanding of conversion: "Because the Eucharist makes present the redeeming sacrifice of the Cross, perpetuating it sacramentally, it naturally gives rise to a continuous need for conversion, for a personal response to the appeal made by Saint Paul to the Christians of Corinth: 'We beseech you on behalf of Christ, be reconciled to God' (2 Cor 5:20)" (§37, p. 48).

For pastors, the pope repeats as principle what in the introduction he had stated as personal testimony: the Eucharist "is the principal and central *raison d'être* of the sacrament of priesthood" (§31, p. 42). However valuable other priestly activity might be, priests must not forget that the Eucharist is their main concern, but they can also be reassured that "they will find in the Eucharistic Sacrifice . . . the spiritual strength needed to deal with their different pastoral responsibilities" (§31, p. 43). Because of the importance of the Mass, and of the priest in presiding, for the whole church, the ordained priesthood is "a gift which the assembly *receives through episcopal succession going back to the Apostles*"; as for the bishop, his key work is making "through the Sacrament of Holy Orders . . . a new presbyter by conferring upon him the power to consecrate the Eucharist" (§29, p. 40).

With such convictions, the pope is naturally anxious about any Catholic community that "does not have a priest to lead it" (§32, p. 43). Even in such circumstances, however, it is not possible to break the bond between Eucharist and priesthood. Rather, the faithful should pray for increased clerical vocations, do what can be done with "non-ordained members of the faithful [who] are entrusted with a share in the pastoral care of a parish," but most of all "keep alive in the community a genuine 'hunger' for the Eucharist, so that no opportunity for the celebration of Mass will ever be missed" (§33, p. 44).

Christ—church—ministry—the sacraments—salvation: these elements that Protestants treat as instrumental or sequential or even separable, the pope treats as parts of one organic reality: "Incorporation into Christ, which is brought about by Baptism, is constantly renewed and consolidated by sharing in the Eucharistic Sacrifice, especially by the full sharing which takes place in sacramental communion" (§22, p. 30). But because the church is constituted and sustained by its life in the sacraments, it becomes itself "a 'sacrament' for humanity, a sign and instrument of the salvation achieved by Christ, the light of the world and the salt of the earth (cf. Mt 5:13-16), for the redemption of all. . . . The Eucharist . . . appears as both *the source* and *the summit* of all evangelization, since its goal is the communion of mankind with Christ and in him with the Father and the Holy Spirit" (§22, p. 31). Because in the Eucharist the church experiences "the profound relationship between the invisible and the visible elements of ecclesial communion," that experience constitutes "the Church as the sacrament of salvation" (§35, p. 46).

To so thoroughly integrate Eucharist and church is, of course, significant for ecumenical relations. The pope obviously approves of increased contacts and better relations among Christian churches. He gives "thanks to the Blessed Trinity for the significant progress and convergence" (§30, pp. 40-41) of ecumenical relations in recent years, and he acknowledges that non-Catholic celebrations of the

Eucharist testify to the celebrators' belief in the significance of Christ, his work and his coming glory. He also refers to his encyclical on Christian unity, *Ut unum sint* ("that they may be one," from John 17) to underscore the imperatives of ecumenicity. And yet he also repeats from that encyclical the assertion that "the path towards full unity can only be undertaken in truth" (§44, p. 54).

In consequence, John Paul affirms with the Second Vatican Council that non-Roman Catholic churches, "especially because of the lack of the sacrament of Orders . . . have not preserved the genuine and total reality of the Eucharistic mystery" (§30, p. 41). The Eucharist, "as the supreme sacramental manifestation of communion in the Church," requires "Baptism and . . . priestly Orders." It must "be celebrated in *a context where the outward bonds of communion are also intact.*" Hence, "it is not possible to give communion to a person who is not baptized or to one who rejects the full truth of the faith regarding the Eucharistic mystery. Christ is the truth and he bears witness to the truth (cf. Jn 14:6; 18:37); the sacrament of his body and blood does not permit duplicity" (§38, pp. 49-50).

For their part, "the Catholic faithful" are not to receive communion when celebrated by other Christians, "so as not to condone an ambiguity about the nature of the Eucharist" (§30, p. 41). Because such groups "lack a valid sacrament of Orders," Catholics "may not receive communion in those communities" (§46, p. 57). In addition, "it is unthinkable to substitute for Sunday Mass ecumenical celebrations of the word or services of common prayer with Christians from the aforementioned Ecclesial Communities, or even participation in their own liturgical services" (§30, p. 41).

Particularly with reference to the Eastern Orthodox churches, exceptions to the general rule of not sharing the Eucharist may occur under "special circumstances" when those who are "separated in good faith from the Catholic Church . . . spontaneously ask to receive the Eucharist from a Catholic minister and are properly disposed" (§45, p. 56).[8]

In the pope's mind, ecumenical hope and Catholic discipline move in the same direction: "In the celebration of the Eucharistic Sacrifice the Church prays that God, the Father of mercies, will grant his children the fullness of his Holy Spirit so that they may become one body and one spirit in Christ" (§43, p. 54), but "precisely because the Church's unity, which the Eucharist brings about, . . . absolutely requires full communion in the bonds of the profession of faith, the sacraments and ecclesiastical governance, it is not possible to celebrate together the same Eu-

[8]From the text, it is not entirely clear how wide this exception extends; footnotes refer to the *Code of Canon Law* for detailed clarification.

charistic liturgy until those bonds are fully re-established" (§44, p. 54). To uphold this position expresses the church's "love for Jesus Christ in the Blessed Sacrament," love "for our brothers and sisters of different Christian confessions—who have a right to our witness to the truth," and love "for the cause itself of the promotion of unity" (§46, p. 57).

After explaining the Eucharist theologically and ecclesiastically, the pope turns in chapter five to "The Dignity of the Eucharistic Celebration." Here the two main concerns are the Eucharist as a stimulus for culture and the Eucharist in its proper celebration. In the Gospels, the solemnity and simplicity of the Last Supper are balanced by the extravagance of the woman at Bethany who anointed Jesus with a costly perfume. From this beginning point, the church has learned to fear "*no 'extravagance'*" in "devoting the best of her resources to expressing her wonder and adoration before the *unsurpassable gift of the Eucharist*" (§48, p. 60). This gift has stimulated "an interior disposition of devotion," but also "*a rich artistic heritage*" (§49, p. 61) that has led to great works of architecture, art and sacred music.

The pope then underscores the need to preserve the proper dignity of the Eucharist and the art it stimulates. Adaptation to local culture is a good thing, but the "important work" of celebrating the Eucharist duly and honoring it appropriately means that "this important work of adaptation" must "be carried out with a constant awareness of the ineffable mystery against which every generation is called to measure itself" and "must be undertaken in close association with the Holy See" (§51, p. 64). Likewise, priests must remember that in presiding over the Eucharist, they celebrate "not only for the community directly taking part in the celebration, but also for the universal Church" (§52, p. 64). Thus, "a misguided sense of creativity" is as dangerous as an over-reaction against formalism. It is vital, rather, to maintain the liturgical forms "chosen by the Church's great liturgical tradition and her Magisterium" (§52, p. 65).

In the encyclical's last substantive chapter, the pope takes up a theme that has historically perplexed and disconcerted evangelicals: "At the School of Mary, 'Woman of the Eucharist.'" Although John Paul acknowledges that direct scriptural evidence linking Mary to the Eucharist is slight, he finds great significance in the fact that Mary is mentioned as being in the Upper Room with the apostles who prayed for the Holy Spirit (Acts 1:14). It is even more pertinent that in "her interior disposition," Mary proved herself to be "*a 'woman of the Eucharist' in her whole life*" (§53, p. 68). Mary's place in Eucharistic theology is guaranteed by a series of conjunctions:

- "If the Eucharist is a mystery of faith which so greatly transcends our understanding as to call for sheer abandonment to the word of God, then there can be no one like Mary to act as our support and guide in acquiring this disposition" (§54, p. 68).
- Furthermore, the materiality of the Eucharist reflects the prior materiality of the incarnation. "At the Annuciation Mary conceived the Son of God in the physical reality of his body and blood, thus anticipating within herself what to some degree happens sacramentally in every believer who receives, under the signs of bread and wine, the Lord's body and blood" (§55, pp. 68-69). "The body given up for us and made present under sacramental signs was the same body which she had conceived in her womb!" (§56, p. 70).
- "There is a profound analogy between the *Fiat* ["let it be"] which Mary said in reply to the angel, and the *Amen* which every believer says when receiving the body of the Lord" (§55, p. 69).

In concluding these reflections, the pope appeals for a "*re-reading of the Magnificat* [from Luke 1] in a Eucharistic key" (§58, p. 71). Especially significant is the fact that when Mary begins to sing, "'My soul magnifies the Lord . . . ,' she already bears Jesus in her womb. She praises God 'through' Jesus, but she also praises him 'in' Jesus and 'with' Jesus. This is itself the true 'Eucharistic attitude'" (§58, p. 71). For communicants today, the edifying application is irresistible: "The Eucharist has been given to us so that our life, like that of Mary, may become completely a *Magnificat!*" (§58, p. 72).

In the encyclical's substantial conclusion, the pope uses expressive language to restate some of the main themes he had treated more academically. The Eucharist exists to encourage an entire life of faith: "Every commitment to holiness, every activity aimed at carrying out the Church's mission, every work of pastoral planning, must draw the strength it needs from the Eucharistic mystery, and in turn be directed to that mystery as its culmination" (§60, pp. 74-75). But it is also always imperative to remember that the Eucharist is a "mystery . . . sacrifice, presence, banquet," which "*does not allow for reduction or exploitation.*" And yet this is a mystery that builds up the church (§61, p. 75). It exists to advance communion with all saints, especially Mary (§62, pp. 76-77). It is a spur to ecumenicity combined with truth: "The treasure of the Eucharist . . . impels us towards the goal of full sharing with all our brothers and sisters to whom we are joined by our common Baptism. But if this treasure is not to be squandered, we need to respect the demands which derive from its being the sacrament of communion in faith and in apostolic succession" (§61, pp. 75-76). And, above all, it exists to make manifest the presence of Christ: "In the humble signs of bread and wine, changed into his body and blood, Christ walks beside us as our strength and our food for the journey, and he enables us to become, for everyone, witnesses of hope" (§62, p. 77).

The pope begins these concluding pages with a deeply personal statement, as he had opened the encyclical itself:

> Allow me, dear brothers and sisters, to share with deep emotion, as a means of accompanying and strengthening your faith, my own testimony of faith in the Most Holy Eucharist. *Ave verum corpus natum de Maria Virgine, vere passum, immolatum, in cruce pro homine!* [Hail, true body, born of the Virgin Mary, truly suffered and slain on the cross for humankind!] Here is the Church's treasure, the heart of the world, the pledge of the fulfilment for which each man and woman, even unconsciously, yearns. A great and transcendent mystery, indeed, and one that taxes our mind's ability to pass beyond appearances. Here our senses fail us: *visus, tactus, gustus in te fallitur,* in the words of the hymn *Adoro Te Devote;*[9] yet faith alone, rooted in the word of Christ handed down to us by the Apostles, is sufficient for us. Allow me, like Peter at the end of the Eucharistic discourse in John's Gospel, to say once more to Christ, in the name of the whole Church and in the name of each of you: "Lord to whom shall we go? You have the words of eternal life" (Jn 6:68). (§59, pp. 73-74)

ASSESSMENT

Evangelical assessment of John Paul's encyclical on the Eucharist is complicated by the fact that evangelicals differ among themselves on the nature and workings of the Lord's Supper. Yet almost all evangelicals should be edified by at least some aspects of this encyclical, in particular its consistent reference to the Scriptures for explicating the meaning of the Eucharist; its focus on the death and resurrection of Christ as the sole provision for human salvation; its depiction of the purpose of life as oriented toward "Jesus . . . his redemptive sacrifice . . . his resurrection . . . the gift of the Holy Spirit . . . adoration, obedience and love of the Father" (§60, pp. 74-75); its charity toward Christians who are not Catholics (the document is strikingly free of the anathemas that once characterized this genre of theology); and its insistence on the knowability of truth as from God. Whatever disagreements evangelicals might have with the pope on the Eucharist or the Eucharist in connection

---

[9]The pope is quoting from a hymn by Thomas Aquinas written at the request of Pope Urban IV when in 1264 he established the Feast of Corpus Christ: "Devoutedly I Adore You." The complete verse is as follows: *Visus, tactus, gustus te fallitur, sed auditu solo tuto creditur; credo quidquid dixit Dei Filios; nil hoc verbo Veritatis verius* (Sight, taste, and touch fail, but hearing can be believed; I believe what the Son of God has said; nothing else offers this word of Truth). Available at <www.preces-latinae.org/thesaurus/Hymni/Adorote.html>.

with the Catholic church, most would benefit from pondering the biblical, Christ-centered, pious, charitable and truth-driven exposition of *Ecclesia de eucharistia.*

Differences among evangelicals come into play most clearly in assessing what the pope claims for the realism of Christ's presence in the Lord's Supper and for the soteriological efficacy of Christ's real presence. To oversimplify, contemporary evangelicals can be described as spread out along a continuum. One end of that continuum is defined by a non-liturgical, non-sacramental view of salvation combined with an informal, or "low" view of the church understood as simply a gathering of believers (or perhaps of an invisible union of all believers throughout the world). It would represent the view of most Baptist, independent, Restorationist and other generic evangelicals as identified by pundits, pollster and scholars. The convictions of most contemporary evangelicals are probably somewhere near this pole.

The other end of the continuum is defined by a view in which the sacraments truly present God to worshipers with saving effect and which embraces a "higher" view of the church understood as a divinely created visible institution with divinely mandated institutional purposes. This pole represents the view of Martin Luther and historical Lutheranism, of some Anglicans/Episcopalians and of a few Methodists as well as Reformed or Calvinist Christians. Although, with its origins in Luther, it is the oldest Protestant stance on the Lord's Supper, the convictions defining this pole would be held by only a small minority of contemporary evangelicals.

What can be called the Baptist, or memorialist, view is well represented in many contemporary statements of faith. The Baptist Faith and Message statement from the Southern Baptist Convention is a good example. Its description of salvation mentions neither church nor sacraments and is focused on the faith of the believing individual.[10] It defines the "New Testament church of the Lord Jesus Christ" as "an autonomous local congregation of baptized believers, associated by covenant in the faith and fellowship of the gospel." And it describes the "ordinance" of the Lord's Supper as "a symbolic act of obedience whereby members of the church, through partaking of the bread and the fruit of the vine, memorialize the death of the Redeemer and anticipate His second coming."[11]

---

[10]"Salvation involves the redemption of the whole man, and is offered freely to all who accept Jesus Christ as Lord and Saviour, who by His own blood obtained eternal redemption for the believer. In its broadest sense salvation includes regeneration, justification, sanctification, and glorification. There is no salvation apart from personal faith in Jesus Christ as Lord." Text taken from Baptist Faith and Message, Southern Baptist Convention (2000) <www.sbc.net/bfm/bfm2000.asp>.

[11]Ibid.

The contrasting view, which might be called the historical or realist position, is stated in part by the Lutheran Augsburg Confession of 1530 when it affirms that "the true body and blood of Christ are truly present under the form of bread and wine in the Lord's Supper and are distributed and received there."[12] The realist position can also be found in several of the Protestant-Catholic dialogues that have taken place since the Second Vatican Council. For example, the Methodist-Catholic dialogue includes a joint agreement on the saving effects of the Lord's Supper: "Both the personal and communal aspects of the Christian life are present in the two sacraments that Methodists and Roman Catholics consider basic. Baptism initiates the individual into the koinonia of the church; in the eucharist, Christ is really present to the believer . . . , who is thus bound together in koinonia both with the Lord and with others who share the sacramental meal."[13] The Anglican-Catholic dialogue also found agreement in strongly realist terms: The Eucharist exemplifies a "sacramental presence in which God uses realities of this world to convey the realities of new creation. Bread for this life becomes the bread of eternal life." In the same dialogue it is also affirmed that, after the Eucharistic prayer, the bread "is truly the body of Christ, the Bread of Life."[14]

Between the polar opposites are a number of historical Protestant positions that ascribe realism and saving efficacy to the Lord's Supper, but without going as far as the Lutherans. Such opinions were held by many of the earliest Protestant reformers—including John Calvin, Martin Bucer, Peter Martyr, John à Lasco, Thomas Cranmer, Nicholas Ridley and Hugh Latimer—who embraced what has sometimes been called the "spiritual real presence" of Christ in the Lord's Supper. Zacharias Ursinus and Kaspar Olevianus expressed this mediating view of "spiritual realism" in the Heidelberg Catechism of 1563: the bread and wine in communion are "not changed" into the body and blood of Christ. Nonetheless, the celebration of communion is properly called "the New Covenant in his blood" and the Supper (in Pauline language) is "'a means of sharing' in the body and blood of Christ," because, "Christ . . . wishes to teach us . . . that as bread and wine sustain this temporal life so his crucified body and shed blood are the true food and drink of souls for eternal life. Even more, he wishes to assure us by this visible sign and

---

[12]From the German text of the Augsburg Confession, in *The Book of Concord: The Confessions of the Evangelical Lutheran Church,* ed. Robert Kolb and Timothy J. Wengert (Minneapolis: Fortress, 2000), p. 44.

[13]Methodist-Catholic dialogue, in *Growth in Agreement: Report and Agreed Statements of Ecumenical Conversation on a World Level,* ed. Harding Meyer and Lucas Vischer (New York: Paulist; Geneva: World Council of Churches, 1984), p. 586, par. 12.

[14]Anglican-Catholic dialogue, in ibid., p. 75, par. 7.

pledge that we come to share in his true body and blood through the working of the Holy Spirit as surely as we receive with our mouth these holy tokens in remembrance of him, and that all his sufferings and his death are our own as certainly as if we had ourselves suffered and rendered satisfaction in our own persons."[15]

The belief that Scripture teaches at least a "spiritual real presence" is maintained by a number of evangelicals today, as expressed, for example, in a recent book from InterVarsity Press: "The Lord's Supper is more than a faded memory of a long-gone person; it brings us his life-giving presence. Communion is not just another name for the sacrament of the Lord's Supper; it describes the very essence of what takes place in that sacrament. Christ brings us into a special communion with himself and with each other so that his life and saving power nourishes our bodies and souls. . . . And this communion with Christ is not merely some spiritual presence, but a Spirit-wrought communion with his actual person, his glorified humanity and his life-giving flesh and blood."[16]

It is not the office of this chapter to adjudicate between evangelical views of the Lord's Supper, but it does make things more interesting to assess the encyclical from the realist pole. As it happens, my own conviction[17] is that the realist position reflects foundational biblical teaching,[18] that it is the historic position of the Christian church[19] and that it perfectly expresses the classical Reformation doctrine of justification by faith.[20]

Whether my kind of sacramental realism is correct or not, using it as a standard to measure the pope's encyclical does allow for extensive interaction with *Ecclesia de eucharistia.* By contrast, from a memorialist perspective, the pope's exposition can be dismissed readily, however much a memorialist might appreciate the evident piety of the pontiff. Since the "ordinances," including the Lord's Supper, are occasions for believers to remember what God has done for them, and so to re-

---

[15]From the Heidelberg Catechism's question and answer nos. 78 and 79, in *The Book of Confessions* (Louisville, Ky.: Presbyterian Church [U.S.A.], 2002), p. 41.

[16]Leonard J. Vander Zee, *Christ, Baptism and the Lord's Supper: Recovering the Sacraments for Evangelical Worship* (Downers Grove, Ill.: InterVarsity Press, 2004), p. 199.

[17]Mark A. Noll, "One Cup—Many Interpretations," *Eternity,* October 1981, pp. 36-41.

[18]Especially as found in Matthew 26, John 6 and 1 Corinthians 10—11.

[19]See, for example, Ignatius in the first decades of the second century: "breaking one bread . . . is the medicine of immortality and the antidote that we should not die but live for ever in Jesus Christ. . . . The eucharist is the flesh of our Saviour Jesus Christ, which flesh suffered for our sins, and which the Father of His goodness raised up" (The Epistles of S. Ignatius, in *The Apostolic Fathers,* ed. J. B. Lightfoot and J. R. Harmer [1891; reprint, Grand Rapids: Baker, 1984], pp. 142, 158).

[20]Particularly the belief that God in mercy comes in human flesh to save sinners apart from any action or intellectual achievement of their own.

experience the blessing they received when they put their trust in Christ; since the ordinances in no sense impart salvation; since church gatherings in which the ordinances are observed are constituted only by the believers who make up these gatherings; and since the pope's affirmation of a Eucharistic real presence, the saving efficacy of the Eucharist, and the validity of the Eucharist only in a Catholic setting and only from an ordained Catholic priest must be considered un- (or anti-) biblical positions—given these circumstances, there does not seem to be much to be gained by following the pope through the details of his exposition. Many memorialists can affirm that at least some Catholics are oriented toward the same goals of redemption in Christ and service to Christ that they are, but from a memorialist point of view this encyclical is wrongheaded.

By contrast, from a Protestant realist perspective, there is much to ponder. The earliest Protestant statements on the Eucharist specified several Catholic errors and offered careful positive statements of what Protestants considered the proper biblical meaning of the sacrament. For instance, Martin Luther in *The Babylonian Captivity of the Church* specified three "captivities" by which Rome had imprisoned the Lord's Supper: the communication of the laity only in the bread while reserving the wine to priests, the mandating of transubstantiation as the required understanding of the real presence and the treatment of "the sacrifice of the mass" as a good work which the church did and in response to which God granted salvation.[21] In 1530, the Augsburg Confession also complained about withholding the cup from the laity and about treating the Mass as a sacrifice (and so a good work done by the church for God). It added the complaint that masses were being bought and sold like common commodities and, most importantly, that celebration of the Roman sacrament had replaced faith with good works.[22]

Positively, Augsburg defined the Eucharist as an expression of God's free gift of salvation "to be used . . . as a comfort to terrified consciences."[23] Luther, always more loquacious, concluded that

> the mass was provided only for those who have a sad, afflicted, disturbed, perplexed and erring conscience, and that they alone commune worthily. For, since the word of divine promise in this sacrament sets forth the forgiveness of sins, let every one draw near fearlessly, whoever he may be, who is troubled by his sins, whether by remorse

---

[21]Martin Luther, *The Babylonian Captivity of the Church* (1520), in *Luther's Works: American Edition*, vol. 36, *Word and Sacrament II*, ed. Abdel Ross Wentz (Philadelphia: Fortress, 1959), pp. 27-57.
[22]*Book of Concord*, pp. 60-62, 68-72 (articles 22, 24).
[23]Ibid., p. 68.

> or by temptation. For this testament of Christ is the one remedy against sins, past, present and future, if you but cling to it with unwavering faith and believe that what the words of the testament declare is freely granted to you. . . . For faith alone means peace of conscience, while unbelief means only distress of conscience.[24]

The Eucharistic theology propounded by Luther and the authors of the Augsburg Confession (mostly Philip Melanchthon) did not say exactly what other Protestant realists felt the Scriptures required them to say about the Lord's Supper. But these criticisms and positive affirmations about the sacrament came close enough to outlining the main themes of a Protestant realist position that they can serve for evaluating *Ecclesia de eucharistia.*

On the specific charges of the early Reformers, it is obvious that John Paul II teaches a Eucharist doctrine closer to what the Protestant Reformers themselves advocated than to what they condemned in the sixteenth century.

1. Distribution of the Eucharist in only one kind and the commercialization of the Eucharist are now rejected as Catholic practice. Where abuses of this sort continue in the Catholic church, they do so in contravention to the church's authoritative teaching.

2. On transubstantiation, John Paul has considerably softened the sharply etched Aristotelian definitions that were once standard Catholic dogma, and also the church's once rigid insistence that everyone affirm just this one view. About the only remnant of that Aristotelianism is the pope's quotation from Paul VI's "Solemn Profession of Faith" (1968), which defines as one of the "boundary" markers in Eucharistic theology the affirmation that "the bread and wine have ceased to exist after the consecration" (§15, p. 23). Martin Luther's prime objection to transubstantiation was that when the church mandated an Aristotelian theory of substances and accidents as the only acceptable belief allowing a person to come to the Mass, it interposed a man-made impediment (in effect, a man-made creation of intellectual works righteousness) between God's gracious provision in the Eucharist and the supplicating sinner who longed for the grace of Christ manifest in the consecrated bread and the wine. For Luther, the essential thing was not *how* Christ was present in the Lord's Supper, but *that* he was so as an expression of God's free grace.[25]

---

[24]Luther, *Babylonian Captivity,* p. 57.

[27]Luther objected specifically to the requirement that, in order to receive the sacrament, the communicant had to believe on pain of excommunication that after the consecration, the bread and wine ceased in their substance to exist. He felt that although transubstantiation was a substandard view (his own conviction was that the body and blood of Christ came to exist *along with* the bread and

In *Ecclesia de Eucharistia* the pope is not quite to Luther's position on transubstantiation, but by treating technical definition as a secondary matter, by insisting that the Eucharist is "a mystery which surpasses our understanding and can only be received by faith" (§15, p. 22), and by underscoring repeatedly the overarching purpose of the Eucharist ("intrinsically directed to the inward union of the faithful with Christ through communion . . . . we receive his body which he gave up for us on the Cross and his blood which he 'poured out for many for the forgiveness of sins' [Mt. 26:28]" [§16, p. 23])—in these ways the pope disarms transubstantiation as the polemical crux that it had been for so many generations of Catholic-Protestant dispute.

3. On the question of how faith interacts with participation in the Eucharist, the encyclical is not as close to the ideal envisioned by Protestant sacramental realists. Faith, even *sola fide,* is present as an element in this document—for example, when the pope says that since human senses fail in comprehending the gift of God in the Eucharist, "faith alone, rooted in the word of Christ handed down to us by the Apostles, is sufficient for us" (§59, p. 74). But as in this quotation, faith is so intimately a part of what has been "handed down to us by the Apostles" and functions so completely within the rubrics of Catholic institutional life, that it is difficult to discern the driving urgency of personal commitment, personal engagement and personal belief that has always been so much a part of the evangelical understanding of not only the Lord's Supper but of all Christian life.[26]

4. The pope's treatment of faith anticipates also his treatment of sacrifice. The encyclical brims over with sacrificial language, but sacrifice does not connote the crude performance of works that Protestants feared and at least some Catholics may have practiced. The stress is rather on the cross, where "reconciliation" was "won once for all by Christ for mankind in every age" (§12, p. 19). Likewise, the definition of the sacrifice of the Mass as a "*memorial* celebration" that "cannot . . . be understood as something separate, independent of the Cross" (§12, p. 20), seems, from an evangelical perspective, to give the work of Christ the unique status it deserves.

Yet the prominence of sacrificial language and the use to which it is put clearly

wine), it did no harm for communicants to believe in transubstantiation—just so long as the church did not mandate it as the only acceptable view. The prime issue was the insistence by the human church that it could dictate the conditions under which sinners could receive divine grace.

[26]See Luther, *Babylonian Captivity,* pp. 53-54: "For it is faith that the priest ought to awaken in us by this act of elevation. And would to God that as he elevates the sign, or sacrament, openly before our eyes, he might also sound in our ears the word, or testament, in a loud, clear voice, and in the language of the people, whatever that may be, in order that faith may be the more effectively awakened."

identify *Ecclesia de eucharistia* as a traditional Catholic document. When the pope says, "the Mass makes present the sacrifice of the Cross; it does not add to that sacrifice nor does it multiply it" (§12, p. 19), and when he affirms that "in giving his sacrifice to the Church, Christ has also made his own the spiritual sacrifice of the Church, which is called to offer herself in union with the sacrifice of Christ" (§13, p. 20), it is once again evident that the institutional life of the Catholic Church enjoys a prominence in defining a foundational Christian reality that evangelicals do not allow for any human institution.

Conclusion

The encyclical's exposition of the Eucharist—as illustrated by its treatment of transubstantiation, faith and sacrifice—points to a larger conclusion about the nature of the Christian faith that so transparently inspired the pope in writing this document. As is obvious from the wording of especially the opening and closing sections, John Paul experienced the Eucharist in its historical Catholic shape as the defining reality of his life. Today, Christians who are not Catholics can observe the pope's way of life and the life to which he calls the Catholic faithful with much more respect, admiration and (hopefully) empathy than was possible in the centuries of all-out Catholic-Protestant antagonism. But from an evangelical perspective, this Catholic way of life still defines a different understanding of Christianity than has been internalized by evangelical habits. Three particulars illustrate the difference.

1. Historically, evangelicals have practiced a Christian faith driven by the quest for forgiveness of sin, for a peaceful conscience before God, and for the exchange of a destructive, human-centered existence for a bountiful, God-centered existence—for, in other words, justification by faith. These emphases can also be found in *Ecclesia de eucharistia.* It is clear that they no longer constitute a religion that Catholicism opposes. But these emphases are not the elements that guide the deep structure of the encyclical. That deep structure is attached more securely to union with Christ, solidarity with Christ's apostles and their successors, and joyful communion with the saints, especially Mary. To those Catholic elements, many evangelicals can now respond with appreciation. But they are not the defining elements of evangelical faith.

Evangelicals should have moved beyond the conclusion that these distinctive Catholic emphases make up an anti-Christian faith. But the suspicion must still linger that, by not emphasizing the centrality of justification by faith, the pope and the Catholic faithful who heed his voice are obscuring the heart of biblical religion and therefore missing what sinners most need to experience in the course of their lives. To put it more precisely, it is not as though Catholics are missing this heart of biblical religion but that, even as they possess and honor the pearl of great price, they do not completely realize what an unfathomable treasure it is.

Of course, Catholics could come to a parallel conclusion in their charitable observations of evangelicals: evangelicals may acknowledge the value of union and communion with Christ, yet they act as if these matters were really not too important.[27]

2. Mentioning the Scripture highlights another perceptible difference though, again, a difference in degree and not in kind. The Bible was obviously crucial to the pope in composing *Ecclesia de eucharistia.* But almost any Protestant reading this document would be struck by the absence of papal consideration of how scriptural preaching provides a necessary complement to the celebration of the Eucharist. In John Paul's earlier letter to bishops on the Eucharist, he does mention "The Table of the Word of God" as a parallel gift to "The Table of the Bread of the Lord," but actual consideration of what is preached from the Bible is very brief.[28] By contrast, classical definitions of the church from the Reformation, as in the Augsburg Confession, stressed "the assembly of all believers among whom the gospel is purely preached and the sacraments administered according to the gospel."[29]

As a historian with Protestant realist views of the sacrament looking back over the last half millennium from the perspective of the early twenty-first century, I am convinced that evangelical-Catholic antagonists saw much too strong a contrast between a Mass-based faith and a Bible-based faith. As defined by the pope in this encyclical, the Mass-based faith is also a biblical faith; as defined by any number of Protestant sacramental realists, a Bible-centered faith is also a Eucharistic faith. But, again, to an evangelical, the danger of not keeping the Scriptures uniquely central for all people in the church and all activities of the church, even the celebration of the Eucharist, is to risk straying beyond God-ordained boundaries into terrain too much exposed to the caprice of mere humans, no matter how godly they may be.

3. To mention caprice is to raise the most significant qualification that a sympathetic evangelical must register about *Ecclesia de eucharistia* since caprice is a

[27]I do not take up here the obvious issue that, if such classical evangelical elements are so important, they need also to be reasserted among those now known as evangelicals, who often fail to appreciate the pearl of great price they have inherited.

[28]*Dominicae cenae,* §10, p. 23.

[29]*Book of Concord,* p. 42 (art. 7).

charge that Catholics have regularly leveled against Protestants. When considering the multitude of Bible-based, yet often contradictory, Protestant opinions that have proliferated since the sixteenth century, it certainly looks like Protestants are the ones who suffer most from human caprice. In historical Protestant-Catholic debate, the Catholic antidote to caprice is the church. But evangelicals worry that this cure can too easily become a pathogen.

Elsewhere I have tried at some length to explain why ecclesiology—not soteriology or sacraments or Scripture or Mary—constitutes the great remaining divide between Catholics and evangelicals who share the "mere Christianity" of Nicene faith.[30] Here it is enough to say that every line of *Ecclesia de eucharistia* breathes a Catholic ecclesiology foreign to evangelical convictions: the God who in his mercy sent Jesus Christ to live and die for the sin of the world, who revealed himself in the written revelation of the Old and New Testaments, who graciously bestows the Holy Spirit to do the work of Christ in the world, who joyfully welcomes sinners into the household of faith—this God also established the Roman Catholic Church as his uniquely authoritative and fully apostolic *ecclesia*.

By contrast, evangelicals say that apostolicity pertains first to the preached word of scriptural salvation and only then to the preacher of the word and the institutions authorizing the preacher—but if and only if the preaching communicates that gracious word. Evangelicals believe in the priesthood of all believers as a doctrine that reflects the inner workings of justification by faith as well as one that exists for the advance of the kingdom of God and the protection of God's children. Many evangelicals are now prepared to honor, respect and even learn from a teacher who can write such an edifying tract as *Ecclesia de eucharistia*. But they are prepared to do so because they recognize in it the truths of the gospel, rather than because its author has been designated by a human institution as the vicar of Christ. In a word, evangelicals believe that the sacred encouragement arising from the Eucharist, which John Paul II so richly describes in this encyclical, does not require, and may even in some circumstances be compromised by, the specifically Catholic commitments that are so integral to the pope's understanding of the holy supper.

[30]Mark A. Noll and Carolyn Nystrom, *Is the Reformation Over? An Evangelical Assessment of Contemporary Roman Catholicism* (Grand Rapids: Baker, 2005), esp. pp. 233-47.

7

Ut Unum Sint and Papal Infallibility

A Response

William J. Abraham

Introduction: Doorway to a New Conversation

For the ecumenical movement, the appearance of *Ut unum sint* in 1995 was a welcome rainbow of hope in the midst of a long season of depressing, inhibiting rain. We can surely say that the ecumenical movement has been one of the most important renewal movements of the twentieth century—so much so that for a period it captured the minds and imaginations of leading theologians and church leaders.[1] Yet it has become abundantly clear that the ecumenical movement is in deep trouble. Despite a radical change of atmosphere in interchurch relations and despite a mountain of literature devoted to ecumenical challenges, progress toward organic, visible unity has stalled. Indeed we now face the prospect of new divisions in and around disputes about the practice of homosexuality.[2] *Ut unum sint* repre-

---

[1]I have discussed the topic of renewal at some length in *The Logic of Renewal* (Grand Rapids: Eerdmans, 2005).

[2]I predict three developments in the decades ahead in the West. First, given the current divisions within modern Christianity, there will be realignment within Christianity in which Christians from within Roman Catholicism, Eastern Orthodoxy, evangelicalism, and the orthodox mainline will come together informally. Second, given that organic, visible unity will not materialize in the foreseeable future, Protestants will turn to developing new denominational identities. Anglicanism is already on this path. Third, given the difficulties in the direction of official ecumenical theology and the acrimonious divisions within their households, Protestant theologians will continue to convert to Eastern Orthodoxy and Roman Catholicism.

sents an extraordinary word of hope and illumination in the midst of ecumenical anxiety and depression.

I first encountered this splendid encyclical at a meeting in New York sponsored by Father Richard John Neuhaus. The encyclical was introduced by Edward Cardinal Cassidy from Australia, who at that time was president of the Pontifical Council for the Promotion of Christian Unity. I was expecting the usual ecumenical niceties wrapped in a carefully crafted vision of the Roman Catholic Church as the one true church of Christ. What struck me at the time—and still strikes me today—was not just the radical change in tone but the very specific proposals that were laid out on the table. They showed Pope John Paul II at his creative best as a theologian and ecclesiastical statesman of the highest order. In a beautifully crafted encyclical he opened a door that until that time seemed firmly locked.

Three elements stood out. There was, first, the reiterated commitment on the part of the Roman Catholic Church to ecumenism.

> It is absolutely clear that ecumenism, the movement promoting Christian unity, *is not just some sort of "appendix"* which is added to the Church's traditional activity. Rather, ecumenism is an organic part of her life and work, and consequently must pervade all that she says and does; it must be like the fruit borne by a healthy and flourishing tree which grows to its full stature.[3]

I saw this commitment close up on my last visit to Karaganda, Kazakhastan, where I have been working over the last ten years with a recently planted evangelical church. The local Roman Catholic bishop had called all the Christian groups together and had even gone so far as to invite the young pastors of this new church to preach in the local Roman Catholic Church. After a very shaky start it is now clear that the Roman Catholic Church has become an indispensable agent in sustaining the commitment to ecumenism across the generations. While others faltered, John Paul II stepped up to take a decisive leadership role in the ecumenical movement.

There was, second, the suggestion that the church of the first millennium could be the basis of unity between the East and the West.

> The Church's journey began in Jerusalem on the day of Pentecost and its original expansion in the *oikoumenē* of that time was centred around Peter and the Eleven (cf. Acts 2:14). The structures of the Church in the East and in the West evolved in reference to that Apostolic heritage. Her unity during the first millennium was maintained within those same structures through the Bishops, Successors of the Apostles,

[3]John Paul II, *Ut unum sint: On Commitment to Ecumenism*, Libreria Editrice Vaticana (May 25, 1995) §20, <http://www.vatican.va/holy_father/john_paul_ii/encyclicals/documents/hf_jp-ii_enc_25051995_ut-unum-sint_en.html>.

> in communion with the Bishop of Rome. If today at the end of the second millennium we are seeking to restore full communion, it is to that unity, thus structured, which we must look.[4]

Of course, everything hangs on how we interpret what constitutes the church of the first millennium; but this is a bold and original proposal deserving of the closest attention. I shall return to this matter later.

Third, there was the astonishing request for help in thinking through how best to spell out the exercise of the papal office as the servant of unity for the future. The request was prefaced by a plea for forgiveness from John Paul II.

> As I acknowledged on the important occasion of a visit to the World Council of Churches in Geneva on 12 June 1984, the Catholic Church's conviction that in the ministry of the Bishop of Rome she has preserved, in fidelity to the Apostolic Tradition and the faith of the Fathers, the visible sign and guarantor of unity, constitutes a difficulty for most other Christians, whose memory is marked by certain painful recollections. To the extent that we are responsible for these, I join my Predecessor Paul VI in asking forgiveness.[5]

The obvious sense of repentance for past mistakes was in itself a remarkable development. The move beyond this to ask for assistance in reforming the exercise of papal primacy showed that the sense of repentance was no mere exercise in ecclesial honesty and humility; it was the doorway to a whole new conversation. The passage concerned deserves to be quoted at length.

> Whatever relates to the unity of all Christian communities clearly forms part of the concerns of the primacy. As Bishop of Rome I am fully aware, as I have reaffirmed in the present Encyclical Letter, that Christ ardently desires the full and visible communion of all those Communities in which, by virtue of God's faithfulness, his Spirit dwells. I am convinced that I have a particular responsibility in this regard, above all in acknowledging the ecumenical aspirations of the majority of the Christian Communities and in heeding the request made of me to find a way of exercising the primacy which, while in no way renouncing what is essential to its mission, is nonetheless *open to a new situation.* For whole millennium Christians were united in "a brotherly fraternal communion of faith and sacramental life. . . . If disagreements in belief and discipline arose among them, the Roman See acted by common sense as moderator."
>
> In this way the primacy exercised its office of unity. When addressing the Ecumenical Patriarch His Holiness Dimitrios I, I acknowledged my awareness that

---

[4]Ibid., §55. This claim is reiterated at §§57, 61.
[5]Ibid., §88.

> "for a great variety of reasons, and against the will of all concerned, what should have been a service sometimes manifested itself in a very different light. But . . . it is out of a desire to obey the will of Christ truly that I recognize that as Bishop of Rome I am called to exercise that ministry. . . . I insistently pray the Holy Spirit to shine light upon us, enlightening all the Pastors and theologians of our Churches, that we may seek—together, of course—the forms in which this ministry may accomplish a service of love recognized by all concerned."
>
> This is an immense task, which we cannot refuse and which I cannot carry out by myself. *Could not the real but imperfect communion existing between us persuade Church leaders and their theologians to engage with me in a patient and fraternal dialogue on this subject, a dialogue in which, leaving useless controversies behind, we could listen to one another, keeping before us only the will of Christ for his Church and allowing ourselves to be deeply moved by his plea "that they may all be one . . . so that the world may believe that you have sent me" (Jn 17:21)*?[6]

This is an extraordinary ecumenical development. On the one hand, there is openness to a new situation; on the other, there is a gracious invitation to think through how best to envisage the ministry of the pope in the service of love and unity. In this chapter I want to respond to this invitation by taking up one aspect of the issue to be addressed, namely, the matter of papal infallibility.

Infallibility as Epistemology

The challenge to be faced at this point is acute. What is at stake is the place (and not just the meaning and nature) of papal infallibility in the life of the church. Clearly this is a crucial issue in that papal infallibility is constitutive of the canonical commitments of the Roman Catholic Church since Vatican I. Moreover, it can be read as the culmination of a vision of the authority of Scripture that has deep roots in the early Christian tradition and that was developed with great ingenuity in the medieval and Protestant traditions. Thus any commitment to the visible, organic unity of the church cannot sidestep the place of papal infallibility in the exercise of papal primacy.

Of course, for some—including many, if not most, evangelicals—the very idea of papal primacy and papal infallibility has been seen as an insuperable barrier to unity. Many church leaders and theologians have seen John Paul II as a charismatic, photogenic bulldog intent on destroying the freedom and new life that had swept across the world in the middle of the twentieth century.[7] They failed to re-

---

[6]Ibid., §§95-96, emphasis mine.

[7]I am relying at this point on my own informal experience in academic circles.

alize that God had given to the whole church a most remarkable pope; his life and work was surely a work of wonderful providence in a century of savage death and theological instability. In *Ut unum sint* he makes it clear that the Roman Catholic Church is fully aware of the challenge presented by the papacy and expresses convictions in a way that is genuinely humble, open and constructive. It is not enough in these circumstances to give in to old hurts and prejudices and to fall back on a policy of ecumenical despair that waits for the Roman Catholic Church to abandon its vision of the papacy. In the wake of the generous invitation to respond in a constructive manner, we have to clear our throats and see where the conversation takes us.

At this point we can take heart from the progress on the doctrine of justification in the Joint Declaration of June 1999. Two generations ago few would have thought it possible to reach canonical agreement; yet the crucial breakthrough is now in place. Equally few would have thought that the *filioque* dispute could be resolved, but this is exactly what has happened in the famous Doctrinal Note of December 13, following John Paul II's address to Patriarch Bartholomew I on June 29, 1995.[8] We can add to the list of surprises the revocation of the anathemas of 1054 on December 7, 1965. So we should refrain from despair in tackling the issue of papal infallibility, even as we realize that papal infallibility presents a unique challenge. Let's proceed and see what can be said.

The specific declaration of papal infallibility as given in Vatican I runs as follows.

> It is a divinely revealed dogma that the Roman Pontiff, when he speaks *ex cathedra,* that is, when, acting in the office of shepherd and teacher of all Christians, he defines, by virtue of his supreme authority, a doctrine concerning faith or morals to be held by the universal Church, possesses through the divine assistance promised to him in the person of the Blessed Peter, the infallibility with which the divine Redeemer willed His Church to be endowed in defining the doctrine concerning faith or morals; and that such definitions of the Roman Pontiff are therefore irreformable of themselves, not because of the consent of the Church (*ex sese, non autem ex consenu ecclesiae*).[9]

I take the doctrine of papal infallibility to be first and foremost an epistemological claim. The evidence for this construal of the doctrine is overwhelming. Thus the doctrine is announced as a divinely revealed dogma; in form it is epis-

---

[8]For details see Olivier Clement, *You Are Peter: An Orthodox Theologian's Reflection on the Exercise of Papal Primacy* (New York: New City Press, 1997), p. 81.

[9]Josef Neuner, and Jacques Dupuis, eds., *The Christian Faith in the Doctrinal Documents of the Catholic Church* (London: Collins, 1983), p. 234.

temological in character. It is equally so in content. The very term *infallibility* is epistemic in nature and usage. Papal infallibility results in a form of doctrinal discourse marked by truth; and the truth concerned is warranted by special divine assistance promised uniquely to the pope. Moreover, there is no doubt that papal infallibility has been received and interpreted by the faithful as an epistemic doctrine. Thus papal infallibility has been taken as a guarantee that the Roman Catholic Church has a unique form of access to the divine will on matters of faith and morals. To be sure, the exercise of papal infallibility is carefully restricted; it applies only in those circumstances in which the pope speaks *ex cathedra* on faith and morals. Furthermore, papal infallibility can be read, of course, in a maximal or minimalist fashion. Minimalists stress the negative significance of not being led astray; maximalists stress the role of the papacy in identifying positive truth in faith and morals. So there is plenty of room for debate on how best to construe its intent; indeed, the Roman Catholic Church shows conspicuous ingenuity in unpacking its doctrinal commitments over time. However, the epistemological nature of the doctrine is not in question. Even if papal infallibility has only been invoked in exceptionally few occasions, it remains as a kind of epistemic nuclear strike, ready to protect the church in its quest for truth and the avoidance of error. The faithful can be sure that the church will get it right on issues crucial to salvation.[10]

Our initial reading of how to think about papal infallibility is confirmed by noting that papal infallibility naturally takes its place within a rich vision of divine revelation. It is not that the pope is the recipient of new revelation. Rather, when disputes arise about the meaning of the special revelation given in Scripture and interpreted in the tradition of the church, the role of the pope is to decide what interpretation best captures the will of Christ. Thus the role of the pope in this vision of divine revelation operates as a matter of last resort. When other practices, such as general councils, fail to provide sufficient illumination or resolution, then the pope makes the critical call. What is needed at that point is appropriate divine assistance. There is no necessity, say, for God to speak in some miraculous manner; the exact mechanism of assistance can be left to divine providence. Thus the doctrine of papal infallibility is one element in a complex vision of divine revelation. Clearly, divine revelation is a pivotal epistemic concept for Christian theology; given this, it is natural to see papal infallibility as an epistemic concept.

One further point needs to be made at this juncture. In order to capture the full

[10]I leave aside at this point how we are to interpret the claim that the Marian dogmas are in fact crucial to salvation.

force of the challenge before us, it is important to note that the epistemological vision of the papal office is not a matter of opinion in the Roman Catholic Church. Papal infallibility is a doctrine that has been canonically defined and adopted. This is a contingent development; there is no necessity that churches formally adopt epistemological proposals. Christians and churches readily, of course, make epistemological claims about the warrants for their truth-claims. Thus it is readily said that this or that theological claim is warranted by Scripture, or by Scripture interpreted in the church, or by a combination of Scripture, tradition, reason and experience. We have a great variety of epistemological proposals floating around space and time. Once developed, Christian communities may then officially adopt this kind of proposal as binding on themselves. At that point they are given a whole new status; they are officially listed as the teaching of the relevant community; they become canonical. This is surely the case as regards papal infallibility. It was officially adopted as canonical at Vatican I and reaffirmed at Vatican II. It is now constitutive of the life and faith of the Roman Catholic Church.

Initially it may appear odd to think of the doctrine of papal infallibility in terms of epistemology. Generally speaking, epistemology has been construed as the careful study of justification, warrant, knowledge, truth and the like.[11] More specifically, issues of justification have been cast in terms of supplying propositional evidence for this or that claim. Thus knowledge has often been seen as justified, true belief, with justification being seen as requiring the citing of relevant evidence. On both counts it might appear that claims about papal infallibility simply fall outside the field of epistemology and that it is, therefore, misplaced to think of papal infallibility in epistemic terms. However, this is a superficial judgment that should readily be rejected. On the one hand, what is at issue is not just epistemology generically construed but rather the epistemology of theology. Papal infallibility comes into the epistemological picture because it is clearly relevant to the justification of theological proposals related to faith and morals in the Christian tradition. Given the divine assistance afforded the pope, he can be relied upon to secure the truth in matters of faith and morals. On the other hand, it has become clear that justification can take the form of appeal to reliable truth-detecting mechanisms and agents as much as appeal to true, evidentiary propositions. Thus it is no longer the case that in epistemology we are restricted to appeal to propositional evidence. It is in fact entirely natural to think of the appeal to papal infallibility in terms of a reliable

[11]Truth is generally kept in the wings as a background concept, but it is clear that questions about truth naturally belong in the field of epistemology despite its exclusion. The traditional definition of knowledge as true, justified belief makes this clear.

truth-transmitting agent lodged at the heart of the Magisterium.[12]

A different way to challenge this vision of papal infallibility would be to insist that the role of the pope is soteriological rather than epistemological.[13] Thus the Petrine office should be seen, it might be said, in its sacramental and liturgical context in which the pope is given a special charism of identifying the truth and avoiding error in order to secure the spiritual welfare of the church and her members. This observation is true, but it is beside the point. The divine assistance furnished the pope to discern truth and avoid error is indeed soteriologically oriented; the ultimate intention is to safeguard the full salvific content of the faith once delivered to the church. However, this does not undercut the fact that the charism exercised is also epistemic in nature. In fact, in this instance the soteriological role of the pope is tied to his epistemic role; epistemology is in the service of soteriology; it is logically prior to soteriology in its fullest expression and effect.

The Problem: Initial Nonstarters

Now that we are relatively clear about the nature and status of the doctrine of papal infallibility—it is epistemic in nature and has been given canonical status in the Roman Catholic Church—we can grasp the ecumenical challenge before us. Given that the Roman Catholic Church is "open to a new situation," how might we envisage "forms in which this ministry may accomplish a service of love recognized by all concerned"? It is obvious that there will be no easy answer to this question, and any answer we give will need to be thought through over time before it should be accepted. We can perceive the enormity of the challenge by exploring some obvious answers that may be initially attractive but that are ultimately unsatisfactory.

One option is simply to insist that all ecclesial communities must sooner or later accept the doctrine of papal infallibility and its exercise. The doctrine is so crucial to the Roman Catholic Church, and the Roman Catholic Church is so crucial to ecumenism, that there can be no ultimate unity without its official adoption by the whole church. Clearly this is a neat and clean solution, but, if it is accepted, then ecumenism, as it has been spelled out over the last century, is over. Ecumenical work on this analysis, while it will still have a host of issues to resolve, will involve in the end the patient effort of convincing those not persuaded of the doctrine of papal infallibility that they have been wrong and need to change their

[12]Those who follow Wilfred Sellars and Donald Davidson in holding that only beliefs can be a warrant for other beliefs will clearly find it difficult to think of papal infallibility as an epistemic concept; but there is surely no need to limit ourselves to the epistemological constraints of Sellars and Davidson at this point.

[13]I am grateful to Scott Hahn for bringing this option to my attention.

minds. Ecumenism collapses in this instance into persuasion and intellectual conversion.

At the other end of the spectrum there is the option of insisting that the Roman Catholic Church abandon the claim of papal infallibility. It would not be difficult to make a case for this in that there are a host of difficulties in the doctrine that are well known and that do not need to be repeated here. Clearly, the option of abandoning the commitment to papal infallibility would also be a neat and clean solution. However, it is an immediate dead end. For one thing, proponents of papal infallibility are more than able to make a case for their position. More importantly, papal infallibility is constitutive of the Roman Catholic Church. Giving up papal infallibility is not just practically and intellectually unlikely, it is ecumenically impossible for the Roman Catholic Church. Again, ecumenism would collapse into protracted exercises in persuasion and intellectual conversion, only this time the specific option would be even less likely to succeed.

In between these two extremes we can envisage an interesting middle way. The core suggestion would be to develop a reinterpretation of papal infallibility that would make it feasible for other churches to adopt it. One way forward would be to interpret the doctrine of papal infallibility more symbolically than literally. Thus it might be seen as symbolic of the ultimate indefectibility of the church in its life and faith. Asserting papal infallibility would be a way of speaking of the efficacious faithfulness of God in upholding the church so as to secure whatever is needed for the spiritual well-being of the faithful. In itself this kind of move would be in keeping with the constant reception and reinterpretation of previous tradition in order to meet the challenges of a new day. The intention behind the original formulation would be honored, but the verbal formulation itself would be reinterpreted so as to express the truth that God will never allow the church officially to adopt anything that would threaten the spiritual welfare of the people of God.

The attraction of this position is that it keeps intact commitment to the doctrine of papal infallibility. The problems, however, are obvious. It is impossible to square this vision of papal infallibility with the plain meaning of the declaration of Vatican I. One does not have to be some kind of insensitive literalist or wooden reader to note that this kind of symbolic reading of the text is an unacceptable stretch. To be sure, Vatican I can be taken as saying that God will not let the church falter when it comes to matters of faith and morals; but it says a lot more than this, so much so that it cannot be reduced to this minimalist reading. In addition, it is difficult to avoid the judgment that what is on offer is not really a new interpretation of Vatican I but a repudiation of Vatican I. This kind of sleight of hand surely hinders rather than helps ecumenical progress.[14]

A Proposal: Doctrinal Consensus, Epistemic Diversity

There is, however, another way that deserves our attention. The core of this suggestion is that the content of the doctrine of papal infallibility remain as robust as desired by its proponents but that its canonical status be refigured in the future. No doubt there may be more than one way to spell out this option, but for the moment the general direction is clear. Papal infallibility would remain as a significant epistemological option in the life of the church, but it would not be required as canonical for the whole church, at least not until such time as it could be formulated in a way that could be endorsed by the whole church. The argument for this move can be made from various angles and in stages.

It is clear that papal infallibility was not a canonical doctrine within the Roman Catholic Church until the late nineteenth century. This does not mean that it was not held, or that papal infallibility was not relied on in theological deliberations. The crucial observation is that it was not canonized; it was left as significant midrash in the life of the Roman Catholic Church. In fact, in the famous Baltimore Catechism it was not deemed constitutive of Roman Catholic teaching. To be sure, papal infallibility was widely believed, and later it was claimed that it was always believed as constitutive of Roman Catholicism, so I am not asking for a return to the exact situation that existed prior to Vatican I. However, there is sufficient analogy here to open up a fresh possibility. Clearly any future united church is going to be different from anything we currently know, so we need not look for an exact replica of the situation prior to Vatican I. Yet in principle we have a situation where papal infallibility does not have the canonical status it enjoyed after Vatican I.

We can extend this line of thinking back to the church prior to the split between East and West that is conventionally dated to 1054. The issue is contentious, but it is historically the case that papal infallibility was not canonical for the whole church in the first millennium. The great churches of the East do not

---

[14]A very different kind of middle way has been proposed by Paul G. McGlasson in *Invitation to Dogmatic Theology, A Canonical Approach* (Grand Rapids: Brazos Press, 2006), p. 208. In this option the Eastern Orthodox Church is invited to abandon its rejection of the *filioque* clause and the Roman Catholic Church to abandon papal infallibility. I applaud McGlasson's intention to champion a legitimate diversity in the theological expressions of the Christian church but find this way ahead unconvincing. In the end it trades on making Barth's epistemology of theology (suitably updated by the work of Brevard S. Childs) confessional and canonical for the church as a whole.

accept papal infallibility to this day. Thus the unity of the church did not depend on official agreement on this matter. Given that *Ut unum sint* proposes that the East and West can come together in communion on the basis of what was in place in the first millennium, we have in hand an even better analogue to that given to us by the Roman Catholic Church prior to Vatican I. In this instance, papal infallibility was thoroughly contested in the church as a whole; it was not as if it was implicitly held across the board. Again, it is important not to overreach at this point. Much has happened across the last millennium, so it would be historically naïve to believe that we can think away crucial developments across the last millennium of Christian experience. However, what we should hope for and expect in the future is not replication. We should expect genuinely new configurations of ecclesial life that have sufficient continuity with earlier history to engender trust and confidence.

There is a deeper line of argument that deserves elaboration. I have insisted heretofore that papal infallibility should be seen as an epistemological doctrine. Regrettably, theologians have paid next to no attention to the status of epistemological doctrines in the life of the church. What I have in mind at this point are not general epistemological doctrines about, say, perception, testimony, deduction, intuition, coherence and the like. What is at stake are proposals about how best to think about the epistemology of Christian theology. Generally such proposals revolve in and around debates about natural theology, special revelation, conscience, Scripture, the *sensus divinitatis,* the *oculis contemplationis* and religious experience. Papal infallibility belongs in fact to a complex epistemology of theology that depends on a positive vision of the relation between faith and reason and that is lodged in a rich account of the relations among Scripture, tradition, the sense of the faithful, the deliberations of the Magisterium and the work of theologians.

Epistemologies of theology are important phenomena. They seek to answer perennial questions that are posed by believers; they have a pivotal role in sustaining the faith of the faithful; they play an important role in evangelism; and they rebut charges of irrationality that constantly crop up in the church's engagement with culture. It is very important the theologians and church teachers be able to cope with questions that arise at this level of theological inquiry. Granting all this, we need to ask: Should the church as a whole be committed to any particular epistemology? Should epistemological proposals, no matter how compelling and attractive, be canonized?

I suggest that epistemological proposals should not be canonized for the following reasons. First, the church of the first millennium was perfectly able to agree on the essentials of its internal life before God without officially adopting any epistemology of theology. The church was able, for example, to develop its canonical Scriptures, its canonical creed, its canonical structures, its canon law, its canon of saints and the like without ever adopting an agreed epistemology of theology. It simply left epistemological options as a matter of acceptable diversity, allowing various visions of divine revelation, inspiration, the authority of Scripture, the status of tradition, the nature of reason and the like to exist and flourish. This is not to say that the church was indifferent to truth or that its teachers did not take epistemological issues seriously. On the contrary, the church had a canon of truth in the Nicene Creed that it developed, adopted and recited in the teeth of fierce opposition. Moreover, the great theologians and teachers of the church were perfectly ready to take up issues of warrant and justification where pertinent to their theological endeavors. However, truth can be adopted, proclaimed and defended in the absence of a canonized epistemology. If we are to take seriously the common faith of the church prior to the division of East and West, then we have to come to terms with its canonical modesty and reserve with respect to epistemologies of theology.

Second, it is clear that if we canonize this or that epistemological proposal, then we need far more agreement than has been generally forthcoming in the history of theology across the centuries. Agreement in general epistemology had never been available to us in philosophy. The effort in the modern period to insist on, say, some kind of classical foundationalism in the West has collapsed in the last generation. Current epistemology is awash in competing theories and insights. Christian philosophers who agree, say, in their commitment to the Nicene Creed are in deep disagreement about how best to secure its truth. The same can be said of Christian theology. There is no agreement on theological method or more generally on the epistemology of theology. Theories in this domain come and go; older insights that we thought were dead ends are recovered and brought to life; conventional interpretations of the classical options undergo radical reformulation and reinterpretation; creative new suggestions are pursued and defended. To look for agreement in the epistemology of theology is to chase a will-o'-the-wisp that is simply not available.

Disagreement and diversity even exist in the case of the history of the epistemology of theology in the Roman Catholic Church. One only has to look at the place of the great work of Thomas Aquinas to see this. Aquinas was clearly given a privileged position in the epistemology of theology after Vatican I. However, over time the reading of Aquinas across a century and more came to reflect the epistemological sensibilities of new generations of theologians and philosophers. Hence even a positive account of the relation between revelation and reason—a position Aquinas clearly instantiates—can come to be expressed in radically different ways.[15] The same applies to the vision of scriptural authority. At Trent, Scripture was construed in terms of divine dictation; this was also true of *Providentissimus Deus,* the fine encyclical of Pope Leo XIII on the study of holy Scripture issued in 1893. This is now clearly discarded and forgotten, even though doctrines of biblical inerrancy still show up in Vatican II. We can even extend this observation to the doctrine of papal infallibility. There is no agreement on how this doctrine is to be read and implemented. Hence what is offered as secure and settled in epistemology turns out to be flexible and relative. The upshot of these observations is this: we simply do not have the kind of clarity and agreement about the crucial issues that crop up in the epistemology of theology to license the canonization of any robust theory for the whole church.

Third, it is clear that if we insist on epistemological agreement, then the prospects for ecumenism are bleak in the extreme. The history of Protestantism bears ample witness to the difficulties. Protestants have split again and again over rival visions of the epistemology of theology. The variations on doctrines of biblical authority are legion and encompass both internal and external considerations. Does Scripture settle matters of church polity? Is it to be used negatively or positively? Must a Christian doctrine or practice be actually derivable from Scripture, or is it enough if it is not forbidden? How are considerations in Scripture to be taken in relation to material drawn from tradition, reason and experience? Different ecclesial bodies have wrangled over these matters since the Reformation, and the divisions they help cause are endless.[16]

One way to think of the doctrine of papal infallibility is, in fact, to see it as one more way to bring these deadly and divisive squabbles to an end once and for all. It is no accident that papal infallibility was canonized at a time when Western Christianity was obsessed with questions about authority and epistemology, and when it became clear that a whole wing of Protestantism was pre-

---

[15]We can see the ground shifting in the way in which the concept of natural law has become somewhat wobbly in recent years. See, for example, Joseph Cardinal Ratzinger (Pope Benedict XVI), *Values in a Time of Upheaval* (San Francisco: Ignatius Press, 2006), p. 38. Pope Benedict XVI accepts that the appeal to natural law has become "a blunt instrument" and radically modifies the appeal to any kind of universal reason.

[16]Note that I am not claiming that divisions arise only because of epistemological differences, but clearly epistemological differences have been prominent in the modern period.

pared to abandon revelation in favor of some vision of reason or religious experience. Papal infallibility on this analysis was the capstone of the effort to secure the authority of Scripture in the West. It is thus no accident that both evangelical and mainline theologians have in recent years turned to the Roman Catholic Church for relief from the great misery of Protestantism. "Modernism" (and the apostasy it harbored) was clearly lurking below the surface. In these circumstances the temptation to insist on canonizing papal infallibility was great indeed; its evangelistic significance in some circles remains substantial. However, we should resist this temptation precisely because it will lead to irreparable division. Once we insist on such substantial, official epistemological agreement as a condition of unity, we are insisting on a burden that cannot in the long term be borne given the diversity of epistemological commitment in the church across space and time. We are, in fact, perpetuating division even as we seek to bring it to an end once and for all.

I trust I have said enough to provide a *prima facie* case for the central proposal of this chapter. My suggestion is that the doctrine of papal infallibility should not be rejected or reinterpreted, but neither should it be proposed as canonical for the life of the church as a whole. Papal infallibility should be given the status that it had in the Roman Catholic Church prior to Vatican I. Those who believe in papal infallibility, including the Bishop of Rome, can continue to hold it, rely on it in their theological deliberations and seek to persuade others to adopt it. However, papal infallibility should not be universally canonical; it should be treated as an exceptionally significant and fruitful option in the epistemology of theology, but it should not be canonized as the only option or as an essential ingredient in the epistemology of theology. This fits with the conviction that the consensus of the church prior to the schism between East and West should be given a privileged position in the life of the church. It also dovetails with a healthy vision of the modest place of epistemological doctrine in the life of the church.

Two Possible Objections

In the final part of this chapter I want now to look at a couple of objections and to identify some implications of my analysis for evangelicalism. The sensitive reader will readily think of two objections at this stage of the argument. In responding to them I shall further elaborate on what might be at stake if this proposal is taken seriously. The first of these takes us to an intrinsic worry that will naturally arise; the second stems from the fact that papal infallibility does not stand alone but may well be linked to issues of jurisdiction and of spiritual completeness in the life of the church.

The intrinsic worry that will naturally arise is this. Surely, it will be said, this proposal rests on the unrealistic assumption that the Petrine office can be neatly divided into two distinct roles so that in one role the pope will operate as Bishop of Rome, as Patriarch of the West, as a moderator and leader of the whole church, and in the other role he will operate as a special epistemic envoy exercising the art of papal infallibility as and when needed. Another way to approach the worry would be this. Surely this proposal suggests that the pope retains the ability to make infallible *ex cathedra* decisions though these decisions are no longer binding on the whole church. Are not these suggestions incoherent and impractical on their face?

I agree that there are internal tensions buried in the proposal, but I do not think they are such that we can claim that they reach the level of incoherence. However the ecumenical future turns out, there will have to be some change in the exercise of papal infallibility, and it is likely that the kind of change needed will involve a novel configuration that may initially appear conceptually demanding. It is not essential at this stage that we know how the different roles assigned to the pope will be exercised. What matters is that we can distinguish between the different roles that will exist, and this we can surely do without undue strain.

As to the problem of practicality, it is important not to cross too many bridges before we get to them. The fact of the matter is that papal infallibility is exercised on very, very few occasions. More importantly, in any united church the office of the pope will be tempered and constrained by a new configuration of the instruments of unity, so that the need for the exercise of papal infallibility may not arise. Or, if the need does arise, the pope will genuinely give expression to the voice of the whole church, and such an operation might legitimately be seen as something natural and efficacious in the instrumentality of the Holy Spirit. It is the latter, that is, giving voice *de facto* and contingently to the mind of the whole church, that really matters rather than a formal canonization of the doctrine of papal infallibility. Over against the latter we can, moreover, surely allow for papal pronouncements that would be binding on part of the church rather the whole church. A church that is genuinely universal will have to allow for legitimate diversity and for provincial or local tradition.

The second issue that needs attention is this. Surely, it will be said, the exercise of papal infallibility does not stand alone. It is integrally related to the exercise of jurisdiction and to the unique spiritual resources safeguarded through communion with the Bishop of Rome in the Roman Catholic Church. Indeed the exercise of jurisdiction and of spiritual safeguarding is warranted precisely by the charism of papal infallibility. So any move to recast the status and function of papal infallibility will have important implications for other ministries of the pope. Clearly we enter here a whole new set of issues, but we should walk forward in faith and hope rather than in suspicion and fear. I do not find this objection immediately successful.

To begin, it is not at all clear that papal infallibility is essential to any and every vision of jurisdiction. The exercise of executive authority in the church can stand on its own as a charism without reference to any notion of infallibility.[17] Moreover, it is obvious that the ministry of executive authority is dispersed through a network of juridical instruments so that the load is carried across a spectrum of offices. So I see no insuperable difficulty on this front. Cardinal Walter Kasper would appear to agree.

> The issue is to disentangle the functions which have accrued to the papacy in the course of time. The important thing is to distinguish the essential and therefore indispensable duties of Petrine ministry from those duties that pertain to the Pope as the first bishop (patriarch or primate) of the Latin Church, or have accrued over time. Such a distinction could also lead to consequences . . . for the restructuring of the Roman Catholic Church and construction of intermediary authorities between the individual bishop, the bishop's conference and Rome.[18]

How are we to respond to the worry about securing the full resources of the church as a whole across space and time? Frankly, it is not at all clear how we should construe claims to possess the fullness of the means of grace in the Roman Catholic Church. Assertions along these lines are not difficult to find, but it is rare to find them spelled out in any detail. It sometimes sounds as if the claim to fullness is to be taken in a personalistic and individualist sense. Thus someone who is not in communion with the Bishop of Rome is lacking in some spiritual gift or quality. This is hard to sustain given the witness of the saints and martyrs outside communion with Rome.[19] The more natural way to take this claim is in a corporate or communal sense. On this reading the claim to fullness can be expressed in the contention that the Roman Catholic Church keeps alive the full panoply of means of grace that God bequeathed to the church. This is a much more plausible claim, but it needs to be spelled out in detail before it can be evaluated. It is not

---

[17]This rule applies also to the teaching capacity of the pope, but I will not chase that important topic here.

[18]Walter Kasper, *That They May All Be One: The Call to Unity* (New York: Burns and Oates, 2004), p. 82.

[19]Happily this theme is taken up at some length in *Ut unum sint.*

enough simply to make this kind of assertion; it is crucial to unpack it specifically and concretely. In the meantime it is foolhardy to make the additional claim that such fullness, however delineated in detail, requires the canonization of the doctrine of papal infallibility. If we go this far, then the great churches of the East and the Roman Catholic Church itself prior to Vatican I were spiritually defective for almost two thousand years. We have at this point reached a *reduction ad absurdum.*

CONCLUSION: A WORD OF HEALING TO EVANGELICALS

It remains to explore briefly the implications of this proposal for evangelicalism. I noted earlier that many evangelicals are indifferent if not hostile to any serious engagement with the Roman Catholic Church. This should not surprise us in that old divisions are still very much alive, and the tensions between evangelicals and Roman Catholics are still in place in various parts of the world. However, many evangelicals in the West long ago discovered that the Roman Catholic Church is a crucial ally and not an enemy in the defense of the faith.[20] Hence, evangelicals can enter into serious engagement with the Roman Catholic Church in good faith and without defensiveness. As they ponder the central thesis of this chapter, there are three implications that deserve mention.

First, it has long been clear that evangelicalism operates best as a leaven within a wider ecclesial configuration rather than as a church or a denomination. Evangelicalism needs the treasures and structures of the wider church to be at its best. Without these treasures, it fragments into polemical, sectarian modes of practice and rhetoric, and it falls into heresy and apostasy. It also too readily creates a host of self-appointed, infallible leaders who have no accountability and who all too often devour the sheep. If we can envisage a church where papal infallibility remains a live option but is not canonized, then a critical barrier to ecumenism has been refigured in a way that will allow evangelicals to make their best contribution to the church as a whole.

Second, if, as I propose, we relativize epistemological proposals in the life of the church, then evangelicals will need to face up to the challenge of this move too. Evangelicals have at times been obsessed with issues of religious epistemology, so much so that epistemological commitments have displaced the gospel and the faith of the church and led to acrimonious division. It has also caused evangelicalism to be the mother of a host of liberal Protestants who readily give away the faith once delivered to the saints in the interests of engagement with high culture. So

---

[20]John Wesley was prescient in his discernment of this possibility in his famous *Letter to a Roman Catholic*, ed. Michael Hurley (Belfast: Epworth, 1968).

exercising canonical modesty with respect to the epistemology of theology will be a healing move for the evangelical tradition as a whole. It will also allow evangelicals to continue to explore the whole range of epistemological issues; most especially it will allow those so inclined to make their case for biblical authority with appropriate passion and freedom.

Third, if evangelicals are to relativize their own epistemologies, and if they are honorably to embrace the treasures and structure of the church, then it is clear that they will need to expand their conventional vision of the work of the Holy Spirit in the church. Evangelicals have rightly focused on the ministry of the Holy Spirit in such arenas as conversion, personal piety, and the production and reading of Scripture. They have, however, tended to set their face against the "institutional church" as something altogether human and even demonic. Thus in their ecclesiologies they have been hard-boiled secularists and functional atheists. It is a real challenge for evangelicals to think of a Petrine office in the church, much less to think of a Petrine office as a charismatic gift in the life of the church. However, once evangelicals come to see that the work of the Holy Spirit in providing ecclesiological structures and offices is not an alternative to the other manifold ministries of the Holy Spirit, then they can, like John Paul II, be "open to a new situation."[21] The great Russian theologian Vladimir Solovyov once said that the united church of the future will embrace the work of Peter, Paul and John. Perhaps one task of evangelicals in ecumenism is to champion the work of Luke.

---

[21] *Ut unum sint,* §95.

8

VERITATIS SPLENDOR

Human Freedom and the Splendor of Truth

Andrew J. Goddard

INTRODUCTION

Veritatis splendor—the splendor of truth—was destined to be one of the most significant of all John Paul II's writings even before he signed it on the Feast of the Transfiguration, August 6, 1993. In the words of John Wilkins, editor of the *Tablet*, "few papal documents of modern times have been awaited with such anticipation."[1] The encyclical's importance is, however, not immediately obvious from either its stated recipients or its subject matter. It is addressed to "Venerable Brothers in the Episcopate"[2] rather than to the wider audience of most other encyclicals (although it is clear the pope was addressing a much larger constituency, particularly teachers of moral theology[3]). Its subject matter—"certain fundamental questions concerning the Church's moral teaching"—is both rather technical and unprecedented (*Veritatis splendor,* §5).[4] Previous papal encyclicals and other encyc-

---

[1]John Wilkins, "Introduction," in *Understanding Veritatis splendor* (London: SPCK, 1994), p. ix. *Veritatis splendor,* though dated August 6, 1993, was not officially released to the press until October 5, 1993.

[2]John Paul II, *Veritatis splendor,* Libreria Editrice Vaticana (August 6, 1993), introductory blessing <http://www.vatican.va/holy_father/john_paul_ii/encyclicals/documents/hf_jp-ii_enc_06081993_veritatis-splendor_en.html>.

[3]Linda Woodhead, "*Veritatis splendor:* Some Editorial Reflections," *Studies in Christian Ethics* 7, no. 2 (1994): 1, begins her reflections by recalling a shy and lonely old man she used to visit who could not talk directly to her about his deep concerns so instead spoke to his dog in her presence!

[4]Unless otherwise noted, in-text references to *Veritatis splendor* will be identified by section number only.

licals of John Paul II address specific ethical subjects[5] while part three of the *Catechism*[6] (being written at the same time as *Veritatis splendor* but appearing before it) offers a significant account of the church's moral teaching. This encyclical is, however, unique in its focus on the structure and method of Christian moral theology. Before examining and offering comment on the letter's content it is, therefore, important to set it in context so as to understand why it was written and why it has proved such a controversial document, especially among Roman Catholic moral theologians.

The Context

The first signal of John Paul's intention to address the church's moral teaching came on August 1, 1987, in his apostolic letter *Spiritus domini,* a reflection on the life of Saint Alphonsus Liguouri, patron saint of confessors and moral theologians.[7] Having extolled Alphonsus' role in, among other areas, the renewal, study and teaching of moral theology, the pope promised to offer his own contribution to the task by "treating more fully and deeply . . . questions concerning the very foundations of moral theology." That promise, fulfilled in this encyclical, must be set in the context of the recent renewal of Catholic moral theology. Although a longer story could, of course, be told, it is Vatican II that, as so often, is crucial. Its decree on priestly training, *Optatam totius,* issued in October 1965, famously stated,

> Likewise let the other theological disciplines be renewed through a more living contact with the mystery of Christ and the history of salvation. Special care must be given to the perfecting of moral theology. Its scientific exposition, nourished more on the teaching of the Bible, should shed light on the loftiness of the calling of the faithful in Christ and the obligation that is theirs of bearing fruit in charity for the life of the world.[8]

The following decades saw a great revival in Catholic moral theology but also growing divergences among Catholic moral theologians. These differences were

---

[5]Most famous are those many encyclicals developing the church's social teaching from *Rerum novarum* (1891) through to John Paul's *Centesimus annus* (1991). John Paul's *Laborem exercens* and *Evangelium vitae* are his other predominantly ethical encyclicals.

[6]*Catechism of the Catholic Church* (London: Geoffrey Chapman, 1994).

[7]<www.vatican.va/holy_father/john_paul_ii/apost_letters/index.htm> links to the text but sadly not in English.

[8]Paul VI, *Decree on Priestly Training "Optatam totius"* (October 28, 1965), §16 <www.vatican.va/archive/hist_councils/ii_vatican_council/documents/vat-ii_decree_19651028_optatam-totius_en.html>.

in relation to both method and conclusions on specific issues, especially in sexual ethics. The *cause célèbre,* of course, became the issue of contraception, after Pope Paul VI issued *Humanae vitae* in July 1968. This upheld the church's traditional teaching by excluding "any action which either before, at the moment of, or after sexual intercourse, is specifically intended to prevent procreation—whether as an end or as a means" and declaring it "a serious error to think that a whole married life of otherwise normal relations can justify sexual intercourse which is deliberately contraceptive and so intrinsically wrong."[9]

Divisions among Roman Catholic moral theologians focused on this subject but were often related to wider and deeper methodological disagreements and conflicts. While there is a great diversity and spectrum of views, it is not too much of a caricature to describe broadly two camps of opinion. A significant number of scholars have distanced themselves from *Humanae vitae* and developed the tradition of Catholic moral thought in ways that are open to a more positive assessment of not only contraception but also such practices as reproductive technologies, divorce and remarriage, and homosexual relationships. A string of significant writers such as Josef Fuchs, Bernhard Häring, Richard McCormick, Lisa Sowle Cahill, Jean Porter and Bernard Hoose have been prominent in dissenting to varying degrees from official teaching and revising traditional methodologies. Some, most famously Charles Curran, have been disciplined by the Vatican as a result of their dissent.[10] In contrast, there has also been a growing number of theologians and philosophers who have participated in the renewal of moral theology called for by Vatican II in a way which, although not uncritical of pre-Vatican II Roman Catholic moral theology, has more clearly developed and upheld traditional moral teaching. These include not only the writers associated with the new natural law thinking (such as John Finnis and Germain Grisez) or a strong focus on defending *Humanae vitae* (for example, Janet E. Smith) but also scholars such as Servais Pinckaers, Martin Rhonheimer, Romanus Cessario, William E. May and Livio Melina, many of whom have particularly emphasized a return to scriptural teaching (especially

[9]Paul VI, *"Humanae vitae": Encyclical of Pope Paul VI on the Regulation of Birth* (July 25, 1968) §14 <www.vatican.va/holy_father/paul_vi/encyclicals/documents/hf_p-vi_enc_25071968_humanae-vitae_en.html>.

[10]One guide to the debates is the collection of articles from across the spectrum of opinion in Charles E. Curran and Richard A. McCormick, eds., *Dissent in the Church,* Readings in Moral Theology 6 (Mahwah, N.J.: Paulist Press, 1988). Curran has offered his own assessment of Pope John Paul's contribution in *The Moral Theology of Pope John Paul II* (Washington, D.C.: Georgetown University Press, 2005) and recently produced a memoir, *Loyal Dissent: Memoir of a Catholic Theologian* (Washington, D.C.: Georgetown University Press, 2006).

the Decalogue and the Sermon on the Mount) and the place of the virtues in Christian moral thought.

This wider context explains both why John Paul II's contribution was so eagerly anticipated and why—in its support for the latter group and criticisms of the former—this encyclical aroused such bitter controversy among Roman Catholics. Germain Grisez boldly stated that "theologians who have been dissenting from the doctrine reaffirmed in this encyclical now have only three choices: to admit that they have been mistaken, to admit that they do not believe God's word, or to claim that the Pope is grossly misinterpreting the Bible."[11] In contrast, Bernhard Haring issued a *cri de coeur* against the document which he claimed "is directed above all towards one goal: to endorse total assent and submission to all utterances of the Pope, and above all on one crucial point: that the use of any artificial means for regulating birth is intrinsically evil and sinful, without exception."[12]

These internal disputes among Roman Catholics have sadly often dominated the interpretation and reception of the encyclical. It is therefore important that the much broader substantive content of the encyclical is properly understood. In particular, its wider and deeper concern of providing a faithful, biblical Christian analysis and response to the moral confusion of contemporary society must be evaluated without everything being filtered through the narrower ecclesial politics within which it arose and to which it also responds.

Structure and Content

After its brief introduction, the encyclical falls into three chapters with a short conclusion focused on Mary. The contrasts between the three parts has produced much comment (including speculation about different drafters) and questions about the degree to which the letter coheres as a whole.[13] The first—"'Teacher, what good must I do . . . ?' Christ and the Answer to the Question About Morality"—offers a widely praised biblical meditation upon the encounter between Jesus

---

[11]Germain Grisez, "Revelation Versus Dissent," in *Understanding Veritatis splendor,* ed. John Wilkins (London: SPCK, 1994), pp. 7-8.

[12]Bernhard Häring, "A Distrust That Wounds," in *Understanding Veritatis splendor,* ed. John Wilkins (London: SPCK, 1994), p. 9. A more sustained and scholarly response to the pope's analysis from those who felt misrepresented is found in Joe Selling and Jan Jans, eds., *The Splendor of Accuracy: An Examination of the Assertions Made by Veritatis splendor* (Kampen: Kok Pharos, 1994).

[13]The best proposal for there being coherence is that of Oliver O'Donovan, who sees "a carefully ordered sequence of forms. It is teleological; it offers a conception of the good. It is deontological, proposing a code of moral commands. It is eschatological, arousing a hope of transcendent perfection" ("A Summons to Reality," in *Understanding Veritatis splendor,* ed. John Wilkins [London: SPCK, 1994], p. 41).

and the rich man (Mt 19).[14] The second, citing Romans 12:2 ("Do not be conformed to this world"), examines certain tendencies in present-day moral theology. It is the most technical and controversial, engaging with some of the disagreements among Catholic theologians. The final chapter again takes a key biblical text as its focus—1 Corinthians 1:17 on not emptying the cross of Christ of its power—and explores "moral good for the life of the Church and of the world" with an "extraordinary discussion of martyrdom."[15]

Introduction. The letter's opening signals two of its great themes—the dignity of human beings ("the splendour of truth shines forth . . . in a special way, in man, created in the image and likeness of God") and the relationship between freedom and truth ("truth enlightens man's intelligence and shapes his freedom"). These are given a Christocentric focus rooted in Scripture (the short introduction cites seventeen biblical texts). The letter's concerns are then identified: seeking "*to reflect on the whole of the Church's moral teaching*" (§4),[16] it does so in the face of the errors of "relativism and scepticism" that lead to humans searching for "an illusory freedom apart from truth itself" (§1), which has even developed in Christian thinking that detaches "human freedom from its essential and constitutive relationship to truth" (§4). The bishops are reminded they share the call to safeguard sound teaching and, faced with "a genuine crisis" (§5), the pope's specific purpose is "to set forth, with regard to the problems being discussed, the principles of a moral teaching based upon Sacred Scripture and the living Apostolic Tradition, and at the same time to shed light on the presuppositions and consequences of the dissent which that teaching has met" (§5).

Chapter one. The opening biblical meditation introduces the letter's key themes and, by rooting them in Scripture, particularly Matthew 19:16 and following, it instantly attracts the attention of many evangelicals. It thus merits a more detailed summary than other chapters.

The young man is taken to represent all who turn to Christ with an essential question about morality ("what good must I do to have eternal life?") (§6). This question is focused on life's meaning rather than rules and shows the connection

---

[14]This gospel narrative and its relationship to Christian ethics is also considered by both Karl Barth in *Church Dogmatics* 2/2 and Dietrich Bonhoeffer in *Discipleship.* Gilbert Meilaender helpfully compares the encyclical's treatment to Barth's in Meilaender, "Grace, Justification Through Faith, and Sin" in *Ecumenical Ventures in Ethics,* ed. Reinhard Hütter and Theodor Dieter (Grand Rapids: Eerdmans, 1998), pp. 65-70.

[15]Stanley Hauerwas, "The Pope Puts Theology Back into Moral Theology," *Studies in Christian Ethics* 7, no. 2 (1994): 18.

[16]Italics indicate emphasis in the original unless otherwise designated.

between moral good and our destiny. Christ's response reveals that God alone—the Good and the source of human happiness—can answer this question, and John Paul emphasizes our need for God's self-revelation. This draws us back to the Decalogue's first table and relationship with God as at the heart of the Law and the good. Realizing "no human effort . . . succeeds in 'fulfilling' the Law" (§11), we find such fulfillment must be a divine gift of sharing in divine Goodness through following Jesus. Before Christ, God's answers concerning the good were found in creation and the natural law and in Israel's history, especially the Decalogue, and so Christ's response closely correlates eternal life and obedience to God's commandments.

Pressed further, Jesus reemphasizes the Decalogue, especially its second table focused on neighbor-love. This shows "the singular dignity of the human person" (§13) whose good the various commandments safeguard by providing "the basic condition for love of neighbour . . . the *first necessary step on the journey towards freedom*" (§13). Jesus brings these to fulfillment by interiorizing their demands and drawing out their full meaning rooted in a loving heart.[17] He himself "*becomes a living and personal Law*" through his total self-giving (§15).

The young man claims to have kept the commandments but is aware this is insufficient. Jesus invites him onto the path of perfection. John Paul II interprets this in the light of the Beatitudes, which promise us the good and are concerned with attitudes and dispositions, offering a self-portrait of the Christ we are called to follow. Respect for the commandments is thus required but must find fulfillment in following Christ, which requires mature human freedom and God's grace.

This reading provides the basis for one of the encyclical's central themes: "human freedom and God's law are not in opposition; on the contrary, they appeal one to the another" (§17). For those who "live 'by the flesh'" the law is experienced as restricting or denying freedom but for those "walking by the Spirit" and following Jesus it is experienced as "the fundamental and necessary way in which to practise love as something freely chosen and freely lived out" (§18). Responding to Jesus' call "involves *holding fast to the very person of Jesus*" (§19) and "Jesus' way of acting and his words, his deeds and his precepts" are what "constitute the moral rule of Christian life" (§20) with the new commandment to imitate Jesus' love by being conformed to him at the depths of our being.

The conversation's poignant end shows God's power—the Spirit—as the key

[17]In the Sermon on the Mount he shows the commandments to be "a path involving a moral and spiritual journey towards perfection, at the heart of which is love" (*Veritatis splendor*, §15).

to these demands of discipleship.[18] Here again we see the priority and exclusivity of grace,[19] but this gift creates the free response in us of love for God and neighbor. Grace and freedom, gift and task are inseparably linked, and, although "*the New Law is the grace of the Holy Spirit given through faith in Christ*" (§24), the moral demands are reinforced and not lessened by this empowering gift.

The pope concludes by stressing the universality of the question and of Christ's answer. Scripture's moral prescriptions "must be *faithfully kept and continually put into practice* in the various different cultures throughout the course of history" (§25). Bishops are entrusted with the task of interpreting the apostles' moral catechesis through both "exhortations and directions connected to specific historical and cultural situations" and "ethical teaching with precise rules of behaviour" (§26). As "a communion both of faith and of life" (§26), the church's unity is damaged by "those who disregard the moral obligations to which they are called by the Gospel" (§26). Bishops therefore must promote and preserve the moral life as, with the Spirit's aid, "*the authentic interpretation* of the Lord's law develops" (§27) in a way that "can only confirm the permanent validity of Revelation and follow in the line of the interpretation given to it by the great Tradition of the Church's teaching and life" (§27).

Faced with "new tendencies and theories" the Magisterium "senses more urgently the duty to offer its own discernment and teaching, in order to help man in his journey towards truth and freedom" (§27). This discernment is the heart of the second chapter.

Chapter two. Building on "the essential elements of Revelation in the Old and New Testament with regard to moral action" (§28), John Paul argues that the crucial issues are human freedom (related to human dignity and conscience) and the crisis of truth. Errors opposing moral law and conscience to nature and freedom deny freedom's dependence on truth expressed in Jesus' words that "you will know the truth, and the truth will make you free" (Jn 8:32).

This is *first* explored in the relation of freedom to law. Drawing on the Thomist tradition, various forms of moral law are discussed within an understanding that God is their source who alone decides what is good and evil. True human freedom accepts God's moral law. It is not a moral autonomy that effectively creates truth and so denies in divine revelation "a specific and determined moral content, universally valid and permanent" (§37). Our reason discovers and applies the law.

[18]"To imitate and live out the love of Christ is not possible for man by his own strength alone. He becomes *capable of this love only by virtue of a gift received*" (ibid., §22).

[19]"Love and life according to the Gospel cannot be thought of first and foremost as a kind of precept. . . . They are possible only as the result of a gift of God who heals, restores and transforms the human heart by his grace" (ibid., §23).

This is not a form of heteronomy but rather what the encyclical calls "participated theonomy" as we participate in the knowledge of good and evil by natural reason and divine revelation. The common, related opposition between nature and freedom is also challenged in the light of Christian teaching on the unity and dignity of the human person.

A central theme of the chapter is the contemporary destruction of law's universality and immutability and John Paul's insistence that negative precepts of natural law "oblige each and every individual, always and in every circumstance." Choosing behavior they prohibit "is in no case compatible with the goodness of the will of the acting person, with his vocation to life with God and to communion with his neighbour" (§52).[20]

The *second* section explores the place where the relationship between freedom and God's law is lived out—the human heart, in moral conscience. Appealing to Romans, the pope rejects the view that conscience is creative, establishing the law. Instead he teaches that conscience confronts us with the law and witnesses internally to our personal (un)faithfulness. It is "a *practical judgment* . . . which makes known what man must do or not do, or which assesses an act already performed by him" (§59). It seeks objective truth but "*is not an infallible judge*" (§62).[21]

The *third* section explores two levels of choices—specific acts and a "fundamental option."[22] Those (called "proportionalists") who claim that the former cannot alter the latter and that whether a specific action is right or wrong is judged not by some universal moral norm but "only on the basis of a technical calculation of the proportion between the 'premoral' or 'physical' goods and evils which actually result from the action" (§65) are strongly criticized.

The *fourth* section focuses on moral evaluation of specific acts. This is determined not, as some claim, by consequences or intention but by the act's object and our freedom's relationship with the good.[23] It is therefore an error to justify, even in the name of love, "deliberate choices of kinds of behaviour contrary to the commandments of the divine and natural law" (§76). There are "intrinsically evil acts"

[20]The pope therefore notes that "the Church has always taught that one may never choose kinds of behaviour prohibited by the moral commandments expressed in negative form in the Old and New Testaments" (ibid., §52).

[21]The encyclical helpfully summarizes traditional Catholic teaching on an erroneous conscience and the need for formation of conscience as we "make it the object of a continuous conversion to what is true and to what is good" (ibid., §64).

[22]A fundamental option "qualifies the moral life and engages freedom on a radical level before God" (ibid., §66), as in the decision to follow Jesus.

[23]"Acting is morally good when the choices of freedom are *in conformity with man's true good* and thus express the voluntary ordering of the person towards his ultimate end: God himself" (ibid., §72).

which radically contradict the good of the person made in God's image.

The chapter closes with an appeal to bishops, elaborated in the third chapter, not simply to warn about errors and dangers but "first of all show the inviting splendour of that truth which is Jesus Christ himself" in whom man "can understand fully and live perfectly, through his good actions, his vocation to freedom in obedience to the divine law summarized in the commandment of love of God and neighbour . . . through the gift of the Holy Spirit, the Spirit of truth, of freedom and of love: in him we are enabled to interiorize the law, to receive it and to live it as the motivating force of true personal freedom" (§83).

Chapter three. In response to the fundamental question of human freedom's submission to the truth of God's law, the church must focus on Christ crucified as he "*reveals the authentic meaning of freedom; he lives it fully, in the total gift of himself* and calls his disciples to share in his freedom" (§85). Freedom's deepest foundation is therefore worship of God and a relationship with truth. Insisting faith and morality must not be separated, John Paul offers further confirmation of the unacceptability of certain ethical views through reflections on martyrdom.[24] This teaching seems intransigent to some but is part of the church's teaching mission in the world and arises out of compassion and love for the person, his or her true good and genuine freedom. Individuals and societies are served by faithfulness here because "only by obedience to universal moral norms does man find full confirmation of his personal uniqueness and the possibility of authentic moral growth" (§96). Illustrating this with examples, the pope warns of the danger, after the fall of communism, of "*an alliance between democracy and ethical relativism*" (§101).

Although keeping the commandments is difficult, God's grace and mercy make it possible. Rather than revising moral norms in the face of our weakness, we are to see "*the proclamation and presentation of morality*" (§107) as part of evangelization. The encyclical therefore closes by describing the specific calling of moral theologians and bishops and the role of the Magisterium.

Conclusion. The conclusion focuses on Mary as Mother of God and Mother of Mercy but within the clear statement that "Christian morality consists, in the simplicity of the Gospel, in *following Jesus Christ,* in abandoning oneself to him, in letting oneself be transformed by his grace and renewed by his mercy" (§119). Thus for man "only the Cross and the glory of the Risen Christ can grant peace to his conscience and salvation to his life" (§120).

---

[24]"The love of God entails the obligation to respect his commandments, even in the most dire of circumstances, and the refusal to betray those commandments, even for the sake of saving one's own life" (ibid., §91).

Some Evangelical Reflections

The encyclical presents such a rich moral theology that it is very difficult to do it justice. The task of offering an evangelical appreciation and evaluation is further complicated by the sad fact that moral theology, and particularly an evangelical methodology in ethics, has not been a great evangelical strength. Many subjects could be discussed, but what follows examines five prominent areas in the encyclical which address issues where evangelicals will both welcome much of the pope's teaching and also raise some serious concerns.

Scripture, gospel and moral theology. One of evangelicalism's hallmarks is its focus on Scripture. This is indisputably also one of the encyclical's hallmarks. As the Old Testament scholar Walter Moberly has noted, "one of the striking aspects of the encyclical is the extent to which appeal to Scripture is made. This is the case both at the level of reference to the scriptural text in support of specific points, and, most importantly, at a conceptual level."[25] William Spohn writes that no papal document in history has "relied as much on Scripture as the source of its argument."[26] Table 8.1 demonstrates this, showing that there are 274 distinct passages of Scripture cited from 35 books of the Bible with 167 explicit quotations within the text and another 165 citations without quotation.[27]

Charles Curran is clearly right to assert that "both implicitly and explicitly, John Paul II emphasizes Scripture as a primary source for moral theology" and that "*Veritatis splendor* heavily relies on scripture to develop its message."[28]

At various points, John Paul II is clear that Scripture is the authority for his teaching. So he writes that "Sacred Scripture remains the living and fruitful source of the Church's moral doctrine" and that the church has to preserve "what the word of God teaches . . . about moral action, action pleasing to God" (§28, cf. also §§5, 25, 49, 57, 67, 81, 82, 110). Various criticisms can and have been made in relation to some of the ways appeal is made to Scripture.[29] Limits of space mean

---

[25]R. W. L. Moberly, "The Use of Scripture," in *Veritatis splendor: A Response,* ed. Charles Yeats (Norwich: Canterbury Press, 1994), p. 8.

[26]William C. Spohn, "Morality on the Way of Discipleship: The Use of Scripture in *Veritatis splendor,*" in *Veritatis splendor: American Responses,* ed. Michael E. Allsopp and John J. O'Keefe (Lanham, Md.: Sheed & Ward, 1995), p. 91.

[27]Data collated from index of scriptural references by Leon Derckx in *The Splendor of Accuracy: An Examination of the Assertions Made by Veritatis splendor,* ed. Joe Selling and Jan Jans (Kampen: Kok Pharos, 1994), pp. 174-81. There are also references to Sirach and Wisdom from the Apocrypha.

[28]Curran, *Moral Theology,* pp. 45, 51.

[29]In addition to the authors cited in previous notes, see also Karl P. Donfried, "The Use of Scripture in *Veritatis splendor,*" in *Ecumenical Ventures in Ethics,* ed. Reinhard Hütter and Theodor Dieter (Grand Rapids: Eerdmans, 1998), pp. 38-49.

Table 8.1. Scriptural Citations in *Veritatis splendor*

Book	Distinct biblical passages referenced	Specific quotations	Citations without quotation
Gen	7	7	2
Ex	9	3	6
Lev	2	2	1
Deut	5	2	3
Josh	1	0	1
Ps	12	10	4
Prov	1	0	1
Is	3	2	1
Jer	3	0	3
Ezek	2	0	2
Dan	1	1	0
Joel	1	0	1
Amos	1	0	1
Mic	1	0	2
OT—14 books	49	27	28
Mt	45	40	20
Mk	9	6	5
Lk	17	7	11
Jn	37	22	25
Acts	8	0	8
Rom	25	17	18
1 Cor	11	6	6
2 Cor	7	4	3
Gal	9	7	10
Eph	15	9	7
Col	4	3	3
1 Thess	3	0	3
1 Tim	4	4	0
2 Tim	5	4	2
Tit	2	0	2
Philem	1	1	0
Heb	3	1	2
Jas	3	1	2
1 Pet	3	1	2
1 Jn	9	7	3
Rev	5	0	5
NT—21 books	225	140	137
Bible—35 books	274	167	165

these cannot be examined here, but they generally reflect a more liberal and critical attitude to Scripture; evangelicals will broadly welcome the encyclical's hermeneutic, particularly when it is contrasted with much of the Roman Catholic moral tradition, by which Scripture was often sidelined.

The danger—to which some evangelicals succumb—is that Scripture can be regularly cited as a guide for living but the ethic as a whole may not be a thoroughly theological and gospel ethic. The best recent evangelical contribution to moral theology opens with these words: "The foundations of Christian ethics must be evangelical foundations; or, to put it simply, Christian ethics must arise from the gospel of Jesus Christ. Otherwise it could not be *Christian* ethics."[30] Although evangelicals will still have questions about aspects of the gospel underlying the encyclical, one of its clear strengths is its insistence that faith and life, gospel and ethics must be connected. The pope writes of the "*serious and destructive dichotomy, that which separates faith from morality,*" and he stresses that Christian faith is "a new and original criterion for thinking and acting in personal, family and social life" (§88). Even more encouraging is the strong emphasis—despite the encyclical's emphasis on law—on grace and the fact that it is "the Gospel which reveals the full truth about man and his moral journey, and thus enlightens and admonishes sinners" (§112). The pope clearly states the priority of divine action both in revelation—"*what man is and what he must do becomes clear as soon as God reveals himself*" (§10)—and in redemption—"*the moral life presents itself as the response* due to the many gratuitous initiatives taken by God out of love for man" (§10). Here, in contrast to much in the tradition of Roman Catholic ethics, the "pope puts theology back into moral theology"[31] and, in a real sense, shows himself to be evangelical.[32]

There is, therefore, much for evangelicals to welcome here, although some might perhaps wish the encyclical had drawn out more explicitly the structure of the biblical narrative or drama. This is clearly implicit in the letter's various discussions of creation, sin, Israel, Christ, the Spirit and new creation but does not provide a clear framework for the encyclical's biblical hermeneutic.[33]

---

[30]Oliver O'Donovan, *Resurrection and Moral Order* (Grand Rapids: Eerdmans, 1986), p. 11.

[31]This is the title of Hauerwas's essay in *Studies in Christian Ethics* 7, no. 2 (1994): 16-18.

[32]L. Gregory Jones writes, "The Pope shows his true evangelical colours in not only mentioning the 'G-word' in polite company, but actually asserting that this character identified as God ought to be central to discussions about how people ought to live. How dare he!" (*First Things* 40 [January 1994]) <http://www.firstthings.com/article.php3?id_article=4405&var_recherche=L.+Gregory+Jones#jones>.

[33]For a recent good example of this method, see Craig G. Bartholomew and Michael W. Goheen, *The Drama of Scripture: Finding Our Place in the Biblical Story* (Grand Rapids: Baker, 2004).

Finally, the encyclical is, fundamentally, Christ-centred in its theology, offering an ethic whose heart is following Jesus and living out his self-giving love (e.g., §§19, 20). In the words of Hauerwas, "Happily John Paul II writes as a theologian profoundly displaying the difference Christ should make for how Christians live as well as how moral theologians think."[34] Nevertheless, other emphases and serious questions have been raised about how to interpret the encyclical as a whole in relation to this claimed Christ-centeredness. Attention has been drawn to the fact we first meet Christ as moral teacher and that this didactic focus perhaps distorts the encyclical's vision. This must, however, be put alongside the equally strong emphasis on Christ crucified, especially in chapter three. Similarly, although, as some have argued, Christ is more central in the first and third chapters, even in the second chapter the technical arguments about freedom, law and intrinsically evil acts seek to be based on the explicit teaching of Christ and on Christ being the fulfillment of the law.

The role of law. One area which has aroused much comment from various quarters is the encyclical's treatment of law.[35] The significance of law is evident to even a casual reader and is demonstrated by the fact that the word *law* appears no less than 237 times in the letter while *commandments* occurs 97 times.[36] For many readers this framework stands in tension with the emphasis on the gospel and the person of Jesus Christ, and it is clear this focus is closely correlated with the letter's concern to reaffirm "*the universality and immutability of the moral commandments,* particularly those which prohibit always and without exception *intrinsically evil acts*" (§115; cf. §4). This is a concern most evangelicals would share, especially in the face of growing moral relativism and the challenges still presented by forms of situation ethics within many Protestant churches. Evangelicals will also be encouraged that the pope does not distinguish between commands (or precepts) and counsels. Nor does he emphasize the importance of works of supererogation, which those in the tradition of the Reformers have often criticized in Catholic moral teaching[37] and which as a framework sometimes claimed biblical warrant from the gospel narrative of the rich ruler.

---

[34]Hauerwas, "Pope Puts Theology Back," p. 16.

[35]A particularly helpful discussion of the whole subject is that of Reinhard Hütter, "'God's Law' in *Veritatis splendor:* Sic et Non," in *Ecumenical Ventures in Ethics,* ed. Reinhard Hütter and Theodor Dieter (Grand Rapids: Eerdmans, 1998), pp. 84-114.

[36]Data from John Paul II, *Veritatis splendor,* Libreria Editrice Vaticana, concordance <http://www.vatican.va/edocs/ENG0222/P.HTM>. The only theological terms used more often are *God* (359), *man* (319), *moral* (310) and *good* (243). Other key terms are less frequent: *church* (218), *life* (209), *freedom* (194), *human* (191), *truth* (184), *Christ* (149), *love* (146), *Jesus* (140) and *person* (112).

[37]See, for example, article 14 of the Church of England's Thirty-Nine Articles.

In relation to the discussion of law, one of the letter's problematic elements is that the term is used to cover a variety of phenomena without being given clear definition and without always acknowledging important differences between the uses. In particular, the opening chapter concentrates on the Law in the sense of the Torah and particularly the Decalogue (§§8-11), but there is then introduced "the law which is inscribed in his heart" (§12) with reference to Romans 2:15. This "natural law" is increasingly significant in the argument, often under the phrase "moral law," a phrase that first appears in the second chapter—§32—and becomes increasingly prominent, embracing natural law and the biblical divine law (Old Law and New Law). Although these distinctions are discussed, shaped by Aquinas's classic discussion (§44),[38] they are ultimately all subsumed under the general category of "(moral) law."

Much evangelical ethics has a prominent place for law and commandments, and the pope's challenging of false views of law, and particularly of its relationship to freedom, are a major contribution to Christian moral theology that must be welcomed. There are, however, two areas where concerns must be raised. First, by focusing on Jesus' words to the rich man concerning the commandments, he fails to do justice both to Jesus' more critical sayings and practice in relation to the law as recorded in the gospels and to Paul's critique of the Law.[39] In the light of these other biblical emphases, such a strong emphasis on moral law in the encyclical must be questioned. Second, his shift from the Law to "moral law" and particularly "natural law" needs more care and nuance. John Paul's emphasis on the Bible—particularly on biblical commandments (e.g., §§25-26)—is welcome. However, there is the danger that other rules, claiming the authority of natural law and reason rather than Scripture, will be given equal weight, an issue of concern in a number of concrete areas.

The pope has a welcome and passionate concern that Christian life is not antinomian but that, in the words of Augustine (quoted in §23), "The law was given that grace might be sought; and grace was given, that the law might be fulfilled." Similarly, his argument (most fully in §§35-53) that our freedom is found in relation to law, not in opposition to it, is vital in our contemporary context. However, most evangelicals will lack his confidence in (and emphasis on) reason and natural law. This is evident in Oliver O'Donovan's warning that "the Pope . . . speaks out

---

[38]The interpretation of Aquinas here is quite a minefield. Hütter, in "'God's Law' in *Veritatis splendor*," pp. 89-92, notes some of the issues in relation to *Veritatis splendor*'s discussion.

[39]This criticism is raised by, among others, both Donfried, "Use of Scripture," pp. 45-46, and Nicholas Peter Harvey, "Comment on *Veritatis splendor*," *Studies in Christian Ethics* 7, no. 2 (1994): 14-15.

of a species of Christian idealism which understands the rationality of moral law as something grounded in the human mind. He offers, indeed, some startling hostages to the claims of unaided natural reason. . . . What is lacking in contemporary trends in moral thought is a sense of moral order in the world. Can he repair this with a stress on moral order in the mind? I am not sure."[40]

Despite these cautions, the underlying concern for upholding moral norms and moral law against certain trends in Christian and secular thinking is one evangelicals will welcome. Few evangelicals use such phrases as "intrinsically evil acts"[41] or encounter the developed Catholic methodology of proportionalist moral thought. However, most of us have engaged with similar approaches in church and society that develop a technical, calculating understanding of moral decision making. These seek to evaluate consequences, relativize traditional moral teachings and elaborate exceptions to biblical rules in the name of wider biblically based moral values such as love or liberation or justice. In responding to these we have much to learn from this encyclical.

Evangelicals will, for reasons already noted in relation to natural law, part company with some specific contents of Roman Catholic teaching on what constitute universal moral prohibitions. Nevertheless, in this encyclical they will find much of value in offering a defense of the existence and place of moral absolutes. In particular, the pope relates such prohibitions to a positive vision of the dignity of the human person. They are therefore not simply understood as expressions of the divine will that we must obey. They are correlated with the very nature of human beings as made in God's image and restored in Christ. Some evangelicals can sometimes present moral teaching as simply a matter of Christian obedience to biblically stated divine commands. It is sometimes in reaction against this that the commands are rejected or redefined or adapted in the light of new circumstances. Evangelicalism would profit if it took up the implicit challenge found in the encyclical and began to develop, as part of its moral theology, a biblically based,

---

[40]O'Donovan, "Summons to Reality," p. 44.

[41]For discussion of this category see Bernd Wannenwetsch, "'Intrinsically Evil Acts'; or Why Abortion and Euthanasia Cannot Be Justified," in *Ecumenical Ventures in Ethics,* ed. Reinhard Hütter and Theodor Dieter (Grand Rapids: Eerdmans, 1998), pp. 185-215; Martin Rhonheimer, "Instrinsically Evil Acts and the Moral Viewpoint: Clarifying a Central Teaching of *Veritatis splendor,*" in *Veritatis splendor and the Renewal of Moral Theology,* ed. J. A. DiNoia and Romanus Cessario (Huntington, Ind.: Our Sunday Visitor, 1999); and various writings of Servais Pinckaers, for example, *The Pinckaers Reader,* ed. John Berkman and Craig Steven Titus (Washington D.C.: Catholic University of America Press, 2005), chapt. 11. A critical response is given by Bernard Hoose, "Circumstances, Intentions and Intrinsically Evil Acts," in *The Splendor of Accuracy: An Examination of the Assertions Made by "Veritatis splendor,"* ed. Joe Selling and Jan Jans (Kampen: Kok Pharos, 1994), pp. 136-52.

Christ-centered anthropology that offered a vision of human flourishing within which biblical commandments clearly made sense as serving "to protect the personal dignity and inviolability of man, on whose face is reflected the splendour of God" (§90). Within this, John Paul's emphasis on the importance of humans as a body-soul unity (e.g., §§46-50) and elements of his own carefully articulated theology of the body could help evangelicals as they respond to new challenges in sexual, medical and social ethics.

There is, however, one element of the pope's arguments in relation to law that evangelicals will emphatically reject. This opens up deeper theological questions about the encyclical. In opposing those who question the traditional teaching about "intrinsically evil acts," one concern is to defend the traditional Catholic teaching about mortal and venial sins and the threat that committing mortal sins presents to a person's salvation (§§49, 68-70). This raises a third area for comment.

Works and faith, salvation and morality. One of the fundamental traditional differences between Roman Catholicism and evangelicalism relates to understandings of justification and salvation, particularly divergent accounts in relation to such areas as faith, works, grace and merit. These are inevitably addressed within an encyclical on moral theology, both implicitly and explicitly, in passing and, at times, in some depth.

Positively, there are many statements that illustrate the fruit of wider ecumenical discussions and the dangers of some traditional evangelical caricatures of papal teaching. In numerous places there is an emphasis on the gracious initiative of God's action for us and in us, in Christ and by the Spirit. The opening paragraph of *Veritatis splendor* begins by reminding us that we are "called to salvation through faith in Jesus Christ," while later the pope writes that

> *following Christ is thus the essential and primordial foundation of Christian morality.* . . . This is not a matter only of disposing oneself to hear a teaching and obediently accepting a commandment. More radically, it involves *holding fast to the very person of Jesus,* partaking of his life and his destiny, sharing in his free and loving obedience to the will of the Father. By responding in faith and following the one who is Incarnate Wisdom, the disciple of Jesus truly becomes *a disciple of God.* (§19)

There are, however, other signs that the Vatican's understanding remains one evangelicals will criticize. Two terms signal this—*condition* and *merit.* Jesus is held to propose the commandments as "the way and condition of salvation" (§12) and "the first and indispensable condition for having eternal life" (§17). In fact, "the performance of good acts . . . constitutes the indispensable condition of and path to eternal blessedness" (§72). Part of the gospel's work is also claimed to be to preserve sinners "from the presumption that they can be saved without merit" (§112).

Underlying these statements is an understanding of the importance of our own human actions (strengthened by divine grace) in transforming and perfecting us. This is at the expense of an evangelical emphasis on the finished and perfect work of Christ for us and apart from us. Here the language of perfection takes on a particular role—"Jesus shows that the commandments must not be understood as a minimum limit not to be gone beyond, but rather as a path involving a moral and spiritual journey towards perfection, at the heart of which is love" (§15). The pope refers three times to a statement of Vatican II (including a relatively rare citation of the Apocrypha in the encyclical) in order to claim that "God willed to leave man 'in the power of his own counsel' (cf. Sir 15:14), so that he would seek his Creator of his own accord and would freely arrive at full and blessed perfection by cleaving to God" (§§34, 38, 71). This means that "attaining such perfection means *personally building up that perfection in himself*" and so "in performing morally good acts, man strengthens, develops and consolidates within himself his likeness to God" (§39). The deeper understanding of humans and their relationship to God is clearly stated—"it is precisely through his acts that man attains perfection as man, as one who is called to seek his Creator of his own accord and freely to arrive at full and blessed perfection by cleaving to him" (§71)—while faith "entails and brings to perfection the acceptance and observance of God's commandments" (§89).

The consequence of this understanding of the significance of human acts in our perfection is related to the discussion of intrinsically evil acts and mortal sin by drawing specifically on Reformation disagreements so as to reaffirm that "as the Council of Trent teaches, 'the grace of justification once received is lost not only by apostasy, by which faith itself is lost, but also by any other mortal sin'" (§68).[42]

This traditional Catholic concern for the effect of human actions on the agent, including their standing before God, lies at the heart of the critique of "fundamental option." John Paul's central criticism is that, in some Catholic moral theologians' recent teaching, specific evil acts cannot alter the status of the believer which is given and secured by their "fundamental choice" for God. Although there are clearly differences between these formulations in Catholic ethics and the Reformers' gospel, there are also many similarities. Saarinen (from the Evangelical Lutheran Church of Finland) therefore comments that "the Council of Trent's *Decree*

[42]Trent is later quoted to the effect that "no one, however much justified, ought to consider himself exempt from the observance of the commandments, nor should he employ that rash statement, forbidden by the Fathers under anathema, that the commandments of God are impossible of observance by one who is justified" (*Veritatis splendor*, §102).

on Justification . . . is quoted throughout *Veritatis Splendor* against those who downplay the importance of external manifestation of moral life. In this way the theology of the Reformation becomes connected with the condemned views of 'certain theologians' who themselves are not Lutherans but liberal Roman Catholics."[43] The seriousness of this from an evangelical perspective is clear in the following passage from the discussion of fundamental option:

> According to the logic of the positions mentioned above, an individual could, by virtue of a fundamental option, remain faithful to God independently of whether or not certain of his choices and his acts are in conformity with specific moral norms or rules. By virtue of a primordial option for charity, that individual could continue to be morally good, persevere in God's grace and attain salvation, even if certain of his specific kinds of behaviour were deliberately and gravely contrary to God's commandments as set forth by the Church.
>
> In point of fact, man does not suffer perdition only by being unfaithful to that fundamental option whereby he has made "a free self-commitment to God." With every freely committed mortal sin, he offends God as the giver of the law and as a result becomes guilty with regard to the entire law (cf. Jas 2:8-11); even if he perseveres in faith, he loses "sanctifying grace," "charity" and "eternal happiness." (§68)

Although not directed at an evangelical understanding of justification by faith alone, apart from works, this rejection clearly also takes aim at that doctrine. Here the evangelical can only in turn reject the pope's stance as one which "simply leaves no room for a Reformation understanding of faith as that *fiducia* which, clinging to Christ, makes us right with God even in our sin."[44]

Evangelical moral theology must, of course, avoid the error of so stressing justification by faith in Christ (apart from any merit of our own) that the seriousness of sin and the need for personal repentance and renewal are downplayed or lost. However, in avoiding these dangers it is necessary clearly to uphold our justification in Christ by faith apart from works and the truth that we always, as believers in Christ, remain *simul justus et peccator.*[45] It is here that the encyclical, for all its

[43]Risto Saarinen, "Protestant Undertones, Averrosit Overtones? The Concept of Nature in *Veritatis splendor,*" in *Ecumenical Ventures in Ethics,* ed. Reinhard Hütter and Theodor Dieter (Grand Rapids: Eerdmans, 1998), p. 119.

[44]Meilaender, "Grace, Justification Through Faith, and Sin," p. 73.

[45]Oliver O'Donovan notes that the Thirty-Nine Articles, "deny *independence* to the individual believer over against what God has done for him in Christ. . . . The relationship between the believer and the one sinless representative of mankind is a relationship of complete dependence. In him we are acceptable and accepted; apart from him we are not acceptable and are not accepted. This relationship is the beginning and end of our justification. It does not change. At all times in our lives . . . we are dependent upon him as sinners upon the sinless one" (*On the 39 Articles* [Carlisle: Paternoster, 1986], p. 80).

strengths, reveals how far it still is from evangelical faith.

The church. Another area where evangelicals must offer criticism (again joined, paradoxically, by many liberal Catholics!) is the encyclical's vision of the church's authority. This is, like justification, another wider and fundamental difference between evangelicalism and Roman Catholicism, and the encyclical's strong emphasis on the Magisterium's teaching and disciplining authority inevitably stands out.

Positively, there are clear and specific statements that tie the Magisterium to Scripture—it is to "'reverently preserve and faithfully expound' the word of God" (§29) and proclaim the commandments of God (§110). There is also a very welcome sense that moral theology is not a detached academic discipline accountable to the methods and politics of the academy but rather, like all theology, an ecclesial task within and serving the community of faith.

Nevertheless, evangelicals will continue to have problems with the ecclesiology found here. First, church tradition continues to be treated as part of the word of God and, along with reason, to play an important role in shaping the authoritative teaching and witness of the Magisterium. Second, the Magisterium's special and unique status is also clearly and strongly reaffirmed through words of Vatican II: "the task of authentically interpreting the word of God, whether in its written form or in that of Tradition, has been entrusted only to those charged with the Church's living Magisterium, whose authority is exercised in the name of Jesus Christ" (quoted in §27). The power and significance of this is most evident in relation to the formation of the believer's conscience[46] and when the pope reminds moral theologians that they "are to set forth the Church's teaching and to give, in the exercise of their ministry, the example of a loyal assent, both internal and external, to the Magisterium's teaching in the areas of both dogma and morality" (§110).

From an evangelical perspective this grants undue and excessive authority to a particular human institution with the danger that it, rather than the Word of God and the Spirit of God, directs and controls the life of the people of God. This concern is only increased when the often strongly negative and critical tone of the encyclical raises the concern that, in the words of an Anglican observer, "the Magisterium expects to be only the subject of prophecy, and never its object."[47]

---

[46]John Paul writes that "in proclaiming the commandments of God and the charity of Christ, the Church's Magisterium also teaches the faithful specific particular precepts and requires that they consider them in conscience as morally binding" (*Veritatis splendor,* §110, cf. §64).

[47]Nigel Biggar, "*Veritatis splendor,*" *Studies in Christian Ethics* 7, no. 2 (1994): 13. Oliver O'Donovan, another evangelical Anglican ethicist, notes that "of course, an Anglican moral theologian does not expect to agree with what the Vatican says about the teaching authority; but I cannot find anything significantly new to choke on here" ("Summons to Reality," p. 45).

Although these are important criticisms, evangelicalism must also recognize its own ecclesiology (in as much as it can, given its interdenominational identity, be said to have one) is challenged by the positive benefits arising from an authoritative Magisterium issuing an encyclical such as this one. Faced with the reality of a post-Christian society, the danger in evangelicalism is that its weak ecclesiology (and at times excessive individualism) will prevent the creation and nurturing of a united, faithful and distinctive Christian moral witness as salt and light in the contemporary world. Instead it risks offering an increasingly divided and compromised moral witness. This is perhaps nowhere more evident than in most Protestant denominations—not least Anglicanism's current debates over sexuality. Biggar, in speaking of the Magisterium as the subject of prophecy, highlights one of the undoubted gifts to the wider church that can come from Rome and perhaps explains why, as O'Donovan writes in the final sentence of his response to the encyclical, "if there is a place for a Petrine office in the Church (a matter on which I keep an open mind), surely this encyclical is a creditable example of the kind of service it may render."[48]

This leads to the concluding more positive area of comment.

The prophetic voice on freedom and truth. The central issue for John Paul II in this encyclical is the relationship between freedom and truth. Here, although clearly concerned about tendencies in Catholic moral theology, his real concern and his greatest contribution is much deeper:

> His concern with ecclesial authority is rooted in a deeper concern over the rising individualism in contemporary society. He questions whether the individual's conscience—and its criteria of "sincerity, authenticity, and 'being at peace with oneself'"—should be the supreme tribunal of moral judgment (32). He questions the loss of an idea of universal and absolute truth.[49]

In the years since the encyclical appeared, its fundamental diagnosis of our society's ills has proved accurate, though sadly the disease continues to spread, often now appearing in various forms under the label of postmodernism.

Whatever evangelicals' disagreements with elements of the encyclical, and despite the fact that a distinctively evangelical response would look significantly different in a number of places, John Paul II's determination to offer a biblically shaped understanding of human freedom and its relationship to God's truth—in

---

[48] O'Donovan, "Summons to Reality," p. 45.

[49] Lois Malcolm, "Freedom and Truth in *Veritatis splendor* and the Meaning of Theonomy," in *Ecumenical Ventures in Ethics*, ed. Reinhard Hütter and Theodor Dieter (Grand Rapids: Eerdmans, 1998), p. 159.

his ordering of creation and his self-revelation, supremely in Christ—produces much rich fruit for those who are concerned, like him, to understand and to evangelize the contemporary Western world. The encyclical is prophetic in its insistence that "autonomy" is a false god. We can only welcome its unmasking of the dangers in believing we are free to determine for ourselves what is good and evil and are called to construct our world creatively as we wish in the pursuit of goods and values we choose. Pope John Paul II offers an alternative vision in which, as humans liberated by Christ and empowered by his Spirit, we must act into and shape the world as creatures who respond to God's truth, to the Creator's giving of order to his creation, and then to the special calling and dignity of all men and women made in God's image. In giving us this encyclical, he left perhaps his most significant legacy, not just for evangelicals but for the whole Christian church as it faces the challenges of the twenty-first century.

PART THREE

Witnessing to Truthful Practice

9

EVANGELIUM VITAE

John Paul II Meets Francis Schaeffer

Nancy R. Pearcey

INTRODUCTION

Should babies have to earn the right to live?[1] If so, where do we draw the line in deciding who qualifies? "It was strongly suggested that we consider abortion after they found our baby had a club foot," said David Wildgrove, who lives in England. He was appalled, knowing that the birth defect is readily corrected, even without surgery. (Splints and casts are used to set the foot in the correct position.) Famous people born with club foot include the poet Lord Byron, actor Dudley Moore and figure skater Kristi Yamaguchi, winner of a 1992 Olympic gold medal. Yet a 2006 study found that in England today, babies with club foot are frequently aborted.

Wildgrove's son was not one of them, however: "We resisted, the problem was treated, and he now runs around and plays football with everyone else."[2]

In *Evangelium vitae,* or the Gospel of Life, John Paul II warns of an "extraordinary increase and gravity of threats"[3] to life in our day. In addition to the ancient scourges of poverty, hunger and war, modern societies confront "new forms of attacks on the dignity of the human being," arising from the application of science

---

[1]I would like to thank the following people for commenting on earlier drafts of this chapter: Jacob Ellens, Joel Garver, Patrick Lee, J. Richard Pearcey, J. Brian Pitts, Alexander R. Pruss and Albert M. Wolters.

[2]Lois Rogers, "Babies with Club Feet Aborted," *The Sunday Times,* May 28, 2006.

[3]John Paul II, *Evangelium vitae . . . on the Value and Inviolability of Human Life,* Libreria Editrice Vaticana (March 25, 1995), §3 <http://www.vatican.va/holy_father/john_paul_ii/encyclicals/documents/hf_jp-ii_enc_25031995_evangelium-vitae_en.html>.

and technology, such as abortion and embryo research. These "crimes against life" have taken on an "even more sinister character" (*Evangelium vitae,* §4)[4] precisely because they are often regarded not as tragedies but as the exercise of individual rights and freedoms. Thus, "paradoxically," the pontiff writes, what were once crimes now "assume the nature of 'rights,' to the point that the State is called upon to give them legal recognition and to make them available through the free services of health-care personnel" (§11).

In the past, practices like abortion were regarded as extreme measures to which people might be driven by crushing poverty or abandonment (the "hard cases"). But now these same practices have been elevated into "legitimate expressions of individual freedom" (§18). Moreover, they are vigorously promoted around the globe by the richest and most powerful nations, which are "haunted" by the specter of demographic growth among the "most prolific and poorer peoples" (§16). Thus many of the most serious perils to human life are "scientifically and systematically programmed threats" (§17) legitimized by the dominant worldviews of the day and carried out under impeccable legal and medical auspices.

These developments are all the more ironic in an age enamored with human rights—an age marked by "a growing moral sensitivity, more alert to acknowledging the value and dignity of every individual as a human being, without any distinction of race, nationality, religion, political opinion or social class." For at the same time, "these noble proclamations are unfortunately contradicted by a tragic repudiation of them in practice" through unprecedented attacks on the elderly, the weak and the newly conceived. These attacks pose a serious threat to the entire culture of human rights—"a threat capable, in the end, of jeopardizing the very meaning of democratic coexistence" (§18).

What is the best strategy for meeting this threat? John Paul identifies several causal factors that urgently require a response, including secularism, materialism and moral relativism. What may be most distinctive about his diagnosis, however—and of greatest interest to evangelicals—is that he locates the decisive turning point in a new definition of the human person (philosophical anthropology). Practices like abortion and euthanasia are justified by a radical mind/body dualism that identifies moral worth solely with mental abilities such as self-awareness and consciousness, while denigrating the human body to the level of raw material that can be readily tinkered with or simply disposed of.

It may seem surprising to say that Western society denigrates the physical body,

---

[4]Unless otherwise noted, in-text citations to *Evangelium vitae* will be identified by section number only.

given that it places a ridiculously high value on physical health and pleasure. But as we will see, John Paul is absolutely right. Indeed, the same mind/body dualism is central not only to morality but also to contemporary science and philosophy. Let's reverse the order and begin by surveying this broader scientific context, which will then equip us to dissect the most contentious moral debates of our day. Finally, we will ask what were the philosophical trends that inspired John Paul to make such a surprising diagnosis.

In the process, we will discover that the same trends inspired Protestant philosophers like Herman Dooyeweerd, and those influenced by him such as Francis Schaeffer. Perhaps this convergence explains why it was John Paul and Schaeffer who spearheaded awareness of the life issues among evangelicals in the first place. As Baptist theologian Timothy George notes, "it was the pope and Francis Schaeffer who got evangelicals on board the pro-life concern."[5] What these two leaders grasped was a crucial shift in the underlying view of the human person—a shift that would create a domino effect from abortion to euthanasia, infanticide, and genetic engineering. Let's find out what gave them both such prophetic insight.

Oh, Let Us Love Irrationally

Since antiquity, most cultures have assumed that a human being is an integrated unity of both physical and spiritual elements. What is novel about our own day is that these two elements have been split apart and redefined in ways that render them outright contradictory. On one hand, the human *body* is treated as nothing but a complex mechanism, in accord with a naturalistic conception of science. On the other hand, the human *person* is defined in terms of ungrounded choice and autonomy, in accord with a postmodern conception of the self. Logically, these two conceptions are irreconcilable, yet they interact in a deadly dualism to shape contemporary debates over abortion, euthanasia, sexuality and the other life issues.

Let's start by uncovering the roots of this dualism in contemporary science—or, more accurately, in *scientism*, the philosophy that science is the sole source of truth. In the field of cognitive science today, most researchers work within a nat-

---

[5]"Pope Gave Evangelicals the Moral Impetus We Didn't Have," *Christianity Today*, interview with Timothy George by Collin Hansen (April 6, 2005) <http://www.ctlibrary.com/ct/2005/aprilweb-only/32.0.html>. George points out that even after the Supreme Court's 1973 *Roe v. Wade* abortion decision, the Southern Baptist Convention passed resolutions supporting the pro-abortion point of view. For a history of resolutions by the SBC on abortion, see <http://www.johnstonsarchive.net/baptist/sbcabres.html>.

uralistic paradigm, which treats the human being as merely a complex mechanism within a closed nexus of cause and effect. For example, in *How the Mind Works,* Stephen Pinker of Harvard writes that when working in the laboratory, he adopts "the mechanistic stance," viewing people as "robots," and the brain as nothing more than a complex data processing machine.

Paradoxically, however, Pinker acknowledges that the same "mechanistic stance" cannot be applied outside the lab to ordinary life. "When those discussions wind down for the day," he writes, "we go back to talking about each other as free and dignified human beings."[6] In other words, when he goes home to his family and friends, the naturalistic paradigm does not work. In everyday experience, we cannot treat people as machines or robots. In that context, Pinker admits, we are forced to acknowledge the reality of moral freedom and human dignity—*even though these concepts have no basis within his own intellectual system.*

The same paradox is expressed by Rodney Brooks of the Massachusetts Institute of Technology. In *Flesh and Machines,* Brooks acknowledges that he operates "on a dual nature" in his behavior, even maintaining "two sets of inconsistent beliefs." On one hand, he insists that a human being is nothing but an automaton—"a big bag of skin full of biomolecules" interacting by the laws of physics and chemistry. Granted, it is not easy, to think of people as mere robots, he writes. Nonetheless, "when I look at my children, I can, when I force myself, . . . see that they are machines."

Does Brooks actually treat his children like machines, though? Of course not. "That is not how I treat them. . . . They have my unconditional love, the furthest one might be able to get from rational analysis."[7] Just so—if what counts as rational is a naturalistic worldview in which people are automatons, then love *is* irrational. Like moral freedom, it cannot be accounted for within the prevailing worldview in science.

The contradiction is stated most starkly by Marvin Minsky, also of the Massachusetts Institute of Technology. In *The Society of Mind* he writes, "The physical world provides no room for freedom of will." Yet "that concept is essential to our models of the mental realm. . . . [And so] we're virtually forced to maintain that belief, *even though we know it's false.*"[8] Here is postmodern irony at its most acute. These leading scientists are promoting scientific naturalism, yet they acknowledge that in actual lived experience they are compelled to live *as if* concepts of freedom

---

[6]Steven Pinker, *How the Mind Works* (New York: Norton, 1997), p. 56.
[7]Rodney Brooks, *Flesh and Machines* (New York: Pantheon, 2002), p. 174.
[8]Marvin Minsky, *The Society of Mind* (New York: Simon and Schuster, 1985), p. 307, emphasis added.

and responsibility were true—all the while "knowing" that they are actually false, according to their own naturalistic worldview.

How can people live with such clashing contradictions? If we think of a worldview as a mental map to guide us in navigating reality, then Christianity provides the only map "big" enough to cover all of human experience. Every other map is too "small." Materialism or naturalism produces a map that covers only what is material or natural—while insisting that anything not found within its own cramped map is not real. But since people actually are created in God's image and live in God's world, at some point they will sense a contradiction between their limited map and their lived experience.

As science journalist John Horgan puts it, based on scientific naturalism, there is no basis even for the concept of a self: "The concept of a unified self, which is a necessary precondition for free will, is itself an illusion." And yet, "no matter what my intellect decides, I'm compelled to believe in free will."[9] Translation: When a map is too small to account for all of human experience, then people are "compelled to believe" in concepts that their own worldview cannot explain.[10]

IS THIS MY FATHER'S WORLD?

In a society dominated by science, it is not surprising that this same contradiction spills over from science into ethics, where it intertwines in a strange and destructive dialectic to create what *Evangelium vitae* calls "the culture of death."

Prior to the Enlightenment, nature was regarded as God's creation, imbued with God's purposes—a *teleological* view of nature. The word comes from the Greek *telos,* which means a thing's purpose or goal or perfect state. For human beings, that perfect state is the image of God. Genesis tells us that was the way humanity was originally created, and it provides the ideal or goal we should all strive to reach. Morality is simply the map telling us how to get there, the directions for reaching the goal, the instruction manual for becoming the person God originally intended us to be.

The most important source of instructions is, of course, God's revelation in Scripture. But another source is nature. We can "read" signs that indicate God's original purpose, traces of God's image that remain even in a fallen world. For example, the biological correspondence between male and female was part of the

---

[9]John Horgan, "More Than Good Intentions: Holding Fast to Faith in Free Will," *The New York Times,* December 31, 2002.

[10]I have developed this form of apologetics argument more fully in *Total Truth: Liberating Christianity from Its Cultural Captivity* (Wheaton, Ill.: Crossway, 2005), pp. 107-11, 217-21, 313-21 and appendix 4.

original creation that God pronounced "very good"—morally good—and therefore it provides a reference point for morality.

Beginning in the Enlightenment, however, Western thought began a gradual process of secularization. Eventually, nature was no longer seen as God's creation, which meant it no longer possessed any signs of purpose or moral goodness—and therefore it no longer provided a basis for moral truths. As philosopher Charles Taylor writes, "the cosmos is no longer seen as the embodiment of meaningful order which can define the good for us."[11] Instead of revealing *God's* will, nature became a morally neutral realm upon which humans may impose *their* will, manipulating it to achieve their own desires and preferences. Nature became a formless, directionless substance that may be directed toward any goals the autonomous self may choose.

In short, a mechanistic cosmos no longer reveals anything about the moral *ends* intended for our lives, but is reduced to a realm of sheer *means* to serve whatever ends we prefer. We can call this view liberalism, employing a definition by the self-described liberal philosopher Peter Berkowitz: "Each generation of liberal thinkers" he says, takes various "dimensions of life previously regarded as fixed by nature" and seeks to show that they are actually "subject to human will and remaking."[12] That is, nature no longer has an intrinsic teleology that we are morally obligated to respect. Instead it is an accidental configuration of matter open to unlimited human control and manipulation. The concept of truth itself was divided into the now-familiar fact/value dichotomy, where "facts" describe the objective world (naturalism) while "values" are subjective preferences imposed on value-free facts (postmodernism).[13]

ARE PEOPLE "PERSONS"?

What did this nonteleological concept of nature mean for morality? Since nature includes the human body, it too was demoted to the level of a mechanism subject to the will of the autonomous self. "With the loss of belief in the spiritual and ethical significance of creation and the human body," explains Roger Lundin of

[11]Charles Taylor, *Sources of the Self: The Making of Modern Identity* (Cambridge, Mass.: Harvard University Press, 1989), pp. 148-49.

[12]Peter Berkowitz, "Rediscovering Liberalism," *The Boston Book Review,* March 1995, p. 12. By using the term *liberal,* we can refer to both secular and religious liberalism.

[13]The impact of the fact/value split is a theme throughout my book *Total Truth.* See also David Schindler, "Biotechnology and the Givenness of the Good: Posing Properly the Moral Question Regarding Human Dignity," *Communio* 31 (Winter 2004), p. 617: "'fact' is now an (empirically-accessed) mechanism whose intelligibility is elicited through human control, while 'value' is the human will's imposition on 'fact' of what is now only nonnaturally 'good'—i.e., 'good' not as given first-intrinsically by nature, but only as posited, instrumentally-arbitrarily, by man."

Wheaton College, these became "essentially amoral mechanisms to be used to whatever private ends we have."[14]

With this background, we have the tools to understand the two-tiered view of the human being (philosophical anthropology) diagnosed by John Paul in *Evangelium vitae.*[15] In scientific naturalism, he writes, the body "is no longer perceived as a properly personal reality" (§23) but as part of subpersonal nature. This allows the postmodern self to treat it as a form of "property, completely subject to his control and manipulation" (§22). The self demands absolute freedom, breaking off any "link with the truth" (§19). That is, there is no longer any "truth of creation which must be acknowledged, or a plan of God for life which must be respected" (§22). As a result, "everything is negotiable, everything is open to bargaining: even the first of the fundamental rights, the right to life" (§20).

John Paul is relying here on an earlier discussion in *Veritatis splendor* (The Splendor of Truth), in which he described an "opposition," a "dialectic, if not an absolute conflict" (§46) in modern thought between the concepts of nature and freedom. When nature is defined as "devoid of any meaning and moral values" (§48), then it is "reduced to raw material for human activity" (§46). That is, nature is no longer *intrinsically* good, revealing the goodness of its Creator, but only *instrumentally* good as it is used to achieve human purposes. Applied to the human being, this nature/freedom dichotomy becomes "a division within man himself." Our identity as persons is equated with the freely choosing self, while the body becomes "extrinsic to the person," a subpersonal possession under our control that can be manipulated to serve our desires (§48).

The same nature/freedom dichotomy was diagnosed by Dooyeweerd, and later illustrated by Schaeffer using the image of two stories in a building.[16] Adapting

---

[14]Roger Lundin, *The Culture of Interpretation: Christian Faith and the Postmodern World* (Grand Rapids: Eerdmans, 1993), p. 102.

[15]John Paul's critique of the contemporary dualistic anthropology is explained in depth by William E. May in a number of articles that can be accessed on his website, <http://www.christendom-awake.org/pages/may/may.html>, especially "Philosophical Anthropology and *Evangelium vitae.*" A similar critique is developed by Patrick Lee in several articles on his website, <http://www2.franciscan.edu/plee/>, especially "The Pro-Life Argument from Substantial Identity," Saint Anselm's College, November 14, 2002. See also Lee's book, *Abortion and Unborn Human Life* (Washington, D.C.: Catholic University of America Press, 1996).

[16]Schaeffer offers critiques of the two-story concept of truth in *Escape from Reason* and *The God Who Is There,* in *The Complete Works of Francis A. Schaeffer,* vol. 1 (Westchester, Ill.: Crossway, 1982). He was influenced by Herman Dooyeweerd's more scholarly analysis in *Roots of Western Culture: Pagan, Secular, and Christian Options* (Zutphen, Netherlands: J. B. van den Brink, 1959; repr., Toronto: Wedge, 1979); *In the Twilight of Western Thought* (Philadelphia: Presbyterian & Reformed, 1960; repr., Nutley, N.J.: Craig, 1972); and his four-volume set *A New Critique of Theoretical Thought,* trans. David H.

that image, we might visualize the contemporary liberal anthropology as illustrated in figure 9.1. Naturalism has demoted the body to a mere physical organism (the "lower story"), controlled by the autonomous self of postmodernism (the "upper story") making ungrounded choices.

FREEDOM

The Self as Autonomous (Postmodernism)

NATURE

The Body as Machine (Naturalism)

Figure 9.1. Liberal view of the human being

THE NEW ABORTION DEBATE

This radical body/self dualism shapes the current form of the abortion debate. In the past, pro-choice arguments simply denied that the fetus is human.[17] ("It's just a blob of tissue.") As a result, pro-life arguments sought to demonstrate that the fetus really is fully human.

Today, however, pro-choice ethicists have taken a new tack. Due to research in genetics and DNA, virtually no ethicist denies that the fetus is human. Science has clearly established that at conception a new being comes into existence—a complete, integral individual capable of internally directed development. The fetus is fully human from the start. Nothing essential is added along the way to transform it into a human being. All he or she needs (gender is determined at conception) is nourishment and an appropriate environment. Put simply, in the process of maturation, one does not become *more* of a human being, only a more *developed* one.

As a result, liberal ethicists have shifted tactics. They now agree that the fetus is human—biologically, physiologically, genetically human (in our diagram, the

Freeman (Ontario: Paideia Press, 1984 [Dutch edition 1935]). In his diagnosis of the nature/freedom dichotomy, Dooyeweerd suggests that, historically, the freedom ideal arose first (during the Renaissance), and it was the drive for human autonomy that motivated the development of a mechanistic conception of nature. (If nature is a machine, then we need only uncover its laws in order to master and manipulate it.) Inevitably, however, the mechanistic paradigm was applied to humans as well (through psychological conditioning, social engineering, genetic manipulation, etc.). Thus, paradoxically, the ideal of freedom eventually led to the loss of freedom. See *Roots,* chap. 6.

[17]I am using the term *fetus* in the popular sense to mean the unborn at any stage, not in the technical sense as the last stage in prenatal development (after zygote, blastocyst and embryo).

lower story). But, they argue, mere membership in the human species confers no moral significance; nor does it warrant legal protection. The deciding factor is the point at which fetus becomes a "person," typically defined in terms of acquiring autonomy or self-awareness (upper story). As John Paul puts it, the contemporary approach "recognizes as a subject of rights only the person who enjoys full or at least incipient autonomy." It "tends to *equate personal dignity with the capacity for verbal and explicit,* or at least perceptible, *communication*" (§19, emphasis in original).

For example, during the 2004 presidential election, Democratic nominee John Kerry surprised voters by agreeing that "life begins at conception." How, then, could he support abortion? Because, as he explained in an interview with Peter Jennings, the fetus is "not the form of life that takes *personhood* in the terms we have judged it to be."[18]

Of course, in ordinary conversation, terms like *human being* and *person* refer to the same thing. A wedge was driven between them legally in *Roe* v. *Wade,* when the U.S. Supreme Court argued that a fetus is human but not a person until some later point in development. Consider: If the *human organism* comes into being at one point in time, while the *person* comes into being at a later point in time, then clearly they are two different things. The court implicitly assumed a body/person separation in which the person inhabits the body like a possession or a vehicle—somewhat as we use a car to take us where we want to go.

This two-story view now prevails among liberal bioethicists.[19] "The life of a human organism begins at conception," says Princeton ethicist Peter Singer, but "the life of a person—. . . a being with some level of self-awareness—does not begin so early."[20] Similarly Joseph Fletcher of situation ethics fame says, "What is critical is *personal* status, not merely *human* status." In his view, genetically defective fetuses and newborns are "subpersonal," and therefore fail to qualify for the right to life.[21]

What exactly is this novel concept of personhood? Ethicists cannot seem to agree on how to define it. For some, the defining feature is cognitive function. Mary Anne Warren at San Francisco State University says personhood rests on the capacity for consciousness, reasoning, self-motivated activity, communication and self-

---

[18]*ABC News,* July 22, 1994.

[19]Leon Kass, chairman of the president's Council on Bioethics, says contemporary bioethics "dualistically sets up the concept of 'personhood' *in opposition* to nature and the body" (*Life, Liberty, and the Defense of Dignity: The Challenge for Bioethics* [San Francisco: Encounter Books, 2002], p. 17; see also p. 286).

[20]Peter Singer, "The Sanctity of Life," *Foreign Policy,* September/October 2005.

[21]Joseph Fletcher, *Humanhood: Essays in Biomedical Ethics* (Buffalo, N.Y.: Prometheus, 1979), p. 11.

awareness.[22] Others focus on the desire to live (on the assumption that life is valuable only if someone wants it). Singer says, "I use the term 'person' to refer to a being who is capable of anticipating the future, of having wants and desires for the future."[23]

Because they disagree over the definition of personhood, liberal ethicists also differ over who has a right to life. Nobel laureate James Watson recommends three days of genetic testing before deciding whether a newborn may live. Singer once suggested a cutoff at twenty-eight days, but more recently said personhood remains a "gray" area even at three years of age.[24] With no objective criterion, personhood is reduced to a subjective expression of what each ethicist personally values.

OTHER FISH TO FRY

The rise of "personhood theory" cast a surprising new light on the abortion debate. It is commonly said that pro-life people are motivated by religious teachings about the soul,[25] whereas pro-choice people rely strictly on science. But the truth is precisely the opposite. For pro-lifers, the moral worth of life becomes an issue only *after* the scientific evidence has established that life exists.[26] Biologically, as we have seen, the consensus is that a new individual emerges at conception. That's when the genetic die is cast. From that moment on, the individual merely unfolds the capacities that belong intrinsically to the kind of being it is—whether a human, a horse or a hummingbird. Pro-lifers argue that we have fundamental worth and dignity simply because we are human, not because of abilities that may come and go at various times in our lives.

Of course, people are much *more* than biological organisms. Yet biology gives

[22]Mary Anne Warren, "On the Moral and Legal Status of Abortion," *The Monist* 57, no. 1 (1973): 43-61. On the inadequacy of such functional criteria for personhood, see Francis J. Beckwith, "Abortion, Bioethics, and Personhood," *The Southern Baptist Journal of Theology* 4, no. 1 (2000): 16-25.

[23]From "FAQ" on Peter Singer's website at <http://www.princeton.edu/~psinger/faq.html>. Ironically, Singer broke his own rule when his mother became ill with Alzheimer's disease and lost many of her cognitive abilities. Instead of ending her life, Singer spent considerable sums of money on her care. See Michael Specter in "The Dangerous Philosopher," *The New Yorker,* September 6, 1999, p. 55.

[24]James Watson, "Children from the Laboratory," *Prism: The Socioeconomic Magazine of the American Medical Association* 1, no. 2 (1973): 12-14, 33-34. Singer is quoted in Mark Oppenheimer, "Who Lives? Who Dies? The Utility of Peter Singer," *Christian Century,* July 3, 2002, pp. 24-29.

[25]The National Abortion Action Coalition says abortion laws are "actually a means of enforcing the *religious* concept that the soul is present in the body from the time of conception." Quoted in Pamela Winnick, *A Jealous God: Science's Crusade Against Religion* (Nashville: Thomas Nelson, 2005), p. 18.

[26]For example, biochemist Dianne N. Irving wrote in 1999, "The question as to when a human being begins is strictly a scientific question, and should be answered by human embryologists—not by philosophers, bioethicists, theologians, politicians" ("When do human beings begin? 'Scientific' myths and scientific facts," on the American Bioethics Advisory Commission website <http://www.all.org/abac/dni003.htm>.

an objective, universally detectable marker of human status. By contrast, when disconnected from biology, liberal definitions of personhood float vaguely without any objective criteria. Which abilities or functions "count" in assigning moral worth? And precisely how developed must they be in order to count? The place where any ethicist draws the line rests ultimately on his or her private philosophy and subjective preference.

"The question is not really about life in any biological sense," writes Yale professor Paul Bloom in the *New York Times*. "It is instead asking about the magical moment at which a cluster of cells becomes more than a mere physical thing." And what "magical" force has the power to convert a "mere physical thing" into a person with a dignity so profound that it is morally wrong to kill it? That "is not a question that scientists could ever answer," Bloom says[27]—implying that it cannot be decided by any objective methods. The liberal definition of personhood is perilously subjective and arbitrary.

The tables have been decisively turned on this issue. One might say that when abortion supporters lost the argument on the scientific level—when they could no longer deny that an embryo is human—then they switched tactics to an argument based on personhood, which relocates the issue to the realm of private philosophy.

This became dramatically clear in a confrontation between Robert George of Princeton and the well-known deconstructionist Stanley Fish. In an article, Fish had repeated the typical stereotype that to be pro-life is religious, while to be pro-choice is scientific.[28] When challenged by George at a meeting of the American Political Science Association, Fish acknowledged that he was mistaken. "Professor George is right," Fish announced. "And he is right to correct me." In a paper presented at that meeting, he wrote: "Nowadays, it is pro-lifers who make the scientific question of when the beginning of life occurs the key one . . . , while pro-choicers want to transform the question into a 'metaphysical' or 'religious' one by distinguishing between mere biological life and 'moral life.'"[29]

---

[27]Paul Bloom, "The Duel Between Body and Soul," *New York Times*, September 10, 2004. For a response, see Patrick Lee and Robert P. George, *First Things* 150 (February 2005): 5-7.

[28]"A pro-life advocate sees abortion as a sin against a God who infuses life at the moment of conception," Fish had written; "a pro-choice advocate sees abortion as a decision to be made in accordance with the best scientific opinion as to when the beginning of life, as we know it, occurs." Stanley Fish, "Why We Can't All Just Get Along," *First Things* 60 (February 1996): 18-26.

[29]Fish continued: "Until recently pro-choicers might have cast themselves as defenders of rational science against the forces of ignorance and superstition, but when scientific inquiry started pushing back the moment when significant life (in some sense) begins, they shifted tactics and went elsewhere in search of rhetorical weaponry." See Deborah Danielski, "Deconstructing the Abortion License," *Our Sunday Visitor*, October 25, 1998.

Of course, many religions, including Christianity, do teach that humans have (or are) spiritual souls.[30] But the issue at stake is not the status of the human spirit. One might even say that the real issue is the status of the human *body*. Abortion is defended by arguments that define personhood solely in terms of nonphysical mental capacities like self-consciousness, while denigrating the physical body to the level of the subpersonal. The body is trivialized as a form of raw material that can be manipulated or destroyed subject only to a utilitarian cost-benefit calculus. In an unexpected twist, it is orthodox Christians who are arguing against secular and religious liberals for a high view of the human body.

The early church faced a pagan culture of world-denying philosophies like Gnosticism and neo-Platonism that defined salvation as the liberation of the soul from the prison-house of the body. At that time, the doctrine of the incarnation—that God himself became flesh (Jn 1:14)—was a revolutionary claim. And it still is today. The Apostle's Creed affirms the "resurrection of the body," which means that we are not saved *out of* the material creation, but that ultimate redemption will *include* the material world. The biblical worldview gives the only firm basis for according a high dignity to embodied life.

OUR BODIES, OUR SELVES

The same denigration of the body underlies arguments for euthanasia. Supporters of voluntary euthanasia (assisted suicide) often argue that human dignity consists in the ability to exercise conscious control over our lives. If that control is lost or threatened due to a debilitating disease or injury, then personhood itself (upper story) is threatened—while all that is left is biological life (lower story), which is assumed to have no intrinsic value. We may "intervene creatively to achieve death by choice," writes Daniel Maguire, when "mere biological life is no longer of any value."[31]

What about *involuntary* euthanasia? Well, if individuals are not even capable of giving informed consent, that itself is taken to mean that they are no longer persons—even though they are obviously still human. This dualistic reasoning emerged, for example, in the Terri Schiavo case. The media presented it as a right-to-die case, but Terri was not dying, so that was not the heart of the debate. The core issue was personhood theory.

---

[30]For a good recent discussion, see John Cooper, *Body, Soul, and Life Everlasting: Biblical Anthropology and the Monism-Dualism Debate* (Grand Rapids: Eerdmans, 1989).

[31]Daniel Maguire, "The Freedom to Die," in *New Theology*, ed. Martin Marty and Dean Peerman (New York: Macmillan, 1973), 10:188-89.

In a television debate, bioethicist Bill Allen was asked point blank, "Do you think Terri is a person?" He replied, "No, I do not. I think having awareness is an essential criterion of personhood."[32] Those who favored cutting off Terri's food and water included neurologist Ronald Cranford, who has defended the same policy even for disabled people who are conscious and partly mobile. For example, a California case involved a brain-damaged man who had learned to scoot around in an electric wheelchair (like Stephen Hawking). Nevertheless, Cranford argued that the man's feeding tube should be removed so that he would die.[33]

According to personhood theory, just being part of the human race is not morally relevant. Individuals must earn their personhood by meeting a set of *additional* criteria—the ability to make decisions, exercise self-awareness and so on. Those who do not make the cut are demoted to "non-persons." Many ethicists have begun to argue that non-persons should be used for research and harvesting organs. Wesley Smith calls this a proposal for "human strip-mining"[34] and warns that it would reduce human life to a marketable commodity.

A Half-Baked Beginning

In stem cell research, embryos are created in the laboratory in order to destroy them and extract their stem cells. These are then cultured and maintained until they multiply into the millions for use in experiments. In the two-story paradigm, embryos are merely biological life anyway (lower story), which means there is nothing wrong with killing them to harvest their parts if a utilitarian calculus suggests some benefit to society.

However, if humans are whole beings with intrinsic dignity at all levels, including the body, then destroying an embryo is morally akin to killing an adult. One of the most basic principles of ethics is that people should be treated only as ends, not as means. (As we say in ordinary conversation, it is wrong to *use* people.) The ethical problem with embryonic stem cell research is that human life is created only to be destroyed for extraneous purposes. Even those who are uncertain whether the embryo is a full person find this troubling since it reduces human life to a mere means. There is something deeply dehumanizing, says Smith, about "treating human life—no matter how nascent—as a mere natural

---

[32] *Court TV*, March 24, 2005. See also Wesley J. Smith, "'Human Non-Person': Terri Schiavo, Bioethics, and Our Future," *National Review* Online (March 29, 2005) <http://article.nationalreview.com/?q=NGI4YWVjZjA4NDExMjM1OTQyODE1NjY4MmViMzcwYmM=>.

[33] Wesley J. Smith, "Dehydration Nation," <www.humanlifereview.com/2003_fall/article_2003_fall_smith.php>.

[34] Smith, "'Human Non-Person.'"

resource to be harvested like a soy bean crop."[35]

In the long term, embryo research is also the crucial step toward full-scale genetic engineering. As we saw earlier, the two-tiered view of human nature is internally contradictory. And since reason rejects a contradiction, many seek to resolve it by simply denying the reality of the upper story altogether, reducing humans to material products of their genes. In that reductionistic paradigm, it may seem that the means to improve humanity is simply to adjust our genes. And embryo research is providing the tools.

A movement calling itself "transhumanism" urges us to take charge of human evolution through gene modification. The underlying assumption is that humanity is merely one step in an evolutionary chain of organisms, a chance configuration of cells that will be surpassed by the next evolutionary stage. Thus human life as it exists today has no inherent dignity or value. As philosopher John Gray writes, Darwin taught us that we are animals—and like all animals we are "only currents in the drift of genes."[36] Nick Bostrom of Oxford, a leading transhumanist, says the movement views "human nature as a work-in-progress, a half-baked beginning that we can learn to remold in desirable ways."[37]

Due to Darwinism, says embryologist Brian Goodwin, "we've lost even the concept of human nature." As a result, that "life becomes a set of parts, commodities that can be shifted around."[38] By the same token, of course, parts can also be shifted between humans and animals. If *Homo sapiens* compose merely another herd of animals, no higher and sometimes lower on the cognitive scale than other animals, then there is no ethical barrier to using transgenic technologies (across species) to splice animal DNA into human DNA in attempts to enhance our capabilities and create a "post-human" race.

WHO'S EXCLUSIVE *NOW?*

Transhumanists often speak in euphoric tones, as though technology were provid-

---

[35]Wesley J. Smith, "Welcome to Our Brave New World," interview by John Zmirak, *Godspy—Faith at the Edge* (December 15, 2004) <http://www.godspy.com/reviews/Welcome-to-Our-Brave-New-World-An-Interview-with-Wesley-Smith-by-John-Zmirak.cfm>. There is a crucial distinction between using adult stem cells (which is not at all morally controversial) and using embryonic ones, a process in which the human embryo is killed.

[36]John Gray, *Straw Dogs* (London: Granta, 2002), chap. 1.

[37]Nick Bostrom, "Transhumanist Values," posted on Bostrom's website at <http://www.nickbostrom.com/ethics/values.pdf>.

[38]Brian Goodwin, interview by David King, *GenEthics News* 11 (March/April 1996): 6-8. Goodwin is author of *How the Leopard Changed Its Spots* (1994; reprint, Princeton, N.J.: Princeton University Press, 2001).

ing the tools to create a genetic utopia. But this is an illusion. What counts most in shaping a humane society is not the level of technology but the prevailing worldview. "If human life does not matter simply and merely because it is human, this means that moral worth becomes subjective and a matter of who has the power to decide," warns Smith. "History shows that once we create categories of differing worth, those humans denigrated by the political power structure as having less value are exploited, oppressed, and killed."[39]

On a similar note, John Paul says that unless we "safeguard the dignity of the person," "there can be no true democracy." The human being will be reduced to a mere "thing," which, like other things we encounter in the world, can be controlled and manipulated" (§§71, 101).

The debate over the life issues is often portrayed as a conflict between those who think the state should be neutral on moral issues, against those want to "force" their beliefs on others. As we have seen, however, the liberal position is far from neutral. It is based on a dualistic anthropology that defines personhood as something that must be earned by achieving some arbitrary standard of cognitive functioning. This is an *exclusive* definition of the human being—that is, some people don't make the cut, don't measure up.

Over against it is a holistic anthropology that treats the person as an integral unity, with intrinsic value at all levels. This is an *inclusive* definition—if you are a member of the human race, you're "in." You have the dignity and status of a full member of the moral community. As theologian David Hart writes, there is "a glory hidden in the depths of every person, even the least of us—even 'defectives' and 'morons' and 'genetic inferiors,' if you will—waiting to be revealed, a beauty and dignity and power of such magnificence and splendor that, could we see it now, it would move us either to worship or to terror."[40]

Hooking Up and Hurting

The same dualistic division of the human being gives the key to liberal attitudes toward sexuality. In a teleological view of nature, the biological structure of our bodies signals a divine purpose for male and female to form covenants for mutual love and the nurturing of new life. But in the two-story view, nature is pictured as

---

[39]Smith, "Welcome to Our Brave New World."

[40]David Hart, "The Anti-Theology of the Body," *The New Atlantis*, no. 9, summer 2005, pp. 65-73. Hart seems to be paraphrasing C. S. Lewis, who calls on Christians "to remember that the dullest and most uninteresting person you talk to may one day be a creature which, if you saw it now, you would be strongly tempted to worship" (*The Weight of Glory* [Grand Rapids: Eerdmans, 1949], pp. 14-15).

a realm of blind, material forces (lower story), which autonomous selves are free to manipulate according to their own desires (upper story). What does that imply for human sexuality? If our biology does not reveal any moral teleology, then we are free to use it any way we choose.

What does this mean in practice? A survey by the Institute for American Values found that 40 percent of college women engage in "hooking up"—physical encounters of various levels with no expectation of any personal relationship. And the trend is trickling down into high schools and junior highs. Hookup partners are referred to as "friends with benefits," but that's a euphemism, because they are not really even friends. The unwritten etiquette is that they never just talk or spend time together. "You just keep it purely sexual, and that way people don't have mixed expectations, and no one gets hurt," explains a *New York Times* article. Many young people have absorbed the idea that romantic relationships are "complicated, messy, and invariably painful. Hooking up . . . is exciting, sexually validating, and efficient."

Except when it isn't. Invariably, people do get hurt. Young people find that it's not so easy to separate personal feelings from what the body does. The article quotes a teenager named Melissa who was depressed because her hookup partner had just broken up with her. "The point of having a friend with benefits is that you won't get broken up with, you won't get hurt," she said.[41] But like Melissa, many find they cannot surgically separate the body from the whole person. As a character says in George Bernard Shaw's *Too True to Be Good,* "When men and women pick one another up just for a bit of fun, they find they've picked up more than they bargained for, because men and women have a top story as well as a ground floor; and you can't have the one without the other."

The mistake people make, a college student told *Rolling Stone,* is to "assume that there are two very distinct elements in a relationship, one emotional and one sexual, and they pretend like there are clean lines between them."[42] Precisely: Hooking up assumes a dualism in which emotional relationships involve persons (upper story), while sexual relationships involve only bodies (lower story).

The body has been "reduced to pure materiality," writes John Paul. "It is simply a complex of organs, functions and energies to be used according to the sole criteria of pleasure and efficiency." The result is that sexuality "is depersonalized and exploited" (§23). A video widely used in public school sex education courses de-

---

[41]Benoit Denizet-Lewis, "Friends, Friends with Benefits and the Benefits of the Local Mall," *The New York Times,* May 30, 2004.

[42]Janet Reitman, "Sex & Scandal at Duke," Rollingstone.com (June 1, 2006) <http://www.rollingstone.com/news/story/10464110/sex__scandal_at_duke/print>.

fines sexual relations as simply "something done by two adults to give each other pleasure."[43] In short, little more than an exchange of services. This is an economic view of sexuality, treating it as a commodity with no moral or social significance. The human body becomes a morally neutral tool that can be used in a purely utilitarian calculus of personal advantage.

John Kavanaugh captures the two-story split in a pithy phrase: "Commodification splits *sexuality* from *selfhood*."[44] Instead of being the embodied expression of our full personhood, sexuality becomes an instrument for release and recreation, or a tool in the competition for power and status.

POMOSEXUALITY

The same two-story dichotomy is at work in the homosexual rights movement. Biological difference is treated as irrelevant to who we are as persons—as "an evolutionary product that just happened to come out as it did."[45] For example, the sex education video quoted earlier defines homosexuality as simply "two people of the same gender giving each other pleasure." If a sexual encounter is just an exchange of physical services, why does it matter what gender you are?

In fact, the cutting edge today is the idea that gender is a social construction, and therefore it can be *de*constructed. In *Omnigender,* Virginia Mollenkott argues that the binary system of masculine and feminine gender is a social invention—and an oppressive one at that.[46] Thus all sexual identities are "up for grabs," as one reviewer notes approvingly. (The reviewer goes on: "Arguments against women's ordination need wholesale revamping since we do not know for sure now what a woman is.")[47]

In *Gender Trouble,* Judith Butler argues that gender is not a fixed attribute but a fluid, free-floating variable that shifts according to personal preference. Butler calls her book "a critique of compulsory heterosexuality," arguing that gender is a fiction, a social artifice, which can be made and remade at will.[48] This is seen as

---

[43]"What Kids Want to Know About Sex and Growing Up," 1992 Children's Television Workshop, a "3-2-1 Contact Extra" special program.

[44]John Francis Kavanaugh, *Following Christ in a Consumer Society: The Spirituality of Cultural Resistance,* rev. ed. (Maryknoll, N.Y.: Orbis Books, 1991), p. 56, emphasis added.

[45]John F. Crosby, "John Paul II's Vision of Sexuality and Marriage," in *The Legacy of Pope John Paul II,* ed. Geoffrey Gneuhs (New York: Herder & Herder, 2000), p. 59.

[46]Virginia Ramey Mollenkott, *Omnigender: A Trans-Religious Approach* (Cleveland: Pilgrim, 2001).

[47]Mary E. Hunt, "Grace—Is a Transgender Person Who Loves Women and Men," *The Witness* 84 (July/August, 2001).

[48]Judith Butler, *Gender Trouble* (New York: Routledge, 1999). See critique by Martha Nussbaum in "The Professor of Parody," *The New Republic,* February 22, 1999.

liberating, a way to practice self-determination and create one's own identity.

On college campuses Butler's theory has become popular among radical students. Calling themselves "transgenders" (or "trannies" for short), they reject the male/female system, cultivating an androgynous look. The *New York Time* reports that some colleges now offer separate bathrooms, housing and sports teams for students who do not identify themselves as either male or female. At Wesleyan, the campus clinic no longer requires students to check *M* or *F* on their health forms. Instead, they are asked to "describe your gender identity history."[49] (Which genders have you been over your lifetime?)

A magazine for homosexuals explains what these trends mean. People "don't want to fit into any boxes—not gay, straight, lesbian, or bisexual ones," the author writes. Instead, "they want to be free to change their minds." The idea that one is born with a certain gender that cannot be changed is so *modernist,* the article says dismissively. Society is moving to a *postmodern* view that says you can choose any gender you want—and then alter it at will.[50] A pomosexual view.[51]

The irony is that Christians are often labeled prudes and Puritans, accused of having a low regard for the body. But the truth is that Christianity has a much *higher* view than today's liberal utilitarian view. The two-story division alienates people from their own bodies, treating gender as having no intrinsic dignity or purpose. Biology is merely an undefined material substratum that can be used for whatever extrinsic purposes the self may impose on it.

Butler herself came to recognize the problem. Critics of her book argued that by divorcing gender from biology, she was ignoring and even denigrating "the materiality of the body."[52] Eventually she agreed, and wrote a follow-up book titled *Bodies That Matter.*[53]

Just so—bodies do matter. In the postmodern body/self bifurcation, there is no respect for the intrinsic good or *telos* (purpose) of the human body, no dignity accorded to the unique capabilities inherent in being male or female. By contrast,

---

[49]Fred Bernstein, "On Campus, Rethinking Biology 101," *The New York Times*, March 7, 2004. See also Gene Edward Veith, "Identity Crisis," *World,* March 27, 2004.

[50]Bret Johnson, *In the Family,* July 1998. Cited in Laura Markowitz, "A Different Kind of Queer Marriage: Suddenly Gays and Lesbians Are Wedding Partners of the Opposite Sex," *The Utne Reader,* 101, September/October 2000, <http://www.utne.com/issues/2000_101/features/1369-1.html>; see also Stephen F. Sternberg, "Can Those Identifying Themselves as Homosexual Experience Change?" *Leadership U*, <www.leaderu.com/stonewall/issues/change.html>.

[51]Carol Queen and Lawrence Schimel, eds., *PoMoSexuals: Challenging Assumptions About Gender and Sexuality* (San Francisco: Cleis Press, 1997).

[52]Butler summarizes her critics in an interview by Peter Osborne and Lynne Segal, "Gender as Performance: An Interview with Judith Butler," *Radical Philosophy* 67 (Summer 1994).

[53]Judith Butler, *Bodies That Matter: On the Discursive Limits of Sex* (London: Routledge, 1993).

the biblical view treats our sexual identity as intrinsically good. Our bodies reveal who we are as whole persons created in God's image. In Genesis 2, when Adam recognizes Eve as kindred to himself, he exclaims, "This at last is bone of my bones and flesh of my flesh" (Gen 2:23). Christ's own commentary on Genesis is that "they are no longer two, but one flesh" (Mt 19:6). Scripture offers a stunningly high view of fleshly union as a union of whole persons.[54]

Even more profoundly, Scripture tells us that marriage is a picture of God's love for his people. We image God not only as individuals but also through communion with one another. "In loving each other," John Paul writes, "Adam and Eve, made visible the love of God, i.e., the love in the Trinity itself."[55] Throughout Scripture, marriage is used as a metaphor for the relationship between God and his people: in the Old Testament, Israel as the unfaithful wife; in the New Testament, the church as the bride of Christ. Our sexual nature possesses a "language" that is meant to proclaim God's own transcendent love and faithfulness.

ZOMBIES AND SPIRITS

Evangelicals reading *Evangelium vitae* can appreciate the way John Paul delves beneath the surface of ethical issues to the underlying two-story worldview. As we have seen, his ethical analysis dovetails neatly with the work of Reformational thinkers like Herman Dooyeweerd and Francis Schaeffer,[56] who likewise diagnose

---

[54]See "The Nuptial Meaning of the Body," General Audience of January 9, 1980, in John Paul II, *The Theology of the Body: Human Love in the Divine Plan* (Boston: Pauline Books and Media, 1997), p. 61.

[55]Cited in Richard M. Hogan, "The Nuptial Meaning of the Body," in *An Introduction to John Paul II's Theology of the Body*, Natural Family Planning Outreach (March 1, 2003), chap. 2 <http://www.nfpoutreach.org/Hogan_Theology_%20Body2.htm>.

[56]Dooyeweerd made the broader argument that *any* nonbiblical worldview will ultimately split into some form of dualism. He identified three major dualisms in Western thought: the Greek matter/form dualism; Thomas Aquinas and the scholastic nature/grace dualism; Immanuel Kant and the humanistic nature/freedom dualism (see *Roots of Western Culture* and *A New Critique*). John Paul would have disagreed with Dooyeweerd's identification of Thomas Aquinas as the source of the nature/grace dualism. Thomists argue that the problematic dualism resulted not from Thomas's formulation (a distinction need not be a separation), but rather from the work of later scholastics in whose hands the two stories became increasingly separate, independent and autonomous: e.g., Cajetan, Molina, Suarez and especially William of Ockham. John Paul was a close friend of Henri de Lubac, a proponent of *nouvelle theologie*, a twentieth-century school of theology that is credited with overcoming the scholastic nature/grace dualism. Dooyweerd acknowledged the positive impact of *nouvelle theologie:* "It is a gladdening symptom of a re-awakening biblical consciousness, that under the influence of Augustinianism an increasing number of Roman Catholic thinkers, belonging to the movement of the so-called *nouvelle theologie*, have begun to oppose this dualistic view. They agree with the Reformed philosophical movement in the Netherlands in advocating the necessity of a Christian philosophy" (*In the Twilight of Western Thought*, p. 141).

Discussions by Catholic thinkers of the problems of the nature/grace dualism are found in Stephen J.

a two-story worldview at the heart of modernity. In tracing its historical genesis, most philosophers begin with the mind/body split of René Descartes. The body, being part of nature, Descartes treated as a machine, operating by the same principles as clocks and automatons. The mind, by contrast, he portrayed as a free, solitary, rational consciousness.

This "ghost in the machine" picture of the human being runs through much of modern thought. Yet it has created enormous difficulties. How could two such opposing substances interact with one another? How could a robotic body and thinking mind function as an integrated whole? "Cartesian dualism breaks man up into two complete substances," writes philosopher Jacques Maritain: "on the one hand, the body which is only geometric extension; on the other, the soul which is only thought." The human being was "split asunder."[57]

Philosophy, too, was split asunder into two opposing streams. To use our image of a building, in the lower story was the Enlightenment, which focused on the mechanistic aspect of nature. The tenuous ghost inhabiting the machine proved easy to exorcise, and before long philosophical materialists were denying the existence of any upper story at all, reducing humans to nothing but complicated mechanisms. Free will and moral responsibility were dismissed as illusions—recall the contemporary examples at the beginning of this chapter. In fact, today there is even a school of thought called *eliminative* materialism that dismisses consciousness itself as an illusion. Based on the popular computational model of the mind, philosophers like Paul Churchland argue that mental states do not exist. They recommend that language about things like beliefs and desires be replaced with statements about the physical mechanisms of the nervous system—the activation of neurons and so on.[58]

Somewhat tongue in cheek, eliminative materialists say humans are essentially zombies—not the movie monsters but "philosopher's zombies," creatures that exhibit typical human behavior while lacking inner consciousness. "It *seems* we have

---

Duffy, *The Dynamics of Grace* (Collegeville, Minn.: Liturgical, Glazier, 1993): "For Thomas there is no two-story religious world"; late scholasticism created "the two-story world"; in Fergus Kerr, *After Aquinas* (Oxford: Blackwell, 2002): de Lubac put "an end to the two-storey view of grace and nature"; and in several essays in *Catholicism and Secularization in America: Essays on Nature, Grace, and Culture,* ed. David L. Schindler (Huntington, Ind.: Our Sunday Visitor, Communio Books, 1990): for example, Walter Kasper diagnoses the problems with a "dualistic and separatist conception" of nature and grace, a "two-story system."

[57]Jacques Maritain, *The Dream of Descartes,* trans. Mabelle Andison (New York: Philosophical Library, 1944), p. 179.

[58]See Nancy Pearcey, "A New Foundation for Positive Cultural Change: Science and God in the Public Square," review of *The Wedge of Truth* by Phillip Johnson, *Human Events* (September 15, 2000).

selves. It *seems* we have minds. It *seems* we are agents," writes Daniel Wegner of Harvard. But it is more "accurate to call all this an illusion." His book is aptly titled *The Illusion of Conscious Will.*[59]

The result is that human beings have been reduced to mechanisms with no higher value than gadgets and gizmos—a view that clears the decks for unbridled experimentation with human life and DNA.

While this radical naturalism was developing in the lower story, a contrary reaction took place in the upper story. Starting with the Romantic movement, the "ghost" in the machine was moved to center stage until it gave rise to a kind of pantheism, in which the universe itself was ultimately the unfolding of a mental or spiritual substance (philosophical idealism).[60] In the philosophy of Hegel and Schelling, the self was elevated to cosmic dimensions and identified with an Absolute Mind or Spirit. Though it was later cut down to size, the lasting legacy has been a conviction that the self is the creator of its own moral universe. The postmodern self surveys the world and is free to put on it whatever construction it chooses.[61]

Clearly, neither of these two currents produces a complete picture of the human being, and thus both have contributed to the strange, internally contradictory dualism we have diagnosed in today's liberal bioethics. As materialism reduces humans to useful gadgets to be tinkered with, the postmodern self rejects all ethical limits on its own desires.

Idols of the Mind

How was it that John Paul II and Herman Dooyeweerd both came to identify dualism as the core problematic of modern thought? The answer is that, as Europeans, both were influenced by continental philosophy, especially phenomenology.[62] Founded by Edmund Husserl in the early twentieth century, phenomenol-

---

[59]Daniel Wegner, *The Illusion of Conscious Will* (Cambridge, Mass.: MIT Press, 2002), pp. 341-42, emphasis added.

[60]A key turning point in the rise of Romanticism was the philosophy of Immanuel Kant. In Dooyeweerd's words, Kant sought to "moderate" the pretensions of mechanistic science "by limiting the validity of the laws of nature to sensorily perceivable phenomena. Above this sensory realm of 'nature' there existed a 'suprasensory' realm of moral freedom which was not governed by mechanical laws of nature but by norms or rules of conduct which presuppose the autonomy of human personality" (*Roots,* p. 171).

[61]For a good history of philosophical idealism, see Robert C. Solomon, *Continental Philosophy Since 1750: The Rise and Fall of the Self* (New York: Oxford University Press, 1988), p. 5. For a critique of the influence of the Cartesian concept of the self on theology, see Fergus Kerr, *Theology After Wittgenstein* (1986; reprint, London: SPCK, 1997).

[62]On Dooyeweerd, see Albert M. Wolters, "The Intellectual Milieu of Herman Dooyeweerd," in *The Legacy of Herman Dooyeweerd,* ed. C. T. McIntire (Lanham, Md.: University Press of America, 1985), pp.

ogy sought to escape the split created by the two conflicting streams that had emerged from the Enlightenment and Romanticism.[63] How? By bringing philosophy back to its touchstone in ordinary life and experience.

Phenomenology took as its starting point the full range of everyday human experience—the "lived world" or "universal human experience." Dooyeweerd called it "pre-theoretical" or "naïve" experience, meaning ordinary experience *before* we begin to philosophize about it.[64] Prior to theoretical study, we experience objects as concrete wholes.[65] As we act in the world, we also experience *ourselves* as integral wholes. We don't say my mouth is eating lunch; we say *I* am eating lunch. Phenomenology seeks to overcome Cartesian dualism by reconnecting the mind and the body. Thinking is an action performed by whole persons embedded in the lived world.

1-19. On John Paul II, see Jaroslaw Kupczak, *Destined for Liberty: The Human Person in the Philosophy of Karol Wojtyla/John Paul II* (Washington, D.C.: Catholic University of America Press, 2000), and Rocco Buttiglione, *Karol Wojtyla: The Thought of the Man Who Became Pope John Paul II* (Grand Rapids: Eerdmans, 1997). Though remaining a Thomist, Wojtyla encountered phenomenology through Roman Ingarden, who had been one of Husserl's students and who was a professor in the philosophy department at the University of Krakow where the future pope was earning his doctorate in philosophy. Wojtyla wrote his doctoral dissertation on Max Scheler, who was also a student of Husserl's and who applied phenomenology to ethics. Both Dooyeweerd and Wojtlya were influenced by the earlier works of Husserl, where phenomenology is presented as a method more than as a metaphysical system; they rejected his later move to philosophical idealism. Other Christians influenced by phenomenology include Dietrich von Hildebrand, Edith Stein, Paul Ricoeur and Gabriel Marcel.

Both Dooyeweerd and Wojtyla were also influenced by neo-Kantianism, especially by Nicolai Hartmann, who countered reductionism by describing human nature as resting on, and including, all the varied "levels" of existence, including the physical, the organic, the sentient, the psychological and the spiritual. A central element in Dooyeweerd's philosophy is his own construal of the levels (his "modal scale"). For a useful introduction, see L. Kalsbeek, *Contours of a Christian Philosophy: An Introduction to Hermann Dooyeweerd's Thought* (Toronto: Wedge, 1975).

[63]The two currents are typically labeled Anglo-analytic and continental thought. By the late nineteenth to early twentieth century, not only Husserl but many other thinkers were actively seeking to overcome the split, including the pragmatists in America. William James labeled the analytic school "tough-minded" and the continental idealists "tender-minded," claiming that his own pragmatism was intended as a means to resolve them. John Dewey battled against what he called "dualism" all his life. See Pearcey, *Total Truth*, chap. 8.

[64]"Naïve experience" is not the same as "naïve realism" or a copy theory of knowledge—because it is not a theory at all. It is rather a "pre-theoretical datum, corresponding with the integral structure" of experience (Dooyeweerd, *In the Twilight of Western Thought*, p. 18).

[65]"This unity of experience is the great discovery of phenomenology," writes Buttiglione. Phenomenology provides a resolution of the two-story bifurcation of the human person "because it begins from unified experience, which is there before abstraction" (*Karol Wojtyla*, pp. 68, 72). In a series of lectures given in 1954-1955, Wojtyla revealed the impact of phenomenology by arguing (in the words of Kenneth Schmitz) that "the empirical basis of philosophical ethics is ordinary human experience." "Our recognition of personal causality" is a matter of "plain human experience." "These are the common facts of ethical life, and they should be included in the starting point of any ethical analysis" (*At the Center of the Human Drama: The Philosophical Anthropology of Karol Wojtyla/Pope John Paul II* [Washington, D.C.: Catholic University of America Press, 1993], pp. 42-47).

For Dooyeweerd, "in the human thinking act, the entire human body is active," explains Yong Joon Choi. "Theoretical thinking is possible from the integral centre of the human nature (heart, soul, spirit) only within the human body."[66] John Paul likewise emphasized action, especially moral action. Having formed his thinking in the crucible of confrontation with an oppressive political regime, he wrote that we experience ourselves as integrated persons most forcefully when we have to "take an active stand upon issues requiring vital decisions and having vital consequences."[67]

Universal human experience also provides a testing ground to evaluate competing worldviews. According to phenomenology, philosophy begins when we *abstract* one aspect from the connected fabric of experience in order to study it and formulate theories about it. But we must always come back and *apply* our theories to the world of ordinary experience. If a worldview fails to explain experience, then it is not an adequate worldview. As Dooyeweerd writes, "Any philosophical theory of human experience which cannot account for this datum [lived experience] in a satisfactory way must be erroneous in its fundamentals."[68] To use our earlier metaphor, a mental map that is "too small" will not be capable of accounting for the full range of human experience.

The same process of abstraction explains how various forms of dualisms arise, including the modern dualism that John Paul and Dooyeweerd both identified. It occurs when we abstract *and then absolutize* some aspect of experience, treating it as the ultimate, all-defining principle—whether nature (as in Enlightenment naturalism) or consciousness (as in Romantic idealism). Thus Dooyeweerd says: "The mechanistic standpoint rests on an overestimation and an absolutization of the mechanical phenemona."[69] And conversely, John Paul notes, "Since the time of

[66]Yong Joon Choi, "Dialogue and Antithesis: A Philosophical Study on the Significance of Herman Dooyeweerd's Transcendental Critique" (Ph.D. diss., 2000), p. 59, available at <http://my.dreamwiz.com/tulip7/CSDS/dialogue.htm>.

[67]Cited in Buttiglione, *Karol Wojtyla,* p. 120. For Wojtyla, "the physical and psychological dynamisms of the whole human person are brought together in action. . . . Action draws together all of the elements in the experience of the person" (Schmitz, *At the Center of the Human Drama,* pp. 65-66).

[68]Dooyeweerd, *In the Twilight of Western Thought,* p. 18.

[69]Dooyeweerd, *Roots,* pp. 172-73. The tendency to absolutize or idolize some aspect of experience is central to Dooyeweerd's analysis of the history of philosophy. Note the many listings under "Absolutization" in the index of *A New Critique.* See also J. M. Spier, *An Introduction to Christian Philosophy* (Philadelphia: Presbyterian and Reformed, 1954), pp. 67-69. Roy Clouser offers a Dooyeweerdian analysis of the way various philosophies of science absolutize some aspect of creation in *The Myth of Religious Neutrality* (Notre Dame, Ind.: University of Notre Dame Press, 1991). David Koyzis applies a Dooyeweerdian analysis to political philosophy: "Liberalism idolizes the individual, socialism the economic class, and nationalism the nation-state or ethnic community" (*Political Visions & Illusions: A Survey and Christian Critique of Contemporary Ideologies* [Downers Grove, Ill.: InterVarsity Press, 2003], p. 38).

Descartes, consciousness has been absolutized."[70] To use religious terms, Western thinkers have tended to *idolize* either nature or consciousness, treating one or the other as ultimate reality. But because neither one is adequate to account for all of experience, the two remain locked in an irresolvable dualism.

A CREATIVE CONVERGENCE

In his earlier struggle against Marxism, the future pope concluded that the central weakness of communism—indeed of all atheistic ideologies—is a deficient doctrine of the human person. In a letter, he once wrote that he was devoting his thinking to "the metaphysical significance and the mystery of the PERSON." As he explained, "the evil of our times consists in a kind of degradation . . . of the fundamental uniqueness of each human person. *This evil is even much more of the metaphysical than of the moral order.*"[71] He was right. The Bible speaks of people being morally lost without Christ, but it is also true that people are *metaphysically* lost when they direct their lives by nonbiblical worldviews. In order to effectively address the moral issues of our day, we must evaluate the underlying worldviews.

Evangelicals reading *Evangelium vitae* will encounter theological teachings that they reject, of course, areas of ongoing disagreement between Catholics and Protestants. But they will also find a critique of the moral crisis in Western culture that is remarkably congruent with the most influential form of worldview analysis being carried out within evangelical and Reformed circles today. One might say that John Paul shows how to *apply* Dooyeweerd's critique of dualism to current ethical issues, while Dooyeweerd provides a deeper and more systematic philosophical *context* for the pope's moral analysis. In dialogue with one another, these two could well produce a surprisingly creative confluence.

---

[70]From a 1979 article, cited in Schmitz, *At the Center of the Human Drama,* p. 39, n. 19. Wojtyla "points out that the radical separation between the two great currents in the Western philosophy [here identified as realism versus idealism] originated in the absolutization of one of the two aspects of human experience"—either inner or outer experience (Kupczak, *Destined for Liberty,* p. 76).

[71]Cited in Avery Cardinal Dulles, "John Paul II and the Mystery of the Human Person," *America* 190, no. 3 (2004): 10-22, emphasis added.

10

DIVES IN MISERICORDIA AND *SOLLICITUDO REI SOCIALIS*

Mercy and Justice

Mark Charlton

INTRODUCTION

Throughout his long pontificate, John Paul II repeatedly reminded his listeners that God is preparing a "great springtime" for Christianity. In anticipation of this, John Paul II called on all members of the church, especially the laity, to commit themselves to a New Evangelization. The New Evangelization would be premised on the belief that "the Gospel of God's love for man, the Gospel of the dignity of the person and the Gospel of life are a single and indivisible Gospel."[1]

With this as a *leitmotif* of his pontificate, John Paul II set about addressing a broad range of issues relating to various dimensions of the task of cultural renewal. His teachings on the deterioration of the West into a "culture of death" and his advocacy for a "culture of life" received wide, albeit often critical, coverage in the media. Many North American evangelicals became familiar with and responded positively to John Paul II's call for the dignity of individuals. Less familiar to many evangelicals is his deep concern and engagement with pressing global social issues such as poverty and underdevelopment, international trade and debt, and unemployment and hun-

[1]John Paul II, *Evangelium vitae . . . on the Value and Inviolability of Human Life,* Libreria Editrice Vaticana (March 25, 1995), §2 <http://www.vatican.va/holy_father/john_paul_ii/encyclicals/documents/hf_jp-ii_enc_25031995_evangelium-vitae_en.html>. Unless otherwise noted, the italics in quotes from church documents are shown as in the original text.

ger. These concerns flowed out of his commitment to an incarnational Christian humanism which takes seriously both the call to gospel evangelization and the commitment to applying a holistic gospel to all dimensions of culture.

In their early history, evangelicals took seriously the call both to engage in evangelization and to promote social reform. However, by the early twentieth century, North American evangelicals had shifted their attention away from social reform issues in order to focus on confronting the challenges posed by modernity and the theological liberalism that was becoming prevalent in mainline denominations and institutions.[2] Gradually, social reform became associated with the "social gospel" of liberal Protestantism, with its more optimistic assessment of human capabilities for bringing about the kingdom of God on earth in the here and now. In reaction, North American evangelicals expressed even greater skepticism about large-scale social projects, preferring to focus on more "personal" forms of evangelism that stressed the inner transformation of the individual rather than the broader transformation of society itself. Because of the popularization of premillennialist theology and a preoccupation with end times through the writings of authors such as Hal Lindsey and Tim LaHaye, a growing segment of North American evangelicalism became pessimistic about having any possible impact on the major socioeconomic issues of the day.[3] While evangelicals were encouraged to undertake personal acts of mercy or charity, engagement with the issues of broader structural change were seen as beyond their scope.

In recent decades, North American evangelicals have become more engaged in public policy issues. Many conservative evangelicals have allied themselves with pro-life Catholics on such issues as abortion, euthanasia and protection of traditional notions of the family. Although North American evangelicals have both concurred with John Paul II's teachings on the dangers of a culture of death and publicly supported Catholic positions on these issues, we still have much to learn from his teachings on broader social issues, particularly those relating to global poverty and underdevelopment.

---

[2]It is important here to add the qualifier *North American* evangelical since British evangelicalism took a somewhat different trajectory and has always been more interested in social issues. This can be seen in the much greater involvement of British evangelicals in the Jubilee 2000 Debt Campaign in comparison with North American evangelicals.

[3]These tendencies have, of course, been challenged in recent decades by a host of writers, including several contributors to this volume. For a summary of the intellectual and social currents which led to the evangelical retreat from social reform, see Mark Noll's *The Scandal of the Evangelical Mind* (Grand Rapids: Eerdmans, 1994). For an argument that these trends reflect a growing spirit of gnosticism among evangelicals, see Philip Lee, *Against the Protestant Gnostics* (New York: Oxford University Press, 1987).

In this chapter we will explore how the social thought of John Paul II, particularly his restatement of the social mission of the church as a fundamental component of the calling of the gospel, can challenge evangelicals to rethink the relationship between the Great Commission to evangelize the world and the struggle for social justice, especially as it relates to the problems of development and underdevelopment. John Paul's reflections on the church's social calling, his focus on the transformation of justice by the mercy of God, and his holistic vision of development can stimulate evangelicals to a develop a more positive and balanced understanding of the social mission of the church as an integral part of the call to evangelize.

We will address these issues through an examination of two of John Paul II's encyclicals, *Dives in misericordia* (Rich in Mercy) and *Sollicitudo rei socialis* (On Social Concern). In these two encyclicals, John Paul II presents a sweeping vision of what it means to apply the New Evangelization in a social context. In seeking to understand this vision, we will concentrate on issues which should be of interest to evangelicals: (1) By what authority does the church address social issues? (2) What is the scriptural and theological basis for engaging in social analysis? (3) How are the problems of development to be understood in the light of the gospel? (4) What is the relationship between sin and social and economic structures? (5) How does a commitment to justice transformed by mercy lead us to practice solidarity? However, before addressing these questions it will be useful to review the origins of these two encyclicals.

Background and Summary of the Two Encyclicals

At first glance, it may seem odd to focus on this particular combination of encyclicals. Chronologically, the publication of *Dives in misericordia*[4] precedes that of *Sollicitudo rei socialis*[5] by seven years. In addition, the two encyclicals are quite different in their subject matter. Technically *Dives in misericordia* is not normally considered to be one of the social encyclicals, but rather is part of a trilogy of encyclicals which focus on the nature of the Trinity. The first part of this trilogy, *Redemptor hominis,* was published in 1979, in the very first year of John Paul II's pontificate. This first encyclical set the tone for his pontificate in many ways by reflecting on the mystery of redemption through the person of Jesus Christ and its

---

[4]John Paul II, *Dives in misericordia,* Libreria Editrice Vaticana (November 30, 1980) <http://www.vatican.va/holy_father/john_paul_ii/encyclicals/documents/hf_jp-ii_enc_30111980_dives-in-misericordia_en.html>.

[5]John Paul II, *Sollicitudo rei socialis . . . for the Twentieth Anniversary of Populorum Progressio,* Libreria Editrice Vaticana (December 30, 1987) <http://www.vatican.va/holy_father/john_paul_ii/encyclicals/documents/hf_jp-ii_enc_30121987_sollicitudo-rei-socialis_en.html>.

relation to the dignity and life of human being.

Dives in misericordia was published the following year on the first Sunday in Advent in 1980. This second encyclical focuses on the character of the divine mercy of God the Father as it is revealed to us through Christ. Six years later the trilogy was completed with the publication of *Dominum et vivificantem* in 1986. Here John Paul II's reflection on the nature of the Trinity is rounded out by a discussion of the role of the Holy Spirit, particularly its life-giving power in assisting in bringing about renewal in human beings, within society and with the church.

Dives in misericordia was written out in long hand in Polish.[6] As result, the text itself has a tightness of argument and flow which is sometimes absent in *Sollicitudo rei socialis.* Although it is not strictly a social encyclical, *Dives in misericordia* is important to consider in this context because it sets out the theology that lies behind some of the fundamental concepts we find in John Paul II's social teaching. In particular, this teaching on the relationship between mercy and justice is critical to an understanding of his call for all Christians to develop the virtue of solidarity as a response to the problems of poverty and injustice that we find in the world.

The encyclical itself is composed of eight sections. The first section begins with a reflection on John 14:9 that "whoever has seen me has seen the Father." In this John Paul II sets out the Christocentric focus of his social thought. Christ is the very center of history, and it is Christ, the "new Adam," who reveals to man who he really is as a human. In revealing to man his true nature, Christ also reveals to him the nature of God the Father, "who is rich in mercy" (Eph 2:4). The modern world is often averse to the notion of a God of mercy, yet John Paul II emphasizes that this message is profoundly needed.

In the next section, John Paul II focuses on the incarnation as the manner in which God becomes "visible in His mercy." When Christ announced that he had been sent to bring the good news to the poor, the blind, the captives and the oppressed, he placed at the heart of his messianic ministry not only God's revelation of divine mercy but also the call for his followers to embody this essential virtue.

John Paul II includes a review of the concept of mercy in the Old Testament. When Christ addressed his own Jewish people, he was speaking to those who had a long history of experiencing the mercy of God. Significantly, John Paul II writes that "this experience was social and communal, as well as individual and interior" (*Dives in misericordia,* §4).

---

[6]For a discussion of the background to John Paul II's writing of this encyclical and the role that the theme of mercy played throughout his pontificate, see George W. Kosicki, *John Paul II: The Great Mercy Pope* (Stockbridge, Mass.: John Paul II Institute of Divine Mercy, 2001).

At the center of *Dives in misericordia,* John Paul II presents an extended reflection of the significance of the parable of the prodigal son. Although neither *mercy* nor *justice* is present in these texts, John Paul II insists that this parable expresses the very essence of divine mercy and how it transforms justice. This is a mercy which through the paschal mystery is passed from "generation to generation." John Paul goes on to discuss the relationship between justice and mercy and its implications for the mission of the church today; we will explore both themes more closely later in this chapter.

The second encyclical we are considering is *Sollicitudo rei socialis.* John Paul II wrote three encyclicals dealing specifically with social issues. *Sollicitudo rei socialis* is in fact the second in this series, being published in 1987, six years following the publication of the first social encyclical *Laborem exercens* (1981). *Sollicitudo rei socialis* was published to commemorate the twentieth anniversary of Pope Paul VI's *Populorum progressio,* which dealt with the problem of the development of peoples, particularly in the context of the challenges facing impoverished developing countries. Pope John Paul's third social encyclical, *Centesimus annus* was published four years later 1991 to honor the one hundredth anniversary of *Rerum novarum,* the encyclical of Pope Leo XIII which is seen as marking the beginning of the modern tradition of Catholic social thought. In contrast to *Dives in misericordia, Sollicitudo rei socialis* is quite different in tone and style. This is due not only to the very different subject matter, but also to the lengthy consultative and writing process of its creation; as a result, it does not read with the same graceful flow as does *Dives in misericordia.*[7]

The timing of the publication of *Sollicitudo rei socialis* and *Centesimus annus* was meant in part to emphasize that John Paul II's teaching on social issues should be seen as a continuation of the tradition of social thought developed by his predecessors. To reinforce this point, *Sollicitudo rei socialis* referred to this body of thought as Catholic social doctrine. While the term *doctrine* had been used by earlier popes in reference to their social teaching, the word did not appear either in John XXIII's encyclical *Pacem in terris* (Peace on Earth) or in the Second Vatican Ecumenical Council's Pastoral Constitution *Gaudium et spes* (On the Church in the Modern World). It may well be that John Paul II wanted to remind Catholics that the social teaching of the church now forms a comprehensive doctrinal corpus which has a certain inner coherence and continuity of its own. Moreover, the reference to social doctrine emphasizes the point that, as doctrine, it forms an

---

[7]On the process by which the encyclical was written, see Robert Suro, "The Writing of an Encyclical," in *Aspiring to Freedom,* ed. Kenneth Myers (Grand Rapids: Eerdmans, 1988), pp. 159-69.

essential component of the faith of Christians and is not merely an optional add-on to the other doctrinal teachings of the church. As John Paul II warns readers in a later section of *Sollicitudo rei socialis,* "anyone wishing to renounce the difficult yet noble task of improving the lot of man in his totality, and of all people . . . that person would be betraying the will of God the Creator" (*Sollicitudo rei socialis,* §30).

At the same time, John Paul II wanted to emphasize his intent to "renew" and "update" the church's teaching on social issues. Catholic social doctrine is not simply a set of abstract, universal principles, set in stone at an earlier date and applied in a mechanistic manner in every situation. John Paul II was well aware that he was speaking to the church as a universal church whose members are spread throughout the world in diverse cultures and socioeconomic and political circumstances. This means that there is no easy blueprint for everyone or every circumstance. The documents of Vatican II had emphasized that the church has "the duty of scrutinizing the signs of the times and of interpreting them in the light of the Gospel" (*Gaudium et spes* §4). Thus Catholic social doctrine demands an ongoing effort to rethink how its principles can be applied in the ever-changing circumstances of human history.

Given that twenty years had passed since Paul VI had reflected on the significance that Catholic social doctrine has for an understanding of the development of peoples, John Paul II noted that it was time to update the church's teaching on these issues by reflecting on changing circumstances and the new challenges facing society so that this "continuity and renewal [would be] proof of the perennial value of the teaching of the Church" (*Sollicitudo rei socialis,* §3).

This need had become a pressing one in the early period of John Paul's pontificate. In South America, the Catholic Church had become increasingly embroiled in the struggle for social justice among the poor. The Marxist-oriented liberation theology was gaining in popularity throughout Latin America and other parts of the developing world.[8] A growing number of liberationist priests were becoming directly involved in the political struggles of their peoples, in some cases taking up political offices while remaining priests, a practice John Paul II actively discouraged and eventually outright prohibited. These moves were decried by many who were sympathetic to the plight of the poor in Latin America; they feared that a

[8]For one of the early influential texts in liberation theology, see Gustavo Gutiérrez, *A Theology of Liberation: History, Politics, and Salvation* (Maryknoll, N.Y.: Orbis, 1973). A critical response to this developing theology was written by Cardinal Ratzinger. See Congregation for the Doctrine of the Faith, "Instruction on Certain Aspects of the Theology of Liberation," *Origins* 14, no. 3 (1984): 194-204.

socially conservative focus would predominate throughout the pontificate of John Paul II, making him insensitive to the plight of those suffering from poverty and oppression.

However, two important incidents occurred in 1987. The first pivotal moment happened during John Paul II's visit to Chile, Argentina and Uruguay that year. There he witnessed firsthand the unrest and turmoil afflicting many Latin American countries as a result of political and economic oppression. While in Chile, a country still under the oppressive control of the military regime of Augusto Pinochet, a disturbance broke out near the site of one of the papal masses. More than thirty people were injured as the police clashed with protestors within sight of the pope. Observers noted that John Paul II appeared deeply troubled by what he had witnessed. The second happened later that year, when John Paul II also visited Poland, where he once again witnessed the unrest of the Polish people, particularly the young, as their struggled for change under the Communist system. Thus, *Sollicitudo rei socialis* can be seen in part as John Paul II's desire to demonstrate that his papacy was sensitive to these turbulent events which were taking place abroad and that the teaching of the modern church indeed had something relevant to say to those facing crisis.[9]

As a document, *Sollicitudo rei socialis* is structured around five main chapters. In the first, John Paul II discusses the "originality" of *Populorum progressio* and explains its significance for the development of Catholic social doctrine in light of Vatican II. Here he notes Paul VI's desire to address the problem of underdevelopment and poverty as a fundamentally ethical and cultural problem, rather than merely an economic or technical one, thus necessitating the church's involvement. Because the problem of development is at its core an ethical and moral one, John Paul II notes that the church has a special competence to address this issue as an "expert in humanity," a claim that I will address in further detail below.

The second chapter of *Sollicitudo rei socialis* provides a survey of the dimension of the problems facing the contemporary world, particularly since the publication of *Populorum progressio.* John Paul II notes that the world is less optimistic about the prospects of global development than it had been twenty years earlier. While some improvements have occurred, he notes that all the generally accepted indicators of development showed a widening gap between rich and poor countries. Rather than being lifted up, many individuals and communities now found themselves being weighed down, not just by a declining standard in living but also by a

---

[9]Cf. Suro, "The Writing of an Encyclical."

growing sense of passivity and dependency.

While these failures had many causes, John Paul II comments on the failures of developing nations themselves, especially of those holding positions of political and economic power who often ignore the plight of the poor. Equally important is the failure of developed nations to cultivate a sense of duty in coming to the assistance of those countries penalized by the economic, financial and social mechanisms unfairly imposed upon them. *Sollicitudo rei socialis* notes how such diverse problems as lack of housing, unemployment and increases in the international debt are only symptoms of a growing problem of underdevelopment.

In addition, John Paul II notes that the crisis of underdevelopment was aggravated by the ideological struggles between the Eastern and Western blocs, a struggle which had in fact intensified during the early part of the 1980s. Although the East-West struggle is essentially a conflict between two different concepts of development, the pope warns that neither the ideologies of liberal capitalism nor Marxist communism are capable in themselves of encouraging a form of true human development.

Chapter three of *Sollicitudo rei socialis* discusses what John Paul II means by "authentic human development." Neither a mere accumulation of goods nor improvements in modern technology will be sufficient to address the problems of underdevelopment. Such a materialist conception of development leads only to new problems of overdevelopment in the West, which means that a few have more while others go with less, a situation that only compounds the sense of injustice. Rather, an authentic vision of development must have at its core an ethical component: individuals must realize that their purpose is not simply the accumulation of wealth but the sharing of their abundance and even necessities in the assistance and care of others. True development, John Paul II notes, involves the respect of the rights of the person and a demonstration of solidarity with others in a spirit to true self-sacrifice.

Having set out the moral component of the concept of development, John Paul II provides a "theological reading of modern problems" in chapter four. Because of the moral character of development, the slow progress of development is frequently caused not only by economic factors but by political and ideological ones. Here John Paul II introduces the notion of "structures of sin," which will be discussed more fully below. Human selfishness and shortsightedness become institutionalized within social structures in a way that magnify and perpetuate the moral evil of individuals within the very structures of the international community. As a result, for John Paul II, the struggle for structural changes in the international system must be accompanied with the necessary conversion of both individuals and institutions.

Finally, chapter four focuses on identifying particular guidelines as a response to the issue identified in the previous parts of the encyclical. Here John Paul II notes that the church has no technical solutions to offer. Nor does he state a preference of one sociopolitical system over another. Rather, he notes that the church must seek to defend human dignity and freedom. Instead of offering an ideology which outlines a blueprint for transforming society, the pope calls on the church to renew its commitment to social justice as an integral part of the gospel call to evangelization.

Although these two encyclicals are quite different in focus, the issues they raise regarding the relationship between the gospel call and the task of social witness, especially in the area of global development, can provide some useful lessons for contemporary North American evangelicals to reflect upon in thinking about how we relate to the wider world outside this continent. We now turn to an examination of some of these issues.

The Church's Competence to Address Social Issues

Many evangelicals are suspicious of calls for engaging in social action, primarily because they wonder whether the church has the authority or competence to address such issues. Is not the mandate of the church to preach Christ? Are not complex social issues like underdevelopment and poverty or international trade and debt beyond the competence of the church to address? How can the church address issues like development when the leaders who often speak on behalf of the church are not themselves economists or development experts? Such concerns are often voiced, not just by Christians themselves, but also by secular critics who argue that church leaders do not have the technical expertise to address such critical social issues and therefore should just stick to "religious" matters outside the public domain. Moreover, many Christians caution against the church tainting itself by becoming involved in such politically charged issues.

John Paul II addresses these concerns directly by acknowledging that, at first glance, complex issues such as the development of peoples do indeed appear to be in the realm of the social and economic sciences and therefore "could seem extraneous to the legitimate concern of the Church as a religious institution" (*Sollicitudo rei socialis,* §8). Nevertheless, John Paul II notes that the tradition of Catholic social teaching since Pope Leo XIII has always asserted that such issues have at their core an ethical and cultural character. It is society's failure to recognize the essential moral nature of these issues that affirms the "legitimacy and necessity of the Church's intervention in this field" (*Sollicitudo rei socialis,* §8).

However, in addressing these issues, the church speaks not as an authority in the area of the social and economic sciences, but rather as an "expert in humanity" (*Sollicitudo rei socialis,* §7). A theme that runs throughout his social encyclicals, and his other teachings dealing with the "culture of death," is that human schemes often go wrong because they are based on a false anthropology. In other words, a distorted understanding of what it means to be human often leads to the imposition of political and economic schemes with disastrous results. Thus, in order to address the most pressing social issues of the day, John Paul II insists that society must have a correct understanding of the true nature of humankind.

John Paul II's view here is no doubt partly influenced by his experience with communism in Eastern Europe, where he saw firsthand the bitter consequences of a political-economic system that failed to respect the dignity of the human person. Despite the deployment of enormous resources and technologies to address social problems, if any scheme for social reform is not "guided by a moral understanding and by an orientation towards the true good of the human race, it easily turns against man to oppress him" (*Sollicitudo rei socialis,* §28). Thus the church's involvement in social issues is not based on some idealistic and overly optimistic myth of human progress, but rather on a realistic reading of social issues in the light of the true nature of humankind.

In *Veritatis splendor,* John Paul II makes it clear that truth is the most important factor in considering questions of both personal and social morality. It is the church's special responsibility to teach the truth about humankind. At the beginning of *Dives in misericordia,* John Paul II notes that his first encyclical *Redemptor hominis* addressed the subject of "the truth about man" (*Dives in misericordia,* §1). Thus, from the beginning John Paul II made the proclamation of the truth of the nature of the human person a central focus of his papacy. Although *Dives in misericordia* focuses on God the Father as revealed through his Son Christ ("whoever has seen me has seen the Father" [Jn 14:9]), John Paul II notes that the revelation of the nature of God the Father as a God of mercy "fully reveals man to himself and brings to light his lofty calling (*Dives in misericordia,* §1, quoting Constitution *Gaudium et spes*).

However, while affirming both the legitimacy and necessity of the church to address complex socioeconomic issues, John Paul II is careful to point out that its role is not to provide a detailed blueprint that is to be applied by decision makers in each country. In both *Sollicitudo rei socialis* and his other social encyclicals, he states that the church has no specific models to present. Such development models can arise only in the context of specific historical circumstances and as a result of the careful reflection of those working most closely with the concrete social, economic, political and cultural aspects of the problem.

This is why John Paul II is careful to assert that Catholic social doctrine is not an ideology in itself, and it does not endorse any specific ideology. The church "does not propose economic and political systems or programs, nor does she show preference for one or the other, provided that human dignity is properly respected and promoted, and provided she herself is allowed the room she needs to exercise her ministry in the world" (*Sollicitudo rei socialis,* §41).

A little later in the same section, John Paul II notes:

> The Church's social doctrine is not a "third way" between liberal capitalism and Marxist collectivism, nor even a possible alternative to other solutions less radically opposed to one another: rather, it constitutes a category of its own. Nor is it an ideology, but rather the accurate formulation of the results of a careful reflection on the complex realities of human existence, in society and in the international order, in the light of faith and of the Church's tradition. Its main aim is to interpret these realities, determining their conformity with or divergence from the lines of the Gospel teaching on man and his vocation, a vocation which is at once earthly and transcendent; its aim is thus to guide Christian behavior. It therefore belongs to the field, not of ideology, but of theology and particularly of moral theology. (*Sollicitudo rei socialis,* §41)

Rather than the articulation of a comprehensive ideological program, John Paul II notes that what Catholic social doctrine offers is "principles for reflection, criteria for judgment, and directives for action."[10] These guidelines are meant primarily to have a "practical orientation" that is "directed towards moral conduct." Thus, John Paul II concludes that when the church "concerns herself with the 'development of peoples,' she cannot be accused of going outside her own specific field of competence and, still less, outside the mandate received from the Lord" (*Sollicitudo rei socialis,* §8).

In setting out this approach, John Paul II challenges us to avoid sliding into an easy dualism whereby we think that the gospel message deals only with spiritual matters, while secular society is left to deal with the social and economic problems that arise in the spheres outside the church. Instead, the necessity for careful social reflection arises directly out of "an application of the word of God to people's lives and the life of society" (*Sollicitudo rei socialis,* §8).

---

[10]*Sollicitudo rei socialis,* §41, and elsewhere. John Paul is particularly insistent on this point, repeating this formula at least six times in different sections of the document.

THE CHRISTOLOGICAL BASIS FOR JOHN PAUL II'S SOCIAL ANALYSIS

Throughout *Sollicitudo rei socialis,* John Paul II repeatedly emphasizes the point that "whatever affects the dignity of individuals and peoples" cannot be treated as a "technical" problem but must be seen in its ethical and moral dimensions. By being willing to address issues such as development, "the Church fulfills her mission to evangelize, for she offers her first contribution to the solution of the urgent problem of development when she proclaims the truth about Christ, about herself and about man, applying this truth to a concrete situation" (*Sollicitudo rei socialis,* §41).

It is important to note here John Paul's assertion that the church's role in addressing social issues is to first proclaim "the truth about Christ." This statement reflects a significantly different approach to writing about social issues than one finds in previous social encyclicals. A reader picking up a copy of Pope Leo XIII's *Rerum novarum* (1891), which marks the beginning of the modern social encyclical tradition, will be struck by the virtual absence of scriptural references and any invocation of the name of Christ. Rather, the social encyclical tradition relied almost exclusively on natural law reasoning for the development of its arguments. By making an appeal to "nature" or "natural law," which was accessible to all people, popes were deliberately addressing their encyclicals not just to fellow Christians but to "all people of good will."

In contrast, the three social encyclicals of John Paul II make no specific reference to natural law in their texts. Certainly, as shown in the discussion on *Vertitas splendor* in chapter eight in this volume, John Paul II continued to believe that natural law reasoning is an important part of the church's intellectual heritage and needs to be preserved. Nevertheless, in writing his social encyclicals he makes no effort to develop further this aspect of Catholic social thought. Rather, he sets out a much more christological basis for approaching social issues. This shift in emphasis reflects an important change in approach signaled by Vatican II when *Gaudium et spes* proclaimed that it was the church's responsibility to "read the signs of the times" in the light of the gospel. As a result, John Paul II's social encyclicals give increased attention not only to historical contextualization, but also to a careful scriptural exegesis and a christological basis for understanding the nature of human dignity.

This focus is important for two reasons. First, as alluded to above, John Paul II believed strongly that secular ideologies and social schemes are bound to fail because they are based on a distorted or false anthropology. In order to get this anthropology right, it is essential to turn to Christ for an understanding of the true nature of man.

As he states in the second paragraph of *Dives in misericordia,* "the truth about man . . . is revealed to us in its fullness and depth in Christ." And again in the same paragraph: "Man and man's lofty calling are revealed in Christ through the revelation of the mystery of the Father and His love" (*Dives in misericordia,* §1).

Second, in establishing a christological basis for understanding the nature of man, it also becomes clear that our involvement in social issues is an important part of the Christian calling to proclaim the gospel message. Again Christ provides the model. John Paul II reminds us of Christ's ministry to the poor, the suffering and the oppressed. "By these actions and words Christ makes the Father present among men" (*Dives in misericordia,* §3). In revealing God's mercy and forgiveness, Christ "demanded from people that they also should be guided in their lives by love and mercy." Twice in this section, John Paul II repeats that demonstrating this mercy is at "the heart of the Gospel ethos."

Authentic Human Development as a Moral Concept

In surveying the current international situation, John Paul II notes that "one of the greatest injustices in the contemporary world" is the fact that "the ones who possess much are relatively few and those who possess almost nothing are many" (*Sollicitudo rei socialis,* §28). John Paul II was acutely aware that the world situation had actually become worse since *Populorum progressio* was published. With this in mind, he calls for a reevaluation of the concept of development. "We have to ask ourselves," he writes, "if the sad reality of today might not be, at least in part, the result of a too narrow idea of development, that is, a mainly economic one" (*Sollicitudo rei socialis,* §15).

He bases this question on the observation that purely economic development alone does not lead to greater human satisfaction and happiness. In fact, he points out that growing levels of poverty and underdevelopment have been accompanied by the phenomenon of "superdevelopment." While some peoples experience growing misery, others live in consumer or consumption-oriented societies where there is "no other horizon than the multiplication or continual replacement of the things already owned with others still better." Despite this overabundance, experience shows that a society based on "pure consumerism" or a "crass materialism" leads ultimately to a feeling of "radical dissatisfaction." While there is an accumulation of ever more goods, "deeper aspirations remain unsatisfied and perhaps even stifled" (*Sollicitudo rei socialis,* §28).

John Paul II uses this contrast to make the point that concepts of development which focus on merely the economic dimension will inevitably fail. Unless the fundamental moral dimension of development is recognized, solely materialistic approaches will only succeed in turning "against man to oppress him" (*Sollicitudo rei socialis,* §28).

For John Paul II, materialistic approaches to development fail because they make the mistake of confusing "having" with "being." It is true that a great many people cannot reach their true human vocation because they are deprived of essential goods. However, many who do have much *also* fail to meet their true human vocation because they are too caught up in what John Paul II calls the "cult of 'having.'" For John Paul II this evidence confirms his contention that development is essentially a moral issue involving the correct ordering of fundamental human values. Thus, getting development right is not a matter of finding the correct economic model, but a matter of establishing the correct order to the hierarchy of values. The "having" of goods must always be subordinate to the good of "being," that is, the achievement of man's true vocation. Simply having more goods does not ensure that humans will flourish. In fact, an excessively narrow conception of development may only turn "against those whom it is meant to benefit" (*Sollicitudo rei socialis,* §28).

As a result, John Paul II concludes that "development cannot consist only in the use, dominion over, and indiscriminate possession of created things and the products of human industry, but rather in subordinating the possession, dominion and use to man's divine likeness and to his vocation to immortality" (*Sollicitudo rei socialis,* §29). Thus, in his view, all approaches to economic and social development which ignore this transcendent reality concerning the nature of the human being are bound to fail. Successful development will occur only when there is a right order of values, especially between "having" and "being." Thus, he notes that "when the 'having' of a few can be to the detriment of the 'being' of many others," it is vital that the church respond by helping to relieve the misery of those suffering by giving not only out of its "abundance," but also out of its "necessities" (*Sollicitudo rei socialis,* §31). John Paul II even suggests that the church may have to sell of some of its own property in order to provide for the poor. The duty to respond to such need and reestablish a proper ordering of values is required not only for individuals, but for societies and nations as well.[11]

[11]It should be noted that John Paul II is not necessarily endorsing a form of socialism here. Writing in *Centesimus annus,* following the end of the Cold War, John Paul II does acknowledge the legitimate role of private property, profit-making and a market economy in the development of nations. But, he also emphasizes the necessity that such capitalist measures be placed in a "strong juridical framework which places it at the service of human freedom in its totality, and which sees it as a particular aspect of that freedom, the core of which is ethical and religious" (*Centesimus annus,* §42).

Sin and the Structural Dimension of Social Problems

Given this emphasis on the moral dimension of development, it is perhaps not surprising that in *Sollicitudo rei socialis* John Paul places significant emphasis on individual attitudes and behaviors. If the problem of development and underdevelopment has a fundamentally moral character, then "the obstacles to development likewise have a moral character" (*Sollicitudo rei socialis,* §35). These obstacles are not technical in nature but essentially "political" in nature because they are obstacles that require an exercise of an "effective political will" to address. Thus, in the chapter entitled "A Theological Reading of Modern Problems," John Paul II seeks to "single out the moral causes which, with respect to the behavior of individuals considered as responsible persons, interfere in such a way as to slow down the course of development and hinder its full achievement" (*Sollicitudo rei socialis,* §35).

This approach has been criticized by those who argue that John Paul's emphasis on personal moral responsibility and the attitudes of the poor themselves minimizes the degree to which oppressive international economic structures contribute to the poverty of many in developing countries. Thus, it has been suggested that John Paul II's encyclical merely reinforces the status quo by focusing so much on individual behaviors.[12]

Such criticisms have the danger of overshadowing the point that John Paul II accentuates throughout the entire document. He wants us to understand that how we view and understand the human person should have a profound impact on how we behave in the socioeconomic realm. If we truly believe in the transcendent dimension of the human person, then we will transform the social and economic character of both our individual behaviors and the institutions that we create.

John Paul II does indeed acknowledge that there are significant structural and systemic barriers to development. For example, he notes that "the instrument chosen to make a contribution to development has turned into a counterproductive mechanism" (*Sollicitudo rei socialis,* §19), and often these mechanisms or structures "suffocate or condition the economies of the less developed countries" (*Sollicitudo rei socialis,* §16).

Although he recognizes the reality of such structures, John Paul II is reluctant to label them as a "structural evil" or "structural sin" in their own right, independent of individual human responsibility. Thus, in an oblique reference to the Marxist assumptions that underlay early forms of liberation theology, John Paul

---

[12]Cf. Mary E. Hobgood, *Catholic Social Teaching and Economic Theory* (Philadelphia: Temple University Press, 1991), p. 194.

notes that he rejects those notions of social sin in which blame is "placed not so much on the moral conscience of an individual, but rather on some vague entity or anonymous collectivity such as the situation, the system, society, structures or institutions" (Apostolic Exhortation *Reconciliatio et Paenitentia*). From his experience of living under a Communist system, John Paul II is well aware that just changing social structures themselves is often insufficient to address the real problems of injustice.

As a result, *Sollicitudo rei socialis* introduces the concept of "structures of sin," but then focuses particularly on the moral behaviors which give rise to them. Economic, social and political structures do not just arise through some operation of impersonal forces; they arise out of the intentional act of the will of morally responsible individuals. Thus, in the case of those structures which become real obstacles to full human flourishing, these "structures of sin" form out of "the accumulation and concentration of many personal sins" (*SRS* §36, fn. 65, quoting from Apostolic Exhortation *Reconciliatio et Paenitentia*). In the case of hindrances to development, "the all-consuming desire for profit" and the "thirst for power" (*Sollicitudo rei socialis,* §37) often combine to create structures which hinder development. For John Paul II, "structures of sin" are always "rooted in personal sin, and thus always linked to the concrete acts of individuals who introduce these structures, consolidate them and make them difficult to remove. And thus they grow stronger, spread, and become the source of other sins, and so influence people's behavior" (*Sollicitudo rei socialis,* §36). This notion is rooted in the personalist philosophy of John Paul II, who always wants us to be aware of the element of human responsibility in all that we do.[13]

The notion that our attitudes and behaviors give rise to structural problems that hinder true human development is emphasized throughout *Sollicitudo rei socialis.* The phrase "structure of sin" is mentioned at least nine times. In one place John Paul reminds us that "the principal obstacle to be overcome on the way to authentic liberation is sin and the structures produced by sin as it multiplies and spreads" (*Sollicitudo rei socialis,* §46). In another he states that "one must denounce the existence of economic, financial and social mechanisms which, although they are manipulated by people, often function almost automatically, thus accentuating the situation of wealth for some and poverty for the rest" (*Sollicitudo rei socialis,* §16).

[13]Although at times John Paul II appears to be taking up the language of liberation theology, his emphasis on personal responsibility clearly differentiates his position from those who suggest that "social sin" is impersonal and anonymous. For a discussion of this point, see Avery Cardinal Dulles, *The Splendour of the Faith: The Theological Vision of Pope John Paul II* (New York: Herder and Herder, 2003), p. 125.

This message is particularly relevant for modern North American evangelicals, who tend to focus on sin as essentially a "personal" matter, something primarily between the individual and God. We also discount the idea of social sin and give even less credence to the notion that "personal sin" may have social consequences. The consequences of this privatization of sin and social responsibility are reflected in studies repeatedly showing that far too often the socioeconomic decisions of believers, including evangelicals, are little different from those of nonbelievers.[14]

John Paul's concept of "structures of sin" helps us realize that social structures do not come into existence independently of human actions and motivations. They arise out of and are deeply rooted in the specific human attitudes and behaviors. Thus, when we act only out of motives such as an "all-consuming desire for profit" or a "thirst for power," our actions will give rise to institutions which reflect and perpetuate these sinful attitudes (*Sollicitudo rei socialis,* §37). Thus, as John Paul warns, our individual concrete sins will "grow stronger, spread, and become the source of other sins, and so influence people's behavior" (*Sollicitudo rei socialis,* §36). As John Paul II emphasizes throughout his teachings, all sin to some extent has a social dimension and is never totally "personal."

This should be a reminder to those of us who live in a North American culture of overabundance and hyper-consumerism that our social and economic behaviors can indeed give rise to destructive structures which institutionalize and perpetuate our "personal" sins. The sins of greed and over-consumption are not just "personal" vices, but are social sins which have consequences far beyond what we can imagine. In our North American social context, so influenced by a neo-liberal economic ideology which emphasizes the supposedly neutral and impersonal laws of the marketplace, we view our personal consumer habits and economic decisions as essentially "private" rather than "public" decisions. John Paul II's focus should provide us with a reminder that all of our "private" decisions ultimately have "public" consequences, and thus we should be ready to take moral responsibility for them.[15] It is clear that John Paul II applies this not only on the individual level, but also on community, national and international levels as well.

This focus on the moral responsibility of the person leads John Paul II to warn that simply working through social justice struggle to change unjust social and

---

[14]See Robert Wuthnow, *God and Mammon in America* (New York: Free Press, 1994), and Ronald J. Sider, *Scandal of the Evangelical Conscience: Why Are Christians Living Just Like the Rest of the World* (Grand Rapids: Baker, 2005).

[15]John Paul's notion that "private" consumerism always has "public" consequences was perhaps inadvertently driven home in the wake of September 11, 2001, when President George W. Bush called on all Americans not to stay home but to drive to their local malls to shop.

economic structures alone will not be enough. There will need to be a more profound change in the underlying personal values and attitudes which give rise to these structures. Thus, for the problems of underdevelopment to be addressed, we must also change "the *spiritual* attitudes which define each individual's relationship with self, with neighbor, with even the remotest human communities, and nature itself; and all of this in view of higher values such as the common good." John Paul continues by stating that Christians will recognize that he is talking about a "conversion," which will involve a transformation of the "relationship to God, to the sin committed, to its consequences and hence to one's neighbor, either an individual or a community" (*Sollicitudo rei socialis,* §38).

SOLIDARITY AS AN INCARNATION OF THE GOSPEL OF MERCY

One might have expected that following this discussion on the structures of sin, John Paul would move directly to a resounding call for all to join in the struggle for social justice and efforts to overthrow these structures. Instead, he moves to a discussion of conversion of attitudes and relationships and then to a lengthy treatment of the concept of solidarity. This latter term is one which is largely foreign to the vocabulary. At best we might associate it with some warm fuzzy feeling of compassion toward the needy or something we have heard sung in a labor union song. How does John Paul II move from a discussion of social sin to conversion to solidarity? The key to understanding this linkage is a reference in the section in *Sollicitudo rei socialis* dealing with "sin" and "structures of sin" when John Paul II writes, "The God who is rich in mercy, the Redeemer of man, the Lord and giver of life, requires from people clear cut attitudes which express themselves also in actions or omissions toward one's one neighbor" (*Sollicitudo rei socialis,* §37).

To understand John Paul II's interpretation, it is helpful to return briefly to his encyclical *Dives in misericordia.* In the face of the growing inequalities and injustices in the world, there is a growing, and justified, clamor for justice. John Paul writes: "It is obvious that a fundamental defect, or rather series of defects, indeed a defective machinery is at the root of contemporary economics and materialist civilization, which does not allow the human family to break free from such radically unjust situations" (*Dives in misericordia,* §11).

However, there seems to be an even deeper problem. Programs which start out with the idea of promoting justice often end up causing further suffering and injustice. John Paul notes that "experience of the past and of our own time demonstrates that justice alone is not enough, that it can even lead to the negation and destruction of itself" (*Dives in misericordia,* §12). Later in that same section he notes that "desacralization" within society often turns in "dehumanization." What John Paul wants us to understand is that unless the struggle for justice in rooted in a proper understanding of the transcendent nature of humans, it can easily degenerate into a tool for further oppression and hatred.

This is why John Paul II emphasizes in *Dives in misericordia* that justice must always be accompanied by mercy—the divine mercy of God the Father, which is revealed to us by his Son, Jesus Christ. To demonstrate what he means, John Paul II provides an extensive exegesis of the parable of the prodigal son. He notes that, having already squandered his inheritance and humiliated his father, the best that the prodigal son could expect was to be hired as a servant, at a servant's wages. In fact, given the hurt and embarrassment that the son's actions had caused to the father, the act of hiring his son as a servant was more than enough to fill the requirement of justice. John Paul points out that the father, out of his deep love for his son, went beyond just the minimal requirements for justice. Seeing his son as he was intended to be in his full dignity, the father sought instead to restore his son to his full dignity. This parable of God's divine mercy, as revealed to us by Christ, is a powerful reminder that justice needs always to be tempered with mercy. In fact, as John Paul notes, mercy serves as a corrective. "True mercy is, so to speak, the most profound source of justice" (*Dives in misericordia,* §14).

Having shown that mercy is necessary to temper and correct justice, John Paul II goes on to remind us that Jesus also taught that we are called not only to receive mercy but to practice it toward others. Obtaining and giving mercy is central to the process of conversion. "This authentically evangelical process [conversion] is not just a spiritual transformation realized once and for all: it is a whole lifestyle, an essential and continuous characteristic of the Christian vocation." Later in that same section, John Paul notes that "mercy becomes an indispensable element for shaping mutual relationships between people, in a spirit of deepest respect for what is human, and in a spirit of mutual brotherhood" (*Dives in misericordia,* §14).

Without the tempering power of mercy, John Paul II warns, a society will be "a world of cold and unfeeling justice." When each claims his or her own rights over the rights of others, society will become merely "an arena of permanent strife between one group and another" (*Dives in misericordia,* §14). John Paul II makes it clear that forgiveness is also not just a "personal" virtue. It is perhaps one of the most important political virtues because it alone can ensure true justice in social relations. As he writes in *Dives in misericordia:* "The fundamental structure of justice always enters into the sphere of mercy. Mercy, however, has the power to confer on justice a new content, which is expressed most simply and fully in forgiveness" (§14).

This discussion in *Dives in misericordia* helps us understand then the emphasis that John Paul places on solidarity as both the fruit of conversion and a Christian virtue whose practice is to be cultivated. In the document *Ecclesia in America,* John Paul II notes that "in order to speak of conversion, the gap between faith and life must be bridged. Where the gap exists, Christians are such only in name" (§26). Thus, for John Paul II our conversion will not be complete unless we revise all aspects of our lives, "especially those related to the social order and the pursuit of the common good" (*Ecclesia in America,* §27).[16] Conversion, or the making of a fundamental change of mentality *(metanoia),* is an ongoing process of "striving to assimilate the values of the Gospel, which contradict the dominant tendencies of the world" (*Ecclesia in America,* §28). For John Paul II then, just as sin always has a social dimension, so too conversion must also have a social dimension in order to demonstrate the fruits of a genuine conversion.

Such conversion will lead us to see the growing interdependence among individuals, communities and nations in a new way. Just as we need to see the concept of development in a new light, so too must we see interdependence as more than just a growing connectedness between nations. Instead we have to see it as a moral category linked to the virtue of solidarity. As a moral concept, solidarity helps us to see each member of society as a true person. John Paul II notes that for Christians, the virtue of solidarity allows us to see our neighbor as "not only a human being with his or her own rights"; that human being "becomes the living image of God the Father, redeemed by the blood of Jesus Christ and placed under the permanent action of the Holy Spirit" (*Sollicitudo rei socialis,* §40).

Solidarity enables us "to see the 'other'—whether a person, people or nation—not just as some kind of instrument, with a work capacity and physical strength to be exploited at low cost and then discarded . . . but as our 'neighbor,' a 'helper' (cf. Gen 2:18-20), to be made a sharer, on a par with ourselves" (*Sollicitudo rei socialis,* §39). This sense of solidarity imposes obligations on all. The wealthy and influential, who possess a greater number of goods, must be ready to share them to the greater good of all. Those who are poor or weak need to do what they can to contribute to the common good in a positive way. Those in between must "not selfishly insist on their own particular interests, but respect the interests of others" (*Sollicitudo rei socialis,* §39).

---

[16]John Paul II, *Post-Synodal Apostolic Exhortation "Ecclesia in America". . on the Encounter with the Living Jesus Christ: The Way to Conversion, Communion and Solidarity in America,* Libreria Editrice Vaticana (January 22, 1999) <http://www.vatican.va/holy_father/john_paul_ii/apost_exhortations/documents/hf_jp-ii_exh_22011999_ecclesia-in-america_en.html>.

His predecessor, Pius XII, had noted that peace is the fruit of justice. John Paul II modifies this by noting that solidarity, the fruit of genuine conversion and mercy, is "the path to peace and at the same time to development. . . . *Opus solidaritatis pax*" (*Sollicitudo rei socialis,* §39).

Conclusions

Since space is limited, I have examined only a few of the key themes which can be drawn out of these two encyclicals. However, these should be sufficient to demonstrate that the teaching of John Paul II can offer many useful insights to us as evangelicals as we seek to address social issues. Perhaps most important is his clear contention that social justice issues and service can be both "evangelical and evangelizing." But, it can be so only if we give careful attention to the social dimensions both of sin and of conversion. This is a message that will continue to have relevance in a consumerist society which is increasingly materialistic and secular. Engagement in social concerns and the struggle for greater social justice is an integral part of the Great Commission which Christ gave to his church. When it is offered in the spirit of Jesus "who came 'to proclaim Good News to the poor' (Lk 4:18) . . . the service of the poor shows forth God's infinite love for all people and becomes an effective way of communicating the hope of salvation which Christ has brought to the world, a hope which glows in a special way when it is shared with those abandoned or rejected by society" (*Ecclesia in America,* §18).

11

LABOREM EXERCENS AND *CENTESIMUS ANNUS*

Work and Economics

Ronald J. Sider

INTRODUCTION

These two encyclicals, released about ten years apart, contain Pope John Paul II's mature thinking on work and economics.

LABOREM EXERCENS

Context. John Paul II issued this encyclical at one of the most dramatic points in his life as pope. Three aspects of the context are especially important: the global economic and political setting, the history of Catholic social teaching, and the earlier life and thought of the pope himself.

When John Paul II released *Laborem exercens*[1] on September 14, 1981, Solidarity, the first independent union in any Communist country, was in the midst of a high-stakes, exceedingly dangerous challenge to the Polish Communist government and indeed to the entire system of communism in Eastern Europe and the Soviet Union. The world watched with anticipation, fear and astonishment as this daring organization of Polish workers, carefully but clearly supported by the Polish pope, demanded dramatic new freedom from their Communist rulers.

---

[1]John Paul II, *"Laborem exercens" . . . on Human Work on the Ninetieth Anniversary of Rerum novarum*, Libreria Editrice Vaticana (September 14, 1981) <http://www.vatican.va/holy_father/john_paul_ii/encyclicals/documents/hf_jp-ii_enc_14091981_laborem-exercens_en.html>.

John Paul II, the former archbishop of Krakow, Poland, returned for a historic pilgrimage to his native country June 2-10, 1979. In those ten days, one-third of all Poles turned out in massive crowds to see the pope in person, to cheer their native son and to listen to his careful but clear call to the Polish people to remember that Christianity had been at the heart of Polish history for a thousand years. He insisted that "the problem of human labor cannot be fully solved without the Gospel."[2] Without frontally defying the Communist authorities, he clearly energized the Polish people to dare to hope and believe that freedom and change were possible.[3]

Just fourteen months later, on August 14, 1980, Lech Walesa led 17,000 workers at the Gdansk shipyards in a daring strike. Subtly but clearly, the pope supported the strikers, and on August 31, 1980, the Polish government signed the first agreement in a Communist country for an independent, self-governing trade union. Furious, the Soviet Union planned an invasion to crush Solidarity in December but inexplicably failed to follow through. With the entire world watching, the crisis continued in the spring and summer of 1981. On September 5, 1981, Solidarity opened its first national congress. As the Soviets conducted threatening military exercises in the Baltic, Solidarity delegates representing over nine million members called for free elections to the Polish parliament and for greater freedom for independent trade unions.

That was the context in the workers' alleged paradise in Communist Poland when the Polish pope on September 14, 1981, issued this famous encyclical on work. As the early sections of the encyclical make clear, however, the conflict with communism was by no means the only aspect of the economic/political context for this encyclical. John Paul II was very aware of the economic changes emerging from automation and technology, growing environmental pollution and the reality of massive poverty throughout the developing world (*Laborem exercens,* §§1, 2). He also was very familiar with the great debate between capitalism and communism about the best way to bring justice to all and the way that both systems seemed to be producing materialistic cultures preoccupied with material things and denying or forgetting deeper spiritual reality.

The second aspect of the context was the long Catholic tradition of social teaching. Starting with Leo XIII's *Rerum novarum* (The Condition of Labor) in

---

[2]Patricia A. Lamoureux, "*Laborem exercens,*" in *Modern Catholic Teaching: Commentaries and Interpretations,* ed. Kenneth R. Himes et al. (Washington, D.C.: Georgetown University Press, 2005), p. 391.

[3]See George Weigel, *Witness to Hope: The Biography of Pope John Paul II, 1920-2005* (New York: Harper, 1999), pp. 304-20.

1891, successive popes had issued a long series of influential encyclicals discussing a wide variety of social issues and developing an elaborate body of sophisticated reflection on societal problems. Those encyclicals clearly supported justice for workers and their unions; they also asserted the importance of private property. *Laborem exercens* builds on these previous papal documents.

John Paul originally intended to issue the encyclical on May 15, 1981, to celebrate the ninetieth anniversary of *Rerum novarum.* But two days before, on May 13, Mehmet Ali Agca almost succeeded in assassinating the pope. During the months of recuperation, John Paul worked further on this encyclical.

The pope's own life provides the third crucial context for understanding *Laborem exercens.* During the Nazi occupation of Poland, Karol Wojtyla (the future John Paul II) worked as a manual laborer in a limestone quarry and then a chemical factory, developing a deep appreciation for the contribution and character of ordinary workers.[4] For the next thirty-plus years, he struggled as Polish priest, bishop and cardinal to understand and interact with communism and its analysis of workers. He was also a distinguished professor of philosophy who had published scholarly books seeking to relate the long Catholic philosophical tradition of Thomism with contemporary philosophy, especially phenomenology and its personalist emphases on the human person. Catholic social teaching had always emphasized the centrality of human dignity, but John Paul's emphasis in this encyclical on the subjective side of work probably derived in part from his philosophical work and careful study of Max Scheler (1874-1928).[5]

Summary. In the introduction to *Laborem exercens*, John Paul II declares that human work (and that includes both manual and intellectual work) "is a key, probably *the essential key,* to the whole social question" (*Laborem exercens,* §3).[6] A proper understanding of work is crucial for any successful solution to society's complex social problems.

In the first major section, "Work and Man," John Paul grounds his analysis of work in the dignity of the human person revealed in Scripture. Genesis' assertion that every human being is made in the image of God and called to exercise dominion over the earth means that "every human being reflects the very action of the Creator of the universe" (*Laborem exercens,* §4). John Paul is quite aware of the harsh aspects of actual human labor, but he insists that through work one achieves

---

[4]Weigel, *Witness to Hope,* pp. 55-58.

[5]See, for example, Derek S. Jeffreys, *Defending Human Dignity: John Paul II and Political Realism* (Grand Rapids: Brazos, 2004), chap. 1; Lamoureux, "*Laborem exercens,*" pp. 404-6.

[6]Emphasis is original in all quotations from John Paul's encyclicals unless noted otherwise.

"*fulfilment* as a human being and indeed, in a sense, becomes 'more a human being'" (*Laborem exercens,* §9). The labor of every single human being enjoys an awesome value.

Central to the analysis is the distinction between the objective and subjective aspects of work. The objective aspect of work refers to the products of human labor: the agricultural, industrial and intellectual things that persons create through their labor (*Laborem exercens,* §5). John Paul appreciates this objective side and the incredible products made possible by modern science and technology. But he believes it is more important to emphasize the subjective side of work.

Drawing both on biblical revelation and his personalist philosophy, he insists that because persons are made in the image of God, they are subjective beings "capable of acting in a planned and rational way, capable of deciding about [themselves], and with a tendency to self-realization." Regardless of what products a worker may produce, his or her work must "all serve to realize his humanity, to fulfil the calling to be a person that is his by reason of his very humanity" (*Laborem exercens,* §6). That means that "work is 'for man' and not man 'for work.'" That also means that work must be organized so that it respects the human dignity of the worker.

A further implication is that we must reject the ancient division of people into different (and differently valued) classes depending on the kind of work they do. The fact that God Incarnate taught a "Gospel of Work" by spending most of his time at manual labor as a carpenter means that "the basis for determining the value of human work is not primarily the kind of work being done but the fact that the one who is doing it is a person" (*Laborem exercens,* §6).

John Paul is insistent. This subjective dimension of work "takes precedence over the objective dimension" (*Laborem exercens,* §10).

Tragically, from the beginning of the industrial age, the worker has often become a mere instrument of production. Rather than organizing work in a way that respects the full dignity of the worker as a person made in God's image, society has developed a "materialistic economism" that focuses primarily on the objective dimension of work rather than the subjective. Workers become mere tools in a complex, materialistic productive process. The "liberal socio-political system" (i.e., capitalistic societies) has paid attention to and protected the initiative of those who possessed capital more than it has respected the rights of workers. The result has been the degradation of workers and their exploitation via unjust wages.

Fortunately, worker solidarity has led to substantial improvement. Precisely because it is called to be the "church of the poor," the church must stand in solidarity with workers as they demand a "just wage" and working conditions that respect their dignity. Unfortunately, "various ideological or power systems"—i.e., both capitalist and Communist societies—still allow "*flagrant injustices*" (*Laborem exercens,* §8).

In addition to being the way that persons achieve the dignity that the Creator intended, work also makes possible two other crucial things. Work enables persons to create the things—the means of subsistence and the things necessary for education—that are essential to found a family. Work also makes it possible to create a society with its vast accumulation over the centuries of buildings, traditions, culture, etc.—"a great historical and societal incarnation of the work of all generations." Thus, through work, each person adds "to the heritage of the whole human family" (*Laborem exercens,* §10).

In the next major section, John Paul analyzes the conflict between labor and capital in contemporary society. Briefly, he outlines the way in which, during the last couple of centuries, a small, influential group of owners of the means of production exploited the vast body of workers by "following the principle of maximum profit," trying to pay the lowest possible wages, and disregarding the health and safety of workers. In response, the Marxist system of "scientific socialism and communism" sought to eliminate class injustice by abolishing private property and establishing collective ownership of the means of production. By establishing a monopoly of power, the Marxists hoped to introduce socialism and eventually communism everywhere (*Laborem exercens,* §11).

John Paul insists that the church's basic response to both capitalism and communism must be the "*priority of labour over capital.*" Every worker makes use of two things: first, the vast wealth of riches that the Creator has given to us in the material world; and second, the slow accumulation of knowledge and tools produced by previous workers that now enable workers to create new, vast, complex products out of the material world given to us by the Creator. "This gigantic and powerful instrument—the whole collection of means of production that in a sense are considered synonymous with 'capital'—is the result of work." All this almost infinitely vast complex of tools, technology and productive capabilities, however, is "only a collection of things." "Man alone is a person" (*Laborem exercens,* §12). Therefore the worker must take priority over capital.

John Paul rejects the Marxist claim that labor and capital must be in conflict. They ought not to be opposed to each other. Labor has produced all the capital that exists. Capital is supposed to serve the worker as a subject. Tragically, in the course of modern history, labor and capital became separated and placed in opposition to each other, and both were viewed as impersonal forces—merely two factors of production. John Paul labels this "fundamental error of thought" "materialism" and "economism" (*Laborem exercens,* §13). Directly or indirectly, this approach assumes that material reality is superior and spiritual reality (including the human person) is inferior or nonexistent. Liberal, capitalist societies developed a "practical materialism." Marxist societies, later, developed a philosophical materialism. Neither system starts by affirming the priority of labor which flows from a biblical understanding of human dignity. To do that will require changes in both theory and practice.

Central to a solution is a reaffirmation of what John Paul believes is the longstanding Christian understanding of private property. Private ownership, as previous papal encyclicals made clear, is right and important. Marxist collectivism is wrong. But the church's understanding of private property also differs from the system of liberal capitalism.

> Christian tradition has never upheld this right [of private property] as absolute and untouchable. On the contrary, it has always understood this right within the broader context of the right common to all to use the goods of the whole of creation: *the right to private property is subordinated to the right to common use.* (*Laborem exercens,* §14)

Private property is legitimate only when it serves labor and thereby serves "the universal destination of goods and the right to common use of them" (*Laborem exercens,* 14).[7]

John Paul therefore explicitly rejects the position of "'rigid' capitalism" that defends "the exclusive right to private ownership of the means of production as an untouchable 'dogma' of economic life." Capital, he insists, is the product of the work of generations of laborers. It is also being created day by day by workers. Therefore proposals such as "*joint ownership of the means of work*" and workers sharing in management and/or profits must be explored (*Laborem exercens,* §14).

Equally clearly, John Paul rejects the notion that communism's elimination of private property will solve the problems. Collectivist systems that "socialize" property wrongly develop a monopoly of power in the hands of the governing authorities. He calls for "a wide range of intermediate bodies with economic, social and cultural purposes" that enjoy "real autonomy with regard to the public powers" (*Laborem exercens,* §14)—just what Solidarity was demanding in Poland!

The next major section takes up the rights of workers in more detail. John Paul

[7]For further discussion of the idea of the "universal destination of goods," see Pontifical Council for Justice and Peace, *Compendium of the Social Doctrine of the Church* (Washington, D.C.: USCCB, 2004), §§328, 329, 481-85.

starts with the obligation to work. Why is this an obligation? First, because God has commanded it. Second, because it is part of human nature made in the image of the Creator to work. And third, we must work in order to serve our family, our society and the whole human family (*Laborem exercens,* §16).

John Paul condemns unemployment as an evil "in all cases." Society must be organized so that all who are able to work have an opportunity to do so. And when workers lose their jobs, there is an "obligation to provide unemployment benefits"—an obligation which flows from everyone's right to life (*Laborem exercens,* §18).

The principle of the common use of goods demands that workers receive a "just wage." Indeed, the presence or absence of a just wage is "the concrete means of *verifying the justice* of the whole socioeconomic system." John Paul defines a just family wage as "a single salary given to the head of the family for his work, sufficient for the needs of the family without the other spouse having to take up gainful employment outside the home" (*Laborem exercens,* §19). He also insists on the right of a worker to a pension, insurance for old age and in case of accident, and a safe working environment.

John Paul vigorously asserts the rights of workers to organize free, independent unions. Noting that modern unions emerged out of the struggle of workers to protect their "just rights" over against the owners of the means of production, he insists that history teaches that unions are "an indispensable *element of social life.*" Rejecting narrow self-centeredness, he says, unions must "secure the just rights of workers within the framework of the common good of the whole of society." Unions must enjoy "the *right to strike,*" but they should use it judiciously. And, he insists, in a statement that must have cheered Solidarity and infuriated the Communist government, unions "should not be subjected to the decision of political parties" (*Laborem exercens,* §20).

John Paul also includes moving statements about the need to overcome the poverty of agricultural workers around the world (*Laborem exercens,* §21), the urgency of providing meaningful, suitable employment for the disabled (*Laborem exercens,* §22), and the importance of treating immigrant workers in the same way other workers are treated (*Laborem exercens,* §23).

In a final section on the spirituality of work, John Paul summarizes some of the key biblical, theological foundations of this encyclical. Created in the divine image, persons share in the work of the Creator and in a sense perfect God's work by developing the resources placed by the Creator in the natural world (*Laborem exercens,* §25). Jesus proclaimed "the Gospel of Work" by his activity as a carpenter and his many positive references to human work (*Laborem exercens,* §26). And since all work inevitably involves toil, the Christian who works also participates in some sense in the suffering which Christ endured on the cross and thereby "collaborates with the Son of God for the redemption of humanity" (*Laborem exercens,* §27).

Assessment. It is not surprising that this powerful encyclical, issued just when an independent trade union in Communist Poland was focusing sharply and dangerously the long-standing twentieth-century clash between Marxism and democratic capitalism, provoked enormous response.[8] Also not surprising is the fact that commentators emphasized what they wanted the pope to say: socialist-leaning Catholic scholar Gregory Baum claimed the encyclical confirmed a shift to the left in Catholic social teaching;[9] Michael Novak, the famous advocate of democratic capitalism, celebrated John Paul II's defense of private property.[10]

I find it unclear at least and quite possibly problematic to say as John Paul does in section twenty-seven that as Christians participate in the toilsome aspects of work, we somehow collaborate with Christ for the redemption of humanity. How does the fact that work is often hard, back-breaking activity enable us to participate in Christ's once-for-all act of redemption in the cross and resurrection? Furthermore, does the pope's argument imply that the more burdensome work is, the greater our participation in Christ's redemptive work? Indeed, might not this idea lead workers experiencing especially harsh and unjust working conditions—wrongly—to embrace them for the sake of Christ rather than protest and oppose the injustice?[11]

Second, the encyclical perhaps fails to strike the right balance between the idealistic vision of what the Christian vision says work should be and the horrible reality that real workers too often experience. John Paul certainly knows—and briefly refers to—the negative reality of real-life working conditions. But he probably should have emphasized this aspect more clearly.

Third, and related to the previous point, there is very little in this encyclical about social sin and structural injustice. If we are to implement the wonderful vision of this encyclical, we must grapple vigorously with the structural realities that

---

[8]See Lamoureux, "*Laborem exercens,*" 408-10 and notes, for references to some of the most important responses.

[9]See Gregory Baum's long introduction to the encyclical in *The Priority of Labor: A Commentary on "Laborem exercens," Encyclical Letter of Pope John Paul II* (New York: Paulist, 1982), especially pp. 80-88.

[10]Michael Novak, "The Pope's Brilliant Encyclical," *National Review* 33 (October 16, 1981): 1210.

[11]See Lamoureux, "*Laborem exercens,*" p. 406 and n. 56.

hinder its implication. It would have been helpful to have John Paul's analysis of that challenge.

Fourth, the encyclical tends to reinforce quite conservative views of the role of women. It does not assert that the husband will (or must) always be the primary breadwinner, but it tends to assume that should be the normal situation. While affirming the freedom of women to choose either to enter the job market or stay at home, the encyclical tends to imply that women are "primarily guardians of children and the home."[12] Much of what John Paul was seeking to affirm about the centrality of the family and the equal value of all work including parenting and homemaking is right and important. I agree completely that a just wage should be enough to enable one parent to be home with younger children rather than forcing both parents to find paid employment outside the home (*Laborem exercens,* §19). But must we assume, as the encyclical does, that the unpaid, at-home parent must almost always be the mother?

In these and other ways, *Laborem exercens* could have been stronger. But on balance, I find this encyclical highly illuminating, theologically strong and very challenging. There are some obvious points at which evangelicals should find it especially attractive. And there are even more where I believe we should learn from it.

There are many areas for which evangelicals can quickly give thanks: the solidly orthodox theological foundations of historic Christianity, the sanctity and importance of the family for society, and the critique of Marxism and affirmation of private property.

Especially striking is the centrality of biblical revelation for the whole encyclical. Many commentators have noted that, while arguments from natural law are certainly present, John Paul makes biblical revelation his starting point.[13] After the introduction, as he begins the first major part of the encyclical, he starts his analysis of work with the book of Genesis and its teaching about the unique dignity of persons made in the image of God. He notes that the sciences offer helpful understanding, but promptly insists that "the source of the church's conviction *is above all* the revealed word of God, and therefore what is a conviction of the intellect is also a conviction of faith" (*Laborem exercens,* §4; my emphasis). Again and again through the encyclical, he returns to the basic biblical foundations that he develops here. Evangelicals who feel that Catholic social teaching is sometimes too exclusively focused on rational arguments based in natural law (and thus it is claimed equally accessible to Christian and non-Christian) can certainly rejoice

[12]Ibid., p. 401; see also pp. 400, 408.
[13]Ibid., pp. 393-94.

that methodically this encyclical starts with, and places the greater emphasis on, biblical revelation.

I believe there are many areas where *Laborem exercens* has important things to teach evangelicals. Here I can only emphasize a few.

The vigorous affirmation of the priority of labor over capital is one such area. Evangelicals in the pro-life movement who (rightly) agree with Catholics on the inestimable dignity of each person (because we are made in the image of God) need to hear how this great pro-life pope argues that precisely this biblical understanding of persons demands that economic structures and arrangements for work must fit with the way God has created us as persons. "Work is 'for man,' and not man 'for work'" (*Laborem exercens,* §6). Evangelical Christians—theologians, ethicists, economists, political scientists and politicians—must engage in a thorough reevaluation of our economic systems and the totality of how they treat and impact persons if John Paul is right that the biblical teaching about the unique dignity of persons requires that labor has priority over capital and material productivity. Economic efficiency, maximizing of profits and volume of material productivity simply do not matter as much as treating each worker, indeed every member of society, as a free, responsible, creative, immeasurably valuable person.

Closely related to this teaching on the priority of labor is John Paul's balanced view of property and his critique of both communism and unrestricted capitalism. He clearly affirms the importance of, and a person's right to, private property. The church's teaching "*diverges* radically" from Marxist collectivism and its misguided rejection of private ownership. At the same time, he insists vigorously that the right to private property is not "absolute and untouchable." It must serve the common good and is "subordinated . . . to the fact that goods are meant for everyone" (*Laborem exercens,* §14). Far too often, in their (correct) rejection of Marxism, evangelicals have uncritically endorsed unrestricted capitalism without analyzing, as John Paul insists we must, how unrestricted capitalism ignores and/or undermines the dignity of persons and promotes a practical materialism. People like Michael Novak and their many evangelical friends are right to celebrate the affirmation of private property found in *Laborem exercens*—provided they hear and implement with equal vigor its demand to avoid the evils of unrestricted capitalism.

Undergirding John Paul's analysis of the priority of labor is his extensive analysis of the subjective side of work. He affirms that the objective side (what we produce) is important. But he spends more time insisting that a Christian approach to work will also place great emphasis on the worker who works. Are the arrangements and structures of work such that they respect and affirm the dignity of the worker as a person created in the image of God? Do they enable the worker to exercise the responsibility and creativity that are essential to human dignity? John Paul insists that we dare not value efficiency and productivity more than respect for the unique character of the worker as a person. To be sure, the encyclical does not offer detailed principles or a careful calculus for deciding how much inefficiency and loss of productivity is right in order to implement this understanding of the subjective side of work. Implementing this teaching will require that kind of complicated analysis. But John Paul's basic insight about the important subjective aspect of work is surely one that all evangelicals should ponder carefully.

Finally, evangelicals need to listen carefully to this encyclical's vigorous endorsement of unions, the right to work and the demand for a just wage. Evangelicals have been far more ready to affirm John Paul's insistence on the obligation to work than to agree with this pope on the right to work and society's moral obligation "to *act against unemployment,* which in all cases is an evil" (*Laborem exercens,* §18). Evangelicals have not understood or embraced the important role of unions that John Paul says are "indispensable" (*Laborem exercens,* §20) to society. A prominent evangelical leader once told me that his unbelieving father told him that if he could show him an evangelical Christian church where the pastor talked about going "to the shop" instead of going "to the office," he would attend. Historically, unions have played an important role in promoting movement toward things that this encyclical endorses—a "just wage," unemployment insurance, insurance for accidents at work, the right to a pension (*Laborem exercens,* §19). If Reinhold Niebuhr is right that promoting a balance of power is an important part of how we create justice in society, then we need strong, democratic unions to balance the power of large corporations. That does not mean we should support everything all unions do; they must be democratic, honest and just. Nor does that mean that evangelicals should develop a one-sided embrace of unions rather than corporations, but it does mean we should recognize the need for stronger unions to balance the concentrated power of large corporations.

CENTESIMUS ANNUS

Context. *Centesimus annus,*[14] released on May 1, 1991, is a careful reflection on the stunning changes and new world that had emerged in the previous two years—historic developments that this Polish pope certainly helped to shape.

---

[14]John Paul II, *Centesimus annus . . . on the Hundredth Anniversary of Rerum novarum,* Libreria Editrice Vaticana (May 1, 1991) <http://www.vatican.va/holy_father/john_paul_ii/encyclicals/documents/hf_jp-ii_enc_01051991_centesimus-annus_en.html>.

Given the series of papal encyclicals which had celebrated the several anniversaries of Leo XIII's *Rerum novarum* in 1891, it was a virtual certainty that John Paul II would mark its hundredth anniversary in 1991 with a new encyclical on social questions. But in 1988, significant voices in the Vatican wondered if the pope would have much new to say in 1991, especially since he had just released the important social encyclical *Solicitudo rei socialis* earlier that year.[15] Then in 1989 and 1990, Solidarity swept to power in Poland, the Soviet Empire collapsed, the Berlin Wall fell, and democratic governments replaced Communist governments across Eastern Europe. John Paul's beloved Poland and the daring workers in Lech Walesa's Solidarity were the vanguard in this astonishing, almost entirely nonviolent revolution. And most people acknowledged that John Paul himself had played a crucial role in inspiring and encouraging these historic changes. To an unusual extent, the world was ready to hear this Polish pope's reflections on these breathtaking changes and ponder his guidance on the future shape of these new societies.

Developments within the Roman Catholic Church also shaped the context in which John Paul decided on the content of this encyclical. Liberation theology in Latin America, led largely by Catholic thinkers, had become a powerful voice for justice for the poor. The pope had criticized its heavy reliance on Marxist thought, but had embraced its "preferential option for the poor."

Also important was the recent emergence of strong, neo-conservative voices, led by Catholic intellectual Michael Novak, arguing vigorously that democratic capitalism fits better with Christian truth than do other systems. They urged the Catholic Church to abandon what they believed was a one-sided concern for the distribution of wealth and embrace market economies as the best way to create wealth and reduce poverty.

These two streams of thought among Catholic intellectuals, plus several important pastoral letters on economic life by national conferences of Catholic bishops, all contributed to the encyclical.[16]

John Paul was centrally engaged in its drafting. He made it very clear what he wanted included and drafted parts himself, writing in his native Polish. He proposed that the Pontifical Council for Justice and Peace organize a conference to seek the counsel of about twenty of the world's most prestigious economists. John Paul met with them during their meeting in Rome in November 1990. And he listened carefully to their recommendation that "capitalism works and communism

---

[15]Daniel Finn, "Commentary on *Centesimus annus*," in *Modern Catholic Teaching: Commentaries and Interpretations*, ed. Kenneth R. Himes et al. (Washington, D.C.: Georgetown University Press, 2005), p. 441.
[16]Ibid., p. 440.

doesn't, that developing nations have no alternatives but to join themselves with the first world, that the pope should express a preference for the poor, that the distribution of investment spontaneously generated in capitalism is morally intolerable for its inequality, and that the economist's vision of *homo economicus* is completely inadequate as a theory of the human person."[17]

Summary. In the introduction, John Paul indicated his intention to offer a "rereading" (*Centesimus annus,* §3) of Pope Leo XIII's great encyclical of 1891 and reflect on the "new things" of recent history.

In chapter one, John Paul summarizes and reflects on the key ideas of *Rerum novarum.* Leo rightly saw that a new form of property (capital) and labor (working for wages in ways that often caused labor to become a mere commodity bought like impersonal things) had led to a dangerous conflict between capital and labor (*Centesimus annus,* §§4, 5).

John Paul celebrates the way that Leo's encyclical created a "lasting paradigm" for the church to use as its moral framework to analyze and judge social realities and suggest a direction for societal improvement. Most people in 1891, however, John Paul notes, did not accept this engagement of the church with societal problems. Most people then embraced the dichotomy in which faith related to a "purely other-worldly salvation" but was to remain "extraneous" to issues dealing with this world (*Centesimus annus,* §5). Leo's encyclical gave the church "citizenship status" and helped create a new understanding that the Christian view of the human person is essential to a satisfactory solution of society's problems. There is "*no genuine solution of the 'social question' apart from the Gospel*" (*Centesimus annus,* §5). Furthermore, the proclamation of the church's social doctrine—showing how the Christian message transforms society—is an essential part of the church's "evangelizing mission" (*Centesimus annus,* §5).

Leo was right to ground his entire vision, including the rights of workers, in the church's understanding of the dignity and worth of the human person (*Centesimus annus,* §§6, 11). He correctly endorsed a qualified right to private property (*Centesimus annus,* §6), the right to form unions (*Centesimus annus,* §7), the right to a just wage (*Centesimus annus,* §8), and the right to discharge one's religious duties and rest on Sunday (*Centesimus annus,* §9).

Leo also stated crucial principles about the relationship of the state and its citizens. The state dare not try to solve every social problem. It must respect the rightful autonomy of other sectors, including the family and economic life (*Cen-*

---

[17]J. C. de Pablo, quoted in ibid., p. 441.

tesimus annus, §11). The state's purpose is to "watch over the common good" (*Centesimus annus,* §11). The state must provide a judicial framework that both safeguards a free economy and promotes economic justice (*Centesimus annus,* §15). However, the "preferential option for the poor" (*Centesimus annus,* §11) means that the state must pay special attention to assisting the poor. "The mass of the poor [unlike the richer class] have no resources of their own to fall back on, and must chiefly depend on the assistance of the State. It is for this reason that wage-earners, since they mostly belong to the latter class, should be specially cared for and protected by the Government." After quoting these words from *Rerum novarum,* John Paul emphasizes this "elementary principle of sound political organization, namely, the more that individuals are defenceless within a given society, the more they require the care and concern of others, and in particular the intervention of governmental authority" (*Centesimus annus,* §10).

In chapter two, "Towards the 'New Things' of Today," John Paul reflects on the historical developments from 1891 to 1989.

The fundamental error of socialism was its anthropology (*Centesimus annus,* §13). It viewed the person as simply a "molecule within the social organism," subordinating the good of the individual to the larger socioeconomic mechanism. It believed that the well-being of individuals could be achieved without their free choice. The result? "The concept of the person as the autonomous subject of moral decision disappears" (*Centesimus annus,* §13). The ultimate source of this mistaken understanding of persons, of course, was atheism and the rationalism of the Enlightenment.

Closely connected with this atheism and rationalism was a fundamental misunderstanding of human freedom which became detached from obedience to the truth. In this misguided view, "the essence of freedom then becomes self-love carried to the point of contempt for God and neighbour, a self-love which leads to an unbridled affirmation of self-interest and which refuses to be limited by any demand of justice" (*Centesimus annus,* §17).

At the end of World War II, Communist totalitarianism spread over half of Europe and beyond. The result was two power blocs, and an "insane" arms race (*Centesimus annus,* §18).

John Paul comments on three different responses to communism. Some nations sought to rebuild democratic societies by social justice—in part to deprive communism of its attractiveness. Other anti-Marxist societies developed "national security" states that ran the risk of destroying freedom and the value of the person in their attempt to protect their people from communism. A third response in affluent consumer societies was to seek to defeat Marxism "on the pure level of materialism" by showing that a free-market society better satisfies material human needs than communism. Unfortunately, this third approach, "insofar as it denies an autonomous existence and value to morality, law, culture and religion, . . . agrees with Marxism, in the sense that it totally reduces man to the sphere of economics" (*Centesimus annus,* §19).

Finally, John Paul notes that in spite of the widespread process of "decolonization," many "Third World countries" are still substantially controlled by foreign structures and their people are very poor. Also, in spite of the growing attention to human rights, led especially by the United Nations, there is still no effective, accepted means for the peaceful resolution of international conflicts. "This seems to be the most urgent problem which the international community has yet to resolve" (*Centesimus annus,* §21).

In chapter three, John Paul reflects on the unexpected and promising events of 1989. He celebrates the fact that, contrary to the widespread assumption that only another war could end the division of Europe, the revolutionary changes happened through nonviolent, peaceful protest.

He discusses three causes of the fall of oppressive regimes in 1989 and 1990. First, the case of Poland shows that when these governments violated the rights of workers, the working people rejected "the ideology which presumed to speak in their name" (*Centesimus annus,* §23).

The inefficiency of the Communist economic system was a second significant cause. Nor was this inefficiency merely a technical economic problem. It was grounded in a "violation of the human rights to private initiative, to ownership of property and to freedom in the economic sector" (*Centesimus annus,* §24). And that violation was grounded in the still deeper Marxist misunderstanding that economics alone can explain the human process. At the heart of every culture—and its view of persons—is its attitude toward "the greatest mystery: the mystery of God" (*Centesimus annus,* §24).

Thus the inadequacy of atheism is the deepest cause of the rejection of communism. "Marxism had promised to uproot the need for God from the human heart, but the results have shown that it is not possible to succeed in this without throwing the heart into turmoil" (*Centesimus annus,* §24). In fact, it was often those who remained faithful to God or rediscovered Christ who led the dramatic revolutions of 1989-1990.

His reflection on the failure of communism prompts John Paul to ponder the way that society should take into account the reality of original sin. "As long as time lasts the struggle between good and evil continues even in the human heart" (*Centesimus annus,* §25). How should the social order take this truth into account? By finding ways to bring personal interest and the interest of society into fruitful harmony. If society seeks to violently suppress self-interest, it must replace it with rigid bureaucratic control that destroys initiative and creativity. "When people think they possess the secret of a perfect social organization which makes evil impossible, they also think that they can use any means, including violence and deceit." Politics then becomes a "secular religion," which mistakenly thinks it can create paradise on earth (*Centesimus annus,* §25).

John Paul offers some reflection on what the newly freed countries of Eastern Europe need. He rejoices in the fact that many, he believes, are now more open to the social doctrine of the church (*Centesimus annus,* §26). He insists that these countries need not just material, but also moral, reconstruction (*Centesimus annus,* §27). Fearing that old national, ethnic and religious hatreds may explode after the collapse of dictatorship, he calls for international structures able to arbitrate such conflicts. And he urges the nations of Western Europe to generously assist Eastern Europe in its reconstruction (*Centesimus annus,* §28).

Aiding Eastern Europe, however, dare not lead to the neglect of the even more serious conditions of poverty in the developing world. Enormous resources for this can become available if the huge military machines of the Cold War are disarmed (*Centesimus annus,* §28). People in more developed economies must change their lifestyles and sacrifice positions of power and income in order to join a worldwide effort to promote development (*Centesimus annus,* §§52, 58). Here, too, John Paul warns against reducing development merely to economics. It must also include respect for every individual's dignity, creativity and freedom—especially "the right to discover and freely to accept Jesus Christ, who is man's true good" (*Centesimus annus,* §29).

Chapter four, "Private Property and the Universal Destination of Material Goods," is the heart of this encyclical. John Paul reaffirms earlier encyclicals which both embraced the right of private property and insisted that it is subordinate to the common good (*Centesimus annus,* §30).

God created the natural world with all its bounty for the well-being of all persons. That is the meaning of the Catholic teaching about the "universal destination of the earth's goods." But earth yields its bounty only when persons work; and when by work persons make part of the earth their own, they rightly acquire property (*Centesimus annus,* §31).

Earlier, the most basic form of ownership was ownership of land. But today, ownership of knowledge, technology and skill is more important in the production of wealth. Also important in the production of wealth today is the initiative and entrepreneurial ability that can see the needs of others and bring together the productive factors that enable them to meet those needs. In this way, John Paul affirms the positive aspects of the modern business economy which is based on "human freedom exercised in the economic field" (*Centesimus annus,* §32).

Private ownership of the means of production is just when it "serves useful work." But it is illegitimate when it "serves to impede the work of others," exploits people and breaks "solidarity among working people." "Ownership of this kind has no justification, and represents an abuse in the sight of God and man" (*Centesimus annus,* §43).

If John Paul sees the positive aspects of modern business economies, he also perceives their problems. Many people today—perhaps the majority—lack the knowledge and opportunity to participate in the modern business economy. They work the land without ownership or crowd into impoverished slums in cities of the developing world. For the great majority of these folk, "the human inadequacies of capitalism and the resulting domination of things over people are far from disappearing" (*Centesimus annus,* §33). Strong nations must forgive substantial debt owed by poor nations and help them become stronger partners in the global economy (*Centesimus annus,* §35).

John Paul approves the expansion of global capitalism. Both nationally and internationally, "the *free market* is the most efficient instrument for utilizing resources and effectively responding to needs" (*Centesimus annus,* §34). Then he quickly adds important qualifications. This is true only when all people have the necessary purchasing power. It is a "strict duty of justice" not to allow poor people to perish (*Centesimus annus,* §34). Our response must be work for a just wage, unemployment and old-age insurance, and trade unions. It is quite clear that a just wage is not the same thing as the market wage. Even if fear or necessity forces workers to accept an inadequate wage offered by a powerful employer, it is still unjust (*Centesimus annus,* §§8, 34). Christian faith "demands that the market be appropriately controlled by the forces of society and by the State, so as to guarantee that the basic needs of the whole of society are satisfied" (*Centesimus annus,* §35).

That does not mean returning to a socialist system (which is really state capitalism). It does not mean rejecting the role of profit for a business. But other human and moral factors are at least as important as profit for a business (*Centesimus annus,* §35).

John Paul is deeply concerned about emerging problems in advanced economies. Modern consumerism emerges from a misguided understanding of persons which focuses only on their material aspects and ignores the spiritual. Persons are created by God to achieve fulfillment only as they give themselves to other persons and ultimately to God (*Centesimus annus,* §41). A great deal of educational and cultural work is necessary to help citizens in wealthy nations "create life-styles in which the quest for truth, beauty, goodness and communion with others for the sake of common growth are the factors which determine consumer choices, savings and investments" (*Centesimus annus,* §36).

John Paul also deplores the environmental destruction which is grounded finally in theological error. When humanity fails to see the natural world as a special gift from God with its own God-given purpose and instead arbitrarily subjects it "without restraint to his will," nature rebels and ecological destruction ensues (*Centesimus annus,* §37).

Even more serious in wealthy nations is the destruction of the "human ecology." Societal structures nurture or hinder living in accordance with the truth (*Centesimus annus,* §38). Unfortunately, many rich societies are destroying "the first and fundamental structure" of the family founded on marriage.

John Paul does not blame these problems primarily on the economic system. It is rather the ethical and cultural system that must be changed (*Centesimus annus,* §39). But that does not mean there is no role for the state. The market has clear advantages: it uses resources most efficiently and provides great opportunity for human freedom. But we dare not embrace an "idolatry" of the market because "there are collective and qualitative needs which cannot be satisfied by market mechanisms." And he insists that "it is the task of the State to provide for the defence and preservation of common goods such as the natural and human environments, which cannot be safeguarded simply by market forces" (*Centesimus annus,* §40).

Toward the end of this section, John Paul raises the fundamental question: Since communism has failed, should all countries, including developing "Third World" nations, embrace capitalism?

> The answer is obviously complex. If by *capitalism* is meant an economic system which recognizes the fundamental and positive role of business, the market, private property and the resulting responsibility for the means of production, as well as free human creativity in the economic sector, then the answer is certainly in the affirmative, even though it would perhaps be more appropriate to speak of a "business economy," "market economy" or simply "free economy." But if by *capitalism* is meant a system in which freedom in the economic sector is not circumscribed within a strong juridical framework which places it at the service of human freedom in its totality,

> and which sees it as a particular aspect of that freedom, the core of which is ethical and religious, then the reply is certainly negative. (*Centesimus annus,* §42)

John Paul is clearly glad communism has collapsed. But he warns against a "radical capitalistic ideology" that fails to see the weaknesses and problems of contemporary market economies (*Centesimus annus,* §§43, 56). He does not believe the church has some new economic model to offer. But he believes that the Catholic Church's social teaching offers an ideal orientation that enables people to modify present practices and structures to promote the common good (*Centesimus annus,* §43).

In chapter five, "State and Culture," John Paul deepens his previous analysis of the state and society. The starting point for a good society must be an understanding of transcendent truth. If there is no objective truth, then politics becomes mere power games and totalitarianism is inevitable (*Centesimus annus,* §44).

John Paul endorses a democratic political order (*Centesimus annus,* §46) and approves of the separation of judicial, legislative and executive powers (*Centesimus annus,* §44). But he worries about the widespread view in democratic societies that "agnosticism and sceptical relativism" are the best conceptual foundations for democracy. He totally disagrees. Only if there is transcendent truth and moral order to which all have an obligation to submit will democracies be able to promote the common good and avoid narrow, self-centered power games that will eventually lead to totalitarianism (*Centesimus annus,* §§46, 47).

With both approval and caution, John Paul asserts his view that the democratic ideal is growing in strength today. He affirms the recognition of basic human rights as the foundation of democracy. Among the most important human rights are the right to life, the right to establish and live in a united family, the right to work that is environmentally responsible and enables one to support oneself and one's dependents, and the right to religious freedom (*Centesimus annus,* §47).

This encyclical clearly calls for a limited state. He insists on the importance of "intermediate communities" (e.g., family, voluntary organizations) which prevent the person from being "suffocated between two poles represented by the State and the marketplace" (*Centesimus annus,* §49). The state must respect and protect the independence of these intermediate communities.

The state must also avoid intervening inappropriately in the economy. For example, the state could not directly guarantee the right to work of all its citizens without wrongly restricting personal choices and controlling every aspect of the economy. Individuals and nongovernmental associations have the primary responsibility to see that all people enjoy the right to work. At the same time, the state also has a significant role: to create and sustain conditions which will ensure job opportunities and to avoid monopolies. And in "exceptional circumstances," when social sectors or business systems are too weak, the state rightly exercises a temporary "substitute function." But this state activity must be brief in order to avoid excessively enlarging the state's sphere or permanently taking over functions that properly belong to other societal sections (*Centesimus annus,* §48).

In this context, John Paul criticizes the "welfare state" or "social assistance state" which intervenes directly and permanently in persons' lives in order to reduce poverty but ends up creating huge government agencies whose rigid bureaucracies do not serve clients well. He appeals to the principle of subsidiarity: "A community of a higher order should not interfere in the internal life of a community of lower order, . . . but rather should support it in case of need" (*Centesimus annus,* §48). People with needs (he mentions refugees, the elderly, the sick and drug abusers) can be helped better by people closest to them who can also better understand that the needs are more than just material.

Finally, John Paul underlines the importance of the Christian contribution to culture. The church's "*specific and decisive contribution to true culture*" is to promote human behavior that exhibits self-control, personal sacrifice, solidarity and readiness to promote the common good. And it does that by preaching the truth about creation and redemption (*Centesimus annus,* §51).

Only a few things in the final chapter demand notice here. John Paul insists that the preceding one hundred years of Catholic social teaching have flowed from the church's commitment to care for human beings (*Centesimus annus,* §53). To do that faithfully, the church combines its understanding of "the meaning of man," which comes from divine revelation (*Centesimus annus,* §55), and the insights that arise from the secular disciplines that deal with humanity (*Centesimus annus,* §59). Believing that this holistic view can contribute to societal improvement, the church gladly shares its social teaching with all people. But she also understands that concrete actions will be more powerful than "internal logic and consistency" in convincing others to embrace this teaching (*Centesimus annus,* 57).

The encyclical ends with a plea for the intercession of Mary.

Assessment. As usual, critics emphasized those things in the encyclical that seemed to support their own views. Economic conservative Michael Novak announced that the encyclical supported "reformed capitalism" and "does everything that many of us had hoped for."[18] British theologian Frank Turner, on the other

---

[18]Quoted in ibid., pp. 459, 461.

hand, suggested that this encyclical "sometimes reads like an unusually well-written Labor Manifesto."[19]

Again, I find a few things to question or qualify while celebrating and embracing most of its teaching.

Evangelicals will not be helped by the plea for Mary's intercession.

I doubt that it is helpful, in commenting on the "preferential option for the poor," to broaden the definition of poverty to "other forms of poverty, especially in modern society—not only economic but cultural and spiritual poverty as well" (*Centesimus annus,* §57). It is certainly true that affluent people experience many devastating problems, but it is confusing to call them poverty. Boredom, loss of meaning, consumerism, cultural values that seriously undermine marriage—all these are serious problems that Christians must address. But they are not the things that the word "poverty" normally designates. To use it in this broader way tends to weaken our concern for the agonizing tragedy of those who die because they lack food or minimal health care.[20]

There are obvious places where one would like to hear more specificity. John Paul clearly rejects communism, preferring democratic capitalism. But he also rejects libertarianism, insisting on an important role for the state. But that does not answer the most pressing contemporary questions. Many of the crucial economic debates today revolve around these questions: In what way and under what circumstances does the state rightly intervene in the economy? What are the principles and criteria for this intervention? How do we know when the greater current danger is "big government" and when it is the lack of concrete economic assistance that government can provide?

John Paul rightly criticizes the "welfare state" that creates dependency, stifles human initiative, and produces excessive, unwieldy bureaucracy. But he does not tell us in any detail at all how that warning fits with his repeated call, elsewhere in the encyclical, for state intervention to implement economic justice for all, especially workers. Some commentators have sensed a contradiction between these different sections.[21] I do not think that is the case. Both points are important and consistent with each other. But John Paul does not provide much detailed help for integrating the two concerns.

As in the case of *Laborem exercens,* however, I believe the positive aspects of the encyclical far outweigh the weaknesses. I view as nothing less than brilliant the

---

[19]Ibid., p. 461.
[20]See also the discussion in ibid., pp. 459-60.
[21]See the people cited in ibid., p. 452.

balanced way that John Paul embraces the right of private property but insists that this right is far from absolute. The principle of subsidiarity (higher orders of society dare not take over what lower orders of society rightly and effectively do) supports this right. The principle of solidarity (everything must contribute to the common good) qualifies it.

It is perhaps also true that this encyclical rightly switches the emphasis from the "right *of*" private property to the "right *to*" private property.[22] The latter is the way John Paul puts it in the opening sentence of section four. Repeatedly in the encyclical he demands that poor people be helped to acquire the resources (land, knowledge, education, technological skills)—i.e., the means of production—so that they can earn their own way and be productive partners in the global economy. All people—especially the poor who lack it—have a right to property (*Centesimus annus,* §§33, 34).

Central to John Paul's balanced vision is the way he insists that society is much larger than the state; that intermediate, nongovernmental institutions (family, voluntary associations, etc.) are crucial to a free, just society; and that the state has a limited, but nonetheless significant, role to play in reducing poverty. All that I find stated superbly in this encyclical.

George Weigel is essentially right, I believe, even though he sometimes overstates it, in arguing that here and elsewhere John Paul insists on the priority of culture. "Culture—not economics and not superior material force—[is] the engine of history."[23] From his long study of communism, John Paul knows that economic factors shape history in important ways, but that finally they are not as important as cultural factors, especially religious faith. In chapter five, John Paul rightly insists on the priority of culture. By preaching the truth about creation and redemption, the church nurtures persons who have the understanding and character to create a culture which produces just, peaceful institutions. John Paul understands the crucial nature of just socioeconomic structures. But more basic still is the foundational culture and essential to that is persons who know and love the truth. "The first and most important task is accomplished within man's heart" (*Centesimus annus,* §51).

Evangelicals will rightly appreciate this emphasis on the centrality of personal transformation as the foundation of a good culture. They should learn from John Paul that this emphasis on personal transformation through faith in Christ must be balanced with an understanding of the power and importance of cultural sys-

---

[22]Ibid., p. 446.
[23]Weigel, *Witness to Hope,* p. 614.

tems and the socioeconomic structures they shape.

What I said of *Laborem exercens* is also true of *Centesimus annus.* Both encyclicals contain very little to which evangelicals should object. They contain a great deal that we embrace and much that biblical revelation and careful thought should prompt us to ponder with an open expectation of having our thinking enriched.

A Historic Convergence?

It is instructive to compare these two encyclicals and the larger body of Catholic social teaching with the recent "For the Health of the Nation: An Evangelical Call to Civic Responsibility," unanimously approved by the board of the National Association of Evangelicals and signed by a broad range of prominent evangelical leaders, including Rick Warren, Chuck Colson and James Dobson.[24] *Laborem exercens* and *Centesimus annus,* of course, focus on economic issues. But even here, John Paul's (and the Catholic Church's) strong commitments to the sanctity of human life, the crucial importance of the family, environmental concern and peacemaking are all clear. Probably the easiest way to develop an overview of official Catholic social teaching is in the Vatican's recently released volume, *Compendium of the Social Doctrine of the Church* (2004). The *Compendium* and "For the Health of the Nation" make it quite clear that both Catholics and evangelicals now share an enormously broad range of commitments for public life. Both are pro-life *and* pro-poor, pro-family *and* pro-creation care, pro-democracy *and* pro-peacemaking. The convergence is enormous. A careful reading of the Vatican's *Compendium* reveals only a few relatively minor areas where evangelicals would disagree.

Together, Catholics and evangelicals represent one-half of all voters in the United States. If these communities were to engage in a sustained, decades-long program of sophisticated cooperation to shape public life in a way that reflects this consistently pro-life agenda, we would substantially reshape American politics. One or both major political parties would move much closer to this evangelical/Catholic vision. The result would be a deeper respect for the sanctity of human life, a renewal of wholesome two-parent families, greater economic justice, a wider care for creation and the growth of freedom, and peace in our world. I pray that this book's discussion by evangelicals of Pope John Paul II's encyclicals will contribute to more extensive efforts to implement this historic convergence.

[24]Ronald J. Sider and Diane Knippers, *Toward an Evangelical Public Policy* (Grand Rapids: Baker, 2005), pp. 363-75.

12

REDEMPTORIS MISSIO

Into All the World

Terrance L. Tiessen

The urgency of the church's missionary mandate was a common theme throughout the apostolic journeys of John Paul II,[1] but *Redemptoris missio* was prompted by the twenty-fifth anniversary of Vatican II's "Decree on Missionary Activity" *(Ad gentes)* and signed on December 7, 1990, which was also fifteen years after Pope Paul VI's *Evangelii nuntiandi.* It has been described as "a concise *summa* of official Roman Catholic thinking on mission today."[2] As the second millennium entered its final decade, John Paul II felt an urgent need to repeat the cry of the apostle Paul, "Woe to me if I do not preach the Gospel!" (1 Cor 9:16) (*Redemptoris missio,* §1).[3] In spite of numerous reasons for encouragement, he feared that missionary activity appeared to be waning, and he wrote this document to stem the "undeniable negative tendency" that he discerned in the church's attitude to global mission (§2). He addresses objections to global mission which were being voiced

[1]Avery Cardinal Dulles, *The Splendor of Faith: The Theological Vision of Pope John Paul II,* rev. and updated ed. (New York: Crossroad, 2003), p. 70.

[2]Stephen B. Bevans, "The Biblical Basis of the Mission of the Church in *Redemptoris Missio,*" in *The Good News of the Kingdom: Mission Theology for the Third Millennium,* ed. Charles Van Engen, Dean S. Gilliland and Paul Pierson (Maryknoll, N.Y.: Orbis, 1993), p. 37.

[3]John Paul II, *Redemptoris missio: On the Permanent Validity of the Church's Missionary Mandate,* Libreria Editrice Vaticana (December 7, 1990), p. 3. The following in-text citations to this encyclical will be cited by section number only.

by members of his own church but which had not been significant when Vatican II was convened.[4] On the other hand, he foresaw "the dawning of a new missionary age, which will become a radiant day bearing an abundant harvest, if all Christians, and missionaries and young churches in particular, respond with generosity and holiness to the calls and challenges of our time" (§92).

JOHN PAUL II'S VISION OF THE CHURCH'S GLOBAL MISSION

In the first of eight chapters, John Paul II establishes the unique role of Jesus Christ as "the one Savior of all, the only one able to reveal God and lead to God" (§5). This does not exclude "participated forms of mediation of different kinds and degrees," but these "acquire meaning and value *only* from Christ's own mediation, and they cannot be understood as parallel or complementary to his" (§5).[5] It is because of this definitive self-revelation of God in Jesus that "the Church is missionary by her very nature" (§5). What makes this missionary activity urgent is "the *radical newness of life* brought by Christ and lived by his followers (§7).

Chapter two expounds the church's mission in relationship to the establishment of the kingdom of God which was prepared in the Old Testament, was "brought about by Christ and in Christ," and is now "proclaimed to all peoples by the Church, which works and prays for its perfect and definitive realization" (§12). Israel was chosen for the blessing of all peoples, and God's plan came to fulfillment in Jesus, who identified the proclamation and establishment of God's kingdom as the purpose of his mission (§13). The kingdom aims at transforming human relationships, bringing about communion between human beings and between people and God (§15). The early church preached Jesus Christ because the kingdom was identified with him (§16).

In our own day, we need to beware of an "anthropocentric" view of the kingdom which reduces it to the meeting of people's earthly needs but also of a "theocentric" understanding which is silent about Christ and his redemption and which undervalues the church (§17). The kingdom of God "cannot be detached either from Christ or from the Church" (§18).

The Holy Spirit, as principal agent of mission, is the subject of chapter three. The church is sent out in mission to the nations with the presence and power of the Holy Spirit to cooperate in the mission of Christ (§23), continuing the work

[4]This point is well demonstrated by José Comblin, "The Novelty of *Redemptoris Missio*," in *Redemption and Dialogue: Reading Redemptoris missio and Dialogue and Proclamation*, ed. William R. Burrows (Maryknoll, N.Y.: Orbis, 1993), p. 232.

[5]Emphasis in encyclical quotations is original unless noted otherwise.

of the early Christians as detailed in Acts (§27). From the beginning, mission is seen to be "a community commitment, a responsibility of the local church, which needs 'missionaries' in order to push forward toward new frontiers" (§27).

Although "the Spirit manifests himself in a special way in the Church and in her members," he "is at work in the heart of every person, through the 'seeds of the Word,' to be found in human initiatives—including religious ones—and in mankind's efforts to attain truth, goodness and God himself" (§28). This guides the church in its relationship with other religions, generating a twofold respect, "for man in his quest for answers to the deepest questions of his life," and "for the action of the Spirit in man" (§29). This work of the Spirit is not an alternative to Christ, but it prepares people for the Gospel and "can only be understood in reference to Christ" (§29).

New horizons and possibilities for mission are identified in chapter four. Old ecclesial distinctions and categories no longer serve us well when Christian cities and countries which were formerly deemed Christian now confront us as mission territories (§32). On the other hand, areas of the world which were once the primary recipients of missionary work now have well-established churches and are sending out personnel to evangelize in other places (§32).

In proclaiming Christ, the church seeks to further human freedom, and religious freedom "remains the premise and guarantee of all the freedoms that ensure the common good of individuals and peoples" (§39). As the second millennium drew to a close, John Paul II found cause for joy at the results of modern missionary activity but also sensed that "the 'ends of the earth' to which the Gospel must be brought are growing ever more distant" (§40).

In chapter five, John Paul II turns his attention to the paths the church must follow in order to achieve its mission. First of these is the witness of the lives of missionaries, of Christian families and of the ecclesial community, which reveal a new way of living (§42). Particularly appealing is the compassion of Christians toward the poor, the weak and those who suffer. Also attractive is a commitment to peace, justice, human rights and human promotion, when it is "directed toward integral human development" (§42). The initial proclamation of the gospel is the permanent priority of Christian mission, and missionaries are enthused by the knowledge that they are responding to the expectation of knowing the truth about God, about humanity, and about how we are to be set free from sin and death, which already exists in individuals and peoples by the work of the Spirit, even unconsciously (§45).

The aim of proclamation is Christian conversion, which is a trinitarian gift of

God. The Spirit opens people's hearts so that they can believe Christ to whom people come only by the Father's drawing (§46). Conversion is "joined to Baptism because of the intrinsic need to receive the fullness of new life in Christ" (§47). All converts are a gift to the church, in that they present a responsibility for religious instruction but also because they "bring with them a kind of new energy, an enthusiasm for the faith," and this urges the whole church toward conversion anew every day (§47).

Conversion and baptism incorporate people into an already existing church and "the mission is not completed until it succeeds in building a new particular church which functions normally in its local setting" (§48). These churches should themselves be active in mission (§49), but the missionary goal will also foster ecumenism because "the division among Christians damages the holy work of preaching the Gospel" (§50).[6] So, to the extent that it is possible, "Catholics should collaborate in a spirit of fellowship with their separated brothers and sisters" (§50).

"Ecclesial basic communities" are a growing phenomenon in the young churches and "are proving to be good centers for Christian formation and missionary outreach" (§51). As the church comes into existence in new cultural situations, inculturation must be pursued without compromising the distinctiveness and integrity of the Christian faith (§52).

Interreligious dialogue is another path of evangelizing mission, not an alternative to it (§55). "The fact that the followers of other religions can receive God's grace and be saved by Christ apart from the ordinary means which he has established does not thereby cancel the call to faith and baptism which God wills for all people" (§55).[7] Another path of mission is found in "action on behalf of integral development and liberation from all forms of oppression" (§58). The church desires the total well-being of all people, but it knows that liberation is best achieved through the gospel which brings people into God's work of building his "kingdom of peace and justice, beginning already in this life" (§59). We also need to be concerned about the North, "which is prone to a moral and spiritual poverty caused by 'overdelopment.' . . . [A] soulless development cannot suffice for human beings, and an excess of affluence is as harmful as excessive poverty" (§59).

The leaders and workers in the missionary task are treated in chapter six. John Paul II holds the bishops, including himself, directly responsible for the evangelization of the world (§63), but he expects this responsibility to be carried out

---

[6]Quoting from *Decree on the Missionary Activity of the Church "Ad gentes,"* §6.
[7]Quoting from his *Letter* to the Fifth Plenary Assembly of Asian Bishops' Conferences, June 23, 1990, §4.

through the evangelistic activity of every disciple of Christ. Christ will stir up a special missionary vocation in the hearts of some individuals who will then commit themselves totally to evangelization (§65). Many of these individuals will carry out their missionary work under the direction of "missionary institutes," which must work in communion with the church and under the guardianship of the bishops (§66).The evangelistic task is not to be left to these specialists, however, but is a responsibility of all diocesan priests who "must have the mind and the heart of missionaries," concerned for non-Christians in their own area but also for all of humanity (§67). A special part in the church's mission is also played by the Institutes of Consecrated Life, both the contemplative and the active orders, which have complementary contributions to make to the missionary work of the whole church.

All the laity are missionaries, by virtue of their baptism, participating, as they do, in the threefold mission of Christ as Priest, Prophet and King (§71). Although they engage primarily in temporal affairs, they should order these in accordance with the will of God and be conscious of the fact that only through them will some people be able to hear the gospel (§§71-74). Since the missionary responsibility is shared by all members of the church, John Paul II expands on the means by which this cooperative effort can be worked out, in chapter seven. This includes "spiritual cooperation through prayer, sacrifice and the witness of the Christian life" (§78); the promotion of missionary vocations, particularly by parents who influence their children by the example of their own Christian lives (§80); and generosity in providing for the great material and financial needs of the missions (§81).

The promotion of missions should be part of "the normal pastoral activity of parishes, associations and groups, especially youth groups," and it should be part of the theological educational curriculum (§83). Care should be taken in this process to emphasize the primary task of bearing witness to salvation in Christ and establishing local churches, lest people be given "an incomplete picture of missionary activity, as if it consisted principally in helping the poor, contributing to the liberation of the oppressed, promoting development or defending human rights" (§83). "Missionary activity demands a specific spirituality" (§87), and this is the focus of chapter eight.

An Evangelical Response to John Paul II's Call to Mission

In reading this encyclical, I was struck by how little of its theology of mission would need to be changed to make it an appropriate address to evangelical church leaders. Accordingly, I will begin my assessment by identifying statements that I expect most evangelicals to appreciate, and then I will mention aspects of John Paul's message which get a mixed reception. Finally, I note items in the encyclical which reminded me why I am still a Protestant.

Perspectives likely to foster general evangelical appreciation and to encourage positive directions in mission. *The careful reading and frequent citation of Scripture.* Since this document aims to call the church to move forward in the implementation of the vision it laid out in *Ad gentes,* that document is quoted more frequently than any other. John Paul II also cites the writings of his papal predecessors, and his own previous work. But this passionate summons to mission is inspired fundamentally by the teaching of Scripture, particularly in the overall vision of the church's mission as the continuation of the original apostolic obedience to Christ's commission, which was itself portrayed in trinitarian terms as the establishing of God's kingdom (§§5, 12).[8] Fine exegetical expositions include the kingdom of God as the context for God's saving mission in which the church participates (§§13-17); the missionary mandate as presented distinctly in the four Gospels (§23); and the missionary activity of the primitive church under the impulse of the Spirit, in Acts (§§24-27).

Affirmation of the uniqueness of Jesus Christ as Savior of the world. Redemptoris Missio is emphatic that "Christ is the one Saviour of all, the only one able to reveal God and lead to God" (§5). Only through Christ and by the work of the Holy Spirit can anyone enter into communion with God so that the extraordinary means God uses to save some of the unevangelized are not "parallel or complementary" to Christ's mediation (§5). The spiritual gifts "that God has bestowed on every people" are inseparable from Jesus Christ (§6).

Zeal for the primacy of evangelism and church planting in the church's mission. It is inspiring to read so impassioned an appeal for the urgency and primacy of missionary activity aimed at conversion (§§1, 3) as a key indication of the vitality of the church (§2). Most evangelicals will appreciate the common affirmation of holistic ministry and the range of ministries to the physical needs and general well-being of people that John Paul II includes within the church's mission to the nations, but they will be particularly heartened by the priority assigned to evangelism and church planting (§19). God has chosen to establish the church as "his co-

---

[8]Marcello Zago notes that "there are twice as many Biblical quotations within the text as there are texts of conciliar or papal origin" ("Commentary on *Redemptoris missio,*" in *Redemption and Dialogue: Reading Redemptoris missio and Dialogue and Proclamation,* ed. William R. Burrows [Maryknoll, N.Y.: Orbis, 1993], pp. 75-76). Stephen Bevans identifies John Paul II's construal of Scripture as similar to the model that David Kelsey identified with B. B. Warfield: "scripture contains certain teachings, certain doctrines, which must be faithfully safeguarded by the church" ("Biblical Basis," p. 39).

worker in the salvation of the world" (§9, cf. §18), but "the principal agents of the Church's mission" are Jesus Christ and his Spirit (§36).

Redemptoris missio is not satisfied with the evangelism or conversion of individuals; it posits that the objective of the mission to the nations is "to found Christian communities and develop churches to their full maturity" (§48, cf. §83). Furthermore, *Redemptoris missio* emphasizes that every one of these newly established local churches, in which "the whole mystery of the Church is contained," is missionary by its very nature (§49). It is to this end that unity of the church is sought, since division among us weakens our witness and unity is "a sign of the work of reconciliation which God is bringing about in our midst" (§50).

The call to total and radical conversion. Redemptoris missio describes conversion as a "dynamic and lifelong process which demands a continual turning away from 'life according to the flesh' to 'life according to the Spirit' (cf. Rom 8:3-13)." To be converted is to accept "by a personal decision, the saving sovereignty of Christ" and to become his disciple (§46). New converts often bring new energy and enthusiasm for the faith into the church, but these people will be disappointed if they find the ecclesial community "lacking fervor and without signs of renewal!" "We cannot preach conversion unless we ourselves are converted anew every day" (§47).

The involvement of all members of the church in Christian mission. John Paul II rightly observes that, at the beginning of the church, the mission to the nations was carried out by some who had a special vocation as missionaries but it was "considered the normal outcome of Christian living, to which every believer was committed through the witness of personal conduct and through explicit proclamation whenever possible" (§27). The special vocation of individuals for missionary service does not diminish at all the responsibility of all disciples of Christ to spread the faith to the best of their ability (§65). Calling the laity to missionary witness is not only a matter of strategic effectiveness; this is their "right and duty based on their baptismal dignity, whereby 'the faithful participate, for their part, in the threefold mission of Christ as Priest, Prophet and King'" (§71).[9]

The description of means by which the general membership of the church cooperate directly in the church's evangelistic and church-planting mission begins with the injunctions to pray, go and give that are standard fare in evangelical missionary conferences (§§78-81), but the statement is well done. It is helpful, for instance, to be reminded that young people are most likely to become career missionaries if they are raised in families with "an intense prayer life, a genuine sense

---

[9]Quoting *Apostolic Exhortation "Christifideles laici,"* §14.

of service to one's neighbor and a generous participation in Church activities" (§80). The call for generous giving reminds readers that all we own is a gift from God (§81). New forms of missionary cooperation are recognized, such as visits to see Christian mission work during international tourist travel and short-term mission trips for young people. Helpful mention is also made of the missionary opportunity provided to the church by the travel of followers of non-Christian religions to traditionally Christian countries for work and study (§82).

The critical role of the young churches in the work of mission. "Attention to the young churches as the protagonists of mission in their own territory and in the world is original in this encyclical,"[10] and evangelicals will appreciate it. In the years since the encyclical was written, we have seen remarkable and exciting growth in the number of missionaries sent out by the churches which are the fruit of original Western missionary activity as well as by churches which have no institutional connection to the missionary work of Western bodies.

The affirmation of religious freedom. Despite the lip service paid to religious freedom as a universal right by member nations of the United Nations, it is becoming increasingly clear that this is a distinctively Christian value. It is firmly grounded by *Redemptoris missio* in the context of God's creation of humankind in the image of God (§8) and is rightly perceived as "the premise and guarantee of all the freedoms that ensure the common good of individuals and peoples" (§39).

Identification of the ways by which Christian mission is carried out in the world. Redemptoris missio begins its discussion of "the paths of mission" with a stirring account of the effectiveness of "evangelical witness," as individuals and communities "reveal a new way of living," empowered by the Spirit for obedience to Christ (§42). This witness will entail care for the poor, the weak and those who suffer, along with a commitment to peace, justice and the well-being of all people. It will also entail "taking courageous and prophetic stands in the face of the corruption of political or economic power," while using the church's own resources "to serve the poorest of the poor and by imitating Christ's own simplicity of life" (§43).

Evangelicals will appreciate the clear description of the proclamation of the gospel as "the permanent priority of mission," because it "opens the way to conversion," by giving birth to faith (§44). "This proclamation is to be made within the context of the lives of the individuals and peoples who receive it," and is to be done "with an attitude of love and esteem" toward the hearers (§44). We are encouraged because we know that the Spirit of God speaks his truth through us and

---

[10]Zago, "Commentary on *Redemptoris missio*," p. 78.

that we are bringing to people what they seek, even if unconsciously (§45). Soberingly, *Redemptoris Missio* notes the powerful effect of martyrdom in the history of the church's missionary work (§45).

The statement on "Incarnating the Gospel in Peoples' Culture" (§§52-54) is excellent. John Paul II warns against "passing uncritically from a form of alienation from culture to an overestimation of culture," since culture is a human creation that is marked by sin and that needs to be redeemed (§54). It is a process to be carried out particularly by Christians within the culture, but not in isolation from the rest of the church and its faithful transmission of the gospel.

The church is keenly interested in the general well-being of the people among whom it exists, but "a people's development does not derive primarily from money, material assistance or technological means, but from the formation of consciences and the gradual maturing of ways of thinking and patterns of behavior" (§58). *Redemptoris missio* helpfully notes that the church needs to be concerned not only about the underdevelopment in the South of the world but also with the "moral and spiritual poverty caused by 'overdevelopment'" in the North, because "an excess of affluence is as harmful as excessive poverty" (§59). Christians are therefore called to "a more austere way of life which will favor a new model of development that gives attention to ethical and religious values" (§59).

Whereas some large evangelical churches have questioned the biblical legitimacy of parachurch mission agencies, *Redemptoris missio* encourages not only individual missionary vocation but also the raising up in the church of "institutes which undertake the duty of evangelization, which is the responsibility of the whole Church, as their special task" (§65). The general philosophy enunciated by *Redemptoris missio* gives us a healthy framework for relationships between churches and parachurch organizations. Mission agencies "are a vital part of the ecclesial community and should carry out their work in communion with it. Indeed, 'every institute exists for the Church and must enrich her with its distinctive characteristics, according to a particular spirit and a specific mission'" (§66).[11] Evangelicalism has little to compare with the monastic institutions founded in the medieval period, but we do well to consider John Paul II's proposal that "institutes of contemplative life" are especially beneficial "in those areas where religious traditions hold the contemplative life in great esteem for its asceticism and its search for the Absolute" (§69). This idea has been echoed by evangelical leaders in Asia.

[11]Citing *Sacred Congregation for Religious and Secular Institutes and Sacred Congregation for Bishops, Directives for Mutual Relations Between Bishops and Religious in the Church "Mutuae Relationes"* (May 14, 1978), §14b.

Analysis of the challenges to Christian mission. Redemptoris missio elucidates both internal and external factors that threaten the church's mission. It warns against an "anthropocentric" theology which reduces Christianity "to merely human wisdom, a pseudo-science of well-being," limiting the goals of missionary work to the merely horizontal dimension (§§11, 17). It is concerned about a "kingdom-centered" theology and practice of mission which promotes the values of the kingdom (peace, justice, freedom, etc.) and fosters dialogue with cultures and religions but which is "silent about Christ" and about redemption and which undervalues the church (§17). Those who fall into this error tend to be silent about the need for conversion or to see it negatively as "proselytizing" (§46).

John Paul II also notes that some in the church hesitate to use the terms *mission* and *missionary* because of "negative historical connotations." They prefer the noun *mission* in the singular and use "the adjective 'missionary' to describe all the Church's activities." But *Redemptoris missio* wisely expresses concern that this may eliminate the church's mission to the nations and the specific vocation to be "life-long missionaries" (§32). In recent years, I have heard evangelical church members denigrate cross-cultural mission work, since we are all "missionaries," so I welcome the encyclical's warning. Religious relativism also undermines mission work among adherents of other religions (§36). Other internal difficulties facing the church's mission include the divisions among Christians, dechristianization within Christian countries, the decrease of missionary vocations, and the negative impact or "counter witness" of "believers and Christian communities failing to follow the model of Christ in their lives."

Difficulties facing the church's mission from outside are identified as including the refusal of some countries to permit missionaries to enter; the prohibition of evangelization, of conversion, and even of Christian worship in some areas; and cultural hindrances in contexts where conversion is seen as "a rejection of one's own people and culture" (§35). In addition to the "vast regions" still needing to be evangelized, particularly in Asia, where Christians are a small minority, special challenges include the massive growth of cities "where human problems are often aggravated by the feeling of anonymity experienced by masses of people" (§37). "The future of the younger nations is being shaped in the cities," and young people, who often compose more than half the populations, present the church with a special challenge. Migration presents the church with new opportunities, and refugees deserve particular attention. Poverty is often the cause of massive migration, and these inhuman situations challenge the Christian community to "become the means for restoring the human dignity of these people," through "the proclamation of Christ and the kingdom of God" (§37). The world of communications, which is turning the world into a "global village" challenges the church not only to use the media to spread the Christian message but "to integrate that message into the 'new culture' created by modern communications" (§37). Other aspects of our time which provide opportunity for ministry include the need for peace, development and the liberation of peoples; the rights of individuals, particularly of minorities; the advancement of women and children; the protection of the created world; culture, scientific research and international relations; and the desperate search for meaning in the midst of consumerism and materialism that presents an opportunity for the proclamation of Christ.

Missionary spirituality. Given the rise of interest in spirituality among evangelicals generally, evangelical missionaries should appreciate the discussion of the specific spirituality demanded by missionary activity. This begins with "a life of complete docility to the Spirit," who gives us "fortitude and discernment" (§87). Missionary work is difficult, and we need to be both led and emboldened by the Spirit. We should follow Christ's model of self-renunciation (Phil 2:5-8), but it is in doing so that "the missionary experiences the consoling presence of Christ" (§88). "Those who have the missionary spirit feel Christ's burning love for souls, and love the Church as Christ did." They give their lives for the neighbor and thereby overcome "barriers and divisions of race, cast or ideology," being "a sign of God's love in the world" (§89). Above all, missionaries are called to holiness; this is more important than up-to-date pastoral techniques, organization skills or deep delving into the biblical and theological foundations of faith (§90). The missionary must be "a contemplative in action," immersed in personal and community prayer and living out the Beatitudes with an inner joy that comes from faith (§91).

Perspectives concerning which evangelical responses will be mixed. *Accessibilism.* Elsewhere, I have identified three perspectives among evangelicals regarding the possibility of the salvation of the unevangelized: ecclesiocentrism, agnosticism and accessibilism.[12] Consistent with Vatican II, John Paul II enunciates a clear statement of the accessibilist understanding. He believes that the Spirit of God works savingly outside the boundaries of the church, applying the unique saving work of Christ (§6) through the Spirit's ministry (§6) in the hearts and minds of some who have no contact with the church and who are therefore ignorant of the gospel (§§5, 9, 10, 20, 28). Acknowledgment of this universal working of the Spirit gives us hope when we encounter non-Christians that God may already be at work in their

[12]Terrance L. Tiessen, *Who Can Be Saved? Reassessing Salvation in Christ and World Religions* (Downers Grove, Ill.: InterVarsity Press, 2004), pp. 32-33.

lives (§3). This provides a bridge for evangelistic work, and it gives us a context for interreligious dialogue, which can be "a part of the Church's evangelizing mission" (§55), as well as a basis for cooperation for common human good (§29).

Gatherings of evangelicals to discuss these issues have not attained consensus, but ecclesiocentrism appears to be particularly strong within the evangelical missionary community, where the fear is often expressed that the church's motivation to make significant sacrifices for gospel proclamation will be undermined if we concede that God may save some people apart from our evangelistic efforts. Evangelicals who affirm ecclesiocentrism will probably be troubled by the direction taken in *Redemptoris missio,*[13] but it may foster discussion of issues that have become even more urgent since its publication. John Paul II demonstrates that one's passion to see people saved and incorporated into a local church, by God's normal means of salvation, the church's proclamation of the gospel, is not threatened by an optimism about the gracious work of God beyond the missionary efforts of the church (§29). He also lays out very helpful guidelines for forms of interreligious dialogue that complement the church's primary work of evangelism without inhibiting that goal. Such dialogue can lead to the mutual enrichment of religious communities and can eliminate "prejudice, intolerance and misunderstandings" (§§55-57). John Paul II "has spoken more positively about the evidence of the presence and working of the Holy Spirit in the non-Christian religions than either Vatican II or Paul VI had done."[14] But, although *Redemptoris missio* speaks of "participated forms of mediation" which "acquire meaning and value only from Christ's own mediation" (§5), John Paul II has never affirmed religious instrumentalism as some other Catholic theologians have done.[15]

Synergism. Evangelicals have reached no consensus on whether God's saving work is synergistic or monergistic, but Calvinists and other monergists will not be happy with the synergism enunciated in *Redemptoris missio.* The libertarian notion

---

[13]See, for instance, Jack Voelkel's ecclesiocentrist response to the Catholic Church's accessibilism as expressed in this encyclical and elsewhere: "Observations of an Evangelical Protestant Missionary in Latin America," in *Redemption and Dialogue: Reading Redemptoris missio and Dialogue and Proclamation,* ed. William R. Burrows (Maryknoll, N.Y.: Orbis, 1993), pp. 186-89.

[14]Frances A. Sullivan, *Salvation Outside the Church? Tracing the History of the Catholic Response* (Mahwah, N.J.: Paulist Press, 1992), p. 196.

[15]Cf. Jacques Dupuis, who posits that members of other religions are "not saved by Christ in spite of, or beside, their own tradition, but in the sincere practice of it, and, in some mysterious way through it" ("A Theological Commentary: Dialogue and Proclamation," in *Redemption and Dialogue: Reading Redemptoris missio and Dialogue and Proclamation,* ed. William R. Burrows [Maryknoll, N.Y.: Orbis, 1993], p. 152).

of human freedom that the encyclical affirms (§8) and the statement that "salvation, which always remains a gift of the Holy Spirit, requires man's cooperation, both to save himself and to save others" (§9, cf. §10) will not be appreciated by monergists but will pose no difficulty for evangelical synergists who are also most likely to be accessibilists.[16] In harmony with evangelical synergists (and to the puzzlement of monergists), *Redemptoris missio* insists that faith in Christ is received as "a gift from on high, not as a result of any merit of our own" (§11).

Universal atonement and universal brotherhood. The report of the Evangelical Roman Catholic Dialogue on Mission (ERCDOM, 1977-1984) noted a difference between the Roman Catholic and the evangelical participants in regard to "the implications of [Christ's] universal salvation and lordship."[17] The Roman Catholic participants understood all people to be "part of the humanity whose new head has overcome sin and death," and they cited John Paul II's statement that "every person, without exception, has been redeemed by Christ, and with each person, without any exception, Christ is in some way united, even when that person is not aware of that."[18] In the same vein, *Redemptoris missio* frequently makes statements such as: "The redemption event brings salvation to all, 'for . . . with each one Christ has united himself forever'" through the mystery of the incarnation (§4).[19] The encyclical speaks of "universal brotherhood," which is to say that "all men and women are sons and daughters of the same Father and brothers and sisters in Christ" (§43). While many evangelicals are happy to agree that Christ died to save everyone, most will stop short of describing everyone as brothers and sisters in Christ.[20]

Evangelization among nominal Christians. At the Lausanne Committee for World Evangelization (LCWE) meeting in Pattaya, in 1980, the group working on Christian witness to nominal Catholics observed that nominalism "is particularly serious in the 'unreformed' Roman Catholic Church because it tends to view Christian initiation largely, if not solely, in terms of baptism, and so regards all the baptized as genuine Christians, even if lapsed."[21] These evangelicals may have been encouraged, ten years later, to read John Paul II's call for "new evangelization"

---

[16]Tiessen, *Who Can Be Saved?* pp. 66-69.

[17]"Evangelical-Roman Catholic Dialogue on Mission [ERCDOM] 1977-1984: Christology; Holy Spirit; Mission; Common Witness—Final Report on Mission" Centro pro unione, Franciscan Friars of the Atonement (1984), chap. 3, pt. 4. <http://www.prounione.urbe.it/dia-int/e-rc/doc/e_e-rc_ev-cath.html>.

[18]*Redemptoris hominis*, §14; cited in ERCDOM, chap. 3, pt. 4.

[19]Quoting from *Redemptor hominis*, §13.

[20]Cf. ERCDOM, chap. 3, pt. 4.

[21]"Christian Witness to Nominal Christians Among Roman Catholics," Lausanne Occasional Paper from the Consultation on World Evangelization held in Pattaya, Thailand, in June 1980, p. 1.

or "re-evangelization" of "groups of the baptized [who] have lost a living sense of the faith" or who "live a life far removed from Christ and his Gospel" (§33). This is the man who, before his ascendancy to the papacy, had invited Billy Graham to preach in Poland and who had overseen a partnership between the Polish Catholic youth renewal movement and Campus Crusade for Christ,[22] but he did not intend evangelistic work done within the Roman Catholic Church to convert people to Protestantism. "Foreign evangelicalism posed no threat to the cultural monopoly held by the Polish Catholic Church," so that evangelicals were viewed as helpers against communism, "but in South America, evangelicals *were* the competition."[23] The call for "new evangelization," in that context, is an effort to maintain the religious primacy of the Roman Catholic Church and to renew its role as "the foundation and integrating factor of Latin American life."[24]

I expect that John Paul II would have been offended by the LCWE group's suggestion that it is "right to encourage members of this church, if they come by God's grace to justifying faith in Christ, to leave their church and join an Evangelical church."[25] Yet, there were some in the group who were hopeful that the Spirit would bring "repentance, renewal, and revival," within the Catholic Church. In predominantly Roman Catholic contexts such as Latin America, the Philippines and southern Europe, many evangelicals assume that those whose lives are transformed by the gospel will leave the Roman Catholic Church and affiliate with fellow believers in evangelical churches.[26] Evangelicals do not see this as "a reprehensible kind of 'sheep-stealing,'" but participants in the Roman Catholic-WEA dialogue acknowledge that Catholics are "understandably offended whenever Evangelicals appear to regard all Roman Catholics as nominal Christians, or whenever they base their evangelism on a distorted view of Catholic teaching and practice."[27] Participants agreed that a distinction must be made "between one's es-

[22]David Scott, "The Pope We Never Knew: The Unknown Story of How John Paul II Ushered Campus Crusade into Catholic Poland," *Christianity Today* (May 2005): 35-36.

[23]Ibid., p. 4.

[24]M. Daniel Carroll R., "The Evangelical-Roman Catholic Dialogue: Issues Revolving Around Evangelization. An Evangelical View from Latin America," *Trinity Journal* 21 NS (2000): 198.

[25]"Christian Witness to Nominal Christians," p. 1. On the other hand, Edward Cardinal Cassidy "spoke in support of evangelicals and Catholics sharing the gospel with each other, especially with those who were nominal in either camp." He deemed it "far more important for one truly to know Jesus and find salvation in him than to belong without conviction to any particular community" (Mark Noll and Carolyn Nystrom, *Is the Reformation Over? An Evangelical Assessment of Contemporary Roman Catholicism* [Grand Rapids: Baker Academic, 2005], p. 159).

[26]Carroll, "Evangelical-Roman Catholic Dialogue," pp. 199-200.

[27]"Church, Evangelization, and the Bonds of *Koinonia:* A Report of the International Consultation Between the Catholic Church and the World Evangelical Alliance (1993-2002)," article 64.

timate of the doctrines and practices of a church and the judgment that bears on an individual's spiritual condition."[28] Both groups repented of "unworthy forms of evangelization which aim at pressuring people to change their church affiliation in ways that dishonor the Gospel, and by methods which compromise rather than enhance the freedom of the believer and the truth of the Gospel."[29]

Cooperation with Roman Catholics in aspects of the church's mission. Redemptoris missio echoes the call of *Ad gentes* for Catholics to "collaborate in a spirit of fellowship with their separated brothers and sisters . . . by a common profession of faith in God and in Jesus Christ before the nations—to the extent that this is possible—and by their cooperation in social and technical as well as in cultural and religious matters" (§50). Participants in the Roman Catholic-WEA dialogue identified "the prospect of our common witness" as "a hope and a challenge."[30] Its possibility will certainly vary from one situation to another.

Tereso Casiño has identified four approaches by evangelicals to this call for engagement with Roman Catholicism:[31] (1) A "rejectionist" perspective predominates in Roman Catholic-dominated countries, such as Latin America,[32] the Philippines and parts of Europe. Roman Catholicism is viewed "solely through a theological grid," and no common ground is found for any form of cooperation. (2) The "conversionist" approach views Roman Catholics as "nominal Christians," who are therefore candidates for evangelization. (3) The "accommodationist" position (identified with signatories of "Evangelicals and Catholics Together [1992-1994]"[33]) recognizes significant theological differences and refuses to compromise evangelical distinctives. But it values dialogue as a means of fostering better relations and mutual understanding, and it fosters partnership in combating the secularizing trends that threaten us equally. (4) "Integrationism" is found primarily among academics. It identifies "specific points to accommodate, reject, or integrate into the evangelical form of daily life," stressing good points of Catholicism but discarding those which are inconsistent with evangelicalism.

---

[28]Ibid., article 65.

[29]Ibid., article 69. Mark Noll and Carolyn Nystrom take note of the widespread conservative evangelical protest concerning "the moratorium on evangelistic outreach to adherents of the Catholic Church," which signatories of ECT I affirmed (*Is the Reformation Over?* p. 156).

[30]"Church, Evangelization," article 79.

[31]Tereso C. Casiño, "Speaking the Truth in Love: Evangelical Perspectives on Dialogue with Roman Catholicism," *Verbum: WEA Theological News* 35, no. 2 (2006): 4.

[32]Cf. Carroll, "Evangelical-Roman Catholic Dialogue," pp. 200, 205.

[33]"Evangelical & Catholics Together: The Christian Mission in the Third Millennium," *First Things* 43 (May 1994): 15-22 <http://www.leaderu.com/ftissues/ft9405/articles/mission.html>.

The differences among evangelicals which Casiño names were noted in the Manila Manifesto (1989):

> Some evangelicals are praying, talking, studying Scripture and working with [Roman Catholic and Orthodox] churches. Others are strongly opposed to any form of dialogue or cooperation with them. All are aware that serious theological differences between us remain. Where appropriate, and so long as biblical truth is not compromised, cooperation may be possible in such areas as Bible translation, the study of contemporary theological and ethical issues, social work and political action. We wish to make it clear, however, that common evangelism demands a common commitment to the biblical gospel.[34]

Perspectives which will generally not be appreciated by evangelicals or where evangelicals may want to challenge the Catholic Church to do better. *Ecclesiology.* Despite the significant improvement in relationships between evangelical bodies and the Roman Catholic Church, even since the issuance of our different ecclesiologies constitute the primary hindrance to our fellowship. The difference strikes us immediately in the introductory "Apostolic Blessing." Granted, *apostolic* is elsewhere used without a capital to identify missionaries and their work (§40), but we know that John Paul II believed himself to be the Vicar of Christ by unique succession from the apostle Peter and this will inevitably trouble us. Similarly, though evangelicals believe that the church of Christ is found in every local church, they will be disconcerted by the assertion that this is only true if churches remain "in communion with the universal Church" (§48), knowing that this is a reference to the Roman Catholic Church unified hierarchically (§51, cf. §63). Commenting on the Latin American situation, Daniel Carroll observes that John Paul II "seemed to be very intentional in reasserting conservative control of the administration and theology of the Latin American Catholic Church," demonstrating "a return to some pre-Vatican [II] postures in relationship to Church hierarchy and dogma."[35]

Those who know the devotion of John Paul II to the Virgin Mary will not be surprised that he concludes by calling the church to "gather in the Upper Room 'together with Mary, the Mother of Jesus' (Acts 1:14)" (§92), but even so the suggestion strikes the evangelical ear strangely. It is not that we deny the importance of Mary's role in the incarnation of our Savior; most of us just don't feel that the biblical narrative gives her the prominence attributed to her in this conclusion to a splendid treatise on the church's mission. The largest stumbling block occurs in

---

[34]The Lausanne Committee for World Evangelization, "The Manila Manifesto" (1989), §9 <http://www.lausanne.org/Brix?pageID=12894 >.

[35]Carroll, "Evangelical-Roman Catholic Dialogue," p. 194.

the penultimate sentence, where John Paul II quotes his earlier encyclical *Redemptoris mater* and entrusts the church, and particularly its missionaries, to Mary's mediation, even though we can be thankful that this mediation is described as "wholly oriented toward Christ and tending to the revelation of his salvific power" (§92). It is precisely this connection of Christian faith and the church's evangelistic mission with the Virgin Mary that makes joint efforts at evangelism extremely difficult.[36]

Religious freedom. Redemptoris missio states that the church strives for religious freedom "in all countries, especially in those with a Catholic majority, where she has greater influence" (§39). This is a commendable goal, but the statement will have a hollow ring for Protestants who have faced significant persecution, both as individuals and as communities, in situations where the Catholic Church is strong and is closely allied with government and social leadership. It is encouraging that the pope wants the Catholic Church to be a community which "respects individuals and cultures" and "honors the sanctuary of conscience" (§39), but this is often not the reality at the local level. In January 1995, five years after *Redemptoris missio* was issued, the Latin American Council of Churches "decided not to invite official representatives of the Catholic Church to its Third General Assembly in Concepción, Chile, because of worsening relations between Catholics and Protestants throughout the continent."[37] The Episcopal bishop of Mexico City observed that the Catholic Church in Mexico had a "superiority complex." "It is the Church of the majority, and therefore it feels that there is no reason to take other Churches into consideration."[38]

We can be thankful that converts from Catholicism are not placed under the death sentence, as in Islamic Shari'ah, but when individuals have their livelihood threatened because of their faith and evangelical churches are treated unjustly because of the disapproval of the Catholic hierarchy in the area, the gap between the encyclical's ideals and the church's practice is painful. Given the hierarchical nature of the Roman Catholic Church, more needs to be done to ensure that the ideals of the Magisterium are realized at the parish level.

---

[36]As Carroll notes, with particular reference to the Latin American situation. Ibid., p. 197. See also in the ERCDOM report the lengthy appendix on "The Role of Mary in Salvation," which expressed the nervousness of evangelicals on this point (ERCDOM, chap. 3, appendix, pt. b).

[37]Thomas P. Rausch, "Catholic-Evangelical Relations: Signs of Progress," in *Catholics and Evangelicals: Do They Share a Common Future?* ed. Thomas P. Rausch (Downers Grove, Ill.: InterVarsity Press, 2000), p. 39.

[38]Sergio Carranza-Gomez, "Ecumenical Relations in Mexico," *Ecumenical Trends* 24 (July/August 1995): 11. Cited by Rausch, "Catholic-Evangelical Relations," p. 39.

CONCLUSION

From the relative length of my commentary on items in this encyclical which I expect to be appreciated by and beneficial to evangelicals, it should be clear that I consider this to be a valuable statement concerning the mission of Christ for and through his church. Given the immensity of the task confronting the church, whom our Lord commissioned to disciple the nations, I hope and pray that the stirring call and wise instruction found in this letter will be heeded, particularly within the Catholic Church for whom it was written, but also within the church universal in the sense that evangelicals understand that catholicity.

13

Slavorum Apostoli

The Enduring Legacy of Cyril and Methodius

Peter Kuzmič

Summary

Slavorum apostoli[1] is the fourth encyclical of the first Slavic pope. It was issued on the occasion of the 1,100th anniversary of the death of Saint Methodius (c. 815-885) in order to honor him and his brother Saint Cyril by exploring and extolling the exemplary lives and labors as well as enduring legacy and universally relevant lessons of these enormously influential "Slavic apostles." They are praised as symbols of the shared spirituality of the Eastern (Byzantine) and Western (Latin) tradition of the still undivided church, and John Paul II upholds them as models of both missionary activity and Christian unity. As their primary evangelizers they brought the gospel, planted the church and profoundly affected the cultures among the Slavic peoples in an area that links Eastern and Western Europe. They are thus seen as bridge-building figures between the East and the West and as symbolically significant for modern-day reestablishment of European unity based on the common heritage of faith and culture.

This encyclical epistle is at the same time a reflection of the Christian witness and foundational impact of the Slavic apostles as well as a profound expression of the well-known longing of John Paul II for the cultural and religious unity and peace of Europe and his repeated calls for a new evangelization of the old continent, now spiritually and morally threatened by forces of secularization. It must

---

[1]John Paul II, *Slavorum apostoli,* Libreria Editrice Vaticana (June 2, 1985) <http://www.vatican.va/holy_father/john_paul_ii/encyclicals/documents/hf_jp-ii_enc_02061985_slavorum-apostoli_en.html>.

therefore be interpreted within the context of the pope's great desire and multiple ecumenical efforts to see the church again as a "body that breathes with both lungs," and Europe (re)discovering its common Christian roots. The document is also potent with politically prophetic dimension related to the reunification of Western and Eastern Europe, pointing to the way to overcome the ideologically imposed division of the continent and providing helpful hints for its political and economic integration based on the universal values of Christian humanism.

CONTEXTUAL INTRODUCTION

This encyclical was written during the Cold War era, marked by the ideological division of Europe, and yet also a time in which the longing for freedom and unity was evident everywhere. The very first sentence announces its intention to celebrate the past in order to influence the present: "The apostles of the Slavs, Saints Cyril and Methodius, are remembered by the Church together with the great work of evangelization which they carried out. Indeed it can be said that their memory is particularly vivid and relevant to our day."

In this section I summarize the first two chapters of the document, the "Introduction" and the "Biographical Sketch" of the famous brothers.[2] The introduction establishes the historical occasion and pontifical precedent for the encyclical. In 1964, Pope Paul VI proclaimed Saint Benedict, the founder of Western Christian monasticism, the Patron of Europe. Pope John Paul II then elevated Eastern saints Cyril and Methodius to the status of "Co-Patrons of Europe" (along with Benedict) in his apostolic letter *Egregiae virtutis* (Men of Extraordinary Virtue) issued on December 31, 1980, a document "dictated by the firm hope of a gradual overcoming in Europe and the world of everything that divides the Churches, nations and peoples" (*Slavorum apostoli,* §2).[3] The year 1980 was significant for three reasons: it was the eleventh centenary of Pope John VIII's official approval of the use of Old Slavonic in the liturgy translated by the famous brothers; it was also the first centenary of Pope Leo XIII's 1880 encyclical epistle *Grande munus,* which extended the cult of Cyril and Methodius to the entire church and provided an official impetus for the growing movement among Slavic catholics to consider them as "the saints of East-West unity." It was also the year which marked the beginning of, as the pope optimistically states, "the happy and promising theological dia-

---

[2]I am very grateful to Judd Birdsall for help in summarizing complex sections of the encyclical to make their presentation clearer for American evangelical audiences.

[3]Unless otherwise noted, all following in-text citations to *Slavorum apostoli* will be identified by section number only.

logue" between the Catholic Church and Orthodox Churches on the island of Patmos, at times a very turbulent and ecumenically disappointing journey for the initially very hopeful pontiff.

John Paul II also had profoundly personal and historically important reasons for elevating the status of Cyril and Methodius. As the first Polish and thus Slavic pope, he expresses feeling a "particular obligation" to encourage the remembrance of the apostles to the Slavs, whose "special charisms have become still better understood in the light of the situations and experiences of our own times." The Second Vatican Council, an event in which the young bishop Karol Wojtyla enthusiastically participated, had opened a new era of reading the "signs of the times" as well as a new openness to and interest in Eastern Christianity, enabling us to "look in a new way—a more mature and profound way—at these two holy figures . . . so that they might be revealed with fresh fullness in our own age and might bear new fruits" (§3).

The most comprehensive biographer of John Paul II and a reliable interpreter of the role of Catholic Christianity in Central and Eastern Europe, George Weigel, reports of a fascinating conversation of the pope with the Czech bishop Jozef (later Cardinal) Tomko in 1979. In the conversation the creative Slavic pope in an almost spontaneous inspiration decided to name Cyril and Methodius "Co-patrons of Europe" as part of a great vision and, as Weigel conveys, as "a powerful symbol of the Church's drive to give back to the peoples of east central Europe their authentic history and culture . . . another potent example of how Christian images had become the primary symbols of a rebirth of cultural integrity and freedom."[4]

The second chapter of *Slavorum apostoli*, "Biographical Sketch," retells the lives of Cyril and Methodius in three distinct sections: pre-missionary careers, mission work and Methodius's continuation of the work after his brother's untimely death.

Cyril and Methodius were born into a privileged family in Thessaloniki, a cultural and economic hub second only to Constantinople in the Byzantine Empire. Their father was a high-ranking senior official in the imperial administration. Methodius (b. 815-820), the elder of the brothers, became a prefect of a province of the empire in which many Slavic people resided. He then retired from public life to a monastery at Mount Olympus in 840. Konstantin, better known under his religious name Cyril (b. 827-828), was a man of exceptional intellectual abilities, recognized early during his studies in Constantinople, leading him already at a young

[4]George Weigel, *Witness to Hope: The Biography of Pope John Paul II* (New York: HarperCollins, 1999), p. 408.

age to the prestigious positions of Librarian of the Archive at the church of Holy Wisdom (Hagia Sophia) and Secretary to the Patriarch of Constantinople. He received the Holy Orders, but then, similar to his brother, surreptitiously withdrew to a monastery on the coast of the Black Sea. Discovered six months later, Cyril was persuaded to accept a position teaching philosophy at what would today be called the University of Constantinople. "By reason of the excellence of his knowledge, he gained the epithet of The Philosopher by which he is still known" (§4). Both had gained some knowledge of the Slavic language in their native city and according to some sources also became fluent in Latin, Hebrew and Arabic. Because of linguistic and diplomatic skills, Cyril was sent on diplomatic mission to the Saracens, after which he again withdrew from public life to join his brother in their commitment to monastic life. From there both were again recruited by the emperor and patriarch in Constantinople to participate as missionary experts in an imperial delegation to the Judaic Khazars in the Crimea. While there they supposedly recovered the relics of the exiled and martyred pope Saint Clement, which later opened their entry to Rome and gained them the approval of Pope Hadrian II.

The Byzantine Emperor Michael III again called upon the Thessaloniki brothers when Prince Rastislav of Greater Moravia (the Slavic region of Central Europe) requested "a Bishop and teacher . . . able to explain to them the true Christian faith in their own language" (§5). Learned linguists and theologians with broad cross-cultural and diplomatic experience, the brothers were ideal candidates for evangelizing the Slavs and representing the Byzantine interests in a region that was "the crossroads of the mutual influences between East and West." Previous efforts among the Slavs had been unsuccessful in large part because of the German missionaries' insistence on using Latin in the life of the church. At this point the pope in a summary way praises the spiritual commitment, sacrifices and successes of their mission amidst antagonistic circumstances.

Cyril and Methodius made the decision at the outset of their ministry to employ the indigenous Slavonic for liturgy and Scriptures. For this purpose Cyril invented the Glagolitic alphabet. Slavic scholars are unanimous in praising it "because of its originality, and because it expresses perfectly all the sounds of the Old Slavic language, which reveals that Constantine was a highly talented philologist and linguist."[5] The script named in honor of Cyril—Cyrillic, used today in slightly revised forms in Russia, Ukraine, Bulgaria, Serbia and Macedonia—is derivative from Glagolitic and was created later by their followers and disciples of Methodius

---

[5]Francis Dvornik, *Byzantine Missions Among the Slavs: SS. Constantin-Cyril and Methodius* (New Brunswick, N.J.: Rutgers University Press, 1970), p. 103.

in Bulgaria, after their forceful expulsion from Moravia.

The brothers' introduction and use of Slavonic caused considerable opposition and was accompanied by constant controversy. German clerics objected to the practice and appealed to Rome. Pope Nicholas I summoned the brothers to give an account of their work. This was just one of the many "journeys, privations, sufferings" the brothers would face, and they bore them all "with strong faith and indomitable hope in God" (§5). On their journey they ministered in the Slavic region of Pannonia (today's southwestern Hungary, northern Croatia and the province of Voivodina in northern Serbia), where they were warmly received by Prince Kocel and then en route in Venice successfully participated in public disputes about their innovative methods of evangelization. They were accompanied by a number of their Slavic disciples who were candidates for ordination. In Rome they were received warmly by newly installed Pope Hadrian II (Nicholas I had died before they arrived), who approved the ordination of their Slavic candidates and, more importantly, the use of Slavonic in the church.

While in Rome, Cyril fell ill and died on February 14 (Feast of Saints Cyril and Methodius), 869. On his deathbed he movingly implored his older brother to continue the mission among the Slavs rather than retire to the Olympus monastery. "Behold, my brother, we have shared the same destiny, ploughing the same furrow; I now fall in the field at the end of my day. I know that you greatly love your Mountain; but do not for the sake of the Mountain give up your work of teaching" (§6).

Methodius honored his brother's dying plea. While in Rome he was consecrated archbishop for the territory of Pannonia, with the ecclesiastical seat in the ancient Sirmium (modern-day Srijem, in the neighboring area of the residence of this author). He returned to ministry in Greater Moravia, which was made very difficult by constant intrigues and fierce persecution from both political powers and ecclesiastical competitors claiming jurisdiction over the territory. The trials included more than two years of imprisonment, which was ended by the personal intervention of John VIII, who, recalling him to Rome in 880, reinstated his ecclesiastical rights and approval of the use of Slavonic.

Church historians would add that the same pope won the support of the East by lifting the anathemization of Patriarch Photius. Interestingly a year or two later a journey in search of a similar approval was made to Constantinople, where both the emperor and Patriarch Photius provided Byzantine legitimacy to his work. The last years of his life were devoted to further Slavonic translation of the Bible, liturgical books, various patristic works and books of Byzantine law. Pope John

Paul II summarizes his own evaluation: "His far-seeing work, his profound and orthodox doctrine, his balance, loyalty, apostolic zeal and intrepid magnanimity gained Methodius the recognition and trust of Roman Pontiffs, of Patriarchs of Constantinople, of Byzantine Emperors and of various Princes of the young Slav peoples" (§7). But, as we have already seen, not all recognized and trusted him. German civil and ecclesiastical leaders persistently harassed him despite his multiple commendations from both Rome and Constantinople. After his death in 885, Methodius's followers would also face severe persecutions and were banished or forced to flee from Moravia to neighboring mission fields.

The encyclical does not mention that with the death of Pope Hadrian II (d. 885) friendly relations with the East came to an end and that his successor Stephen V forbade the Slavonic liturgy, alienated the Slavs and pushed them into the now already increasingly antagonistic Orthodox camp. That marked the end of the mission in Moravia, which came under strict Latin control, although the ecumenical providence as a result of persecution brought the disciples of Cyril and Methodius and their linguistic and literary work to Slavic Balkans where, as proudly claimed by Byzantine and Slavic historians, they successfully planted Slavic Orthodox Christianity in (greater) Bulgaria. Although omitting the names of the persecutors and confessional blunders with far-reaching negative consequences for further development of European Christianity, made by highest ecclesiastical authorities, John Paul II concludes the biographical section of the encyclical by summarizing this painful part of history with his recognizably delicate ecumenical skill:

> To tell the truth, after the death of Methodius the work of the holy Brothers suffered a grave crisis, and persecution of their followers grew so severe that the latter were forced to abandon their missionary field. Nonetheless, their sowing of the Gospel seed did not cease to bear fruit, and their pastoral attitude of concern to bring the revealed truth to new peoples while respecting their cultural originality remains a living model for the Church and for their missionaries of all ages. (§7)

EVANGELIZERS AND CHURCH PLANTERS

John Paul presents the missionary activity of the brothers in chapters three and four of the encyclical under the titles "Heralds of the Gospel" and "They Planted the Church."

Although Byzantine in origin and culture, Cyril and Methodius became "apostles of the Slavs in the full sense of the word" (§8). In providing biblical precedence for leaving one's homeland to go to a foreign land, John Paul II recounts the calling of Abraham from Ur in Genesis 12 and the Macedonian call of Paul in Acts 16. "Divine Providence," through the voice of the emperor and patriarch in Constantinople, similarly called Cyril and Methodius to leave their homeland and familiar surroundings in order to take the message of salvation, as the evangelicals would say, to the unreached Slavic people. The encyclical quotes in part the moving request from Prince Rastislav to Emperor Michael III: "Many Christian teachers have reached us from Italy, from Greece and from Germany, who instruct us in different ways. But we Slavs . . . have no one to direct us towards the truth and instruct us in an understandable way" (§9). The qualifications and experience of Cyril and Methodius made them obvious candidates. Both brothers held prestigious positions and longed even more for a secluded contemplative life. Rather than pursue their own ambitions, they obeyed the call with a "profoundly Christian response," as expressed in the words of Constantine to the emperor: "However tired and physically worn out I am, I will go with joy to that land . . . for the sake of Christian faith" (§9).[6]

John Paul goes on to develop a biblical basis and christological foundation for the mandate of the brothers by equating their response to the obedience of "the Great Commission," as we evangelicals would describe it, and quotes the words of Jesus from Mark 16:15 and Matthew 28:19. In obedience to the command of the risen Lord, "the preachers and teachers of the Slav peoples let themselves be guided by the apostolic ideal of Saint Paul" (§9), and Galatians 3:26-28 is quoted in full.

Following the example of the biblical apostle to the nations, Cyril and Methodius, motivated by redemptive love and guided by wisdom, identified with Slavic "future believers. . . . They desired to become similar in every aspect to those to whom they were bringing the Gospel; they wished to become part of the peoples and share their lot in everything" (§9). This "lot" included complex issues regarding the identity of the Slavic nations in initial stages of their formation and under military and cultural pressure from the Romano-Germanic Empire as well as amidst the growing ecclesiastical tension between the East and West. And yet, immense suffering in ministry "did not deflect either of them from their tenacious resolve to help and to serve the good of the Slav peoples and the unity of the universal Church" (§10).

For evangelization to succeed and Christian faith to take root, the brothers knew they had to translate the Scriptures and seminal Christian works into the

---

[6]For a more detailed account of the calling, see Franc Grivec, *Slavenski blagovjesnici Sveti Ćiril i Metod* (Zagreb: Kršćanska sadašnjost, 1985), pp. 48-49.

Slavic vernacular. Such an undertaking demanded not only the translation of words but also "to transpose correctly Biblical notions and Greek theological concepts into a very different context of thought and historical experience" (§11). Cyril and Methodius became astute students of Slavic culture and enlisted other coworkers, native Slavs, in their translation project. For their pioneering work, John Paul II, in praising their motives and methodology, makes observations similar to those we read in many reports of Bible societies and of the evangelical Wycliffe missionary Bible translators. "The effort to learn the language and to understand the mentality of the new peoples to whom they wished to bring the faith was truly worthy of the missionary spirit." He then hails the brothers as "true models for all missionaries who in every period have accepted Saint Paul's invitation to become all things to all people in order to redeem all" (§11).

This author, having lived through the renaissance of exclusive nationalistic movements and resultant interethnic wars in former Yugoslavia that began six years after the writing of this encyclical, appreciates the prophetic note of the concluding paragraph of chapter three. It deserves to be quoted in full:

> Perfect communion in love preserves the Church from all forms of particularism, ethnic exclusivism or racial prejudice, and from any nationalistic arrogance. This communion must elevate and sublimate every purely natural legitimate sentiment of the human heart. (§11)

One of the treasured mementos in the personal collection of this author is a medal received from John Paul II during his first visit to the Republic of Croatia, former Yugoslavia, September 10-11, 1994. One-third of this young and, due to Serbian aggression, fiercely nationalistic country was still under the Serbian occupation, and the war was raging in the neighboring Bosnia and Herzegovina. John Paul addressed about one million Croats in a very moving sermon boldly calling for peace, forgiveness and reconciliation. Referring to the Lord's prayer he cried "Our Father . . . you invite us to repudiate violence and build a society based on brotherhood and solidarity. Our father," he continued, "would it not be but intolerable hypocrisy to pray to you while harboring feelings of anger, or even intentions of violence and revenge?" The prayer and the message were tough for most of the Croats suffering injustices and loss of lives and territory. I watched the facial expressions of the stunned President Franjo Tudjman, a former Communist general recently turned nationalist who now heard the most famous visitor say in the largest gathering in the history of this nation that when God is pushed aside, then "there is the risk of idolizing a nation, a race, a party and justifying in their name hatred, discrimination and violence."

Tudjman has only recently been privately reprimanded by Franjo Cardinal Kuharic because of rhetoric and attitudes now publicly condemned by the pope. The pontiff went even further, calling upon Croatian Catholics to "become apostles of the new concord between peoples." The peacemaking pope proclaimed in almost flawless Croatian—*mir*, a Croatian and all-Slavic word for "peace." "*Mir*," he cried, "is not a utopia but is the only realistic approach. To forgive and to be forgiven is the only way to peace. Progress in the Balkans has only one name, peace, *mir*." The applause to this demanding message was not very enthusiastic, but everyone understood that it was the voice from beyond. The pope illustrated the call for reconciliation with an almost poetic story of the two rivers. It deserves an extensive quote as it illustrates in a concrete historical setting what *Slavorum apostoli* teaches in terms of general principle to be applied to the divided churches and nations of Europe.

> In this region that is tested so seriously today, faith must become once again the force which brings people together and bears fruit, much like the rivers that pass through these countries. Like Sava, a river whose source is in Slovenia, that flows through your beloved country and then on along the Bosnian-Croatian border to Serbia, where it joins the Danube. The Danube is another large river that connects Croatia and Serbia with the other countries of Eastern, Central and Western Europe. The two rivers meet, much in the same way that the peoples that live on their shores are called upon to meet. The two Christian churches, the Eastern and the Western, must lead the effort because, in these parts, they have always lived together. The metaphor of the two rivers makes quite clear the path God wants you to take in this troubled moment of your history. It is the path of unity and peace and no-one should avoid it. It is the path that reason tells you to take, even before faith does. Has your history not created so many ties between your peoples that you are bound in a way that can never be undone? Is it not true that your languages, for all their differences, are so similar that you can communicate and understand each other better than you can with languages spoken in other parts of Europe?[7]

In the overall composition of the encyclical, the chapter "They Planted the Church of God" lays ground for the subsequent reflections on catholicity, ecumenical significance and the contemporary relevance of Slavic apostles' far-reaching pioneering mission. In terms of Catholic-Orthodox relations, this most complex chapter of the encyclical clearly intends to portray the Slavic apostles as "authentic precursors of ecumenism" (§14).

---

[7]The integral text of the speech was published as an appendix in Ivan Pavao II, *Testament za Treće tisućljeće* (Zagreb: Prometej, 2000).

Cyril and Methodius were ethnic Greeks but "Slavs at heart," and their guiding theological vision was "the Church as one, holy and universal"[8] (§12). John Paul, in what critics would perceive as a euphemistic simplification, summarizes their controversial ecclesial context: "Already in their time certain differences between Constantinople and Rome had begun to appear as pretexts for disunity, even though the deplorable split between the two parts of the same Christian world was still in the distant future" (§12).

The well-educated and cross-culturally experienced brothers knew that some ancient national Christian traditions in the East used the indigenous language (Georgian and Syriac are explicitly mentioned) in their liturgies and "were therefore not afraid to use the Slavonic language . . . and to make it into an effective instrument for bringing the divine truths" to the Slavic recipients. As John Paul says, bringing in two modern social concepts, they did this "out of love of justice and with a clear apostolic zeal for peoples then developing" (§12). In contrast to this Eastern approach, the Roman West had long viewed Latin as an indispensable tool for uniting Europe. In the minds of the German clerics in Moravia, the coercive imposition of Latin was a justifiable measure to maintain order and unity. The brothers from Greece believed, however, as did the modern Slavic pope, in establishing unity through love, not force, and by respect for cultural and ethnic diversity.

The encyclical takes special effort here and in other places to emphasize that despite the injustices they suffered at the hands of Western Christians, Cyril and Methodius remained deferential to the Bishop of Rome. "In following this programme of harmony and peace [note again the use of modern notions], . . . though subjects of the Eastern Empire and believers subject to the Patriarchate of Constantinople, they considered it their duty to give an account of their missionary work to the Roman Pontiff" (§13). To the historical experts and Orthodox critics, these lines of argument, used in several places, are not only biased in favor of the papal authority and jurisdiction, but also simplifications ignoring the competitive political realities and territorial claims that made compromises of this kind necessary. It is true, however, to claim, as the encyclical does, that the brothers' respect for both East and West was extraordinary in the difficult ninth century; was animated by their vision of the church as one, holy, catholic and apostolic; and thus remains exemplary for our times. They believed that every culture and regional church had their unique contribution to make within the larger Christendom.

---

[8]For an evangelical missiological recasting of the marks of the church, see Charles van Engen, *God's Missionary People* (Grand Rapids: Baker, 1991).

John Paul repeatedly insists on the ecumenical significance of the brothers: "For us today their apostolate also possesses the eloquence of an ecumenical appeal: it is an invitation to restore, in the peace of reconciliation, the unity that was gravely damaged after the time of Cyril and Methodius, and, first and foremost, the unity between the East and the West" (§13). Then and now again, West could be western, the East eastern, and Slavs Slavic as long as they all enriched the "Catholic 'pleroma' . . . with their evangelical insight that the different conditions of life of the individual Christian Churches can never justify discord, disagreement and divisions in the profession of the one faith and in the exercise of charity" (§13).

For their bridge-building efforts, Cyril and Methodius are hailed by John Paul II as "authentic precursors of ecumenism"[9] (§14). The Second Vatican Council defined ecumenism as "those activities and enterprises which, according to various needs of the Church and as opportunities offer, are initiated and organized to promote Christian unity" (§14). Disunity goes against the expressed will of Christ and provides a stumbling block to an unbelieving world. Fidelity to the ancient ecumenical councils and willingness to dialogue with those who opposed their ideas makes the brothers exemplary missionary promoters of the unity of the church. The Second Ecumenical Council of Constantinople and its "unalterable profession of faith of all Christians" are explicitly mentioned in the final sentence of this chapter (§15).

The evangelicals will warmly respond to the concern for unity arising from the missionary engagement of the church in various cultures. They agree with Richard Neuhaus's reminder: "Always in [John Paul's] vision, unity and evangelization are inseparably joined. The unity of Christians is a great good in itself but always, as in John 17, it is a necessary part of the invitation to the world to believe in the one whom the Father has sent. As was the case in Edinburgh in 1910, but was then largely forgotten by the movement to which Edinburgh gave birth, ecumenism must always be vivified by the missionary mandate."[10] Evangelicals would add the historical note that the first effective initiatives leading to ecumenical cooperation and search for Christian unity had been undertaken by those engaged in world evangelization in the nineteenth century, and we would remind our Catholic

---

[9]This designation was suggested to John Paul II four years earlier in a letter from the Ukrainian Cardinal Slipyj. See Jaroslav Pelikan, *Confessor Between East and West: A Portrait of Ukrainian Cardinal Josyf Slipyj* (Grand Rapids: Eerdmans, 1990), p. 37 (see the fascinating chapter "The Disputed Legacy of Cyril and Methodius," pp. 23-37).

[10]Richard John Neuhaus, "A New Thing: Ecumenism at the Threshold of the Third Millennium," in *Reclaiming the Great Tradition: Evangelicals, Catholics and Orthodox in Dialogue,* ed. James S. Cutsinger (Downers Grove, Ill.: InterVarsity Press, 1997), p. 51.

friends of the powerful story and impact of the Student Voluntary Movement. The approaching centenary of that groundbreaking Edinburgh conference and the upcoming Third International Lausanne Congress for World Evangelization (2010) will undoubtedly reemphasize these themes and provide further evidence for the strong link between world missions and the search for unity among the followers of Christ. The evangelicals, as opposed to some more liberal ecumenical ventures, will also continue to insist on fidelity to the teachings of the early church while engaging modern cultures and responding to the moral challenges of contemporary societies. In this sense one can also expect further growth and greater international resonance to the movement and documents of Evangelicals and Catholics Together.[11] One should also point to a very influential contemporary evangelical model in the person and ministry of John R. W. Stott for simultaneous fidelity to historic orthodoxy, creative involvement in evangelism and openness to dialogue with those who disagree. A dialogue between evangelicals and Catholics along the lines proposed might well prove fruitful.

FOUNDATIONAL CATHOLICITY AND CULTURAL DIVERSITY

The following section is a summary and evaluation of the central theological reflection of the encyclical—"Catholic Sense of the Church" (chapter five) and its briefer missiological explication under the title "The Gospel and Culture" (chapter six).

The encyclical appropriately links the ministerial practice of Cyril and Methodius to the intentions, vision and outcomes of the Second Vatican Council, whose principal task was "that of reawakening the self-awareness of the Church and, through interior renewal, of impressing upon her a fresh missionary impulse for the proclamation . . . beyond all the frontiers that yet divide our planet" (§16). It underscores the world-encompassing dimension of catholicity, and in a lengthy quote from *Lumen gentium* (Dogmatic Constitution on the Church) affirms that in this universality "each individual part of the Church contributes through its special gifts to the good of the other parts and of the whole Church. Thus through the common sharing of gifts and through the common effort to attain fullness in unity, the whole and each of its parts receive increase" (§16). Evangelicals will agree with this understanding of the mutuality and complementarity of gifts and ministries as taught by the apostle Paul in Romans 12:1, Corinthians 12—14 and Ephesians 4.

The encyclical again endorses Cyril and Methodius's "catechetical and pastoral

---

[11]"Evangelical & Catholics Together: The Christian Mission in the Third Millennium," *First Things* 43 (May 1994): 15-22.

method," which showed respect for the life and language of the Slavs; it then provides examples of their use of Scriptures in their disputations. To those who questioned their use of a language other than the three approved (Hebrew, Greek and Latin), often referred to as "tri-linguists," Cyril in effective polemical style forcefully replied: "Tell me: do you hold this because you consider God is so weak that he cannot grant it, or so envious that he does not wish it?" (§17). Historical and logical arguments were supported by the brothers' frequent quotation of relevant Scriptures, especially from the "missionary" Psalms calling upon "all nations" to praise God in their own tongues.

The Catholic Church's understanding of catholicity does not imply any attempt to absorb all humanity into one homogeneous entity. Rather, because the gospel speaks to every context, the church allows for contextual expression of faith. "The Gospel," states the encyclical, "does not lead to the impoverishment or extinction of those things which every individual, people and nation and every culture throughout history recognizes and brings into being as goodness, truth and beauty. On the contrary, it strives to assimilate and to develop all these values: to live them with magnanimity and joy and to perfect them by the mysterious and ennobling light of Revelation" (§18). Moreover, constantly incorporating new converts and cultures, the church's catholicity is "not something static, outside history and flatly uniform" but it—and now the encyclical again effectively underscores the multicultural dimension with the theological foundation—"wells up and develops every day as something new from the unanimous faith of all those who believe in God, One and Three, revealed in Jesus Christ and preached by the Church through the power of the Holy Spirit" (§18). John Paul goes on to define the manifestation of catholicity in terms of its ethical attitudes and outcomes: "The catholicity of the Church is manifested in the active joint responsibility . . . of all for the sake of the common good" (§19). The brothers exemplify that all-encompassing vision in which "all individuals, all nations, cultures and civilizations have their own part to play and their own place in God's mysterious plan and in the universal history of salvation" (§19).

The church's diversity and dynamic catholicity are sustained by the active and loving participation of all its members. All peoples have a role to play in God's redemptive plan. The Slavic peoples became the "heirs of the promise made by God to Abraham" and thus "took their destined place in the Church" because of the missionary efforts of Cyril and Methodius, whose message was "transmitted through preaching and instruction in accordance with the eternal truths, at the same time being adapted to the concrete historical situation" (§20).

As heirs of both the Christian religion and the Greco-Byzantine civilization, Cyril and Methodius showed remarkable sensitivity to the delicate relationship between the gospel and culture. Their work both christianized Slavic culture and enriched Christianity with Slavic culture. In the pope's estimation, their ministry provides "a model for what today is called 'inculturation,' the incarnation of the Gospel in native cultures and also the introduction of these cultures into the life of the Church" (§21).

At this point the Slavic pope elaborates the importance of Cyril and Methodius in laying linguistic and literary foundations for further development of Slavic civilization. Their particular contribution to Slavic cultures was, of course, the written language, "their original and ingenious creation of an alphabet." By this invention and translation work the brothers and their disciples "conferred a capacity and cultural dignity upon the Old Slavonic liturgical language, which became . . . also the official and literary language, and even the common language of the more educated classes of the greater part of the Slav nations" (§21). Glagolitic and the later Cyrillic would play as significant a role in the historical development of the Slavic nations as Latin played in the West. What's more, the common use of "Old Church Slavonic," as it is now called, actually outlasted Latin by several centuries. The encyclical lists many of the locales and church traditions in which the language was used. It is still used today in the Byzantine liturgy of Slavonic Eastern churches throughout Europe, as well as in the Roman liturgy of some Catholics in Croatia.

THE MEANING OF THE SLAVIC MILLENNIUM FOR THE NEW EUROPEAN MILLENNIUM

In "The Significance and Influence of the Christian Millennium in the Slav World" (chapter seven), John Paul focuses on the application of the historical lessons learned from the ninth-century mission to the Slavs. He emphasizes the profound contemporary relevance of their lives, methods and message as the copatrons of Europe for the unity of the Slavic peoples and of the continent as modern peoples of the area search for identity and mission in the world eleven centuries later.

Cyril and Methodius's missionary work "can be considered the first effective evangelization of the Slavs." Although their initial efforts were concentrated in Greater Moravia, Methodius became the missionary and pastoral leader of a wider region, encompassing and influencing parts of present-day Slovakia, the Czech Republic, Hungary, and parts of Austria, Slovenia, Croatia, Bulgaria, FYR Macedonia and even Serbia. The encyclical, though pointing to the intermingling of

Latin and Slavic languages and rites and related tensions, nevertheless makes the important and universally valid point that "Christianization of the people was not possible without using the native language" (§23). Wherever the Cyrillic alphabet was later used and strong monastic life cultivated, as is true in most of the Slavic Balkans, the influence of Cyril and Methodius was of formative significance. From southeastern Europe, Christianity moved eastward to Ukraine and Russia, and the pope announces the upcoming celebration of the millennial anniversary of the baptism of Saint Vladimir, leader of the Kiev Rus (§24), in which he no doubt desired to participate.

Cyril and Methodius were early recognized as the fathers of Slavic Christianity and culture. They made an "outstanding contribution to the formation of the common Christian roots of Europe, roots which by their strength and vitality are one of the most solid points of reference, which no serious attempt to reconstruct in a new and relevant way the unity of the Continent can ignore" (§25).

This serious historical reminder is at the same time a warning about the direction the new secularized Europe was already taking. It was written almost a quarter of a century before the same pope would unsuccessfully argue that the Christian roots of the continent deserve a mention in the preamble of the constitution of the European Union.

The legacy of the brothers from Thessaloniki, says the pope, "remains for the Slavs deeper and stronger than any division" and points to the necessity of recognizing Christian unity along with its diversity in terms of ecclesiastical origins, traditions and cultures (§25). John Paul again draws a historical analogy with multiple directional references for the developments in present Europe:

> Ever since the ninth century, when in Christian Europe a new organization was emerging, Saints Cyril and Methodius have held out to us a message clearly of great relevance for our own age, which precisely by reason of the many complex problems of a religious, cultural, civil and international nature, is seeking a vital unity in the real communion of its various elements. (§26)

Following that broader political and ecumenical argument, Cyril and Method are praised again as examples for missions among younger churches, for they began their missionary endeavor with a posture of "full respect for the culture already existing among the Slav peoples, but together with religion they eminently and unceasingly promoted and extended that culture" (§26).

John Paul II in his characteristic fashion pleads again for the recognition of the common religious heritage of Catholicism and Orthodoxy and the imperative to overcome their painful division. Cyril and Methodius here again provide a model, for they had an abiding respect for both Rome and Constantinople and a passion for the unity of the one church. Thus they serve even today as "the connecting links or spiritual bridge between the Eastern and Western traditions, which both come together in the one great Tradition of the universal Church." John Paul II expresses his well-known hope that the "sister Churches of East and West" will rediscover a "visible Unity in perfect and total communion" (§27). As if to set at ease his Orthodox critics, he is quick to note that true unity "is neither absorption nor fusion" but "a meeting in truth and love, granted to us by the Spirit." The lives and mission of the holy brothers demonstrate that such a meeting is indeed possible and desirable.

The entire world, shown in microcosm in Europe, desperately desires peace and unity in place of the "divisions and antagonisms . . . which threaten to cause a frightful destruction of lives and values" (§27). The church, the encyclical states, is called by God to play a key role in building the unity of humanity. But she cannot fulfill this role if she is not actively engaged in the world as were Cyril and Methodius. "Being Christians in our day means being builders of communion in the Church and in society. This calls for openness to others, mutual understanding, and readiness to cooperate through the generous exchange of cultural and spiritual resources." The final paragraph of this prophetic chapter universalizes the humanistic and global intention of this encyclical "case study" by joining it to the statement of the Vatican II's *Lumen gentium:*

> One of the fundamental aspirations of humanity today is to rediscover unity and communion for a life truly worthy of man on the worldwide level. The Church, conscious of being the universal sign and sacrament of salvation and of the unity of the human race, declares her readiness to accomplish this duty of hers, to which "the conditions of this age lend special urgency so that all people joined more closely today by various social, technical, and cultural bonds can achieve as well full unity in Christ." (§27; *Lumen gentium,* §45)

In the conclusion (chapter eight) of *Slavorum apostoli,* Pope John Paul II reiterates the rightness and importance of celebrating the life and impact of Cyril and Methodius. He expresses the "profound happiness I will share in this celebration as the first son of the Slav race to be called, after nearly two millennia, to occupy the episcopal see that once belonged to Peter in this city of Rome" (§28).

The memory of Cyril and Methodius is made especially relevant by virtue of the fact that they labored fruitfully and peaceably in a time when "hostile tensions were increasingly threatening the peace and life of the nations, and even threatening the sacred bonds of Christian brotherhood" (§29). In a lengthy prayer to conclude the epistle, John Paul II entrusts to God the work and memory of Cyril and Methodius and offers a number of poignant and pointed petitions on behalf of the Slavs, the majority of whom lived at the time under Communist totalitarian regimes. Some statements appear, at least implicitly, to appeal for greater religious liberty: "May they follow, in conformity with their own conscience, the voice of your call." Interceding for Slavic Christians, the pope prays, "May they render to you due praise in private and in public life" (§30). Cognizant that Christians were often seen as political threats by Communist leaders, the pope beseeches God, "May their membership of the Kingdom of your Son never be considered by anyone to be contrary to the good of their earthly homeland" (§30).

The pope then broadens the subject of his prayer from the Slavs to all Europeans. One sees immediately the painful Cold War context in which this stirring petition is offered to God:

> But also grant to the whole of Europe, O Most Holy Trinity, that through the intercession of the two holy Brothers it may feel ever more strongly the need for religious and Christian unity and for a brotherly communion of all its peoples, so that when incomprehension and mutual distrust have been overcome and when ideological conflicts have been conquered in the common awareness of the truth, it may be for the whole world an example of just and peaceful coexistence in mutual respect and inviolate liberty. (§30)

Concluding Ecumenical and Evangelical Observations

Changes brought about by the Second Vatican Council and the comprehensive vision of the first Slavic pope for renewal and unity of European Christianity, especially the reconciliation between the East and the West, have awakened a new interest in the nature and significance of the ninth-century mission of the "Slavic apostles," "Saints of Christian unity," Cyril and Methodius. Prior to that a considerable renaissance of the studies of their lives and a development of Cyril-Methodian tradition among the Slavic peoples of Central and Southern Europe took place in the eighteenth and nineteenth centuries, as they aspired for national liberation and sought for unifying symbols and pan-Slavic alliances. It has been long recognized that their apostolic activity transcends the East-West exclusivities while at the same time it affirms Slavic cultural and linguistic identities. On the religious side, the Cyril-Methodian idea was significant for two reasons: spiritual renewal and sought-after establishment of unity between the Roman and Orthodox churches. One of the most visible proponents of that grand vision was the renowned Bishop Josip Juraj Strossmayer of Djakovo, who is also known as the defender of the Slavonic liturgy among the Croat peoples and less known as a supporter of the translation of Scriptures into the vernacular languages a whole century before Vatican II.[12]

This encyclical emphatically underlines what is well known of John Paul II, namely, how deeply he was committed to a "dialogue of love" between Catholic and Orthodox churches. He understood himself to be providentially placed in a unique position as the first Slavic pope and, as this author has heard him say, "a Slav among the Latins and a Latin among the Slavs." It is the combination of his background and pontifical position that enabled him to build bridges across the European ecclesiastical divide.

At the end of the same month that *Slavorum apostoli* was issued, at the celebration of the twenty-fifth anniversary (June 28, 1985) of the Vatican's Secretariat for Christian Unity, John Paul declared the Catholic commitment to ecumenism to be "irrevocable." His ecumenical activities over the next decade heightened and provided ample evidence of his impressive millennial vision to see the East and West fully reconciled and united by the arrival of the Great Jubilee. He had often spoken of the sad reality of the second millennium as the millennium of Christian division and of his dream that the third millennium be a millennium of Christian unity. In May 1995 he issued his significant encyclical *Ut unum sint,* in which he reiterated the priority and urgency of full unity with the Orthodox, but also, surprising many in both Orthodox and Protestant camps, invited his non-Catholic brothers to help him rethink the nature of the primacy of the Roman bishop so as to enhance the movement toward Christian unity. A month later he welcomed the Ecumenical Patriarch Bartholomew I. During the celebration of the solemn Mass on the Feast of Saints Peter and Paul, these two leaders of Catholic and Orthodox Christianity were symbolically seated beside each other on identical presidential chairs, while the gospel was chanted in both Latin and Greek and both delivered homilies. In his homily the pope, as he had done ten years earlier in *Slavorum apostoli,* emphasized that unity was the requirement of the evangelization of the new millennium. "We cannot remain separated!" John Paul insisted. It is in the light of this sincere longing for reconciliation and unity that we must also read the apostolic letter

---

[12]The author is proud to be associated with the university that bears the name of Josip Juraj Strossmayer in the city of Osijek, Croatia, and has written about his ecumenical vision and support for Bible translation into vernacular South Slavic languages. See Peter Kuzmič, *Vuk-Daničićevo Sveto Pismo i Biblijska društva* (Zagreb: Kršćanska sadašnjost, 1983).

Tertio millennio adveniente (The Coming Third Millennium)[13] and understand its unprecedented confessions of the sins that Catholics have committed against Christian unity. Forgiveness, reconciliation and unity would bring about, John Paul was convinced, a "new springtime of evangelization." All these subsequent millennial visions and ecumenical themes were already announced and partially elaborated a decade earlier in *Slavorum apostoli.*

From the perspective of its noble intentions it is, however, unfortunate that this ecumenically framed encyclical does not draw on any parallel Orthodox reflection about the catholicity of the mission of Cyril and Methodius and their creative engagement with the Slavic culture. In a thematic 1985 edition of the *International Review of Mission (IRM),* published by the World Council of Churches in Geneva, John Meyendorff, then dean of Saint Vladimir's Orthodox Theological Seminary in New York, makes for an Orthodox theologian an astonishingly strong case that "one should recognize that Christian mission requires new forms, new ways of including the whole of today's humanity, of today's world, into its realm. But these new forms cannot simply be imported as such from the fallen world, uncritically; they must be adapted to the unchanging content of the Christian gospel and manifest this content in a way that would be consistent with the holy tradition of the one catholic tradition. So, authentic Christian creativity requires this effort of selection, of discernment, as well as boldness in accepting new things."[14]

Meyendorff, one of the leading Orthodox participants in the ecumenical movement, goes on to conclude his article "Christ as Word: Gospel and Culture" by, similarly to John Paul, praising Cyril and Methodius as models of both, representatives of "authentic catholicity" and innovative bridge-builders between tradition and contemporary culture.

> In their own days, Saint Cyril and Methodius were eminent witnesses of such creativity, not only because—as so many missionaries before and after them—they were able, culturally and linguistically, to identify with a social group that needed to hear the gospel, but because they were able to be both traditional and innovative, both faithful and critical. As Orthodox Byzantines, they opposed, as an obvious "innovation," the interpolation of the common creed with the unfortunate *Filioque* clause, but they were respectful of the venerable Church of Rome (which helped them against the Germans) and translated not only the Byzantine liturgy, but also the

---

[13]John Paul II, *Apostolic Letter "Tertio millennio adveniente"... on Preparation for the Jubilee of the Year 2000,* Libreria Editrice Vaticana (November 10, 1994) <http://www.vatican.va/holy_father/john_paul_ii/apost_letters/documents/hf_jp-ii_apl_10111994_tertio-millennio-adveniente_en.html>.

[14]John Meyendorff, "Christ as Word: Gospel and Culture," *International Review of Mission* 74 (1985): 256.

> Latin rite into Slavic. The authentic "catholicity" and dynamism of their ministry should remain as our model even today. To emulate that model is the best way of commemorating the 1100th anniversary of St Methodius' death.[15]

The same issue of *IRM* published "The Influence of the Moravian Mission on the Orthodox Church in Czechoslovakia," written by His Beatitude Dorotheos, Metropolitan of Prague and all Czechoslovakia. Here the story and the mission of Cyril and Methodius are recounted and their extraordinary missionary and cultural achievements praised similarly to John Paul's account. Dorotheos does this, however, with much less ecumenical sensitivity and openness as it exalts them almost exclusively as "sainted protectors of Orthodoxy." It emphasizes that their mission was "spreading Orthodoxy" and that this was the main cause of their brutal persecution by the Roman-approved rulers and clergy. "No one among the learned men of Slavic antiquity can be compared with this holy pair . . . but . . . only Orthodoxy has fully preserved the Cyrillo-Methodian tradition in religious life."[16] Like John Paul in *Slavorum apostoli,* Metropolitan Dorotheos recognizes that "the sainted brothers of Salonica brought peace and mutual understanding among the Slavic tribes who often suffered from internecine struggle" and expresses hope that "the holy brothers will become a bridge that will bring together the Slavs, still divided in their religion." Credit is then given to the present-day ecumenical movement for its attempts at "removing the alienation among Christians," and yet the conclusion is that "if the Christian world achieves the desired togetherness, it will have to be renewed internally by being drawn into the primordial divine truth of Orthodoxy, of the times of the ecumenical councils."[17]

In search for responses and reactions to *Slavorum apostoli* in the Orthodox world, one comes to the conclusion that it has in rare cases barely registered, but has been occasionally sharply criticized for inappropriate "romanization" of the Byzantine brothers and as another instrument of unacceptable "uniatism." What comes as the greatest ecumenical disappointment is, however, how conspicuously this important document was ignored by most serious Orthodox publications.[18]

---

[15]Ibid., pp. 256-57.

[16]Metropolitan Dorotheos, "The Influence of the Moravian Mission on the Orthodox Church in Czechoslovakia," *International Review of Mission* 74 (1985): 228.

[17]Ibid. For a contrary, though more conciliar in tone, presentation of an American Catholic bishop, see Donald Wuerl [bishop of Pittsburgh], "Models of Evangelization," *Columbia,* January 2003, pp. 22-23.

[18]To cite just two examples among important publications in English language: Ken Parry et al., eds., *The Blackwell Dictionary of Eastern Christianity* (Oxford: Blackwell, 1999); Anthony-Emil N. Tachiaos, *Cyril and Methodius of Thessalonica: The Acculturation of the Slavs* (Crestwood, N.Y.: St Vladimir's Seminary Press, 2001). This is even more true among the Orthodox in Greece and most of the Slavic nations.

Some Orthodox critics interviewed by this author believe that the encyclical may have added to the growing strain between East and West in the nineties and that ignoring it saves the relationship from further controversy. Those who appreciate gestures of "repentance for historical sins" that came from John Paul II a decade later emphasize that the theme of *Slavorum apostoli* was a contextually most appropriate place to alleviate some of the burdens of the most painful memory, bitterness and distrust of the East against Rome. "The crusaders' contemptuous treatment of Eastern and Oriental clergy, the sacrileges perpetrated during the sack of Constantinople, the establishment of Latin patriarchates: all led to lasting resentment. Eastern Orthodoxy came to see the pope as an enemy and the Western church as a predatory adversary."[19] Others consider this encyclical to be just another expression of the tendency of the West to underestimate the degree of differences which divide it from the Christianity of the East.

Critically minded (church) historians consider the encyclical's weakness to be in the over-idealized portraits of the brothers, written in a semi-hagiographical style and without sufficiently distinguishing between fact and fiction in the uncritical use of some semi-legendary accounts of their lives.

This mixture of legend and history may be somewhat understandable, for much still remains obscure, though detailed and reliable studies of the lives and work of Cyril and Methodius do exist.[20] The encyclical appears also to downplay the entanglement of Rome with the imperial ambitions and military struggles of regional rulers for control of territory and ecclesiastical jurisdiction serving nonspiritual purposes. The limited aim of this review cannot examine the plausible general objection that *Slavorum apostoli* is an overstretched comprehensive argument that attempts to instrumentalize a ninth-century Christian mission for modern political and ecumenical purposes.

Evangelicals in general appreciate the vision, the message and the brave actions of this dynamic pope whose leadership helped dismantle the totalitarian one-party Marxist regimes in the former Soviet-bloc countries. His strong convictions about truth, freedom, human rights, dignity of all persons, solidarity, justice and democracy are universally admired. His message "Do not fear!" has resonated across all national, confessional and denominational lines and has encouraged millions living under the persecution not to give up their dreams of freedom. He was un-

---

[19]Parry et al., *Blackwell Dictionary of Eastern Christianity*, p. 147.

[20]See Dvornik, *Byzantine Missions;* Grivec, *Slavenski blagovjesnici;* A. P. Vlasto, *The Entry of the Slavs into Christendom: An Introduction to the Medieval History of the Slavs* (Cambridge: Cambridge University Press, 1970).

doubtedly "the principal evangelist of the final revolution," a leader of "a revolution of the human spirit, frequently informed by a reinvigorated Christian . . . faith, which proved to be the irresistible force that the communist enterprise could not finally withstand."[21] No one can forget the pictures of the first papal visit of John Paul to his native Poland, where millions followed his movements and messages of hope. That visit has helped create the climate conducive to the birth of a freedom movement that led from Polish Solidarity to the final tearing down of the Berlin Wall and to full liberation of Eastern Europe. The examples of this brave, theologically and morally orthodox and evangelistically inclined pope and the sacrificial life of Mother Teresa of Calcutta have caused many evangelicals to rethink and change their attitude toward the Roman Catholic Church.

All informed and open-minded evangelicals respond warmly and resonate positively to many topics addressed in this document, especially those of world evangelization, church planting, importance of Bible translation into vernacular languages, and relation of gospel and culture,[22] all so splendidly highlighted in *Slavorum apostoli*. During the recent anniversaries of the brothers, the already extensive bibliography of their lives and work has increased significantly. Most of the studies, however, are focused on the historical and linguistic aspects of their story. This encyclical letter encourages the more recent science of missiology to pay greater attention to the research of their outstanding and innovative ways to transmit the transcultural elements of the gospel into a culture whose foundations they have laid. There is an increasing convergence between evangelical and Catholic missiologists[23] in a number of areas touched upon and elaborated in this document, though at times different terminology is employed, as is the case with the Catholic use of *inculturation* and evangelical preference for *contextualization*. The evangelicals living in the Slavic nations are grateful for the cross-fertilizing potentialities of *Slavorum apostoli* and for the way in which it opened up several new dimensions of ecumenical endeavors. They hope that these and related issues might be further explored in a "trialogue" that would go beyond the insufficiently inclusive metaphor of "two lungs." With the document's geographical focus, injection of many fertile ideas related to the search for Christian unity and missionary work, and contemporary relevance, one would like to find in it at least a fleeting reference

---

[21]George Weigel, *The Final Revolution: The Resistance Church and the Collapse of Communism* (Oxford: Oxford University Press, 1992), p. 13.

[22]Compare to John Stott, ed., *Making Christ Known: Historic Mission Documents from the Lausanne Movement, 1974-1989* (Grand Rapids: Eerdmans, 1997).

[23]See Basil Meeking and John Stott, eds., *Evangelical-Roman Catholic Dialogue on Mission, 1977-1984* (Grand Rapids: Eerdmans, 1986).

to the Hussite movement or the importance of the Moravian mission.

The encyclical reminds Christians on all sides that a true dialogue of love is most essential for relationships between churches and that it must be rooted in complete obedience to the Lord. Such attitudes and commitments should help the confessional majorities in post-Communist lands to recognize the legitimacy of evangelical bodies, affirm their full religious liberties and assure the human rights of evangelical believers in the contexts where a new, though archaic—antidemocratic and antiecumenical—homogenization of the new nations along exclusively ethno-religious lines often leads to marginalization and discrimination of religious minorities. The Catholic and Orthodox communities need to recognize that authentic evangelicals by the very nature of their Christocentric faith, built on apostolic foundation, also organically belong to the "*una, sancta, catholica, apostolica*" church.

Slavorum apostoli is a welcome reminder to Catholics and evangelicals alike that post-apostolic missions did not begin with the sixteenth-century Jesuits going to China and William Carey taking the gospel to India. There are rich lessons to be learned from chapters in history often neglected by modern (especially Western) church historians. The pioneering mission of Cyril and Methodius is a case in point. Evangelicals especially need to recover the lessons of the whole spectrum of church and missions history because they seem to be generally deficient in both an understanding of history, which they read selectively, and a theology of history. It is the sad experience of this author to observe that in most evangelical seminaries in Eastern Europe the students learn more about John Wycliffe or William Tyndale than about Cyril and Methodius. Placing *Slavorum apostoli* on the reading lists in church history could be a good beginning.

As a fellow Slav and evangelical Christian minister involved in both wholistic mission and ecumenical dialogues as well as the promotion of human rights at the very crossroads of Europe, I have at numerous times expressed appreciation for the extraordinary role of the author of *Slavorum apostoli* in building the bridges of reconciliation between West and East and extending horizons of human freedom everywhere. In fact, I have argued that he deserves to enter history as John Paul the Great.[24] The encyclical reviewed here articulates his understanding of providential workings in history and his comprehensive vision necessary to help shape the future of both reconciled Christianity and liberated humanity.

---

[24]Peter Kuzmič, *Vrijeme i vječnost: Etika, politika, religija* (Osijek: Matica hrvatska, 2006). It is regrettable that the collapse of communism did not bring about the desired reconciliation; instead it has fostered a rebirth of rivalry, mutual suspicions and recriminations that have been tearing apart Slavic Christianity and Christian Europe for more than a millenium.

14

Ex corde ecclesiae and the Trouble with Truth

David Lyle Jeffrey

Context

At first blush, the *Apostolic Constitution on Catholic Universities,* more frequently referred to in Catholic circles as *Ex corde ecclesiae,*[1] might seem to be of tangential interest to evangelicals, even evangelicals charged specifically with the maintaining of church-related or interdenominational but evangelical institutions of higher learning. But to think so would be a mistake, I believe, not withstanding the apparent inattentiveness of a host of venerable evangelical commentators to date.

It may be unsurprising to those familiar with evangelical history that, despite the recent rise to prominence in evangelical circles of books and articles dealing with the formation of a Christian worldview and integration of faith and learning in the Christian college curriculum, relatively few such studies take anything like a full measure of the wealth and weight of historic Catholic reflection on these matters. More surprising, perhaps, is that key writings of Pope John Paul II, whose pontifical oversight of the Roman Catholic Church produced much in the way of thoughtful address to issues and problems more closely than ever analogous to those faced by evangelical colleges in North America especially, have also been largely overlooked by most evangelical re-

[1]John Paul II, *Apostolic Constitution of the Supreme Pontiff John Paul II on Catholic Universities [Ex corde ecclesiae],* Libreria Editrice Vaticana (August 15, 1990) <http://www.vatican.va/holy_father/john_paul_ii/apost_constitutions/documents/hf_jp-ii_apc_15081990_ex-corde-ecclesiae_en.html>.

flection on the subject. By way of example, V. James Mannoia's *Christian Liberal Arts: An Education That Goes Beyond* (2000), David S. Dockery and Gregory Alan Thornbury's *Shaping a Christian Worldview: The Foundation of Christian Higher Education* (2002), Douglas V. Henry and Bob Agee's edited collection entitled *Faithful Learning and the Christian Scholarly Vocation* (2003) and Harry Lee Poe's *Christianity in the Academy: Teaching at the Intersection of Faith and Learning* (2004), good books on their subject though they are, all remain at least visibly innocent of the most powerful late twentieth-century advocate for substantially the thesis they advocate. Nicholas Wolterstorff's *Educating for Shalom: Essays on Christian Higher Education* (2004), Duane Litfin's *Conceiving the Christian College* (2004) and David K. Naugle's *Worldview: The History of a Concept* (2002) each refer briefly to John Paul's encyclical *Fides et ratio,* and Naugle additionally cites *Redemptor hominis* (1979), but none note, as well they might (and in my view doubtless should), the central relevance of *Ex corde ecclesiae* for negotiating some of the critical difficulties now facing Christian higher education in general.

Arthur F. Holmes, in *Building the Christian Academy,* can be credited at least with recognizing the rightful place of *Ex corde* within a larger conversation among Protestants in higher education. Holmes observes an ecumenical convergence concerning the necessary centrality to Christian higher learning of an intellectually and theologically coherent "world vision," as *Ex corde* phrases it, and he cites approvingly Richard John Neuhaus's commentary on the document.[2] But there is much more to recommend this undeniably controversial document to careful consideration by non-Catholics. In particular, *Ex corde,* though perhaps to some degree belated in its publication for its own environment, can help evangelicals to anticipate more constructively some of the challenges which almost inevitably will arise for their own mission statements.

Summary

Evangelical and Reformed readers will doubtless be struck with the generous and pertinent use of biblical idiom throughout this papal document. As in other encyclicals, not only the Gospels but also the General Epistles predominate (especially James and 1 John). Consistently in his introduction the late pope underscores the connection between historic Christian views of education and the

[2]Arthur F. Holmes, *Building the Christian Academy* (Grand Rapids: Eerdmans, 2001), pp. 108, 114-15; Richard John Neuhaus, "The Christian University: Eleven Theses," *First Things,* January 1996, pp. 20-22.

development and practice of biblical virtues. Accordingly, though it is the hypertrophy of the disciplines and the dominance of technology which now necessitate an urgent attention to the "*search for meaning*" in education generally, for John Paul II it remains the timeless obligation of the Christian educator to "guarantee that the new discoveries be used for the authentic good of individuals and of human society as a whole" in such a way that the *meaning of persons,* in their "moral, spiritual and religious dimension," remains at the forefront both of research and of teaching (§7).[3] Likewise, though he affirms that the intellectual life should be a source of deep personal enrichment to both teacher and student, he believes that it must nonetheless always be characterized by a "selfless search for truth and for the wisdom that comes from above" (§2).

Even a quick glance at the introduction gives a reliable indication of the case to be made. In the first three small pages of this brief document, virtue words such as *love, joy, hope* and *wisdom,* as well as the predictable *knowledge* and *reason* each occur two or three times. The word *truth,* however, occurs in this same brief space fourteen times, and in every instance with a full register of biblical and traditional Christian theological meaning. In one paragraph (§4) of the introduction, where the word is used an emphatic seven times, we have come unmistakably to the heart of the motive which prompts the entire text. This motive is transparent—a pastoral concern to reverse what John Paul II and others regard as a loss of full-bodied Christian purpose in many Catholic institutions of higher learning such that, in a fashion emulating trendy vices of the world more than the practice of historic Christian virtues, many Catholic universities seem to have exchanged the pursuit of intrinsic goods for a cultivation of instrumental goods:

> Without in any way neglecting the acquisition of useful knowledge, a Catholic University is distinguished by its free search for the whole truth about nature, man and God. The present age is in urgent need of this kind of disinterested service, namely of *proclaiming the meaning of truth,* that fundamental value without which freedom, justice and human dignity are extinguished . . . a Catholic University is completely dedicated to the research of all aspects of truth in their essential connection with the supreme Truth, who is God . . . [thus] dedicating itself to every path of knowledge, aware of being preceded by him who is "the Way, the Truth, and the Life." (§4)

Here, in his frankly biblical insistence on the integration of Truth, is both the central claim and distinctive characteristic of Christian education as the late

[3]Unless otherwise noted, all following in-text citations to *Ex corde ecclesiae* will be identified by section number only.

pope sees it. But any insistence that there is an ordered relation of more or less empirical truths (such as the truths of a discipline) to a bedrock or core theological truth is nowadays suspect, and not least in the classrooms of Catholic and other traditionally Christian colleges. In some environments a more radical skepticism rejects even the postulate of mind-independent truth itself, and theories of "truth" as merely a matter of social construction had made their way into the curriculum on many North American Catholic campuses as early as the 1970s, typically in social science disciplines, but also in philosophy, educational theory and literary criticism. In short, ideas which might be regarded as fundamentally alien to Christian intellectual presupposition had been institutionalized in church-related colleges and universities long before *Ex corde ecclesiae* appeared in 1990.

Nor is this a trivial or readily dismissable consideration for educational environments in what we have tended to think of as "evangelical" colleges and universities. Discussions of the nature and intellectual place of religious truth tend nowadays to be among the testiest and least productive on many of our own campuses. Many of us might, if we were fully candid, admit to participation in academic conversations where even a tentative gesture in the direction of nonsubjectively defined (i.e., mind-independent) truth has immediately put into the air a distinct whiff of impropriety, even scandal. Likewise, almost any member of a college or university community can anticipate the point at which such skepticism is bound to erupt into controversy among the faculty: namely, the point at which any serious connection of the presupposition of an integrated reality or Truth to the question of academic freedom arises. Hence, we should be able to imagine with some sympathy the largely adversarial response among North American Catholic colleges, and Catholic universities especially, to the promulgation of *Ex corde ecclesiae.*[4]

A Rock of Offense

Resistance to this apostolic constitution, tacit and epistemological or explicit and political, has tended to be shaped by the degree to which an audience takes seriously the implications of John Paul II's explicit presuppositions regarding truth. Some of this resistance, to be sure, is subphilosophical. There is certainly a disturbing sense in which, as Jean Cardinal Daniélou put it, in our time the very no-

[4]In response, a restatement of *Ex corde ecclesiae* appeared in 1993 arguing for unity around a "shared baptismal belief in the truths that are rooted in Scripture and tradition, as interpreted by the church, concerning the mystery of the Trinity." This attempt at a more minimalist theological consensus has not been particularly successful at the political level. See Joseph A. Fiorenza, "*Ex corde ecclesiae:* An Application to the United States," *Origins* 29 (1999): 404.

tion of truth has become *scandaleuse,* a scandal to many, so that in many quarters even to speak of truth "raises the hackles."[5] Back in the 1960s Daniélou devoted a superb little book to that traditionally Christian conviction regarding external truth upon which, as the great scientist Henri Poincaré has likewise observed, both the possibility of morality and the practice of science depend.[6] The question which drives Daniélou's meditative argument remains directly pertinent: "How is it that to affirm the existence of truth seems [to so many] to be tantamount to dogmatism and intolerance?"[7] To Daniélou's answer, and to his defense of truth, notably influential for several encyclicals of the late Pope John Paul II, I am gratefully indebted in this analysis, not least because he broadens the base of his reflection to include specific spiritual (and hence psychological and sociological) elements.

But the encyclical of the late pontiff which first comes to mind in this connection is actually *Veritatis splendor* (1993).[8] There John Paul II challenged dissent within the church itself concerning its traditional moral teaching and scriptural authority, which he linked to a pervasive "detaching [of] human freedom from its essential and constitutive relationship to truth" (§8). Whereas on the biblical view, he said, "human freedom and God's law are not in opposition" (§17),

> certain currents of modern thought have gone so far as to *exalt freedom to such an extent that it becomes an absolute, which would then be the source of values.* (§32)

I think we can safely assume that John Paul II refers not only to the ascendancy of philosophical pragmatism here, as, for example, in Richard Rorty's more extravagant reductions of truth to what William James once called "the expedient in our way of thinking,"[9] but also to existentialist, materialist and radical Protestant notions of the supremacy of the will, which can, in the application, come to pretty much the same thing. This is why John Paul II can speak in the next sentence of

> the direction taken by doctrines which have lost the sense of the transcendent or which are explicitly atheist. The individual conscience is accorded the status of a su-

---

[5]Jean Daniélou, *The Scandal of Truth,* trans. W. J. Kerrigan (Baltimore: Helicon, 1962), p. 2. Originally published as *Scandaleuse vérité* (Paris: Librairie Arthème Fayard, 1961).

[6]Henri Poincaré, *The Value of Science: Essential Writings of Henri Poincaré,* ed. and trans. Stephen Jay Gould (New York: Modern Library, 2001), pp. 189-90. Originally published as *La valeur de la science* in 1905.

[7]Daniélou, *The Scandal of Truth,* p. 2.

[8]John Paul II, *Veritatis splendor,* Libreria Editrice Vaticana (August 6, 1993) <http://www.vatican.va/holy_father/john_paul_ii/encyclicals/documents/hf_jp-ii_enc_06081993_veritatis-splendor_en.html>.

[9]William James, *Pragmatism,* ed. Bruce Kuklick (Indianapolis: Hackett, 1981), chap. 2; cf. Richard Rorty, *Consequences of Pragmatism: Essays, 1972-1980* (Minneapolis: University of Minnesota Press, 1982), passim.

> preme tribunal of moral judgment which hands down categorical and infallible decisions about good and evil. (§32)

The use of *infallible* here strikes me as a nice touch: Every man his own pope. Most of us have known at least an adolescent or two who could at some point identify with this presumption. In most such cases, an established opposition of freedom to truth is at least tacit. In many a campus controversy, of course, it becomes explicit.

In a campus debate at my own university over the prerogatives of academic freedom, one of the interlocutors posed a strategic question: "There are two parties [in contest] here," he said, "the Truth party and the Liberty party. I am myself of the Liberty party. Which are you?" The casual antithesis presupposed by this debater's question has, in secular contexts, long ceased to be surprising. The context of this event, however, was not secular. And the question posed what for a Christian worldview must be a false dichotomy, highlighting the tension that Daniélou and John Paul II have so pertinently characterized under the headings, respectively, of the scandal and the splendor of truth.

What I observed then I would reiterate here now: as most definitions make clear, academic freedom is deemed by those of us in the academy as necessary to the pursuit of *truth,* and thus to an authentic learning environment. It is less frequently observed that, on this account, academic freedom is ostensibly valued and defended as an instrumental good. Logically, it is not freedom per se but truth that is ultimately to be loved and sought as the chief end of academic inquiry.

Because our local debates had been more specifically about the meaning of academic freedom in a Christian university, I then added a codicil concerning a much-abused saying of Jesus. In this saying, the relationship between freedom and truth is characterized as reciprocal, apposite rather than opposite.

> *If* you continue in my word, *[then]* you are truly my disciples; and you will know the truth, and the truth will make you free. (Jn 8:31-32)

Here it appears that truth is in fact a necessary condition for our freedom, or at least that the authentic experience of either requires the experience of both. This reciprocity is the bedrock or substratum of the 1993 encyclical's statement that "Human freedom and God's law are not in opposition; on the contrary, they appeal one to the other" (§17). Contrawise, however, "those who live 'by the flesh' experience God's law as a burden, and indeed as a denial or at least a restriction of their own freedom" (§18). These two points from *Veritatis splendor* extend to the episcopate the formulation already addressed to the universities in *Ex corde ecclesiae* (1990).

When *Ex corde ecclesiae* describes itself as an "Apostolic Constitution . . . on Catholic Universities" it is already, of course, asserting something characteristically Catholic, namely, that in their initial purpose, history and tradition such universities derive their authority from fidelity to apostolic and evangelical truth. But in a fashion strikingly parallel to most older Protestant universities, many Catholic institutions of higher learning have recently (in one way or another) let it be known that they, too, wish all that "doctrinal stuff" could be relegated to a titular acknowledgment or perhaps the footnotes of their own mission statements. That is, as with most of the Protestant institutions upon which George Marsden[10] has commented, many in Catholic academic communities have for similar reasons come to regard freedom itself—narrowly defined as the individual scholar's right to a kind of insular autonomy—as the highest good.

In such an environment, *Ex corde* immediately announces itself as a document which has "not come to bring peace, but a sword" (Mt 10:34). Let me recall just two examples, which may easily stand for all:

> It is the honour and responsibility of a Catholic University to consecrate itself without reserve to *the cause of truth*. This is its way of serving at one and the same time both the dignity of man and the good of the Church, which has "an intimate conviction that truth is (its) real ally . . . and that knowledge and reason are sure ministers to faith." (§4)[11]

In this first extract we immediately encounter that word which "divides soul from spirit . . . ; it is able to judge the thoughts and intentions of the heart" (Heb 4:12). In a Protestant learning environment as well, such terms as *honor, responsibility* and *serving* are to be expected. But *Ex corde* doesn't stop there; it adds words like *consecrate, without reserve,* not just to academic truths, but to the very *cause of truth,* i.e., the Lord of the universe. Moreover, as the citation of John Henry Cardinal Newman makes evident, these terms are advanced as the dedications at the heart of the Catholic university because they presume that the heart's affections in a Christian university will grow *ex corde ecclesiae*—out of the heart of the faithful church.

The second polarizing statement renders this presupposition explicit:

> One consequence of its essential relationship to the Church is that the *institutional* fidelity of the University to the Christian message includes a recognition of and ad-

[10]George M. Marsden, *The Soul of the American University: From Protestant Establishment to Established Nonbelief* (New York: Oxford University Press, 1994).

[11]Quoting John Henry Newman, *The Idea of a University* (London: Longmans, Green, 1931), p. 11.

herence to the teaching authority of the Church in matters of faith and morals. Catholic members of the university community are also called to a personal fidelity to the Church with all this implies. (§27)

Now here is a statement which, if politically problematic in many American Catholic universities, might well be regarded as impossible altogether in their Protestant counterparts. The first reason for this, of course, is that by and large our own churches no longer have any "teaching authority." In fact, as I have now come to understand it, there is a meaningful sense in which one may say of those Baptists who call themselves "moderate," that the very idea of "the teaching authority of the Church" would seem to have been pretty much anathema at any point in their history.[12] While this case represents an extreme, it may safely be said that among contemporary evangelical and pentecostal groups there is a more general acceptance of this viewpoint than there used to be, and that even Reformed communities have tended to be less able to shape their educational institutions on the basis of a presumption that faculty will recognize the authority of their church in matters of the content of faith and moral standards.

So here again we approach common ground, muddy ground though it is. Just as there are widely divergent Protestant practices, even sharply divergent notions of what it is to be a Christian today, so likewise now—or at least it seems so—there is an unprecedentedly wide divergence among Catholics. It might be thought that formally and *de jure,* Catholics have some distance to go before catching up with the more extreme among Protestants, but, *de facto,* many of the same tendencies are apparent.[13] The fundamental challenge raised by *Ex corde ecclesiae* has accordingly now become radical in a way inconceivable in earlier centuries; that is, its presupposition, namely, that the center *must* hold if anything resembling a Catholic education is long to persist, has been greeted by the faculty in many American and European Catholic colleges and universities as if it were illegitimate, even intolerant.

It is only fair in this context, however, to confess to analogous complexities to be

---

[12]Harry Leon McBeth, *Texas Baptists: Sesquicentennial History* (Dallas: Baptistway, 1998); Walter B. Shurden, *The Baptist Identity: Four Fragile Freedoms* (Macon: Smith and Helwys, 1993).

[13]See, e.g., Sally M. Furay, "Preserving the Mission into the Future," *Current Issues in Catholic Higher Education* 23, no. 1 (2003): 51-60; and David Holenback, "Strength in Mission Through Solidarity: Catholic Higher Education in a Divided World," *Current Issues in Catholic Higher Education* 23, no. 1 (2003): 5-14. More recently, J. Michael Miller, Secretary of the Congregation for Catholic Education, gave an address at the University of Notre Dame titled "Challenges Facing American and European Catholic Universities: A View from the Vatican," in which he suggested that for nominally Catholic universities in which "secularization . . . proves to be irrevocably entrenched, it might be a matter of truthfulness and justice for such an institution to be considered no longer officially Catholic."

found closer to home. A Texas Baptist pastor I had never met before recently appeared at my office door to offer a prayer—I think possibly on my behalf. By way of introduction he offered a sympathetic admonition: "Coming from way up north," he said, "you just wouldn't understand. Down here a Baptist can be anything from a snake-handler to a Unitarian." It has occurred to me since then that there may be more commonality across this wide spectrum than the good reverend's comment suggests, but, ironically, that commonality may consist simply of that very individualism which has widened the spectrum. Nonconformity resists the very idea of a common lot or a common prayer: its purpose is individuality; its reflex is to resist authority. Unsurprisingly, then, our most characteristic Protestant self, putatively evangelical or not, can be independent to the point of being not all that teachable.

Most Protestants have maintained such notions of teaching authority as we have either through historic confessions and creeds or, at least among evangelicals and Baptists of various stripes, by repeated affirmation of the central authority of the Scriptures themselves. I think most historians of the subject would agree that as long as vigorous local expectations of a strong lay literacy and biblical knowledge prevailed, such groups have remained reasonably coherent in their respective identities, and this gave a certain form and governing principles to our colleges as well. During a multi-denominational conference on the role of Scripture in the academic disciplines (at Wheaton College in May 2004), I suggested that these were necessary conditions, but that there was little reason to suppose their sufficiency. I suggested further that an apparent decline in biblical literacy over the last three or four decades coupled with a tendency in evangelical circles to condone or even to encourage subjective and therapeutic self-authorization in its place poses an increasingly serious problem for ongoing coherence of community as well as for cogency of teaching in many of our churches and in our schools.

I acknowledge that not everyone in the free-church tradition sees this as a problem. Yet in my view it is a substantial problem. What troubled me then and still troubles me is the way in which, for practical purposes, it can appear as though the authority of the Protestant individual has increasingly come to trump the authority of the Scriptures as well as of the church.[14] We temporize, we pick and

---

[14]There has been some recent resistance however. See, e.g., *A Baptist Manifesto,* for an alternative and more catholic view: Mikael Broadway, Curtis Freeman, Barry Harvey, James William McClendon Jr., Elizabeth Newman and Philip Thompson, "Re-Envisioning Baptist Identity: A Manifesto for Baptist Communities in North America," *Baptists Today* 15, no. 10 (1997): 8-10; *Perspectives in Religious Studies* 24 (Fall 1997): 303-10. More recently, Steve Harmon, *Towards Baptist Catholicity: Essays on Tradition and the Baptist Vision* (Carlisle, U.K.: Paternoster, 2006), argues for a reconnection of Baptist theology and polity to a kind of essentialist Catholic tradition.

choose, and our children follow suit with diminishing substantive ecclesial options. At the level of the university we have done little enough to redress this dissipation of "common" truth. Rather, in a manner nowadays increasingly familiar among Catholics as well, we have frequently set our faces like flint against *anything* that would constrain our choices. We have accordingly come to resist anything that might be construed as imposing, even by inference, obligations to search out and take our bearings from universal truth or truths.

At the risk of perhaps too intimate an ecumenical suggestion, I think this is actually one scandal that we share. Worse, to the degree that we share it, we risk becoming, intellectually as well as ethically, indistinguishable from secular pragmatists who have no faith pretensions at all.

The Stumble

Almost the first datum in basic philosophical reflection is a simple demonstration of the probability of truth independent of the mind. Subsequent logical thought depends upon it. As Socrates in the *Cratylus* is at pains to show, to hold subjectively with Protagoras that "Man is the Measure of all things" is immediately to bring the possibility of intelligible dialectic to a halt.[15] If truth is to be meaningful as a term, it must preserve that meaning in some sort of at least provisionally objectifiable sense. In *rational* beings, Aquinas in his *De veritate* tells us, "the true denotes that to which the intellect tends."[16] So far from being a self-referential construct, the "true expresses correspondence of being to the knowing power, for all knowing is produced by an assimilation of the knower to the thing known" and our "knowledge of a thing is a consequence of this conformity." "Therefore," he concludes, our knowledge of anything "is an effect of *its* truth."[17] As if engaging the conversation with Socrates and Hermogenes, Aquinas allows that while there is a limited sense in which the practical intellect "causes" things, and is in that sense a "measure of what it causes," with respect to our speculative or receptive and reflective intelligence, "natural things from which our intellect gets its scientific knowledge" can more aptly be said to "measure our intellect," while in turn "these things are themselves measured by the divine intellect, in which are all created things." This works in pretty much the same way, he adds by way of analogy, "as works of art find their origin in the intellect of an artist."[18]

---

[15]Plato *Cratylus* 386A.
[16]Thomas Aquinas *De veritate* 1.16.1.
[17]Ibid., 1.1, emphasis in original.
[18]Ibid., 1.2.

Aquinas follows closely upon Augustine and especially Anselm in this regard,[19] in positing a "Supreme Truth," self-subsistent, which is not to be confused with "the truth of any particular thing; but," as Anselm has it, "when some thing is in accordance with Supreme Truth, then we speak of the truth or rightness of a thing."[20] This truth, Aquinas will argue (with Anselm as a reference point), is indestructible: truths do not change, for "even when true and correct things are destroyed, the truth or correctness by which they are true remains. "There is, therefore," he concludes, "only one truth."[21] *Per consequens,* for Aquinas as for Augustine and Anselm before him, "Truth . . . is properly and primarily in the divine intellect. In the human intellect it exists properly but secondarily," because there "it exists only because of a relation" to the truths of nature or divine truth.[22] However unfashionable in some academic quarters, such a "realist" or correspondence theory of truth seems to me pretty well indispensable for making sense of Christian theology, be it Catholic or evangelical.

This point may seem too obvious to require mention. But in what follows I am depending upon it because the thesis of *Ex corde* depends upon it fundamentally. As a working assumption, it recurs in several places. In the preamble we are told that

> a Catholic university is completely dedicated to the research of all aspects of truth in their essential connection with supreme Truth, who is God. (§4)

In addressing (in part one) the identity and mission of a Catholic university, the text reminds us that the integration of knowledge, *fides et ratio,* requires that a Catholic university in particular

> *has to be a "living union" of individual organisms* dedicated to the search for truth . . . [since] it is necessary *to work towards a higher synthesis* of knowledge, in which alone lies the possibility of satisfying that thirst for truth which is profoundly inscribed on the heart of the human person. (§16)[23]

Consequently—and problematically so for views of the university which make freedom rather than truth the supreme educational value—*Ex corde* wants to insist upon the Catholic university as a covenanting community that has institutional autonomy and "guarantees its members academic freedom" only "so long as the

[19]See Anselm *De veritate,* chap. 13.
[20]Ibid.
[21]Thomas Aquinas *De veritate* 1.4.3.
[22]Ibid., 1.4.8 especially.
[23]Quoting from John Paul II, "Allocution to the International Congress on Catholic Universities," April 25, 1989, n. 4: *Acta apostolicae sedis* 81 (1989): 1219.

rights of the individual person and of the community are preserved within the confines of truth and the common good" (§12). The problem with this attempt to balance individual freedom with a community commitment to extra-mental, transpersonal truth is that in our time pretty much only a radically orthodox Christian—Catholic or Protestant—is willing to be so "confined"—that is, to try to achieve the balance.

I underscore here the most controversial element in *Ex corde* precisely so that we can register adequately how it is that such a deep commitment to Truth polarizes, divides like a sword. What is for some the *splendor veritatis,* the brightness of the truth which not only lights our way (Ps 119:105) but before whose precepts we willingly self-efface or, in biblical idiom, "freely obey," is simultaneously a *scandale profonde* for others who do not receive this Truth as truth. Indeed, for such persons, even to link religious truth and the common good in this way is to impose a stumbling block. To suggest further that the exercise of individual academic freedom in a Christian university ought to be in some measure conditioned by a commitment to common institutional purpose can be, in effect, to enrage the bull. In recent years it has become apparent to some Catholic and evangelical intellectuals who exchange views on these matters that in this respect we now find ourselves dodging about in the same corral.

In the perspective of our ongoing conversations at Baylor, for example, I have found it interesting to reflect on four of the principles that *Ex corde* considers to be essential to a Catholic university if it is to be, in fact, meaningfully Catholic:

1. a Christian inspiration not only of individuals but of the university community as such;
2. a continuing reflection in the light of the Catholic faith upon the growing treasure of human knowledge, to which it seeks to contribute by its own research;
3. fidelity to the Christian message as it comes to us through the Church;
4. an institutional commitment to the service of the people of God and of the human family in their pilgrimage to the transcendent good which gives meaning to life. (§13)[24]

I was not part of the drafting of our own vision statement, *Baylor 2012.* Indeed, if memory serves, I contributed not so much as a sentence to its final text. (I do, however, warmly endorse it as a statement of purpose.) But any who are

[24]Quoting from *L'Université Catholique dans le monde moderne: Document final du 2ème Congrès des Délégués des Universités Catholiques,* Rome, November 20-29, 1972, §1.

familiar with our particular Baptist vision statement will recognize immediately how much these two documents hold in common. Exchange the word *church* for the *Scriptures, Catholic* for *Christian,* and the principles are, at the presuppositional level, nearly interchangeable. But to get to the heart of our internal conflicts and evident faculty resistance in both cases, it is necessary to consider the practical implication of these first principles, namely, the conviction embodied in both texts that there is an undergirding view of Truth to which the faithful Christian intelligence is obligated—and which is to be experienced not as a burden but as a blessing.[25]

For *Ex corde*, to be "both a University and Catholic, it must be both a community of scholars . . . in which Catholicism is vitally present and *operative*" (§14, emphasis added), a "place of research" in which "research necessarily includes *(a)* the search for an *integration of knowledge, (b)* a *dialogue between faith and reason, (c)* an *ethical concern,* and *(d)* a *theological perspective*" (§15).[26] Finally, through the emphasis on interdisciplinarity, in which "the specific contributions of philosophy and theology" (§16) will play an enabling part, *Ex corde* asks that the theological potential of all the disciplines obtain curricular consideration (§§19-20).

For *Baylor 2012,* in the full text of which these statements are printed in the form of a cross, there are likewise a series of "foundational assumptions" or "core convictions." These include:

- That human decisions should be guided by God as His will and nature are revealed in the crucified and risen Jesus Christ;
- That all truth is open to inquiry, though many truths will elude us and others may be accessible only through divine revelation;
- That human life has a meaning and a purpose that is not simply a matter of human choice;
- That we have a fallen nature that needs both healing and direction;
- That we are a created part of nature but have been given responsibility as stewards—made in the image of God—for its care and management;
- That we find the highest order of personal fulfillment in working constructively for the betterment of others, and that we have an obligation to do so;
- That we need to be active, regularly worshiping members of the body of Christ

[25]See Etienne Gilson, "The Intelligence in the Service of Christ the King," in *A Gilson Reader: Selections from the Writings of Etienne Gilson,* ed. Anton C. Pegis (New York: Image, 1957), pp. 34-35.

[26]Emphasis in quotations from the encyclical is original unless noted otherwise.

as a context of our spiritual growth, as a source of encouragement, and as a partnership in the work of God's kingdom;

- That human beings flourish best in a functional and beautiful physical environment and among colleagues who respect, love, forgive, and support one another.

To all this is added an additional affirmation:

> *And that a university can be such a physical and social environment. Because the Church, the only truly democratic and multi-cultural community, is not identical with any denomination, we believe that Baylor will serve best, recruit more effectively, and both preserve and enrich its Baptist identity more profoundly, if we draw our faculty, staff, and students from the full range of Christian traditions. (*Baylor 2012,* preamble)

Though the *Baylor 2012* formulations are more in the form of a traditional mission statement, and in language and formula recognizably of an evangelical Protestant character, there are evident similarities to *Ex corde,* and a careful reading of both documents will discover many overlapping purposes.

Yet here also, in both texts, we find the very nub of the conflict each statement of purpose engenders. This conflict is not, I think, primarily about infelicities of formulation or lacunae which doubtless might be pointed to in either text. Resistance on the part of faculty (principally but not exclusively) in universities as diverse as Baylor and Notre Dame as well as in colleges as different as Wheaton or Calvin on the one hand and Ave Maria or Marymount on the other has revealed not merely a friction concerning method or emphasis but an impasse as to undergirding theological and philosophical conviction. That is, our parallel contretemps concerns not simply how we may go about the search for Truth but whether, at least in the ultimate sense, a curriculum should ever presume such a search for ultimate truth in the first place. The more vigorous animosities arise not merely, as often suggested, from some sort of propriety or scruple about mixing the categories of faith and reason to the detriment of one or the other sphere (though the systematic development of integrated faith and learning is relentlessly advocated throughout *Ex corde* [§§1, 7, 15-17, 19, 20, 22, 23, 34, 38, 46, 48]). I am inclined to think, rather, that what both partisans and opponents recognize (in either document) is that to postulate, systematically, extra-mental truth which ultimately coheres as one Truth in the Divine Intellect is to advocate for an authority irrefragably higher than the individual self as contingent for intellectual and community life. To the non-Christian mind—or to the mind that does not yet realize, perhaps, that it has left the gospel behind—such advocacy, however gently stated, can appear as a species of tyranny.[27]

How is it then that what is freedom for some is tyranny for others? At bottom, we can see, it is because the former group accepts the idea of self-transcending truth and actually, as Aquinas says, finds in the contemplation of such a unifying truth the greatest of pleasures,[28] while among the latter group, as Augustine notes, even for such a notion of truth to be seriously entertained engenders hatred.[29] Augustine is silently quoting Terence when he makes this remark *(veritas odium parit),* but is clearly reflecting upon real hostility aimed at himself personally as a result of his preaching the gospel among the Donatists as well as the pagans. It strikes me that a comparable hostility has been sometimes evident in the debates surrounding *Ex corde* and *Baylor 2012,* and that this should have been predictable.

Why did we at Baylor, in our own case, not foresee the magnitude of our internal opposition more clearly? Various factors have been suggested in retrospect. Some of my colleagues suspect that the cause may possibly be that, though our traditions are *reflexively* oriented to the Bible as distinctly revelatory of Truth, we have probably become habituated to a kind of subcultural insincerity on this very point. Examples of selective cognition abound. In biblical terms, truth is opposed not only to the open lie (Prov 12:17; Is 59:4; Rom 9:1; 1 Tim 2:4, 7) but to dissimulation (Heb 10:22), self-deception (Ps 15:2; 1 Jn 1:8), self-fashioning (Jn 5:31-32; 8:40-46), and envy and self-promotion (Jas 3:14). For those who are acculturated to the world of academic and religious websites, or who are survivors in a zone of ecclesiastical politics, the ruthless logic of Scripture on this point can appear so unrealistic as to be forgettable. But there has been another less self-contradictory thesis, namely, that our own statement of vision for a theologically and morally consistent Christian set of educational objectives was lamentably belated—that is, that it came too late to turn the tide of an already institutionalized *de facto* secularization. This also just happens to be the view of many Catholic academics about *Ex corde,* among both its supporters and its critics.

If you grant that the repentant psalmist was right about God desiring truth in the inward parts (Ps 51:6), then even for many of us most concerned to advocate

---

[27]To put this another, doubtless less charitable, way: when smart people believe themselves to have outgrown God, they are not, as a result, necessarily "godless." As G. K. Chesterton, C. S. Lewis and others have famously observed, it is frequently the case that another god has emerged in place of the first, namely, a deification of their own intelligence. That this transference is seldom enough a self-conscious evolution does not mitigate the effective religious authority of the new state of mind (a.k.a. deity) in ordering the affections.

[28]Thomas Aquinas *Summa Theologiae,* 1-2, 38.4.

[29]Augustine *Confessions* 10.23.

for a curriculum thoughtfully grounded in Christian worldview presuppositions, an examination of conscience, a *miserere mei* and maybe even a trip to the confessional, is probably in order at this point. More plainly put, perhaps we have failed to reckon adequately with the degree to which, for a serious Christian, a sincere will to truth carries with it a commitment to holiness, to the pursuit of sanctity (Jn 17:17-19; Eph 4:24). This is not merely a matter of personal piety. There are things to think about here for college communities less evidently secularized in their current covenants and understanding of mission. For one thing, evangelical and Reformed Christian institutions of higher learning have typically dared to presume, as a condition of authentic membership, a sincere and active commitment to the communal pursuit of truth and right living. This form of constraint can on occasion make some of us uncomfortable, but I cannot see, as a confessing Christian in a confessedly Christian university, how to duck away from it. (We should doubtless all be grateful that the truth *[ʿemeth]* of God is in Scripture so often conjoined to his mercy [e.g., Pss 25:10; 61:7; 85:10; 86:15; 89:14; 98:3; Prov 3:3; 14:22; 16:6; 20:28, etc.].) But to think that a statement of conduct can by itself provide a sufficient guard against loss of faith identity in the college setting would be folly indeed. Serious shared commitment to the ordering of intellectual affections to a central theological Truth, now more than ever, is indispensable. For an evangelical who can accept that point, it is not merely the content of *Ex corde* which is then of great value, but also some reflection on the consequences of its coming too late for many Catholic universities.

LIGHT, JOY AND TRUTH

It is appropriate that we return now to language borrowed from Saint Augustine in the introduction to *Ex corde* (§1), namely his phrase *gaudium de veritate,* "joy on account of truth." In this joy, Augustine believes, the blessed life consists; we live and move and have our being in Truth, that God who he says is his light, his *lumen* and his *splendor.*[30] We have not time here to analyze in detail Augustine's argument in book ten of the *Confessions,* but it may suffice to observe that his stated concern is to order his own intellectual affections in such a way as to *act* in accordance with the Truth he seeks and serves. Augustine recognizes, as presumably do we, that Truth divides, that even though there may be empirical evidence that it gives joy to some, there are others, as he says, who perhaps do not "desire true happiness." This adverse disposition occurs, he says, even among those who profess to seek truth

[30]Augustine *Confessions* 10.23.33; cf. Thomas Aquinas *De male* 9.1, "It is actually natural for man to strive for knowledge of truth."

> simply because truth is loved in such a [weak] way that those who love some other thing want *it* to be the truth. . . . Thus they hate the real truth for the sake of that other thing which they love in its place. They love truth when it enlightens them, they hate truth when it accuses them.[31]

Summarily, the notion of happiness held by such people reduces to a kind of self-affirmation; they desire learning as a kind of therapy for their habits of mind and will, and it is in fact a kind of freedom from the constraints of truth which is their chief objective. But this cannot be true happiness, or true freedom either, Augustine says, because its critical prerequisite is a self-deception of which the self is at some level aware.

In this sense, ironically, the only authentic freedom is in conformation of our own will to the Truth in God.

> True happiness is to rejoice in the truth, for to rejoice in the truth is to rejoice in you, O God, who are the Truth, you, my God, my true Light, to whom I look for salvation. This is the happiness that all desire.[32]

On Augustine's view, those who cannot imagine a freedom which is not self-defined will miss out on real freedom altogether. Yet for those who have found in God Truth itself, there is perpetual delight, a "holy joy."[33] For these folk the brightness (splendor) of the Truth enlightens everything else it touches, allowing the scholar to live, as John Milton puts it, "beholding the bright countenance of truth in the quiet and still air of delightful studies."[34]

What both an English Protestant intellectual such as Milton and a French Catholic mathematician and scientist like Henri Poincaré (at least in this statement) could agree upon, then, is that, in Poincaré's words, "the search for truth should be the goal of our activities" and is "the sole end worthy of them." And Poincaré adds, "If we wish more and more to free man from material cares it is that he may be able to employ the liberty obtained in the study and contemplation of truth."[35]

It is in his conviction that regard for truth precedes liberty rather than the other way around that we recognize in Poincaré a Christian thinker. He, too, acknowledges that on occasion "truth can frighten us" and that partial truth can be deceptive. But he holds firmly to the principle that in the end Truth is one, that it is accordingly

---

[31]Augustine *Confessions* 10.23.
[32]Ibid.
[33]Ibid., 10.24.
[34]Milton, preface, *Reason of Church Government,* in *John Milton: Paradise Lost: An Authoritative Text, Backgrounds and Scources,* ed. Scott Elledge, 2nd ed. (New York: W. W. Norton, 1975; 1993), l.5.
[35]Poincaré, *Value of Science,* p. 190.

incumbent upon the fearless intellect to seek both scientific truth and moral truth without an artificial imposition of boundaries between them. "Whoever loves the one," he insists, "cannot help loving the other. . . . *These two truths when discovered give the same joy; each when perceived beams with the same splendor,* so that we must see it or close our eyes."[36] This affirmation, from one who at the beginning of the twentieth century was doubtless the world's premiere mathematical scientist, is consonant with Augustine the fourth-century theologian and John Paul II the late twentieth-century pontiff both in logic and in language. They share an affirmation of joy in truth, I would suggest, which will be present wherever a learning community faithful to the gospel is gathered. Such scholars can, in Augustine's sense, "rest" in this joy, not merely because divine truth is our shield and defense (Ps 91:4; Eph 6:14), constantly being renewed despite our own reflective and analytical inconsistency (Pss 100:5; 117:2), but because of the promise of Jesus in the gospel that the Spirit of Truth will guide us to truth (Jn 16:3). He is, after all, the "true Light" who enlightens everyone (Jn 1:9), for it is Jesus alone who can say, as John Paul II is delighted to remind us, *Ego sum via, et veritas, et vita* (Jn 14:6), whose very name in John's apocalyptic vision is revealed as "Faithful and True" (Rev 19:11; cf. 1 Jn 5:20). On this view, "joy in the Truth" is fully the possession of those alone who love the truth, as Pascal[37] and the beloved disciple agree (1 Jn 2—4).

Perhaps one needs to share in this deepest of all affections to have much affection for any vision of Christian higher education such as *Ex corde ecclesiae*. But if this is the case, then it follows that obtaining a deeply Christian account of the relationship between personal intellectual freedom, on the one hand, and the religious liberty of institutions to operate out of a commitment to shared religious truth, on the other, will be indispensable if we are to succeed in our stated missions. Despite much misunderstanding and controversy, I therefore continue to think that achieving a balance between our institutional freedom to advance a religious educational mission (something repeatedly sustained by the courts)[38] and encouraging the mature exercise of academic freedom (in its original purpose) among our colleagues and students is an effort in which we must persevere. If we

[36]Ibid., p. 190.

[37]Blaise Pascal *Pensées* 14.864.

[38]Various Supreme Court decisions have upheld the right of colleges and universities, acting as speakers under the provisions of the First Amendment, to assert their right to a distinctive intellectual and religious mission. For a full account see James D. Gordon III, "Individual and Institutional Academic Freedom at Religious Colleges and Universities," *Journal of College and University Law* 2 (2003): 30; and Michael W. McConnell, "Academic Freedom in Religious Colleges and Universities," *Law and Contemporary Problems* 53 (1990): 303, 305.

are to grow successfully through our own debates about how to achieve a high order of faithfully Christian learning, and move toward that "joy in truth" of which *Ex corde* speaks, a peace deeper than political compromise with those who have effectively secularized part or all of their intellectual categories will be necessary. I realize as I set these words down that the peace we seek must be a "peace . . . which surpasses all understanding" (Phil 4:7). For such harmony to become normative within as well as across ecclesial boundaries, we may need to experience the grace of a true repentance, as well, frankly, as "deeds consistent with repentance" (Acts 26:20). By these means, if by any, we may yet have hope to share more widely in the "joy of truth"—at least until we finally arrive at what Dante describes as "pure light: light intellectual, full of love, love of true good full of joy, joy that transcends every sweetness."[39] That light alone, of course, shall be *splendor sine occasu,* brightness never-ending, when he who *is True Truth* shall make even the sun in our galaxy a dull redundancy.

[39]Dante Alighieri *Paradiso* 30.39-42.

EPILOGUE

Our Common Teacher

Timothy George

I first heard of Karol Wojtyla when I was a graduate student at Harvard University studying with the great church historian George Huntston Williams.[1] Williams had first met the Polish bishop at Vatican II and developed a strong friendship with him during a sabbatical year in Krakow. Williams would later write a major intellectual biography of the pope, *The Mind of John Paul II,* and would become the first Protestant theologian to be admitted by the new pope into the Order of Saint Gregory the Great. When we were planning a Festschrift for Williams, I wrote to his friend inviting him to send special greetings on this occasion. By the time his letter arrived, he had already been summoned to Rome and elected to succeed John Paul I. In the *tabula gratulatoria,* we recorded his name: "*olim,* Karol Cardinal Wojtyla, *nunc,* His Holiness John Paul II." I still cherish that letter along with another I received several years ago from *olim,* Joseph Cardinal Ratzinger, *nunc,* Pope Benedict XVI.

Many people are not aware that on the day Karol Wojtyla was acclaimed as the new Pope John Paul II in Rome, an American evangelist, Billy Graham, was filling his pulpit back in Poland. Graham's preaching missions behind the Iron Curtain, beginning in Hungary in 1977 and including Poland (at the invitation of

---

[1]This essay first appeared as "John Paul II: An Appreciation," *Pro Ecclesia* 14, no. 3 (2005): 267-70, and is used by permission.

Wojtyla) and Russia, became, along with the pope's own courageous call to Christian fidelity, a mighty solvent in the loosening of a system of totalitarianism and terror. One can hardly image two more unlikely allies in twentieth-century Christianity. But in the receding tide of history, it is not at all surprising that Billy Graham, heir to a radical Protestant tradition that referred to the Bishop of Rome as the antichrist, should call the late pope "the greatest Christian leader of our time."

John Paul II was the first non-Italian European to become pope since the Dutchman Adrian VI was elected to that office in 1522, and he was the first Slavic pope ever. His major ecumenical project, and perhaps the greatest disappointment of his papacy, was to heal the breach with the East. In one of the first of his many papal travels, he went to Turkey in 1979 to meet Ecumenical Orthodox Patriarch Dimitrios I, and this visit led to the establishment of an international dialogue commission. But his overtures to the churches and "separated brethren" of the West were significant, dramatic and perhaps of more lasting import in the ongoing quest for Christian unity. In 1983, on the 500th anniversary of the birth of Martin Luther, he became the first pope ever to visit a Lutheran church. This initiative gave impetus to an intensive dialogue, promulgated by able theologians on several continents, related to the material principle of the Reformation. Whatever its weaknesses, and I think there are some, the *Joint Declaration on Justification* (1999)[2] will be long remembered as a landmark breakthrough. Churches that had mutually condemned one another for half a millennium found a way to jointly affirm the central meaning of the gospel of God's free and undeserved grace in Jesus Christ.

Many of these themes came together in John Paul II's 1995 encyclical, *Ut unum sint* (That All May Be One). In this document, the pope took an extraordinary step. Recognizing that the doctrine of papal primacy was a serious obstacle to Christian unity among many believers around the world, the pope invited theologians and church leaders from all Christian traditions to offer counsel to him about how he might more effectively exercise the Petrine Office in the service of the unity of Christ-followers everywhere. The ongoing work of Evangelicals and Catholics Together and the recent discussions of the World Evangelical Alliance-Roman Catholic Church dialogue team are a partial, though tentative, response to this papal plea.

Another of the pope's encyclicals, also from 1995, *Evangelium vitae* (The Gospel of Life) helped to solidify, and gave theological rationale for, Roman Catholic–

[2]<http://www.vatican.va/roman_curia/pontifical_councils/chrstuni/documents/rc_pc_chrstuni_doc_31101999_cath-luth-joint-declaration_en.html>.

evangelical cobelligerency on issues related to the sanctity of human life, especially abortion, euthanasia and the increasingly dehumanizing manipulation of human genetics.

Pope John Paul II will be remembered for many things, but perhaps chief among them will be his role as a teacher of the church. His magisterial (small *m*) ministry has not been without effect among evangelical believers. Only thirty years ago, in 1974, the Southern Baptist Convention went on record supporting the policy of abortion-on-demand as set forth in *Roe* v. *Wade*. That America's largest Protestant denomination, and many other evangelicals as well, have since become leading advocates of the "culture of life" is due not only to courageous leaders within their ranks, such as the late Dr. Francis Shaeffer, who called for the development of a vibrant public moral culture, but also to the steady, persuasive and encompassing moral teachings of the Holy Father.

The pope's emphasis on the integrity of each human person before God was at the heart of his own moral vision. In a letter written in 1968 to the great Jesuit theologian Henri de Lubac, then Karol Cardinal Wojtyla pointed to the horrific tragedies that had beset Europe, East and West, in their own lifetimes: unspeakable genocide, unlimited warfare, and the wholesale destruction of human freedom and human rights. At the root of these horrors, the Polish bishop suggested, was "a degradation, indeed a pulverization, of the fundamental uniqueness of each human person." Today when one visits the John Paul II Cultural Center in Washington, D.C., one is shown a video presentation that opens with a scan of a galaxy in outer space, and then focuses more narrowly, frame by frame, on the earth, on the city, on a single child—a little girl—sitting on the stairs of the National Cathedral. We see her face, then her hand, her thumb, her skin, closer and closer, to the very cells that pulsate with life within her body, the single life of one child, eternally precious, because made forever in the image of God.

Evangelicals and Roman Catholics have shared a torturous history of conflict and mutual condemnation, and this still goes on in many places where these two communities of faith are frequently the most vibrant forms of Christian witness in the region. Increasingly, too, evangelicals and Roman Catholics are among those often called upon to suffer and even die for the faith once delivered to the saints. In *Ut unum sint*, Pope John Paul II called us to remember "the courageous witness of so many martyrs of our century, including members of churches and ecclesial communities not in full communion with the Catholic Church." Evangelicals and Roman Catholics have been brought together by what I have called elsewhere "an ecumenism of the trenches." As we draw closer to Jesus Christ, we will surely draw closer to one another. We will discover that we are comrades in a struggle, not a struggle against one another, and not really a struggle against those outside the Christian faith who reject the light of divine grace because they have fallen in love with the darkness which surrounds them; no, our conflict is with the evil that loiters in the noonday, and slithers through the midnight hour. Against such principalities and powers, John Paul II, our common teacher, calls us to recognize the splendor of truth and the fullness of life, that luminous presence the New Testament calls the glory of God in the face of Christ.

Contributors

William J. Abraham is Albert Cook Outler Professor of Wesley Studies and University Altshuler Distinguished Teaching Professor at Perkins School of Theology, Southern Methodist University.

Michael Beaty is chair and professor of philosophy, the Department of Philosophy, Baylor University.

Mark Charlton is academic vice president and professor of political science at St. Mary's University College, Calgary, Alberta.

Avery Cardinal Dulles, S.J., is Laurence J. McGinley Professor of Religion and Society at Fordham University.

C. Stephen Evans is University Professor of Philosophy and Humanities at Baylor University.

Timothy George is the dean of Beeson Divinity School and executive editor for *Christianity Today.*

Andrew J. Goddard is tutor in Christian ethics at Wycliffe Hall, Oxford University.

David Lyle Jeffrey is Distinguished Professor of Literature and the Humanities, Honors College, Baylor University.

Derek Jeffreys is associate professor of humanistic studies and religion at the University of Wisconsin—Green Bay.

Peter Kuzmič is Eva B. and Paul E. Toms Distinguished Professor of World Missions and European Studies at Gordon-Conwell Theological Seminary and director of the Evangelical Theological Seminary in Osijek, Croatia.

Mark A. Noll is Francis A. McAnaney Professor of History at the University of Notre Dame.

J. I. Packer is the Board of Governors' Professor of Theology at Regent College.

Nancy R. Pearcey is scholar for worldview studies at Philadelphia Biblical University and the author of *Total Truth: Liberating Christianity from Its Cultural Captivity,* study guide edition (Wheaton, Ill.: Crossway, 2005).

Tim Perry is associate professor of theology at Providence College.

Clark H. Pinnock is emeritus professor of systematic theology at McMaster Divinity College.

Ronald J. Sider is professor of theology, holistic ministry and public policy at Palmer Seminary, Eastern University.

Terrance L. Tiessen is emeritus professor of theology and ethics at Providence Theological Seminary.

Name Index

Page numbers in bold indicate the most pertinent pages for a given person.

Subject Index

Page numbers in bold indicate the most pertinent pages for a given topic.

Scripture Index